THE ESSENTIAL SELF

AN INTRODUCTION TO LITERATURE

THE ESSEN

AN INTRODUCTION

PAUL BERRY

McGRAW-HILL BOOK COMPANY

TO LITERATURE

Honolulu, Hawaii

New York   St. Louis   San Francisco   Auckland   Düsseldorf   Johannesburg   Kuala Lumpur   London
Mexico   Montreal   New Delhi   Panama   Paris   São Paulo   Singapore   Sydney   Tokyo   Toronto

THE ESSENTIAL SELF: AN INTRODUCTION TO LITERATURE

1 2 3 4 5 6 7 8 9 0 K P K P 7 9 8 7 6 5

This book was set in Times Roman by Black Dot, Inc.
The editors were Jean Smith, Ellen B. Fuchs, and David Dunham;
the cover was designed by Scott Chelius;
the production supervisor was Charles Hess.
Kingsport Press, Inc., was printer and binder.

Library of Congress Cataloging in Publication Data
Main entry under title:

The Essential self.

    Bibliography: p.
    1. Literature—Collections. I. Berry, Paul,
date
PN6014.E75   820'.8   75-12626
ISBN 0-07-005048-1

ACKNOWLEDGMENTS

Woody Allen, "Mr. Big." Copyright © 1971 by Woody Allen. Reprinted from *Getting Even* by Woody Allen, by permission of Random House, Inc.

W. H. Auden, "The Unknown Citizen" and "Musée des Beaux Arts." Copyright 1940 and renewed 1968 by W. H. Auden. Reprinted from *Collected Shorter Poems 1927–1957* by W. H. Auden. Reprinted in the United States by permission of Random House, Inc., and reprinted in Canada by permission of Faber & Faber Ltd.

John Barth, "The Remobilization of Jacob Horner." From *The End of the Road* by John Barth. Copyright © 1958, 1967 by John Barth. Reprinted by permission of Doubleday & Company, Inc.

Black Hawk, "Farewell, My Nation! Farewell, Black Hawk." From the *Autobiography of Black Hawk,* dictated to Antoine LeClair, edited by Donald Jackson. Reprinted by permission of The University of Illinois Press.

Richard Brautigan, "The Kool Aid Wino." From the book *Trout Fishing in America* by Richard Brautigan. Copyright © 1967 by Richard Brautigan. Used with permission of Delacorte Press/Seymour Lawrence.

Claude Brown, "Turning It Around." Reprinted with permission of The Macmillan Publishing Co., Inc., from *Manchild in the Promised Land* by Claude Brown. Copyright © 1965 by Claude Brown.

Albert Camus, "The Guest." From *Exile and the Kingdom* by Albert Camus, translated by Justin O'Brien. Copyright © 1957, 1958 by Alfred A. Knopf, Inc. Reprinted by permission of the publisher.

Rachel Carson, "The Obligation to Endure." Chapters 1 and 2 of *Silent Spring.* Copyright © 1962 by Rachel L. Carson, . Reprinted with the permission of the publisher, Houghton Mifflin Co.

Irene Castañeda, "A Personal Chronicle of Crystal City." Reprinted by permission of Irene Castañeda.

John Ciardi, "The Act of Language." Reprinted by permission of the author and *The Saturday Evening Post.* © 1960 by the Curtis Publishing Co.

E. E. Cummings, "the Cambridge ladies," "in Just," "o sweet spontaneous earth." Copyright 1923, 1951 by E. E. Cummings. Reprinted from his volume *Complete Poems 1913–1962,* by permission of Harcourt Brace Jovanovich, Inc. "anyone lived in a pretty how town," copyright 1940 by E. E. Cummings; copyright 1968 by Marion Morehouse Cummings. Reprinted from *Complete Poems 1913–1962* by E. E. Cummings by permission of Harcourt Brace Jovanovich, Inc. "next to

Philip Larkin, "Poetry of Departures." Reprinted from *The Less Deserved* by permission of The Marvell Press, England.

D. H. Lawrence, "Love Was Once a Little Boy." From *Phoenix II: Uncollected, Unpublished and Other Prose Works* by D. H. Lawrence, edited by Warren Roberts. Copyright 1925 by Centaur Press; copyright renewed 1953 by Frieda Lawrence. Reprinted by permission of The Viking Press, Inc., and by permission of Laurence Pollinger Ltd. and the Estate of the late Mrs. Frieda Lawrence.

Archibald MacLeish, "Ars Poetica" and "The End of the World." From *Collected Poems 1917–1952.* Copyright 1952 by Archibald MacLeish. Reprinted with the permission of the publisher, Houghton Mifflin Co.

Bernard Malamud, "Black Is My Favorite Color." Reprinted with the permission of Farrar, Straus & Giroux, Inc., from *Idiots First* by Bernard Malamud. Copyright © 1963 by Bernard Malamud.

Carson McCullers, "Sucker." From *The Mortgaged Heart*, edited by Margarita Smith. Copyright © 1971 by Floria V. Lasky, Executrix of the Estate of Carson McCullers. Reprinted with the permission of the Houghton Mifflin Co., publishers.

Joe McGinniss, "Politics, A Con Game" (Chapter 2 from *The Selling of the President*). Copyright © 1969 by Joemac, Incorporated. Reprinted by permission of Simon & Schuster, Inc.

Flannery O'Connor, "A Good Man Is Hard to Find." Copyright 1953 by Flannery O'Connor. Reprinted from her volume *A Good Man Is Hard to Find and Other Stories* by permission of Harcourt Brace Jovanovich, Inc.

Sylvia Plath, "Daddy" and "The Applicant." From *Ariel* by Sylvia Plath. Copyright 1963 by Ted Hughes. Reprinted by permission of Harper & Row, Publishers, Inc. Also by permission of Olwyn Hughes, Literary Agent. *Ariel* was also published by Faber & Faber Ltd., copyright © 1965 by Ted Hughes.

Plato, "The Allegory of the Cave." From *The Republic of Plato*, translated by Benjamin Jowett, 4th ed., 1953. Reprinted by permission of The Clarendon Press, Oxford.

Edwin Arlington Robinson, "Miniver Cheevy" and "Richard Cory." "Miniver Cheevy" (copyright 1907 Charles Scribner's Sons) is reprinted by permission of Charles Scribner's Sons from *The Town Down the River* by Edwin Arlington Robinson. "Richard Cory" is reprinted by permission of Charles Scribner's Sons from *The Children of the Night* by Edwin Arlington Robinson.

Theodore Roethke, "My Papa's Waltz," "Dolor," "Elegy for Jane," and "I Knew a Woman." "My Papa's Waltz," copyright 1942 by Hearst Magazines, Inc. "Dolor," copyright 1943 by Modern Poetry Association, Inc. "Elegy for Jane," copyright 1950 by Theodore Roethke. "I Knew a Woman," copyright 1954 by Theodore Roethke. From the book *The Collected Poems of Theodore Roethke.* Reprinted by permission of Doubleday & Co., Inc.

Bertrand Russell, "A Free Man's Worship." From *Mysticism and Logic* by Bertrand Russell. Reprinted with permission of George Allen &

Unwin Ltd., Book Publishers.

Paul Simon, "The Sound of Silence." © 1964 by Paul Simon. Used with the permission of the publisher.

Gary Snyder, "Four Poems for Robin." From *The Back Country* by Gary Snyder. Copyright © 1968 by Gary Snyder. Reprinted by permission of New Directions Publishing Corporation.

Sophocles, *King Oedipus*. Translated by William Butler Yeats. Reprinted with permission of Macmillan Publishing Co., Inc., from *Collected Plays of William Butler Yeats*, copyright 1934, 1952 by Macmillan Publishing Co., Inc. Also by permission of M. B. Yeats, Miss Anne Yeats, and Macmillan Co. of Canada.

Wallace Stevens, "Peter Quince at the Clavier." Copyright 1923 and renewed 1951 by Wallace Stevens. Reprinted from *The Collected Poems of Wallace Stevens,* by permission of Alfred A. Knopf, Inc.

Dylan Thomas, "Do Not Go Gentle into That Good Night," "Fern Hill," and "The Force That through the Green Fuse Drives the Flower." From *The Poems of Dylan Thomas.* Copyright 1939, 1946 by New Directions Publishing Corporation, 1952 by Dylan Thomas. Reprinted by permission of New Directions Publishing Corp. J. M. Dent & Sons Ltd., Publishers, and the Trustees for the Copyrights of the late Dylan Thomas have given their permission for Canadian rights for the use of *Collected Poems* by Dylan Thomas.

Alvin Toffler, "The Accelerative Thrust." From *Future Shock* by Alvin Toffler. Copyright © 1970 by Alvin Toffler. Reprinted by permission of Random House, Inc.

Kurt Vonnegut, Jr., "Report on the Barnhouse Effect." Copyright 1950 by Kurt Vonnegut, Jr. Originally appeared in *Collier's.* Reprinted by arrangement with the publisher, Delacorte Press/Seymour Lawrence.

Tom Wicker, "Kennedy Without Tears." Reprinted by permission of William Morrow & Co., Inc. Copyright © 1964 by Tom Wicker. First published in *Esquire* Magazine.

William Carlos Williams, "Yachts," "Tract," and "The Red Wheelbarrow." From *Collected Earlier Poems* by William Carlos Williams. Copyright 1938 by New Directions Publishing Corporation. Reprinted by permission of New Directions Publishing Corporation.

William Butler Yeats, "The Second Coming," "Leda and the Swan," and "Sailing to Byzantium." "The Second Coming" is reprinted with the permission of the Macmillan Publishing Co., Inc., from *Collected Poems* by William Butler Yeats, copyright 1924 by Macmillan Publishing Co., Inc., renewed 1952 by Bertha Georgie Yeats. Also by permission of M. B. Yeats, Miss Anne Yeats, Macmillan & Co., Ltd., London, and Basingstoke and Macmillan Co. of Canada. "Sailing to Byzantium" and "Leda and the Swan" are reprinted with permission of Macmillan Publishing Co., Inc., from *Collected Poems* by William Butler Yeats, copyright 1928 by Macmillan Publishing Co., Inc., renewed 1956 by Georgie Yeats. Also by permission of M. B. Yeats, Miss Anne Yeats, Macmillan of London, and Basingstoke and Macmillan Co. of Canada.

TO
NINA
THE BEST OF READERS

CONTENTS

INTRODUCTION

Introductions to anthologies are something like the speeches of politicians at Fourth of July picnics—most of those in attendance would rather get on with the hot dogs and the good times. Only a nod then to the usual voice clearing about an editor's intentions and on to the picnic. Students, teachers, and casual readers may find any number of themes running through the selections of this book. Only three of these themes, however, appear as a result of my intent. The overriding concept that appears within deals with the self, the person we have the most trouble pleasing, the person we have to rely on, the one who sometimes keeps us up nights. Two secondary themes offer different perspectives for viewing this self, one in the revelation of values through the choices we make and the other by a glimpse of the inner person struggling with the impact of science and technology.

One has only to compare contemporary society with the society of the last century to understand why literature has shifted its focus gradually but certainly to inner concerns. Witness the causes: people engulfed by artificial environments; the rise of psychology and its promise of knowing oneself; the growth of human control over nature; alienation; the accelerating pace of life; the multiplication of things any sensible person would fear; the elevation of personal expectations; the inundation of the senses by mass communications. Small wonder we find the self in stress and writers of talent charting that stress. Each of us faces new questions about who we are, how and why we act as we do, what experiences and influences have formed our identities, where our responsibilities lie, and what forms our adaptations of self can and should take. It is the responses of great writers to these questions that you will find here. I hope that the reader will find illumined in their works that most intriguing and elusive of all people, one's self.

Of the two subthemes, the first explores how people reveal the core of self as they face and make decisions. If, as John Barth suggests in "The Remobilization of Jacob Horner," "Choosing is existence," then a close look at the nature of choices and the values on which they rest may do much to improve our grasp of humanity. The reader will find that among the fiction selections the choices that characters face range from routine to incredible, from mortal to pointless, and that the values these choices call forth display the rich diversity of human motivation. Among the fiction selections, the stories by Brown, Hemingway, Barth, Camus, Vonnegut, and Hawthorne examine most intensely the nature of choice and its impact on the self. The theme is so pervasive throughout the poetry selections that it serves little purpose to point out its presence in a particular poet's work. Among the essayists Russell, Gregory, Black Hawk, Ciardi, and Carson give the issue special scrutiny.

The other subtheme in the book deals with the impact of science and technology on our beliefs and conduct. Our perverse concern with understanding life, controlling it, and improving it inevitably leads to realizations and decisions for which we are often ill prepared. The realizations we can accept, ignore, or dispute. In the decisions, however, we often find greater problems, for in them we see at risk deep personal values and sometimes the entire social order. For example, doctors who face the choice of sustaining a life and generals who control silos filled with nuclear warhead missiles face intensely troubling questions raised by science and technology. And for that matter so do other individuals, a woman facing an abortion, a politician leaking news to the media, a pharmaceutical firm manager producing an oversupply of amphetamines for the market. Perplexing problems all, and all of them posed by the inexorable growth of science and technology.

In the stories by Barth and Vonnegut the revelation of values and self through choices linked to science appears most visibly. Auden, Eliot, MacLeish, Plath, and Simon, among the poets, give the matter particularly telling attention, and Toffler, Carson, Plato, and McGinniss, among the essayists, survey the issue from various vantage points.

The reader should recognize that each of these thematic approaches offers only a different perspective on what remains as the same essential theme, the evolving, struggling self, boundless in its shapes, dilemmas, and responses.

Part One

Short Stories

Like a work of art, a good piece of fiction doesn't yield much unless we bring something of ourselves to it. Rather than a *meaning*, fiction offers us an experience, one in which we participate as we read. Having done so, we are somehow the larger for it, and we carry away from the encounter something of value—an understanding, a new sensitivity, a feeling, or perhaps simply a sense of enjoyment. Just how much one takes from involvement with a story depends as much on the sensibilities and openness of the reader as it does on the talents of the writer. This selection of stories has as its main intent improving those sensibilities and enlarging that openness, being at once a vehicle for enjoyment and a tool for honing literary perceptions.

Short stories offer a form of literary experience marked by a quick exposition of characters, conflict, and setting, a unity of impact, and an economy of plot. Most of all, however, short stories of lasting value rely on intriguing characters, people who capture and hold our interest. To be sure, an intriguing plot alone can sometimes carry a story, particularly if it creates enough suspense; but a first-rate piece of short fiction can do with precious little plot as long as it has characters that interest us, people whose lives tell us more about ourselves. Consequently, the stories arranged here have been chosen not only for their memorable characters, but for the glimpses these characters offer us of the self under stress, of the identity in question, of the roles sought and played.

Each of these revelations of self is part of a gallery of portraits centering on the interior person. In Claude Brown's "Turning It Around" we find an autobiographical account of a young man reaching a critical point where he must break with his roots in the black ghetto of New York or very probably face an early and tragic end. In Hemingway's "The Short Happy Life of Francis Macomber" the protagonist fails as he faces a crucial choice. Then, in the agony of his cowardice and his wife's rejection, he discovers his sense of self. In "The Remobilization of Jacob Horner," John Barth gives us an antihero, a young man so paralyzed by the absurdity of life that he must learn to use absurd rules if he is to function as a human being. Young Goodman Brown, Hawthorne's allegorical hero, explores the nature of evil and, after a fantastic brush with it, comes away forever changed, his self bent by the experience. And so on through the gallery of characters. You will recognize, in the situations that many of these protagonists confront, the subtheme of self as revealed through the exercise of values in important choices. Finally you will find most particularly in Kurt Vonnegut's "Report on the Barnhouse Effect," a strong link between choices, the impact of science, and the struggling self.

Carson McCullers (1917–1967)

After studying writing at Columbia University and New York University, McCullers struck it big with her fine first novel, The Heart Is a Lonely Hunter. *She followed this with a number of successful short stories, novels, and plays. The people in her works are often frustrated in their search for love and acceptance. The physical abnormality of many of her characters reflects her own life, for from her mid-twenties on a series of strokes left her left side completely paralyzed.*

Sucker

It was always like I had a room to myself. Sucker slept in my bed with me but that didn't interfere with anything. The room was mine and I used it as I wanted to. Once I remember sawing a trap door in the floor. Last year when I was a sophomore in high school I tacked on my wall some pictures of girls from magazines and one of them was just in her underwear. My mother never bothered me because she had the younger kids to look after And Sucker thought anything I did was always swell.

Whenever I would bring any of my friends back to my room all I had to do was just glance once at Sucker and he would get up from whatever he was busy with and maybe half smile at me, and leave without saying a word. He never brought kids back there. He's twelve, four years younger than I am, and he always knew without me even telling him that I didn't want kids that age meddling with my things.

Half the time I used to forget that Sucker isn't my brother. He's my first cousin but practically ever since I remember he's been in our family. You see his folks were killed in a wreck when he was a baby. To me and my kid sisters he was like our brother.

Sucker used to always remember and believe every word I said. That's how he got his nick-name. Once a couple of years ago I told him that if he'd jump off our garage with an umbrella it would act as a parachute and he wouldn't fall hard. He did it and busted his knee. That's just one instance. And the funny thing was that no matter how many times he got fooled he would still believe me. Not that he was dumb in other ways—it was just the way he acted with me. He would look at everything I did and quietly take it in.

There is one thing I have learned, but it makes me feel guilty and hard to figure out. If a person admires you a lot you despise him and don't care—and it is the person who doesn't notice you that you are apt to admire. This is not easy to realize. Maybelle Watts, this senior at school, acted like she was the Queen of Sheba and even humiliated me. Yet at this same time I would have done anything in the world to get her attentions. All I could think about day and night was Maybelle until I was nearly crazy. When Sucker was a little kid and on up until the time he was twelve I guess I treated him as bad as Maybelle did me.

Now that Sucker has changed so much it is a little hard to remember him as he used to be. I never imagined anything would suddenly happen that would make us both very different. I never knew that in order to get what has happened straight in my mind I would want to think back on him as he used to be and compare and try to get things settled. If I could have seen ahead maybe I would have acted different.

I never noticed him much or thought about him and when you consider how long we have had the same room together it is funny the few things I remember. He used to talk to himself a lot when he'd think he was alone—all about him fighting gangsters and being on ranches and that sort of kids' stuff. He'd get in the bathroom and stay as long as an hour and sometimes his voice would go up high and excited and you could hear him all over the house. Usually, though, he was very quiet. He didn't have many boys in the neighborhood to buddy with and his face had the look of a kid who is watching a game and waiting to be asked to play. He didn't mind wearing the sweaters and coats that I outgrew, even if the sleeves did flop down too big and make his wrists look as thin and white as a little girl's. That is how I remember him—getting a little bigger every year but still being the same. That was Sucker up until a few months ago when all this trouble began.

Maybelle was somehow mixed up in what happened so I guess I ought to start with her. Until I knew her I hadn't given much time to girls. Last fall she sat next to me in General Science class and that was when I first began to notice her. Her hair is the brightest yellow I ever saw and occasionally she will wear it set into curls with some sort of gluey stuff. Her fingernails are pointed and manicured and painted a shiny red. All during class I used to watch Maybelle, nearly all the time except when I thought she was going to look my way or when the teacher called on me. I couldn't keep my eyes off her hands, for one thing. They are very little and white except for that red stuff, and when she would turn the pages of her book she always licked her thumb and held out her little finger and turned very slowly. It is impossible to describe Maybelle. All the boys are crazy about her but she didn't even notice me. All I could do was sit and look at her in class—and sometimes it was like the whole room could hear my heart beating and I wanted to holler or light out and run for Hell.

At night, in bed, I would imagine about Maybelle. Often this would keep me from sleeping until as late as one or two o'clock. Sometimes Sucker would wake up and ask me why I couldn't get settled and I'd tell him hush his mouth. I suppose I was mean to him lots of times. I guess I wanted to ignore somebody like Maybelle did me. You could always tell by Sucker's face when his feelings were hurt. I don't remember all the ugly remarks I must have made because even when I was saying them my mind was on Maybelle.

That went on for nearly three months and then somehow she began to change. In the halls she would speak to me and every morning she copied my homework. At lunch time once I danced with her in the gym. One afternoon I got up nerve and went around to her house with a carton of cigarettes. I knew she smoked in the girls' basement and sometimes outside of school—and I didn't want to take her candy because I think that's been run into the ground. She was very nice and it seemed to me everything was going to change.

It was that night when this trouble really started. I had come into my room late and Sucker was already asleep. I felt too happy and keyed up to get in a comfortable position and I was awake thinking about Maybelle a long time. Then I dreamed about her and it seemed I kissed her. It was a surprise to wake up and see the dark. I lay still and a little while passed before I could come to and understand where I was. The house was quiet and it was a very dark night.

Sucker's voice was a shock to me. "Pete? . . ."

I didn't answer anything or even move.

"You do like me as much as if I was your own brother, don't you Pete?"

I couldn't get over the surprise of everything and it was like this was the real dream instead of the other.

"You have liked me all the time like I was your own brother, haven't you?"

"Sure," I said.

Then I got up for a few minutes. It was cold and I was glad to come back to bed. Sucker hung on to my back. He felt little and warm and I could feel his warm breathing on my shoulder.

"No matter what you did I always knew you liked me."

I was wide awake and my mind seemed mixed up in a strange way. There was this happiness about Maybelle and all that—but at the same time something about Sucker and his voice when he said these things made me take notice. Anyway I guess you understand people better when you are happy than when something is worrying you. It was like I had never really thought about Sucker until then. I felt I had always been mean to him. One night a few weeks before I had heard him crying in the dark. He said he had lost a boy's beebee gun and was scared to let anybody know. He wanted me to tell him what to do. I was sleepy and tried to make him hush and when he wouldn't I kicked at him. That was just one of the things I remembered. It seemed to me he had always been a lonesome kid. I felt bad.

There is something about a dark cold night that makes you feel close to someone you're sleeping with. When you talk together it is like you are the only people awake in the town.

"You're a swell kid, Sucker," I said.

It seemed to me suddenly that I did like him more than anybody else I knew—more than any other boy, more than my sisters, more in a certain way even than Maybelle. I felt good all over and it was like when they play sad music in the movies. I wanted to show Sucker how much I really thought of him and make up for the way I had always treated him.

We talked for a good while that night. His voice was fast and it was like he had been saving up these things to tell me for a long time. He mentioned that he was going to try to build a canoe and that the kids down the block wouldn't let him in on their football team and I don't know what all. I talked some too and it was a good feeling to think of him taking in everything I said so seriously. I even spoke of Maybelle a little, only I made out like it was her who had been running after me all this time. He asked questions about high school and so forth. His voice was excited and he kept on talking fast like he could never get the words out in time. When I went to sleep he was still talking and I could still feel his breathing on my shoulder, warm and close.

During the next couple of weeks I saw a lot of Maybelle. She acted as though she really cared for me a little. Half the time I felt so good I hardly knew what to do with myself.

But I didn't forget about Sucker. There were a lot of old things in my bureau drawer I'd been saving—boxing gloves and Tom Swift books and second rate fishing tackle. All this I turned over to him. We had some more talks together and it was really like I was knowing him for the first time. When there was a long cut on his cheek I knew he had been monkeying around with this new first razor set of mine, but I didn't say anything. His face seemed different now. He used to look timid and sort of like he was afraid of a whack over the head. That expression was gone. His face, with those wide-open eyes and his ears sticking out and his mouth never quite shut, had the look of a person who is surprised and expecting something swell.

Once I started to point him out to Maybelle and tell her he was my kid brother. It was an afternoon when a murder mystery was on at the movie. I had earned a dollar working for my Dad and I gave Sucker a quarter to go and get candy and so forth. With the rest I took Maybelle. We were sitting near the back and I saw Sucker come in. He began to stare at the screen the minute he stepped past the ticket man and he stumbled down the aisle without noticing where he was going. I started to punch Maybelle but couldn't quite make up my mind. Sucker looked a little silly—walking like a drunk with his eyes glued to the movie. He was wiping his reading glasses on his shirt tail and his knickers flopped down. He went on until he got to the first few rows where the kids usually sit. I never did punch Maybelle. But I got to thinking it was good to have both of them at the movie with the money I earned.

I guess things went on like this for about a month or six weeks. I felt so good I couldn't settle down to study or put my mind on anything. I wanted to be friendly with everybody. There were times when I just had to talk to some person. And usually that would be Sucker. He felt as good as I did. Once he said: "Pete, I am gladder that you are like my brother than anything else in the world."

Then something happened between Maybelle and me. I never have figured out just what it was. Girls like her are hard to understand. She began to act different toward me. At first I wouldn't let myself believe this and tried to think it was just my imagination. She didn't act glad to see me any more. Often she went out riding with this fellow on the football team who owns this yellow roadster. The car was the color of her hair and after school she would ride off with him, laughing and looking into his face. I couldn't think of anything to do about it and she was on my mind all day and night. When I did get a chance to go out with her she was snippy and didn't seem to notice me. This made me feel like something was the matter—I would worry about my shoes clopping too loud on the floor, or the fly of my pants, or the bumps on my chin. Sometimes when Maybelle was around, a devil would get into me and I'd hold my face stiff and call grown men by their last names without the Mister and say rough things. In the night I would wonder what made me do all this until I was too tired for sleep.

At first I was so worried I just forgot about Sucker. Then later he began to get on my nerves. He was always hanging around until I would get back from high school, always looking like he had something to say to me or wanted me to tell him. He made me a magazine rack in his Manual Training class and one week he saved his lunch money and bought me three packs of cigarettes. He couldn't seem to take it in that I had things on my mind and didn't want to fool with him. Every afternoon it would be the same—him in my room with this waiting expression on his face. Then I wouldn't say anything or I'd maybe answer him rough-like and he would finally go on out.

I can't divide that time up and say this happened one day and that the next. For one thing I was so mixed up the weeks just slid along into each other and I felt like Hell and didn't care. Nothing definite was said or done. Maybelle still rode around with this fellow in his yellow roadster and sometimes she would smile at me and sometimes not. Every afternoon I went from one place to another where I thought she would be. Either she would act almost nice and I would begin thinking how things would finally clear up and she would care for me—or else she'd behave so that if she hadn't been a girl I'd have wanted to grab her by that white little neck and choke her. The more ashamed I felt for making a fool of myself the more I ran after her.

Sucker kept getting on my nerves more and more. He would look at me as though he sort of blamed me for something, but at the same time knew that it wouldn't last long. He was growing fast and for some reason began to stutter when he talked. Sometimes he had nightmares or would throw up his breakfast. Mom got him a bottle of cod liver oil.

Then the finish came between Maybelle and me. I met her going to the drug store and asked for a date. When she said no I remarked something sarcastic. She told me she was sick and tired of my being around and that she had never cared a rap about me. She said all that. I just stood there and didn't answer anything. I walked home very slowly.

For several afternoons I stayed in my room by myself. I didn't want to go anywhere or talk to anyone. When Sucker would come in and look at me sort of funny I'd yell at him to get out. I didn't want to think of Maybelle and I sat at my desk reading *Popular Mechanics* or whittling at a toothbrush rack I was making. It seemed to me I was putting that girl out of my mind pretty well.

But you can't help what happens to you at night. That is what made things how they are now.

You see a few nights after Maybelle said those words to me I dreamed about her again. It was like that first time and I was squeezing Sucker's arm so tight I woke him up. He reached for my hand.

"Pete, what's the matter with you?"

All of a sudden I felt so mad my throat choked—at myself and the dream and Maybelle and Sucker and every single person I knew. I remembered all the times Maybelle had humiliated me and everything bad that had ever happened. It seemed to me for a second that nobody would ever like me but a sap like Sucker.

"Why is it we aren't buddies like we were before? Why—?"

"Shut your damn trap!" I threw off the cover and got up and turned on the light. He sat in the middle of the bed, his eyes blinking and scared.

There was something in me and I couldn't help myself. I don't think anybody ever gets that mad but once. Words came without me knowing what they would be. It was only afterward that I could remember each thing I said and see it all in a clear way.

"Why aren't we buddies? Because you're the dumbest slob I ever saw! Nobody cares anything about you! And just because I felt sorry for you sometimes and tried to act decent don't think I give a damn about a dumb-bunny like you!"

If I'd talked loud or hit him it wouldn't have been so bad. But my voice was slow and like I was very calm. Sucker's mouth was part way open and he looked as though he'd knocked his funny bone. His face was white and sweat came out on his forehead. He wiped it away with the back of his hand and for a minute his arm stayed raised that way as though he was holding something away from him.

"Don't you know a single thing? Haven't you ever been around at all? Why don't you get a girl friend instead of me? What kind of a sissy do you want to grow up to be anyway?"

I didn't know what was coming next. I couldn't help myself or think.

Sucker didn't move. He had on one of my pajama jackets and his neck stuck out skinny and small. His hair was damp on his forehead.

"Why do you always hang around me? Don't you know when you're not wanted?"

Afterward I could remember the change in Sucker's face. Slowly that blank look went away and he closed his mouth. His eyes got narrow and his fists shut. There had never been such a look on him before. It was like every second he was getting older. There was a hard look to his eyes you don't see usually in a kid. A drop of sweat rolled down his chin and he didn't notice. He just sat there with those eyes on me and he didn't speak and his face was hard and didn't move.

"No, you don't know when you're not wanted. You're too dumb. Just like your name—a dumb Sucker."

It was like something had busted inside me. I turned off the light and sat down in the chair by the window. My legs were shaking and I was so

tired I could have bawled. The room was cold and dark. I sat there for a
long time and smoked a squashed cigarette I had saved. Outside the yard
was black and quiet. After a while I heard Sucker lie down.

I wasn't mad any more, only tired. It seemed awful to me that I had
talked like that to a kid only twelve. I couldn't take it all in. I told myself I
would go over to him and try to make it up. But I just sat there in the cold
until a long time had passed. I planned how I could straighten it out in the
morning. Then, trying not to squeak the springs, I got back in bed.

Sucker was gone when I woke up the next day. And later when I
wanted to apologize as I had planned he looked at me in this new hard
way so that I couldn't say a word.

All of that was two or three months ago. Since then Sucker has grown
faster than any boy I ever saw. He's almost as tall as I am and his bones
have gotten heavier and bigger. He won't wear any of my old clothes any
more and has bought his first pair of long pants—with some leather
suspenders to hold them up. Those are just the changes that are easy to
see and put into words.

Our room isn't mine at all any more. He's gotten up this gang of kids
and they have a club. When they aren't digging trenches in some vacant
lot and fighting they are always in my room. On the door there is some
foolishness written in Mercurochrome saying "Woe to the Outsider who
Enters" and signed with crossed bones and their secret initials. They have
rigged up a radio and every afternoon it blares out music. Once as I was
coming in I heard a boy telling something in a low voice about what he
saw in the back of his big brother's automobile. I could guess what I didn't
hear. *That's what her and my brother do. It's the truth—parked in the car.*
For a minute Sucker looked surprised and his face was almost like it used
to be. Then he got hard and tough again. "Sure, dumbell. We know all
that." They didn't notice me. Sucker began telling them how in two years
he was planning to be a trapper in Alaska.

But most of the time Sucker stays by himself. It is worse when we are
alone together in the room. He sprawls across the bed in those long
corduroy pants with the suspenders and just stares at me with that hard,
half sneering look. I fiddle around my desk and can't get settled because
of those eyes of his. And the thing is I just have to study because I've
gotten three bad cards this term already. If I flunk English I can't graduate
next year. I don't want to be a bum and I just have to get my mind on it. I
don't care a flip for Maybelle or any particular girl any more and it's only
this thing between Sucker and me that is the trouble now. We never speak
except when we have to before the family. I don't even want to call him
Sucker any more and unless I forget I call him by his real name, Richard.
At night I can't study with him in the room and I have to hang around the
drug store, smoking and doing nothing, with the fellows who loaf there.

More than anything I want to be easy in my mind again. And I miss
the way Sucker and I were for a while in a funny, sad way that before this
I never would have believed. But everything is so different that there
seems to be nothing I can do to get it right. I've sometimes thought if we

could have it out in a big fight that would help. But I can't fight him because he's four years younger. And another thing—sometimes this look in his eyes makes me almost believe that if Sucker could he would kill me.

FOR FURTHER CONSIDERATION

Aristotle observed two basic forms of plot in fiction: a recognition (a change from ignorance to knowledge) and a reversal (the change of a situation to its opposite). Describe the recognitions and reversals that occur in "Sucker." What impact do these recognitions and reversals have on the sense of self manifested by the narrator and by Sucker?

Bernard Malamud (1914–   )

Malamud has established himself as one of America's premier short story writers and novelists, winning the National Book Award and the Pulitzer Prize. He exhibits great interest in people's physical, mental, and moral staying power in a harsh world, and he makes it clear that humor is one of the best weapons in the struggle. Malamud grew up in Brooklyn, worked hard to survive the Depression, and now teaches and writes at Bennington College, Vermont.

Black Is My Favorite Color

Charity Sweetness sits in the toilet eating her two hardboiled eggs while I'm having my ham sandwich and coffee in the kitchen. That's how it goes only don't get the idea of ghettoes. If there's a ghetto I'm the one that's in it. She's my cleaning woman from Father Divine and comes in once a week to my small three-room apartment on my day off from the liquor store. "Peace," she says to me, "Father reached on down and took me right up in Heaven." She's a small person with a flat body, frizzy hair, and a quiet face that the light shines out of, and Mama had such eyes before she died. The first time Charity Sweetness came in to clean, a little more than a year and a half ago, I made the mistake to ask her to sit down at the kitchen table with me and eat her lunch. I was still feeling not so hot after Ornita left but I'm the kind of a man—Nat Lime, forty-four, a bachelor with a daily growing bald spot on the back of my head, and I could lose frankly fifteen pounds—who enjoys company so long as he has it. So she cooked up her two hardboiled eggs and sat down and took a small bite out of one of them. But after a minute she stopped chewing and she got up and carried the eggs in a cup in the bathroom, and since then she eats there. I said to her more than once, "Okay, Charity Sweetness, so have it your way, eat the eggs in the kitchen by yourself and I'll eat when you're done," but she smiles absentminded, and eats in the toilet. It's my fate with colored people.

Although black is still my favorite color you wouldn't know it from my luck except in short quantities even though I do all right in the liquor store business in Harlem, on Eighth Avenue between 110th and 111th. I speak with respect. A large part of my life I've had dealings with Negro people, most on a business basis but sometimes for friendly reasons with genuine feeling on both sides. I'm drawn to them. At this time of my life I should have one or two good colored friends but the fault isn't necessarily mine. If they knew what was in my heart towards them, but how can you tell that to anybody nowadays? I've tried more than once but the language of the heart either is a dead language or else nobody understands it the way you speak it. Very few. What I'm saying is, personally for me there's only one human color and that's the color of blood. I like a black person if not because he's black, then because I'm white. It comes to the same thing. If I wasn't white my first choice would be black. I'm satisfied to be white because I have no other choice. Anyway, I got an eye for color. I appreciate. Who wants everybody to be the same? Maybe it's like some kind of a talent. Nat Lime might be a liquor dealer in Harlem, but once in the jungle in New Guinea in the Second War, I got the idea when I shot at a running Jap and missed him, that I had some kind of a talent, though maybe it's the kind where you have a marvelous idea now and then but in the end what do they come to? After all, it's a strange world.

Where Charity Sweetness eats her eggs makes me think about Buster Wilson when we were both boys in the Williamsburg section of Brooklyn. There was this long block of run-down dirty frame houses in the middle of a not-so-hot white neighborhood full of pushcarts. The Negro houses looked to me like they had been born and died there, dead not long after the beginning of the world. I lived on the next street. My father was a cutter with arthritis in both hands, big red knuckles and swollen fingers so he didn't cut, and my mother was the one who went to work. She sold paper bags from a second-hand pushcart in Ellery Street. We didn't starve but nobody ate chicken unless we were sick or the chicken was. This was my first acquaintance with a lot of black people and I used to poke around on their poor block. I think I thought, brother, if there can be like this, what can't there be? I mean I caught an early idea what life was about. Anyway I met Buster Wilson there. He used to play marbles by himself. I sat on the curb across the street, watching him shoot one marble lefty and the other one righty. The hand that won picked up the marbles. It wasn't so much of a game but he didn't ask me to come over. My idea was to be friendly, only he never encouraged, he discouraged. Why did I pick him out for a friend? Maybe because I had no others then, we were new in the neighborhood, from Manhattan. Also I liked his type. Buster did everything alone. He was a skinny kid and his brothers' clothes hung on him like worn-out potato sacks. He was a beanpole boy, about twelve, and I was then ten. His arms and legs were burnt out matchsticks. He always wore a brown wool sweater, one arm half unraveled, the other went down to the wrist. His long and narrow head had a white part cut straight in the short woolly hair, maybe with a ruler there, by his father, a barber but too drunk to stay a barber. In those days though I had little myself I was old enough to know who was better off, and the whole block of colored houses made me feel bad in the daylight. But I went there as much as I could because the street was full of life. In the night it looked different, but it's hard to tell a cripple in the dark. Sometimes I was afraid to walk by the houses when they were dark and quiet. I was afraid there were people looking at me that I couldn't see. I liked it better when they had parties at night and everybody had a good time. The musicians played their banjos and saxophones and the houses shook with the music and laughing. The young girls, with their pretty dresses and ribbons in their hair, caught me in my throat when I saw them through the windows.

But with the parties came drinking and fights. Sundays were bad days after the Saturday night parties. I remember once that Buster's father, also long and loose, always wearing a dirty gray Homburg hat, chased another black man in the street with a half-inch chisel. The other one, maybe five feet high, lost his shoe and when they wrestled on the ground he was already bleeding through his suit, a thick red blood smearing the sidewalk. I was frightened by the blood and wanted to pour it back in the man who was bleeding from the chisel. On another time Buster's father was playing in a crap game with two big bouncy red dice, in the back of an alley between two middle houses. Then about six men started fist-fighting there, and they ran out of the alley and hit each other in the street. The neighbors, including children, came out and watched, everybody afraid but nobody moving to do anything. I saw the same thing near my store in Harlem, years later, a big crowd watching two men in the street, their breath hanging in the air on a winter night, murdering each other with switch knives, but nobody moved to call a cop. I didn't either. Anyway, I was just a young kid but I still remember how the cops drove up in a police paddy wagon and broke up the fight by hitting everybody they could hit with big nightsticks. This was in the days before LaGuardia. Most of the fighters were knocked out cold, only one or two got away. Buster's father started to run back in his house but a cop ran after him and cracked him on his Homburg hat with a club, right on the front porch. Then the Negro men were lifted up by the cops, one at the arms and the other at the feet, and they heaved them in the paddy wagon. Buster's father hit the back of the wagon and fell, with his nose spouting very red blood, on top of three other men. I personally couldn't stand it, I was scared of the human race so I ran home, but I remember Buster watching without any expression in his eyes. I stole an extra fifteen cents from my mother's pocketbook and I ran back and asked Buster if he wanted to go to the movies. I would pay. He said yes. This was the first time he talked to me.

So we went more than once to the movies. But we never got to be friends. Maybe because it was a one-way proposition—from me to him.

Which includes my invitations to go with me, my (poor mother's) movie money, Hershey chocolate bars, watermelon slices, even my best Nick Carter and Merriwell books that I spent hours picking up in the junk shops, and that he never gave me back. Once he let me go in his house to get a match so we could smoke some butts we found, but it smelled so heavy, so impossible, I died till I got out of there. What I saw in the way of furniture I won't mention—the best was falling apart in pieces. Maybe we went to the movies all together five or six matinees that spring and in the summertime, but when the shows were over he usually walked home by himself.

"Why don't you wait for me, Buster?" I said. "We're both going in the same direction."

But he was walking ahead and didn't hear me. Anyway he didn't answer.

One day when I wasn't expecting it he hit me in the teeth. I felt like crying but not because of the pain. I spit blood and said, "What did you hit me for? What did I do to you?"

"Because you a Jew bastard. Take your Jew movies and your Jew candy and shove them up your Jew ass."

And he ran away.

I thought to myself how was I to know he didn't like the movies. When I was a man I thought, you can't force it.

Years later, in the prime of my life, I met Mrs. Ornita Harris. She was standing by herself under an open umbrella at the bus stop, crosstown 110th, and I picked up her green glove that she had dropped on the wet sidewalk. It was in the end of November. Before I could ask her was it hers, she grabbed the glove out of my hand, closed her umbrella, and stepped in the bus. I got on right after her.

I was annoyed so I said, "If you'll pardon me, Miss, there's no law that you have to say thanks, but at least don't make a criminal out of me."

"Well, I'm sorry," she said, "but I don't like white men trying to do me favors."

I tipped my hat and that was that. In ten minutes I got off the bus but she was already gone.

Who expected to see her again but I did. She came into my store about a week later for a bottle of scotch.

"I would offer you a discount," I told her, "but I know you don't like a certain kind of a favor and I'm not looking for a slap in the face."

Then she recognized me and got a little embarrassed.

"I'm sorry I misunderstood you that day."

"So mistakes happen."

The result was she took the discount. I gave her a dollar off.

She used to come in about every two weeks for a fifth of Haig and Haig. Sometimes I waited on her, sometimes my helpers, Jimmy or Mason, also colored, but I said to give the discount. They both looked at me but I had nothing to be ashamed. In the spring when she came in we used to talk once in a while. She was a slim woman, dark but not the most dark, about thirty years I would say, also well built, with a combination nice legs and a good-size bosom that I like. Her face was pretty, with big eyes and high cheek bones, but lips a little thick and nose a little broad. Sometimes she didn't feel like talking, she paid for the bottle, less discount, and walked out. Her eyes were tired and she didn't look to me like a happy woman.

I found out her husband was once a window cleaner on the big buildings, but one day his safety belt broke and he fell fifteen stories. After the funeral she got a job as a manicurist in a Times Square barber shop. I told her I was a bachelor and lived with my mother in a small three-room apartment on West Eighty-third near Broadway. My mother had cancer, and Ornita said she was very sorry.

One night in July we went out together. How that happened I'm still not so sure. I guess I asked her and she didn't say no. Where do you go out with a Negro woman? We went to the Village. We had a good dinner and walked in Washington Square Park. It was a hot night. Nobody was surprised when they saw us, nobody looked at us like we were against the law. If they looked maybe they saw my new lightweight suit that I bought yesterday and my shiny bald spot when we walked under a lamp, also how pretty she was for a man of my type. We went in a movie on West Eighth Street. I didn't want to go in but she said she had heard about the picture. We went in like strangers and we came out like strangers. I wondered what was in her mind and I thought to myself, whatever is in there it's not a certain white man that I know. All night long we went together like we were chained. After the movie she wouldn't let me take her back to Harlem. When I put her in a taxi she asked me, "Why did we bother?"

For the steak, I wanted to say. Instead I said, "You're worth the bother."

"Thanks anyway."

Kiddo, I thought to myself after the taxi left, you just found out what's what, now the best thing is forget her.

It's easy to say. In August we went out the second time. That was the night she wore a purple dress and I thought to myself, my God, what colors. Who paints that picture paints a masterpiece. Everybody looked at us but I had pleasure. That night when she took off her dress it was in a furnished room I had the sense to rent a few days before. With my sick mother, I couldn't ask her to come to my apartment, and she didn't want me to go home with her where she lived with her brother's family on West 115th near Lenox Avenue. Under her purple dress she wore a black slip, and when she took that off she had white underwear. When she took off the white underwear she was black again. But I know where the next white was, if you want to call it white. And that was the night I think I fell in love with her, the first time in my life though I have liked one or two nice girls I used to go with when I was a boy. It was a serious proposition. I'm the kind of a man when I think of love I'm thinking of marriage. I guess that's why I am a bachelor.

That same week I had a holdup in my place, two big men—both

black—with revolvers. One got excited when I rang open the cash register so he could take the money and he hit me over the ear with his gun. I stayed in the hospital a couple of weeks. Otherwise I was insured. Ornita came to see me. She sat on a chair without talking much. Finally I saw she was uncomfortable so I suggested she ought to go home.

"I'm sorry it happened," she said.

"Don't talk like it's your fault."

When I got out of the hospital my mother was dead. She was a wonderful person. My father died when I was thirteen and all by herself she kept the family alive and together. I sat shive for a week and remembered how she sold paper bags on her pushcart. I remembered her life and what she tried to teach me. Nathan, she said, if you ever forget you are a Jew a goy will remind you. Mama, I said, rest in peace on this subject. But if I do something you don't like, remember, on earth it's harder than where you are. Then when my week of mourning was finished, one night I said, "Ornita, let's get married. We're both honest people and if you love me like I love you it won't be such a bad time. If you don't like New York I'll sell out here and we'll move someplace else. Maybe to San Francisco where nobody knows us. I was there for a week in the Second War and I saw white and colored living together."

"Nat," she answered me, "I like you but I'd be afraid. My husband woulda killed me."

"Your husband is dead."

"Not in my memory."

"In that case I'll wait."

"Do you know what it'd be like—I mean the life we could expect?"

"Ornita," I said, "I'm the kind of a man, if he picks his own way of life he's satisfied."

"What about children? Were you looking forward to half-Jewish polka dots?"

"I was looking forward to children."

"I can't," she said.

Can't is can't. I saw she was afraid and the best thing was not to push. Sometimes when we met she was so nervous that whatever we did she couldn't enjoy it. At the same time I still thought I had a chance. We were together more and more. I got rid of my furnished room and she came to my apartment—I gave away Mama's bed and bought a new one. She stayed with me all day on Sundays. When she wasn't so nervous she was affectionate, and if I know what love is, I had it. We went out a couple of times a week, the same way—usually I met her in Times Square and sent her home in a taxi, but I talked more about marriage and she talked less against it. One night she told me she was still trying to convince herself but she was almost convinced. I took an inventory of my liquor stock so I could put the store up for sale.

Ornita knew what I was doing. One day she quit her job, the next day she took it back. She also went away a week to visit her sister in Philadelphia for a little rest. She came back tired but said maybe. Maybe is maybe so I'll wait. The way she said it it was closer to yes. That was the winter two years ago. When she was in Philadelphia I called up a friend of mine from the Army, now CPA, and told him I would appreciate an invitation for an evening. He knew why. His wife said yes right away. When Ornita came back we went there. The wife made a fine dinner. It wasn't a bad time and they told us to come again. Ornita had a few drinks. She looked relaxed, wonderful. Later, because of a twenty-four hour taxi strike I had to take her home on the subway. When we got to the 116th Street station she told me to stay on the train, and she would walk the couple of blocks to her house. I didn't like a woman walking alone on the streets at that time of the night. She said she never had any trouble but I insisted nothing doing. I said I would walk to her stoop with her and when she went upstairs I would go back to the subway.

On the way there, on 115th in the middle of the block before Lenox, we were stopped by three men—maybe they were boys. One had a black hat with a half-inch brim, one a green cloth hat, and the third wore a black leather cap. The green hat was wearing a short coat and the other two had long ones. It was under a street light but the leather cap snapped a six-inch switchblade open in the light.

"What you doin' with this white son of a bitch?" he said to Ornita.

"I'm minding my own business," she answered him, "and I wish you would too."

"Boys," I said, "We're all brothers. I'm a reliable merchant in the neighborhood. This young lady is my dear friend. We don't want any trouble. Please let us pass."

"You talk like a Jew landlord," said the green hat. "Fifty a week for a single room."

"No charge fo' the rats," said the half-inch brim.

"Believe me, I'm no landlord. My store is 'Nathan's Liquors' between Hundred Tenth and Eleventh. I also have two colored clerks, Mason and Jimmy, and they will tell you I pay good wages as well as I give discounts to certain customers."

"Shut your mouth, Jewboy," said the leather cap, and he moved the knife back and forth in front of my coat button. "No more black pussy for you."

"Speak with respect about this lady, please."

I got slapped on my mouth.

"That ain't no lady," said the long face in the half-inch brim, "that's black pussy. She deserve to have evvy bit of her hair shave off. How you like to have evvy bit of your hair shave off, black pussy?"

"Please leave me and this gentleman alone or I'm gonna scream long and loud. That's my house three doors down."

They slapped her. I never heard such a scream. Like her husband was falling fifteen stories.

I hit the one that slapped her and the next I knew I was lying in the gutter with a pain in my head. I thought, goodbye, Nat, they'll stab me for sure, but all they did was take my wallet and run in three different directions.

Ornita walked back with me to the subway and she wouldn't let me go home with her again.

"Just get home safely."

She looked terrible. Her face was gray and I still remembered her scream. It was a terrible winter night, very cold February, and it took me an hour and ten minutes to get home. I felt bad for leaving her but what could I do?

We had a date downtown the next night but she didn't show up, the first time.

In the morning I called her in her place of business.

"For God's sake, Ornita, if we got married and moved away we wouldn't have that kind of trouble that we had. We wouldn't come in that neighborhood any more."

"Yes, we would. I have family there and don't want to move anyplace else. The truth of it is I can't marry you, Nat. I got troubles enough of my own."

"I coulda sworn you love me."

"Maybe I do but I can't marry you."

"For God's sake, why?"

"I got enough trouble of my own."

I went that night in a cab to her brother's house to see her. He was a quiet man with a thin mustache. "She's gone," he said, "left for a long visit to some close relatives in the South. She said to tell you she appreciate your intentions but didn't think it will work out."

"Thank you kindly," I said.

Don't ask me how I got home.

Once on Eighth Avenue, a couple of blocks from my store, I saw a blind man with a white cane tapping on the sidewalk. I figured we were going in the same direction so I took his arm.

"I can tell you're white," he said.

A heavy colored woman with a full shopping bag rushed after us.

"Never mind," she said, "I know where he live."

She pushed me with her shoulder and I hurt my leg on the fire hydrant.

That's how it is. I give my heart and they kick me in my teeth.

"Charity Sweetness—you hear me?—come out of the goddamn toilet!"

FOR FURTHER CONSIDERATION

Malamud raises several basic questions about ethnic background, equality, and the self. First, to what extent does one's ethnic background control one's sense of self? Second, to what extent is the self trapped in an ethnic stereotype? For example, could Nat Lime find acceptance as an

equal in the black ghetto? Third, does Lime delude himself about his
ability to accept a black person as an equal?

Claude Brown (1937–   )

In his superb Manchild in the Promised Land, *Claude Brown presents an
autobiographical account of the incredible hardships and risks that
accompany growing up in a major city ghetto. The passage which follows
is from the book.*

Turning It Around

Most of the cats my age, sixteen, seventeen, eighteen, were just coming
out of the house. They were just being cut loose from their parents. The
first thing they usually did was run out and start using drugs to be hip, to
be accepted into the street life, to be down. I didn't have to do that,
because I had come up in the street life. I knew all the old hustlers, the
hustlers who had become successful now, the hustlers who used to be
fences, used to be whores, the hustlers I used to sell stolen goods to when
I was just ten, eleven, twelve. I knew these people from way back, and
now they had big Cadillacs, they had restaurants. Some of them had little
nightclubs, after-hours places. I'd see these people on the street, and we'd
stop and talk. All the young cats my age envied me and looked upon me as
an older cat. Most people thought I was older. They had put out the story
at one time that I was a young-looking little midget, a cat who was really
twenty-one or twenty-two. It was the only way some of the cats my age
could explain my being so far ahead of them in street life.

   Mama used to get down on me about hanging out with Reno. She'd
say that she knew he'd be going to jail one day soon and that I'd be going
with him. At the same time, she was always getting down on me about
bringing certain chicks to the house. She used to say I always brought
nasty girls to the house. It became a real hassle.

   Dad knew I was doing something, but he didn't know exactly what.
They didn't know I was dealing pot, because I didn't have people coming to the house. He'd say, "Yeah, you gon be up there in jail where all
them other bad boys is you used to hang around with." He was always
riding me.

   I got tired of it after a while. I got tired of them telling me who to hang
out with and who to associate with. I felt that this shit was childish, and
since I was out and working, I didn't have to take it.

   I got fed up one day and moved out. I told Mama I'd found a place up
on Hamilton Terrace and was moving. Mama didn't believe me until I
started packing my stuff. Dad didn't say anything; he started mumbling to
himself. Mama started crying and said I shouldn't be leaving. I didn't have

anybody outside. She said a boy of sixteen should still be living with his family.

I didn't feel that way about it. I told them that I was tired of living with them, that I just couldn't take that sort of thing any more. They were kind of old-fashioned and countryfied. The way I saw it, they couldn't understand anything. I just packed up one night and pulled out. I left Dad squawking and Mama crying and moved up on Hamilton Terrace to a nice little room. This was where all the young hustlers lived.

The only other fellow I knew in Harlem who used to sell a lot of nice pot was Tommy Holloway, and he lived on Hamilton Terrace too. He was the one who got me my room up there. Tommy dressed real nice. He showed me a lot of stuff. He showed me what fences to buy clothes from if I wanted to get the best. He even cut me into the good drygoods thieves so that I would never get burned by fences.

This was where I felt I was supposed to be; it was where all the slick people were living. This was the set I wanted to be in.

It hurt Mama. Dad didn't care. He thought I was going to end up in jail anyway. Behind this, I could associate with anybody I wanted to. Mama kept telling me, "You can come home," every time I came around. I told her that I had my own home now and that I wasn't going to come back there any more. She said, "Come by and get a good meal." I'd stop by and give them money. After a while, they stopped asking me where I'd gotten it.

After I'd moved, Reno got busted, and he was in the Tombs. I didn't swing with anybody for a while. There was Tony Albee, who was about a year older than me, but he was just coming out. He'd been a nice boy, and he had just come up from down South in 1950. He had never gone through all the stuff that I had gone through. He hadn't been through the gang-fighting stage. He'd never smoked pot until I gave him a reefer one night. The cat was at a party, and I gave him a joint. He said he liked it, and he started trying to get tight with me, but the cat was a farmer. I didn't let him get but so tight. I used to let him run errands for me. He used to do what I told him to. If I went someplace and told him to wait, he'd wait. After a while, I started liking the guy.

He started hanging around. He said he wanted to start dealing pot. I said okay, and I gave him a couple of ounces and told him, "You can give me fifty dollars when you sell the stuff." I had to show him how to roll pot. He was a real country boy all the way.

People started saying that he was my partner. He turned out to be a real nice guy, so I didn't mind. He stayed close to me and used to try to dress the way I did. He'd buy clothes from the same people I got mine from. He'd never worn anything but cheap Charlie's shoes before, but now he started wearing custom-made. I guess he wanted to start acting just like me, and he had to start someplace. If he wanted to get into the street life, he had to start swinging with somebody who was already into it. I was into it kind of good, so I was a good person for him to start with.

When Reno came back on the street scene, he found out that Tony and I were tight. He said he didn't like him and that I shouldn't be hanging out with a farmer. I told him that the cat was all right with me and that I was going to swing with him for a while. Reno started staying away from me, and he started telling other cats that I was swinging with a lame, an old farmer. He was putting me down. I thought, Fuck it, I don't need him. But I still liked the cat and still admired him. I'd see him, and if he needed anything, I'd whip some money on him. Or we'd get high together.

Sometimes Tony would come around and try to talk with him. Tony might say, "Hi, Reno," but Reno would ignore him and then walk.

I guess it was something that Tony deserved, in a way, because he had been a nice boy for so long. Reno and Danny and Butch and Kid and I were with the dirty side. We were always the ones that people said would probably be in jail or dead before we were twenty-one. I think a lot of those "good boy" cats believed their parents when they were telling them that kind of stuff. Guys like Reno had to get their revenge on those cats, I guess, and now the "bad boys'" day had come. We were the elite in the neighborhood. We were the people who were into all the happenings, and these cats were trying to get in.

I guess we all kind of had it in for the righteous-doing folks in the neighborhood because they had messed with all of us when we were just kids coming up. They were always squealing on us and stuff like that. But I don't think anybody had as much reason to get back at them as Reno and his family. Most of them were pretty nice. Bucky was a nice guy. Mac was kind of lame and didn't have a lot of heart, but he was damn nice. He was a natural athlete. He was tall and lanky; he could play a whole lot of basketball, and he could run real fast. He had everything needed to become a good athlete, everything but confidence. Maybe if Miss Jamie had just shown him a little bit that she cared and tried to give him a little bit of self-respect, he would have made out all right. But she didn't do that, so the cat just never had any heart.

I guess it was harder on the girls than it was on anybody. Dixie started tricking when she was thirteen. She was big for her age, and "nice" ladies used to point at her and say, "Oh, ain't that a shame." But it wasn't. The shame of it was that she had to do it or starve. When she got hip and went out there on the street and started turning tricks, she started eating and she stopped starving. And I thought, Shit, it ain't no shame to stop starvin'. Hell, no.

Babe, Dixie's younger sister, was kind of ugly. She tried tricking, but she was just too ugly to make any money. Babe and Dixie were both sent to Hudson State Training School for Girls. When Dixie came out, she moved from Miss Jamie's and got a nice little place downtown. She made it on her own. Babe was too young to make it, so she just kept going back to Hudson. She said that she liked it there. It was the first place she'd been where people didn't make her feel she was out of place.

When Dixie got to be thirteen, there was nobody to tell her not to trick. She figured that since her mother was laying so many cats, why shouldn't she be tricking, especially if it was going to mean money and food. She used to feed the whole family sometimes, and that was a damn job, but the people in the neighborhood just kept looking down on her. They used to say that they didn't want their daughters hanging out with Dixie. But some of their daughters were giving away more cunt than Dixie was selling.

Reno was always in the Tombs for jostling. The Tombs used to be his winter home. He said he didn't mind being down there in the wintertime, but he liked to be out on the streets in the fresh air and living and partying in the summertime, when so much was happening out on the streets. I guess to most people, it would have seemed like a hard life to be spending all your winters down in the Tombs, but it wasn't so bad. Life out on the street for some people was harder. It was much harder to be out there working every day than to be in the Tombs. Jail wasn't hard for anybody who knew how to live down there and get by.

A few weeks after I moved to Hamilton Terrace, a panic was on. You couldn't get any pot. Cocaine was pretty nice, but nobody used cocaine much but the hustlers, and it wasn't an all-night thing with them. You could sell a hundred dollars' worth of cocaine if you made all the bars up to 148th Street. You could sell it to the pimps, the whores, all the hustlers out there at night. But there weren't many customers for cocaine on the street, not like pot. Cats who were working would hardly come up and give you five dollars for a tiny cap of cocaine or ten or twenty dollars for a little tin of cocaine. It was too expensive for the average person, and you couldn't be selling it to the hustlers every night, because they couldn't afford to be blowing all their money on cocaine.

I had a little money in the bank, but I was scared that wasn't going to last too long. So I got a job working at a joint called Hamburger Heaven. This was a real drag. It was something terrible. It was on Madison Avenue, and you had to be a real Tom. Most of the cats there were from the South and weren't too hip. They hadn't been in New York long, and they didn't know anything. Most of them were really dumb—farmers.

I stayed with that for a while. The thing that bothered me most—I didn't know it would, because I'd never thought about it before—was that only white people came in there. I started off as a busboy. Later I became a waiter—white coat, black tie, and black pants. You had to smile at the white folks, hoping they'd throw a big tip on you. You had to watch what you said, and you had to watch the way you acted, because they had an old, dumbhead waiter who was a real Tom.

If you said anything to one of the customers and didn't put a "sir" on it, he'd run up there and say, "Boy, what's wrong with you?" and all this kind of simple shit. It was pretty hard to take, but I needed a job.

I stayed on for about a year. Behind the panic coming on, I couldn't get any pot, so I wasn't dealing anything then. I still had my contacts, and as soon as the stuff came in again, I would go back into business.

The first time I heard the expression "baby" used by one cat to address another was up at Warwick in 1951. Gus Jackson used it. The term had a hip ring to it, a real colored ring. The first time I heard it, I knew right away I had to start using it. It was like saying, "Man, look at me. I've got masculinity to spare." It was saying at the same time to the world, "I'm one of the hippest cats, one of the most uninhibited cats on the scene. I can say 'baby' to another cat, and he can say 'baby' to me, and we can say it with strength in our voices." If you could say it, this meant that you really had to be sure of yourself, sure of your masculinity.

It seemed that everybody in my age group was saying it. The next thing I knew, older guys were saying it. Then just about everybody in Harlem was saying it, even the cats who weren't so hip. It became just one of those things.

The real hip thing about the "baby" term was that it was something that only colored cats could say the way it was supposed to be said. I'd heard gray boys trying it, but they couldn't really do it. Only colored cats could give it the meaning that we all knew it had without ever mentioning it—the meaning of black masculinity.

Before the Muslims, before I'd heard about the Coptic or anything like that, I remember getting high on the corner with a bunch of guys and watching the chicks go by, fine little girls, and saying, "Man, colored people must be somethin' else!"

Somebody'd say, "Yeah. How about that? All those years, man, we was down on the plantation in those shacks, eating just potatoes and fatback and chitterlin's and greens, and look at what happened. We had Joe Louises and Jack Johnsons and Sugar Ray Robinsons and Henry Armstrongs, all that sort of thing."

Somebody'd say, "Yeah, man. Niggers must be some real strong people who just can't be kept down. When you think about it, that's really something great. Fatback, chitterlin's, greens, and Joe Louis. Negroes are some beautiful people. Uh-huh. Fatback, chitterlin's, greens, and Joe Louis . . . and beautiful black bitches."

Cats would come along with this "baby" thing. It was something that went over strong in the fifties with the jazz musicians and the hip set, the boxers, the dancers, the comedians, just about every set in Harlem. I think everybody said it real loud because they liked the way it sounded. It was always, "Hey, baby. How you doin', baby?" in every phase of the Negro hip life. As a matter of fact, I went to a Negro lawyer's office once, and he said, "Hey, baby. How you doin', baby?" I really felt at ease, really felt that we had something in common. I imagine there were many people in Harlem who didn't feel they had too much in common with the Negro professionals, the doctors and lawyers and dentists and ministers. I know I didn't. But to hear one of these people greet you with the street thing, the "Hey, baby"—and he knew how to say it—you felt as though you had something strong in common.

I suppose it's the same thing that almost all Negroes have in common, the fatback, chitterlings, and greens background. I suppose that regardless of what any Negro in America might do or how high he might rise in social status, he still has something in common with every other Negro. I doubt that they're many, if any, gray people who could ever say "baby" to a Negro and make him feel that "me and this cat have got something going, something strong going."

In the fifties, when "baby" came around, it seemed to be the prelude to a whole new era in Harlem. It was the introduction to the era of black reflection. A fever started spreading. Perhaps the strong rising of the Muslim movement is something that helped to sustain or even usher in this era.

I remember that in the early fifties, cats would stand on the corner and talk, just shooting the stuff, all the street-corner philosophers. Sometimes, it was a common topic—cats talking about gray chicks—and somebody might say something like, "Man, what can anybody see in a gray chick, when colored chicks are so fine; they got so much soul." This was the coming of the "soul" thing too.

"Soul" had started coming out of the churches and the nightclubs into the streets. Everybody started talking about "soul" as though it were something that they could see on people or a distinct characteristic of colored folks.

Cats would say things like, "Man, gray chicks seem so stiff." Many of them would say they couldn't talk to them or would wonder how a cat who was used to being so for real with a chick could see anything in a gray girl. It seemed as though the mood of the day was turning toward the color thing.

Everybody was really digging themselves and thinking and saying in their behavior, in every action, "Wow! Man, it's a beautiful thing to be colored." Everybody was saying, "Oh, the beauty of me! Look at me. I'm colored. And look at us. Aren't we beautiful?"

Around November of 1953, I went up to Wiltwyck. I hadn't seen Papanek since I'd gotten out of Warwick for the last time. I guess I didn't want to see him. I'd resigned myself to the fact that I was in street life for good. I'd be going to jail soon, and I'd be doing a lot of time. I liked Papanek, but we could only be but so tight, because I was going the crime way. That's all there was to it.

I went up to Wiltwyck for Thanksgiving to visit the people and see what the place looked like. Maybe it was a kind of homesickness that took me up there. When I left, Papanek drove me to Poughkeepsie to catch a train back to New York City.

He said, "What are you doing, Claude? Are you going to school?"

"No, I'm goin' to school next term, when it starts in February. I'm gonna go to night school." I was only joking with him.

"Yeah, that's good. You can really do it if you want to, and I'm glad to hear that you want to."

I looked at him and said to myself, Well, damn, this cat really believes me. I just didn't think too much more of it after that.

Before I left Wiltwyck, I had been talking to Nick and had told him that I was dealing pot. He was a hip guy and knew how life was on the streets and knew something about Harlem, so I just came out and told him, "Like, man, I'm dealin' pot, and I'll probably be in jail in another couple-a months or so. But right now, I'm doin' good."

He could see I was doing good. He saw the way I dressed. After that Nick started telling me about what Papanek was saying to people about me. He said, "Papanek really thinks a lot of you. He thinks you're gonna make out just great. He keeps tellin' people that Claude Brown is gonna be a real success."

I said, "Yeah, man. Uh-huh. I'm gon be a real success. I'm liable to be the biggest drug dealer in Harlem. . . . Nobody from here is gonna make it too far. I don't think anybody is gonna make it farther than Floyd Patterson has made it." Floyd was Golden Gloves champion at that time. I said, "Maybe Wiltwyck ought to be satisfied with that."

Nick finally said, "Well, Claude, you never know how the cards are stacked up for you, and if it's in the cards, maybe Papanek is right."

I looked at Nick, and I thought, Damn, what the hell is wrong with Nick? He must be gettin' old. Here I just told the cat that I was into the street life and was dealin' pot and cocaine. I just looked at him and said, Poor Nick, to myself. Aloud I said, "Yeah, man. You never know," and I just forgot about it until I got in the car with Papanek and he started asking that business about school.

I'd always been aware throughout my delinquent life of the age thing, and I knew that I didn't have a sheet yet. I knew that I didn't have a criminal record as long as I was sent to the Wiltwycks and Warwicks. But I also knew that since I was sixteen and out on my own, the next time I was busted, I'd be fingerprinted. I'd have a sheet on me for the rest of my life. I thought, Yeah, I could still make it, but, shit, what would I want to make it for? I knew I didn't want to go to school, because I would have been too dumb and way behind everybody. I hadn't been to school in so long; and when I was really in school, I played hookey all the time and didn't learn anything. I couldn't be going to anybody's school as dumb as I was.

I got back out on the streets, and I forgot about what I'd told Papanek on the ride from Wiltwyck to Poughkeepsie. I knew what I was going to do, and there was nothing to think about. When I got back to New York, I did the same things I'd been doing. I kept on working. I kept on dealing pot. I kept on dealing a little cocaine.

One night, I was uptown on 149th Street. I had gone to see some cute little girl up that way. She was a beautiful little brown-skinned girl with long, jet-black hair. She looked like an Indian, so everybody called her Cherokee. I had come out of Cherokee's house about twelve-thirty or one o'clock, and as I started into the hall leading to the outside, somebody from behind the stairs called my name.

"Sonny!"

I said, "Yeah," and turned around. The first thing I saw was a gun in a hand. Then I saw a cat. I'd seen him around. They called him Limpy. I don't know why. He had a sort of hunched back, but he didn't have a limp.

He just said, "Sonny, I want all your shit. I don't want to have to kill you."

I knew he was a junkie, and I knew about junkies. When their habit comes down on them, you can't play with them. It's kill or be killed. I didn't have a gun at the time, because last time I'd gotten busted, I'd lent my gun to Danny.

"Look, Sonny, I don't want to kill you, man. All I want is your shit, now. It's, like, I gotta have it." He started talking real fast. He seemed to be nervous but not scared. His habit was down on him, and he was trying to say all this before anything happened. He wanted to explain.

I liked the way he respected me, and I thought maybe he was a little "religious." He must have seen a look in my eye, and he said, "Now, look, nigger, I'm not scared-a you, and I'll kill you if I have to. But I don't want to. All I want is what you got on you."

I didn't say anything, and he started toward me. I said, "Man, I ain't got nothin'."

"Look, Sonny, I don't want to hear that shit." He put the gun up to my face.

"If that's all you want, man, go on and take it."

"Where is it, man? Don't get crazy and try anything, because my habit's down on me; I got to have some drugs. And I'll kill you, nigger, if you make me."

I told him where the drugs were. I had them in an eyeglass case in my inside jacket pocket.

He reached in there, got it, and looked in it. He said, "Okay, like, you stay here, man. You in my neighborhood now, and I know the backyard; I know the people and everything around here, so don't try and act like you crazy."

He told me to just stay there for about two minutes, and he ran in the backyard. He just took the drugs and was gone. He took about a hundred and ten dollars' worth of coke and pot from me. He'd sell it for horse.

I felt bad. Nobody had ever stuck me up or shit like that. I knew that this would get around, and you couldn't deal any drugs if you were going to be letting cats stick you up and take it. I knew that I'd have to get a gun, and that when cats heard about it—cats like Bubba Williams, Big Freddie, Reno, and Tommy Holloway—they would also want to hear that the guy had been killed. This was the way the people in our set did things. You didn't go around letting anybody stick you up. Shit, if you let somebody stick you up and go on living behind it, you didn't have any business dealing drugs. Everybody who wanted some free drugs would come by and try to stick you up. I didn't want to, but I knew I had to get another piece and find that cat.

The cat pulled a fadeaway. Danny heard about it. Danny and I were still tight. He was coming around. Cocaine couldn't do much for Danny, because Danny was strung out on smack. When you're using heroin, nothing else is going to do but so much for you. I used to always give Danny money to cop, or if I came by some horse by accident—somebody might have given me some for some cocaine—I used to give it to Danny. Danny was a cat who appreciated this sort of thing.

I saw him the day after Limpy had stung me in the hallway on 149th Street. I went up to him, and I said, "I got to get me a piece, baby."

He said, "Yeah, I heard about it, Sonny, but I want to ask you somethin', and I mean it from the bottom of my heart."

"Sure, Danny, you know, speak your piece, baby."

Then Danny said, "Look, Sonny; like, I know you, man, from way back. We came outta the house together, you know?"

"Yeah. So, what you want to ask me, Danny?"

"Do you really want to burn this cat, man? I mean, you want to waste Limpy?"

I said, "Look, man, it's like you said; we came the street way together, and you know how that shit is. You know if I don't kill that mother-fucker, I can't come out on the street any more with any stuff in my pocket talkin' about I'm gon deal drugs. Niggers will be laughin', comin' up in my collar, and sayin', 'Give me what you got.' I mean, if I did that kinda shit, if I let the cat go on livin', mother-fuckers would be tryin' to rob me without a gun. That would be the end of it all."

He said, "Yeah, I know how that shit, is, Sonny. But, like, look, man, you got a whole lot goin' for you. You got a lot on the ball. I never told you this before, but I think you're smarter than all these niggers out here, Sonny. And I think if anybody on Eighth Avenue ever makes it, I think it could be you."

I said, "Danny, what you talkin' about?" That shit surprised me. This wasn't supposed to be coming from Danny. This just wasn't him, and it wasn't the stuff we used to talk about. I said, "What's wrong with you?"

"Look, Sonny, I got a piece, but I'm not gon let you have it. What I want you to do is forget about Limpy, not just forget about him, but let me take him, man, let me worry about him."

Danny had been strung out for about four years. I guess he felt that he didn't have much going for him. His folks had cut him loose; he couldn't go home. None of his relatives wanted him coming by. He was ragged all the time. He'd been in and out of jail. He'd been down to Kentucky a couple of times for the cure. He'd been to a place called Brothers Island. He'd been a whole lot of places for a cure. He'd caused everybody a whole lot of trouble. He felt that life was over for him.

"Look, Sonny, I'm already through. Like, I'm wasted. You got somethin' to live for, but me, I can't lose no more. So let me take care-a the nigger for you, and we'll be squared away. You did a whole lot for me, man. I remember the times I was sick and you gave me some drugs. I couldn't go anywhere but to you. I feel if there's one nigger out here on the street who I owe somethin' to, one nigger I should give my life for, man, it's you. And, besides, I'm not really givin' my life. I'm already fucked up. I gave my life the first time I put a little bit-a horse in my nose."

"Look, Danny, thanks a lot, man, but we're not back in the short-pants days. If somebody stings me out here, it's not like somebody bigger than me fuckin' with me in school or some shit like that. We're out here man for man and playin' for keeps, baby. Everybody's gotta be his own man, you know?"

"Okay, Sonny, like I kinda understand it, but I'm still not gon give you my piece, man, because I don't want you to do it. And if I see the nigger before you do, I'm gon beat you to him."

"Yeah, Danny, like, thanks a lot, baby," and I walked. I went up to Robby Ohara. Robby Ohara was a stickup artist, and he used to sell all the guns in the neighborhood. He lived in my building. Just about all the criminals lived in my building.

Robby had heard what happened to me, and when I came up to his crib and said, "Robby, I need a piece right away," he asked me what kind of piece I wanted. I told him I wanted something small but effective, like a .25 automatic.

He said, "All right." He went into another room, came out, and threw me a .25. He said, "You know how to use it?"

It was a Spanish-made gun, and he showed me some things about it. I took out some money. He said, "Forget it, Sonny, that nigger is suppose to be dead. That's a gift from me."

Robby was a killer, and he understood this sort of thing. I took the piece and left.

I looked for Limpy for about a week or more, and I couldn't find him. After a while, I heard that he had gotten busted trying to stick up a doctor in his office. Somebody said he'd gotten shot about four times. This took me off the hook and saved my face, but I still had the piece. I knew that the next time somebody stung me, I was going to have to kill him. I started thinking about it. It didn't seem right for me to be killing a junkie, because these cats were usually harmless. And when they weren't harmless, it wasn't really them, it was smack that was at fault.

I started talking to Tony. I said, "Look, Tony, I'm gonna give up dealin' pot."

He said, "Yeah, I'm gon give it up too," but I knew he couldn't because he didn't have a job.

I told my customers I was going out of business, and I started sending them to Tony and other people who were dealing. A lot of cats who were dealing stuff would ask me, "Look, Sonny, you need some money? You can't get any good stuff?" I guess they just didn't want to see me stop dealing. I told them I didn't need anything and didn't want anything.

I started going to night school. I went to Washington Irving, because that was the first one I had heard about. When I'd come uptown, I'd see the cats on the corner at night. They were still making that money, teasing me, and laughing. They called me Schoolboy and said that I must be dealing pot downtown someplace, that I was pulling everybody's leg about school. Some of the cats I knew said I wouldn't go to school even when I had the truant officer after me, so why should I be going now.

But after a while, they saw that I was serious, and everybody stopped teasing me about it. I hadn't felt too bad when they were teasing me, because I knew they couldn't call me square or lame. Most of the cats who were out there on the corners dealing stuff now were the newcomers. Most of the cats I came up with were in jail or dead or strung out on drugs. I'd been out in street life long before these cats even knew how to roll a reefer. I could do what I wanted. I could turn square now, even straighten up if I wanted too, and not worry about anybody naming me a lame. I'd been through the street-life thing. At seventeen, I was ready to retire from it. I'd already had ten or eleven years at it.

FOR FURTHER CONSIDERATION

Individuals often make critically important decisions on the basis of vague inner promptings, only to realize later that the decision expressed deeply felt values. When Sonny chooses to quit street life and acquire an education, what does it suggest about his essential values? About his sense of self? What makes the decision a difficult one?

Some social observers feel that the measure of maturity appears in the individual's ability to recognize choices, and to make choices and live with their consequences. Do you agree that these attributes offer a measure of maturity?

Ernest Hemingway (1899–1961)

Everybody knows about Hemingway. World War I Italian Ambulance Corps; wounded; tragic romance; newspaper writing; expatriate days in Paris and Spain; fishing off Cuba; volunteer in the Spanish Civil War; obsessed with boxing, bullfights, big-game hunting; hard drinking, a man's man, several wives, a Nobel Prize winner. A spare style, with language, grammar, rhythm, and sound understating situations and suggesting toughness and courage in the face of loss, nothingness, and death. "Francis Macomber" captures it all in a classic conflict and a matchless portrayal of a woman.

The Short Happy Life of Francis Macomber

It was now lunch time and they were all sitting under the double green fly of the dining tent pretending that nothing had happened.

"Will you have lime juice or lemon squash?" Macomber asked.

"I'll have a gimlet," Robert Wilson told him.

"I'll have a gimlet too. I need something," Macomber's wife said.

"I suppose it's the thing to do," Macomber agreed. "Tell him to make three gimlets."

The mess boy had started them already, lifting the bottles out of the canvas cooling bags that sweated wet in the wind that blew through the trees that shaded the tents.

"What had I ought to give them?" Macomber asked.

"A quid would be plenty," Wilson told him. "You don't want to spoil them."

"Will the headman distribute it?"

"Absolutely."

Francis Macomber had, half an hour before, been carried to his tent from the edge of the camp in triumph on the arms and shoulders of the cook, the personal boys, the skinner and the porters. The gun-bearers had taken no part in the demonstration. When the native boys put him down at the door of his tent, he had shaken all their hands, received their congratulations, and then gone into the tent and sat on the bed until his wife came in. She did not speak to him when she came in and he left the tent at once to wash his face and hands in the portable wash basin outside and go over to the dining tent to sit in a comfortable canvas chair in the breeze and the shade.

"You've got your lion," Robert Wilson said to him, " and a damned fine one too."

Mrs. Macomber looked at Wilson quickly. She was an extremely handsome and well-kept woman of the beauty and social position which had, five years before, commanded five thousand dollars as the price of endorsing, with photographs, a beauty product which she had never used. She had been married to Francis Macomber for eleven years.

"He is a good lion, isn't he?" Macomber said. His wife looked at him now. She looked at both these men as though she had never seen them before.

One, Wilson, the white hunter, she knew she had never truly seen before. He was about middle height with sandy hair, a stubby mustache, a very red face and extremely cold blue eyes with faint white wrinkles at the corners that grooved merrily when he smiled. He smiled at her now and she looked away from his face at the way his shoulders sloped in the loose tunic he wore with the four big cartridges held in loops where the left breast pocket should have been, at his big brown hands, his old slacks, his very dirty boots and back to his red face again. She noticed where the baked red of his face stopped in a white line that marked the circle left by his Stetson hat that hung now from one of the pegs of the tent pole.

"Well, here's to the lion," Robert Wilson said. He smiled at her again and, not smiling she looked curiously at her husband.

Francis Macomber was very tall, very well built if you did not mind that length of bone, dark, his hair cropped like an oarsman, rather thin-lipped, and was considered handsome. He was dressed in the same sort of safari clothes that Wilson wore except that his were new, he was thirty-five years old, kept himself very fit, was good at court games, had a number of big-game fishing records, and had just shown himself, very publicly, to be a coward.

"Here's to the lion," he said. "I can't ever thank you for what you did."

Margaret, his wife, looked away from him and back to Wilson.

"Let's not talk about the lion," she said.

Wilson looked over at her without smiling and now she smiled at him.

"It's been a very strange day," she said. "Hadn't you ought to put your hat on even under the canvas at noon? You told me that, you know."

"Might put it on," said Wilson.

"You know you have a very red face, Mr. Wilson," she told him and smiled again.

"Drink," said Wilson.

"I don't think so," she said. "Francis drinks a great deal, but his face is never red."

"It's red today," Macomber tried a joke.

"No," said Margaret. "It's mine that's red today. But Mr. Wilson's is always red."

"Must be racial," said Wilson. "I say, you wouldn't like to drop my beauty as a topic, would you?"

"I've just started on it."

"Let's chuck it," said Wilson.

"Conversation is going to be so difficult," Margaret said.

"Don't be silly, Margot," her husband said.

"No difficulty," Wilson said. "Got a damn fine lion."

Margot looked at them both and they both saw that she was going to cry. Wilson had seen it coming for a long time and he dreaded it. Macomber was past dreading it.

"I wish it hadn't happened. Oh, I wish it hadn't happened," she said and started for her tent. She made no noise of crying but they could see that her shoulders were shaking under the rose-colored, sun-proofed shirt she wore.

"Women upset," said Wilson to the tall man. "Amounts to nothing. Strain on the nerves and one thing'n another."

"No," said Macomber. "I suppose that I rate that for the rest of my life now."

"Nonsense. Let's have a spot of the giant killer," said Wilson. "Forget the whole thing. Nothing to it anyway."

"We might try," said Macomber. "I won't forget what you did for me though."

"Nothing," said Wilson. "All nonsense."

So they sat there in the shade where the camp was pitched under some wide-topped acacia trees with a boulder-strewn cliff behind them, and a stretch of grass that ran to the bank of a boulder-filled stream in front with forest beyond it, and drank their just-cool lime drinks and avoided one another's eyes while the boys set the table for lunch. Wilson could tell that the boys all knew about it now and when he saw Macomber's personal boy looking curiously at his master while he was putting dishes on the table he snapped at him in Swahili. The boy turned away with his face blank.

"What were you telling him?" Macomber asked.

"Nothing. Told him to look alive or I'd see he got about fifteen of the best."

"What's that? Lashes?"

"It's quite illegal," Wilson said. "You're supposed to fine them."

"Do you still have them whipped?"

"Oh, yes. They could raise a row if they chose to complain. But they don't. They prefer it to the fines."

"How strange!" said Macomber.

"Not strange, really," Wilson said. "Which would you rather do? Take a good birching or lose your pay?"

Then he felt embarrassed at asking it and before Macomber could answer he went on, "We all take a beating every day, you know, one way or another."

This was no better. "Good God," he thought. "I am a diplomat, aren't I?"

"Yes, we take a beating," said Macomber, still not looking at him. "I'm awfully sorry about that lion business. It doesn't have to go any further, does it? I mean no one will hear about it, will they?"

"You mean will I tell it at the Mathaiga Club?" Wilson looked at him now coldly. He had not expected this. So he's a bloody four-letter man as well as a bloody coward, he thought. I rather liked him too until today. But how is one to know about an American?

"No," said Wilson. "I'm a professional hunter. We never talk about our clients. You can be quite easy on that. It's supposed to be bad form to ask us not to talk though."

He had decided now that to break would be much easier. He would eat, then, by himself and could read a book with his meals. They would eat by themselves. He would see them through the safari on a very formal basis—what was it the French called it? Distinguished consideration—and it would be a damn sight easier than having to go through this emotional trash. He'd insult him and make a good clean break. Then he could read a book with his meals and he'd still be drinking their whisky. That was the phrase for it when a safari went bad. You ran into another white hunter and you asked, "How is everything going?" and he answered, "Oh, I'm still drinking their whisky," and you knew everything had gone to pot.

"I'm sorry," Macomber said and looked at him with his American face that would stay adolescent until it became middle-aged, and Wilson noted his crew-cropped hair, fine eyes only faintly shifty, good nose, thin lips and handsome jaw. "I'm sorry I didn't realize that. There are lots of things I don't know."

So what could he do, Wilson thought. He was all ready to break it off quickly and neatly and here the beggar was apologizing after he had just insulted him. He made one more attempt. "Don't worry about me talking," he said. "I have a living to make. You know in Africa no woman ever misses her lion and no white man ever bolts."

"I bolted like a rabbit," Macomber said.

Now what in hell were you going to do about a man who talked like that, Wilson wondered.

Wilson looked at Macomber with his flat, blue, machine-gunner's eyes and the other smiled back at him. He had a pleasant smile if you did not notice how his eyes showed when he was hurt.

"Maybe I can fix it up on buffalo," he said. "We're after them next, aren't we?"

"In the morning if you like," Wilson told him. Perhaps he had been wrong. This was certainly the way to take it. You most certainly could not tell a damned thing about an American. He was all for Macomber again. If you could forget the morning. But, of course, you couldn't. The morning had been about as bad as they come.

"Here comes the Memsahib," he said. She was walking over from her tent looking refreshed and cheerful and quite lovely. She had a very perfect oval face, so perfect that you expected her to be stupid. But she wasn't stupid, Wilson thought, no, not stupid.

"How is the beautiful red-faced Mr. Wilson? Are you feeling better, Francis, my pearl?"

"Oh, much," said Macomber.

"I've dropped the whole thing," she said, sitting down at the table. "What importance is there to whether Francis is any good at killing lions? That's not his trade. That's Mr. Wilson's trade. Mr. Wilson is really very impressive killing anything. You do kill anything, don't you?"

"Oh, anything," said Wilson. "Simply anything." They are, he thought, the hardest in the world; the hardest, the cruelest, the most predatory and the most attractive and their men have softened or gone to pieces nervously as they have hardened. Or is it that they pick men they can handle? They can't know that much at the age they marry, he thought. He was grateful that he had gone through his education on American women before now because this was a very attractive one.

"We're going after buff in the morning," he told her.

"I'm coming," she said.

"No, you're not."

"Oh, yes, I am. Mayn't I, Francis?"

"Why not stay in camp?"

"Not for anything," she said. "I wouldn't miss something like today for anything."

When she left, Wilson was thinking, when she went off to cry, she seemed a hell of a fine woman. She seemed to understand, to realize, to be hurt for him and for herself and to know how things really stood. She is away for twenty minutes and now she is back, simply enamelled in that

American female cruelty. They are the damnedest women. Really the damnedest.

"We'll put on another show for you tomorrow," Francis Macomber said.

"You're not coming," Wilson said.

"You're very mistaken," she told him. "And I want *so* to see you perform again. You were lovely this morning. That is if blowing things' heads off is lovely."

"Here's the lunch," said Wilson. "You're very merry, aren't you ?"

"Why not? I didn't come out here to be dull."

"Well, it hasn't been dull," Wilson said. He could see the boulders in the river and the high bank beyond with the trees and he remembered the morning.

"Oh, no," she said. "It's been charming. And tomorrow. You don't know how I look forward to tomorrow."

"That's eland he's offering you," Wilson said.

"They're the big cowy things that jump like hares, aren't they?"

"I suppose that describes them," Wilson said.

"It's very good meat," Macomber said.

"Did you shoot it, Francis?" she asked.

"Yes."

"They're not dangerous, are they?"

"Only if they fall on you," Wilson told her.

"I'm so glad."

"Why not let up on the bitchery just a little, Margot," Macomber said, cutting the eland steak and putting some mashed potato, gravy and carrot on the down-turned fork that tined through the piece of meat.

"I suppose I could," she said, "since you put it so prettily."

"Tonight we'll have champagne for the lion," Wilson said. "It's a bit too hot at noon."

"Oh, the lion," Margot said. "I'd forgotten the lion!"

So, Robert Wilson thought to himself, she *is* giving him a ride, isn't she? Or do you suppose that's her idea of putting up a good show? How should a woman act when she discovers her husband is a bloody coward? She's damn cruel but they're all cruel. They govern, of course, and to govern one has to be cruel sometimes. Still, I've seen enough of their damn terrorism.

"Have some more eland," he said to her politely.

That afternoon, late, Wilson and Macomber went out in the motor car with the native driver and the two gun-bearers. Mrs. Macomber stayed in the camp. It was too hot to go out, she said, and she was going with them in the early morning. As they drove off Wilson saw her standing under the big tree, looking pretty rather than beautiful in her faintly rosy khaki, her dark hair drawn back off her forehead and gathered in a knot low on her neck, her face as fresh, he thought, as though she were in England. She waved to them as the car went off through the swale of high grass and curved around through the trees into the small hills of orchard bush.

In the orchard bush they found a herd of impala, and leaving the car they stalked one old ram with long, wide-spread horns and Macomber killed it with a very creditable shot that knocked the buck down at a good two hundred yards and sent the herd off bounding wildly and leaping over one another's backs in long, leg-drawn-up leaps as unbelievable and as floating as those one makes sometimes in dreams.

"That was a good shot," Wilson said. "They're a small target."

"Is it a worth-while head?" Macomber asked.

"It's excellent," Wilson told him. "You shoot like that and you'll have no trouble."

"Do you think we'll find buffalo tomorrow?"

"There's a good chance of it. They feed out early in the morning and with luck we may catch them in the open."

"I'd like to clear away that lion business," Macomber said. "It's not very pleasant to have your wife see you do something like that."

I should think it would be even more unpleasant to do it, Wilson thought, wife or no wife, or to talk about it having done it. But he said, "I wouldn't think about that any more. Anyone could be upset by his first lion. That's all over."

But that night after dinner and a whisky and soda by the fire before going to bed, as Francis Macomber lay on his cot with the mosquito bar over him and listened to the night noises it was not all over. It was neither all over nor was it beginning. It was there exactly as it happened with some parts of it indelibly emphasized and he was miserably ashamed at it. But more than shame he felt cold, hollow fear in him. The fear was still there like a cold slimy hollow in all the emptiness where once his confidence had been and it made him feel sick. It was still there with him now.

It had started the night before when he had wakened and heard the lion roaring somewhere up along the river. It was a deep sound and at the end there were sort of coughing grunts that made him seem just outside the tent, and when Francis Macomber woke in the night to hear it he was afraid. He could hear his wife breathing quietly, asleep. There was no one to tell he was afraid, nor to be afraid with him, and, lying alone, he did not know the Somali proverb that says a brave man is always frightened three times by a lion; when he first sees his track, when he first hears him roar and when he first confronts him. Then while they were eating breakfast by lantern light out in the dining tent, before the sun was up, the lion roared again and Francis thought he was just at the edge of camp.

"Sounds like an old-timer," Robert Wilson said, looking up from his kippers and coffee. "Listen to him cough."

"Is he very close?"

"A mile or so up the stream."

"Will we see him?"

"We'll have a look."

"Does his roaring carry that far? It sounds as though he were right in camp."

"Carries a hell of a long way," said Robert Wilson. "It's strange the way it carries. Hope he's a shootable cat. The boys said there was a very big one about here."

"If I get a shot, where should I hit him," Macomber asked, "to stop him?"

"In the shoulders," Wilson said. "In the neck if you can make it. Shoot for bone. Break him down."

"I hope I can place it properly," Macomber said.

"You shoot very well," Wilson told him. "Take your time. Make sure of him. The first one in is the one that counts."

"What range will it be?"

"Can't tell. Lion has something to say about that. Won't shoot unless it's close enough so you can make sure."

"At under a hundred yards?" Macomber asked.

Wilson looked at him quickly.

"Hundred's about right. Might have to take him a bit under. Shouldn't chance a shot at much over that. A hundred's a decent range. You can hit him wherever you want at that. Here comes the Memsahib."

"Good morning," she said. "Are we going after that lion?"

"As soon as you deal with your breakfast," Wilson said. "How are you feeling?"

"Marvellous," she said. "I'm very excited."

"I'll just go and see that everything is ready," Wilson went off. As he left the lion roared again.

"Noisy beggar," Wilson said. "We'll put a stop to that."

"What's the matter, Francis?" his wife asked him.

"Nothing," Macomber said.

"Yes, there is," she said. "What are you upset about?"

"Nothing," he said.

"Tell me," she looked at him. "Don't you feel well?"

"It's that damned roaring," he said. "It's been going on all night, you know."

"Why didn't you wake me," she said. "I'd love to have heard it."

"I've got to kill the damned thing," Macomber said, miserably.

"Well, that's what you're out here for, isn't it?"

"Yes. But I'm nervous. Hearing the thing roar gets on my nerves."

"Well then, as Wilson said, kill him and stop his roaring."

"Yes, darling," said Francis Macomber. "It sounds easy, doesn't it?"

"You're not afraid, are you?"

"Of course not. But I'm nervous from hearing him roar all night."

"You'll kill him marvellously," she said. "I know you will. I'm awfully anxious to see it."

"Finish your breakfast and we'll be starting."

"It's not light yet," she said. "This is a ridiculous hour."

Just then the lion roared in a deep-chested moaning, suddenly guttural, ascending vibration that seemed to shake the air and ended in a sigh and a heavy, deep-chested grunt.

"He sounds almost here," Macomber's wife said.

"My God," said Macomber. "I hate that damned noise."

"It's very impressive."

"Impressive. It's frightful."

Robert Wilson came up then carrying his short, ugly, shockingly big-bored .505 Gibbs and grinning.

"Come on," he said. "Your gun-bearer has your Springfield and the big gun. Everything's in the car. Have you solids?"

"Yes."

"I'm ready," Mrs. Macomber said.

"Must make him stop that racket," Wilson said. "You get in front. The Memsahib can sit back here with me."

They climbed into the motor car and, in the gray first daylight, moved off up the river through the trees. Macomber opened the breech of his rifle and saw he had metal-cased bullets, shut the bolt and put the rifle on safety. He saw his hand was trembling. He felt in his pocket for more cartridges and moved his fingers over the cartridges in the loops of his tunic front. He turned back to where Wilson sat in the rear seat of the doorless, box-bodied motor car beside his wife, them both grinning with excitement, and Wilson leaned forward and whispered,

"See the birds dropping. Means the old boy has left his kill."

On the far bank of the stream Macomber could see, above the trees, vultures circling and plummeting down.

"Chances are he'll come to drink along here," Wilson whispered. "Before he goes to lay up. Keep an eye out."

They were driving slowly along the high bank of the stream which here cut deeply to its boulder-filled bed, and they wound in and out through big trees as they drove. Macomber was watching the opposite bank when he felt Wilson take hold of his arm. The car stopped.

"There he is," he heard the whisper. "Ahead and to the right. Get out and take him. He's a marvellous lion."

Macomber saw the lion now. He was standing almost broadside, his great head up and turned toward them. The early morning breeze that blew toward them was just stirring his dark mane, and the lion looked huge, silhouetted on the rise of bank in the gray morning light, his shoulders heavy, his barrel of a body bulking smoothly.

"How far is he?" asked Macomber, raising his rifle.

"About seventy-five. Get out and take him."

"Why not shoot from where I am?"

"You don't shoot them from cars," he heard Wilson saying in his ear. "Get out. He's not going to stay there all day."

Macomber stepped out of the curved opening at the side of the front seat, onto the step and down onto the ground. The lion still stood looking majestically and coolly toward this object that his eyes only showed in silhouette, bulking like some super-rhino. There was no man smell carried toward him and he watched the object, moving his great head a little from side to side. Then watching the object, not afraid, but hesitating before going down the bank to drink with such a thing opposite him, he saw a man figure detach itself from it and he turned his heavy head and swung away toward the cover of the trees as he heard a cracking crash and felt the slam of a .30–06 220-grain solid bullet that bit his flank and ripped in sudden hot scalding nausea through his stomach. He trotted, heavy, big-footed, swinging wounded full-bellied, through the trees toward the tall grass and cover, and the crash came again to go past him ripping the air apart. Then it crashed again and he felt the blow as it hit his lower ribs and ripped on through, blood sudden hot and frothy in his mouth, and he galloped toward the high grass where he could crouch and not be seen and make them bring the crashing thing close enough so he could make a rush and get the man that held it.

Macomber had not thought how the lion felt as he got out of the car. He only knew his hands were shaking and as he walked away from the car it was almost impossible for him to make his legs move. They were stiff in the thighs, but he could feel the muscles fluttering. He raised the rifle, sighted on the junction of the lion's head and shoulders and pulled the trigger. Nothing happened though he pulled until he thought his finger would break. Then he knew he had the safety on and as he lowered the rifle to move the safety over he moved another frozen pace forward, and the lion seeing his silhouette now clear of the silhouette of the car, turned and started off at a trot, and, as Macomber fired, he heard a whunk that meant that the bullet was home; but the lion kept on going. Macomber shot again and every one saw the bullet throw a spout of dirt beyond the trotting lion. He shot again, remembering to lower his aim, and they all heard the bullet hit, and the lion went into a gallop and was in the tall grass before he had the bolt pushed forward.

Macomber stood there feeling sick at his stomach, his hands that held the Springfield still cocked, shaking, and his wife and Robert Wilson were standing by him. Beside him too were the two gun-bearers chattering in Wakamba.

"I hit him," Macomber said. "I hit him twice."

"You gun-shot him and you hit him somewhere forward," Wilson said without enthusiasm. The gun-bearers looked very grave. They were silent now.

"You may have killed him," Wilson went on. "We'll have to wait a while before we go in to find out."

"What do you mean?"

"Let him get sick before we follow him up."

"Oh," said Macomber.

"He's a hell of a fine lion," Wilson said cheerfully. "He's gotten into a bad place though."

"Why is it bad?"

"Can't see him until you're on him."

"Oh," said Macomber.

"Come on," said Wilson. "The Memsahib can stay here in the car. We'll go to have a look at the blood spoor."

"Stay here, Margot," Macomber said to his wife. His mouth was very dry and it was hard for him to talk.

"Why?" she asked.

"Wilson says to."

"We're going to have a look," Wilson said. "You stay here. You can see even better from here."

"All right."

Wilson spoke in Swahili to the driver. He nodded and said, "Yes, Bwana."

Then they went down the steep bank and across the stream, climbing over and around the boulders and up the other bank, pulling up by some projecting roots, and along it until they found where the lion had been trotting when Macomber first shot. There was dark blood on the short grass that the gun-bearers pointed out with grass stems, and that ran away behind the river bank trees.

"What do we do?" asked Macomber.

"Not much choice," said Wilson. "We can't bring the car over. Bank's too steep. We'll let him stiffen up a bit and then you and I'll go in and have a look for him."

"Can't we set the grass on fire?" Macomber asked.

"Too green."

"Can't we send beaters?"

Wilson looked at him appraisingly. "Of course we can," he said. "But it's just a touch murderous. You see we know the lion's wounded. You can drive an unwounded lion—he'll move on ahead of a noise—but a wounded lion's going to charge. You can't see him until you're right on him. He'll make himself perfectly flat in cover you wouldn't think would hide a hare. You can't very well send boys in there to that sort of a show. Somebody bound to get mauled."

"What about the gun-bearers?"

"Oh, they'll go with us. It's their *shauri*. You see, they signed on for it. They don't look too happy though, do they?"

"I don't want to go in there," said Macomber. It was out before he knew he's said it.

"Neither do I," said Wilson very cheerily. "Really no choice though." Then, as an afterthought, he glanced at Macomber and saw suddenly how he was trembling and the pitiful look on his face.

"You don't have to go in, of course," he said. "That's what I'm hired for, you know. That's why I'm so expensive."

"You mean you'd go in by yourself? Why not leave him there?"

Robert Wilson, whose entire occupation had been with the lion and the problem he presented, and who had not been thinking about Macomber except to note that he was rather windy, suddenly felt as though he had opened the wrong door in a hotel and seen something shameful.

"What do you mean?"

"Why not just leave him?"

"You mean pretent to ourselves he hasn't been hit?"

"No. Just drop it."

"It isn't done."

"Why not?"

"For one thing, he's certain to be suffering. For another, some one else might run onto him."

"I see."

"But you don't have to have anything to do with it."

"I'd like to," Macomber said. "I'm just scared, you know."

"I'll go ahead when we go in," Wilson said, "with Kongoni tracking. You keep behind me and a little to one side. Chances are we'll hear him growl. If we see him we'll both shoot. Don't worry about anything. I'll keep you backed up. As a matter of fact, you know, perhaps you'd better not go. It might be much better. Why don't you go over and join the Memsahib while I just get it over with?"

"No, I want to go."

"All right," said Wilson. "But don't go in if you don't want to. This is my *shauri* now, you know."

"I want to go," said Macomber.

They sat under a tree and smoked.

"Want to go back and speak to the Memsahib while we're waiting?" Wilson asked.

"No."

"I'll just step back and tell her to be patient."

"Good," said Macomber. He sat there, sweating under his arms, his mouth dry, his stomach hollow feeling, wanting to find courage to tell Wilson to go on and finish off the lion without him. He could not know that Wilson was furious because he had not noticed the state he was in earlier and sent him back to his wife. While he sat there Wilson came up. "I have your big gun," he said. "Take it. We've given him time, I think. Come on."

Macomber took the big gun and Wilson said:

"Keep behind me and about five yards to the right and do exactly as I tell you." Then he spoke in Swahili to the two gun-bearers who looked the picture of gloom.

"Let's go," he said.

"Could I have a drink of water?" Macomber asked. Wilson spoke to the older gun-bearer, who wore a canteen on his belt, and the man unbuckled it, unscrewed the top and handed it to Macomber, who took it noticing how heavy it seemed and how hairy and shoddy the felt covering was in his hand. He raised it to drink and looked ahead at the high grass with the flat-topped trees behind it. A breeze was blowing toward them and the grass rippled gently in the wind. He looked at the gun-bearer and he could see the gun-bearer was suffering too with fear.

Thirty-five yards into the grass the big lion lay flattened out along the ground. His ears were back and his only movement was a slight twitching up and down of his long, black-tufted tail. He had turned at bay as soon as he had reached this cover and he was sick with the wound through his full belly, and weakening with the wound through his lungs that brought a thin foamy red to his mouth each time he breathed. His flanks were wet and hot and flies were on the little openings the solid bullets had made in his tawny hide, and his big yellow eyes, narrowed with hate, looked straight ahead, only blinking when the pain came as he breathed, and his claws dug in the soft baked earth. All of him, pain, sickness, hatred and all of his remaining strength, was tightening into an absolute concentration for a rush. He could hear the men talking and he waited, gathering all of himself into this preparation for a charge as soon as the men would come into the grass. As he heard their voices his tail stiffened to twitch up and down, and, as they came into the edge of the grass, he made a coughing grunt and charged.

Kongoni, the old gun-bearer, in the lead watching the blood spoor, Wilson watching the grass for any movement, his big gun ready, the second gun-bearer looking ahead and listening, Macomber close to Wilson, his rifle cocked, they had just moved into the grass when Macomber heard the blood-choked coughing grunt, and saw the swishing rush in the grass. The next thing he knew he was running; running wildly, in panic in the open, running toward the stream.

He heard the *ca-ra-wong!* of Wilson's big rifle, and again in a second crashing *carawong!* and turning saw the lion, horrible-looking now, with half his head seeming to be gone, crawling toward Wilson in the edge of the tall grass while the red-faced man worked the bolt on the short ugly rifle and aimed carefully as another blasting *carawong!* came from the muzzle, and the crawling, heavy, yellow bulk of the lion stiffened and the huge, mutilated head slid forward and Macomber, standing by himself in the clearing where he had run, holding a loaded rifle, while two black men and a white man looked back at him in contempt, knew the lion was dead. He came toward Wilson, his tallness all seeming a naked reproach, and Wilson looked at him and said:

"Want to take pictures?"

"No," he said.

That was all any one had said until they reached the motor car. Then Wilson had said:

"Hell of a fine lion. Boys will skin him out. We might as well stay here in the shade."

Macomber's wife had not looked at him nor he at her and he had sat by her in the back seat with Wilson sitting in the front seat. Once he had reached over and taken his wife's hand without looking at her and she had removed her hand from his. Looking across the stream to where the gun-bearers were skinning out the lion he could see that she had been able to see the whole thing. While they sat there his wife had reached forward and put her hand on Wilson's shoulder. He turned and she had leaned forward over the low seat and kissed him on the mouth.

"Oh, I say," said Wilson, going redder than his natural baked color.

"Mr. Robert Wilson," she said. "The beautiful red-faced Mr. Robert Wilson."

Then she sat down beside Macomber again and looked away across the stream to where the lion lay, with uplifted, white-muscled, tendon-marked naked forearms, and white bloating belly, as the black men fleshed away the skin. Finally the gun-bearers brought the skin over, wet and heavy, and climbed in behind with it, rolling it up before they got in, and the motor car started. No one had said anything more until they were back in camp.

That was the story of the lion. Macomber did not know how the lion had felt before he started his rush, nor during it when the unbelievable smash of the .505 with a muzzle velocity of two tons had hit him in the mouth, nor what kept him coming after that, when the second ripping crash had smashed his hind quarters and he had come crawling on toward the crashing, blasting thing that had destroyed him. Wilson knew something about it and only expressed it by saying, "Damned fine lion," but Macomber did not know how Wilson felt about things either. He did not know how his wife felt except that she was through with him.

His wife had been through with him before but it never lasted. He was very wealthy, and would be much wealthier, and he knew she would not leave him ever now. That was one of the few things that he really knew. He knew about that, about motor cycles—that was earliest—about motor cars, about duck-shooting, about fishing, trout, salmon and big-sea, about sex in books, many books, too many books, about all court games, about dogs, not much about horses, about hanging on to his money, about most of the other things his world dealt in, and about his wife not leaving him. His wife had been a great beauty and she was still a great beauty in Africa, but she was not a great enough beauty any more at home to be able to leave him and better herself and she knew it and he knew it. She had missed the chance to leave him and he knew it. If he had been better with women she would probably have started to worry about him getting another new, beautiful wife; but she knew too much about him to worry about him either. Also, he had always had a great tolerance which seemed the nicest thing about him if it were not the most sinister.

All in all they were known as a comparatively happily married couple, one of those whose disruption is often rumored but never occurs, and as the society columnist put it, they were adding more than a spice of *adventure* to their much envied and ever-enduring *Romance* by a *Safari* in what was known as *Darkest Africa* until the Martin Johnsons lighted it on so many silver screens where they were pursuing *Old Simba* the lion, the buffalo, *Tembo* the elephant and as well collecting specimens for the Museum of Natural History. This same columnist had reported them *on the verge* at least three times in the past and they had been. But they always made it up. They had a sound basis of union. Margot was too beautiful for Macomber to divorce her and Macomber had too much money for Margot ever to leave him.

It was now about three o'clock in the morning and Francis Macomber, who had been asleep a little while after he had stopped thinking about the lion, wakened and then slept again, woke suddenly, frightened in a dream of the bloody-headed lion standing over him, and listening while his heart pounded, he realized that his wife was not in the other cot in the tent. He lay awake with that knowledge for two hours.

At the end of that time his wife came into the tent, lifted her mosquito bar and crawled cozily into bed.

"Where have you been?" Macomber asked in the darkness.

"Hello," she said. "Are you awake?"

"Where have you been?"

"I just went out to get a breath of air."

"You did, like hell."

"What do you want me to say, darling?"

"Where have you been?"

"Out to get a breath of air."

"That's a new name for it. You *are* a bitch."

"Well, you're a coward."

"All right," he said. "What of it?"

"Nothing as far as I'm concerned. But please let's not talk, darling, because I'm very sleepy."

"You think that I'll take anything."

"I know you will, sweet."

"Well, I won't."

"Please, darling, let's not talk. I'm so very sleepy."

"There wasn't going to be any of that. You promised there wouldn't be."

"Well, there is now," she said sweetly.

"You said if we made this trip that there would be none of that. You promised."

"Yes, darling. That's the way I meant it to be. But the trip was spoiled yesterday. We don't have to talk about it, do we?"

"You don't wait long when you have an advantage, do you?"

"Please let's not talk. I'm so sleepy, darling."

"I'm going to talk."

"Don't mind me then, because I'm going to sleep." And she did.

At breakfast they were all three at the table before daylight and Francis Macomber found that, of all the many men that he had hated, he hated Robert Wilson the most.

"Sleep well?" Wilson asked in his throaty voice, filling a pipe.

"Did you?"

"Topping," the white hunter told him.

You bastard, thought Macomber, you insolent bastard.

So she woke him when she came in, Wilson thought, looking at them both with his flat, cold eyes. Well, why doesn't he keep his wife where she belongs? What does he think I am, a bloody plaster saint? Let him keep her where she belongs. It's his own fault.

"Do you think we'll find buffalo?" Margot asked, pushing away a dish of apricots.

"Chance of it," Wilson said and smiled at her. "Why don't you stay in camp?"

"Not for anything," she told him.

"Why not order her to stay in camp?" Wilson said to Macomber.

"You order her," said Macomber coldly.

"Let's not have any ordering, nor," turning to Macomber, "any silliness, Francis," Margot said quite pleasantly.

"Are you ready to start?" Macomber asked.

"Any time," Wilson told him. "Do you want the Memsahib to go?"

"Does it make any difference whether I do or not?"

The hell with it, thought Robert Wilson. The utter complete hell with it. So this is what it's going to be like. Well, this is what it's going to be like, then.

"Makes no difference," he said.

"You're sure you wouldn't like to stay in camp with her yourself and let me go out and hunt the buffalo?" Macomber asked.

"Can't do that," said Wilson. "Wouldn't talk rot if I were you."

"I'm not talking rot. I'm disgusted."

"Bad word, disgusted."

"Francis, will you please try to speak sensibly?" his wife said.

"I speak too damned sensibly," Macomber said. "Did you ever eat such filthy food?"

"Something wrong with the food?" asked Wilson quietly.

"No more than everything else."

"I'd pull yourself together, laddybuck," Wilson said very quietly. "There's a boy waits at table that understands a little English."

"The hell with him."

Wilson stood up and puffing on his pipe strolled away, speaking a few words in Swahili to one of the gun-bearers who was standing waiting for him. Macomber and his wife sat on at the table. He was staring at his coffee cup.

"If you make a scene I'll leave you, darling," Margot said quietly.

"No, you won't."

"You can try it and see."

"You won't leave me."

"No," she said. "I won't leave you and you'll behave yourself."

"Behave myself? That's a way to talk. Behave myself."

"Yes, Behave yourself."

"Why don't *you* try behaving?"

"I've tried it so long. So very long."

"I hate that red-faced swine," Macomber said. "I loathe the sight of him."

"He's really *very* nice."

"Oh, *shut up*," Macomber almost shouted. Just then the car came up and stopped in front of the dining tent and the driver and the two gun-bearers got out. Wilson walked over and looked at the husband and wife sitting there at the table.

"Going shooting?" he asked.

"Yes," said Macomber, standing up. "Yes."

"Better bring a woolly. It will be cool in the car," Wilson said.

"I'll get my leather jacket," Margot said.

"The boy has it," Wilson told her. He climbed into the front with the driver and Francis Macomber and his wife sat, not speaking, in the back seat.

Hope the silly beggar doesn't take a notion to blow the back of my head off, Wilson thought to himself. Women *are* a nuisance on safari.

The car was grinding down to cross the river at a pebbly ford in the gray daylight and then climbed, angling up the steep bank, where Wilson had ordered a way shovelled out the day before so they could reach the parklike wooded rolling country on the far side.

It was a good morning, Wilson thought. There was a heavy dew and as the wheels went through the grass and low bushes he could smell the odor of the crushed fronds. It was an odor like verbena and he liked this early morning smell of the dew, the crushed bracken and the look of the tree trunks showing black through the early morning mist, as the car made its way through the untracked, parklike country. He had put the two in the back seat out of his mind now and was thinking about buffalo. The buffalo that he was after stayed in the day-time in a thick swamp where it was impossible to get a shot, but in the night they fed out into an open stretch of country and if he could come between them and their swamp with the car, Macomber would have a good chance at them in the open. He did not want to hunt buff with Macomber in thick cover. He did not want to hunt buff or anything else with Macomber at all, but he was a professional hunter and he had hunted with some rare ones in his time. If they got buff today there would only be rhino to come and the poor man would have gone through his dangerous game and things might pick up. He'd have nothing more to do with the woman and Macomber would get over that too. He must have gone through plenty of that before by the look of things. Poor beggar. He must have a way of getting over it. Well, it was the poor sod's own bloody fault.

He, Robert Wilson, carried a double size cot on safari to accommodate any windfalls he might receive. He had hunted for a certain clientele, the international, fast, sporting set, where the women did not feel they were getting their money's worth unless they had shared that cot with the white hunter. He despised them when he was away from them although he liked some of them well enough at the time, but he made his living by them; and their standards were his standards as long as they were hiring him.

They were his standards in all except the shooting. He had his own standards about the killing and they could live up to them or get some one else to hunt them. He knew, too, that they all respected him for this. This Macomber was an odd one though. Damned if he wasn't. Now the wife.

Well, the wife. Yes, the wife. Hm, the wife. Well he'd dropped all that. He looked around at them. Macomber sat grim and furious. Margot smiled at him. She looked younger today, more innocent and fresher and not so professionally beautiful. What's in her heart God knows, Wilson thought. She hadn't talked much last night. At that it was a pleasure to see her.

The motor car climbed up a slight rise and went on through the trees and then out into a grassy prairie-like opening and kept in the shelter of the trees along the edge, the driver going slowly and Wilson looking carefully out across the prairie and all along its far side. He stopped the car and studied the opening with his field glasses. Then he motioned to the driver to go on and the car moved slowly along, the driver avoiding wart-hog holes and driving around the mud castles ants had built. Then, looking across the opening, Wilson suddenly turned and said,

"By God, there they are!"

And looking where he pointed, while the car jumped forward and Wilson spoke in rapid Swahili to the driver, Macomber saw three huge, black animals looking almost cylindrical in their long heaviness, like big black tank cars, moving at a gallop across the far edge of the open prairie. They moved at a stiff-necked, stiff-bodied gallop and he could see the upswept wide black horns on their heads as they galloped heads out; the heads not moving.

"They're three old bulls," Wilson said. "We'll cut them off before they get to the swamp."

The car was going a wild forty-five miles an hour across the open and as Macomber watched, the buffalo got bigger and bigger until he could see the gray, hairless, scabby look of one huge bull and how his neck was a part of his shoulders and the shiny black of his horns as he galloped a little behind the others that were strung out in that steady plunging gait; and then, the car swaying as though it had just jumped a road, they drew up close and he could see the plunging hugeness of the bull, and the dust in his sparsely haired hide, the wide boss of horn and his outstretched wide-nostrilled muzzle, and he was raising his rifle when Wilson shouted, "Not from the car, you fool!" and he had no fear, only hatred of Wilson, while the brakes clamped on and the car skidded, plowing sideways to an almost stop and Wilson was out on one side and he on the other, stumbling as his feet hit the still speeding-by of the earth, and then he was shooting at the bull as he moved away, hearing the bullets whunk into him, emptying his rifle at him as he moved steadily away, finally remembering to get his shots forward into the shoulder, and as he fumbled to re-load, he saw the bull was down. Down on his knees, his big head tossing, and seeing the other two still galloping he shot at the leader and hit him. He shot again and missed and he heard the *carawonging* roar as Wilson shot and saw the leading bull slide forward onto his nose.

"Get that other," Wilson said. "Now you're shooting!"

But the other bull was moving steadily at the same gallop and he missed, throwing a spout of dirt, and Wilson missed and the dust rose in a cloud and Wilson shouted, "Come on. He's too far!" and grabbed his arm and they were in the car again, Macomber and Wilson hanging on the sides and rocketing swayingly over the uneven ground, drawing up on the steady, plunging, heavy-necked, straight-moving gallop of the bull.

They were behind him and Macomber was filling his rifle, dropping shells onto the ground, jamming it, clearing the jam, then they were almost up with the bull when Wilson yelled "Stop," and the car skidded so that it almost swung over and Macomber fell forward onto his feet, slammed his bolt forward and fired as far forward as he could aim into the galloping, rounded black back, aimed and shot again, then again, then again, and the bullets, all of them hitting, had no effect on the buffalo that he could see. Then Wilson shot, the roar deafening him, and he could see the bull stagger. Macomber shot again, aiming carefully, and down he came, onto his knees.

"All right," Wilson said. "Nice work. That's the three."

Macomber felt a drunken elation.

"How many times did you shoot?" he asked.

"Just three," Wilson said. "You killed the first bull. The biggest one. I helped you finish the other two. Afraid they might have got into cover. You had them killed. I was just mopping up a little. You shot damn well."

"Let's go to the car," said Macomber. "I want a drink."

"Got to finish off that buff first," Wilson told him. The buffalo was on his knees and he jerked his head furiously and bellowed in pig-eyed, roaring rage as they came toward him.

"Watch he doesn't get up," Wilson said. Then, "Get a little broadside and take him in the neck just behind the ear."

Macomber aimed carefully at the center of the huge, jerking, rage-driven neck and shot. At the shot the head dropped forward.

"That does it," said Wilson. "Got the spine. They're a hell of a looking thing, aren't they?"

"Let's get the drink," said Macomber. In his life he had never felt so good.

In the car Macomber's wife sat very white faced. "You were marvellous, darling," she said to Macomber. "What a ride."

"Was it rough?" Wilson asked.

"It was frightful. I've never been more frightened in my life."

"Let's all have a drink," Macomber said.

"By all means," said Wilson. "Give it to the Memsahib." She drank the neat whisky from the flask and shuddered a little when she swallowed. She handed the flask to Macomber who handed it to Wilson.

"It was frightfully exciting," she said. "It's given me a dreadful headache. I didn't know you were allowed to shoot them from cars though."

"No one shot from cars," said Wilson coldly.

"I mean chase them from cars."

"Wouldn't ordinarily," Wilson said. "Seemed sporting enough to me though while we were doing it. Taking more chance driving that way

across the plain full of holes and one thing and another than hunting on
foot. Buffalo could have charged us each time we shot if he liked. Gave
him every chance. Wouldn't mention it to any one though. It's illegal if
that's what you mean."

"It seemed very unfair to me," Margot said, "chasing those big
helpless things in a motor car."

"Did it?" said Wilson.

"What would happen if they heard about it in Nairobi?"

"I'd lose my licence for one thing. Other unpleasantnesses," Wilson
said, taking a drink from the flask. "I'd be out of business."

"Really?"

"Yes, really."

"Well," said Macomber, and he smiled for the first time all day.
"Now she has something on you."

"You have such a pretty way of putting things, Francis," Margot
Macomber said. Wilson looked at them both. If a four-letter man marries
a five-letter woman, he was thinking, what number of letters would their
children be? What he said was, "We lost a gun-bearer. Did you notice it?"

"My God, no," Macomber said.

"Here he comes," Wilson said. "He's all right. He must have fallen
off when we left the first bull."

Approaching them was the middle-aged gun-bearer, limping along in
his knitted cap, khaki tunic, shorts and rubber sandals, gloomy-faced and
disgusted looking. As he came up he called out to Wilson in Swahili and
they all saw the change in the white hunter's face.

"What does he say?" asked Margot.

"He says the first bull got up and went into the bush," Wilson said
with no expression in his voice.

"Oh," said Macomber blankly.

"Then it's going to be just like the lion," said Margot, full of
anticipation.

"It's not going to be a damned bit like the lion," Wilson told her. "Did
you want another drink, Macomber?"

"Thanks, yes," Macomber said. He expected the feeling he had had
about the lion to come back but it did not. For the first time in his life he
really felt wholly without fear. Instead of fear he had a feeling of definite
elation.

"We'll go and have a look at the second bull," Wilson said. "I'll tell
the driver to put the car in the shade."

"What are you going to do?" asked Margaret Macomber.

"Take a look at the buff," Wilson said.

"I'll come."

"Come along."

The three of them walked over to where the second buffalo bulked
blackly in the open, head forward on the grass, the massive horns swung
wide.

"He's a very good head," Wilson said. "That's close to a fifty-inch spread."

Macomber was looking at him with delight.

"He's hateful looking," said Margot. "Can't we go into the shade?"

"Of course," Wilson said. "Look," he said to Macomber, and pointed. "See that patch of bush?"

"Yes."

"That's where the first bull went in. The gun-bearer said when he fell off the bull was down. He was watching us helling along and the other two buff galloping. When he looked up there was the bull up and looking at him. Gun-bearer ran like hell and the bull went off slowly into that bush."

"Can we go in after him now?" asked Macomber eagerly.

Wilson looked at him appraisingly. Damned if this isn't a strange one, he thought. Yesterday he's scared sick and today he's a ruddy fire eater.

"No, we'll give him a while."

"Let's please go into the shade," Margot said. Her face was white and she looked ill.

They made their way to the car where it stood under a single, wide-spreading tree and all climbed in.

"Chances are he's dead in there," Wilson remarked. "After a little we'll have a look."

Macomber felt a wild unreasonable happiness that he had never known before.

"By God, that was a chase," he said. "I've never felt any such feeling. Wasn't it marvellous, Margot?"

"I hated it."

"Why?"

"I hated it," she said bitterly. "I loathed it."

"You know I don't think I'd ever be afraid of anything again," Macomber said to Wilson. "Something happened in me after we first saw the buff and started after him. Like a dam bursting. It was pure excitement."

"Cleans out your liver," said Wilson. "Damn funny things happen to people."

Macomber's face was shining. "You know something did happen to me," he said. "I feel absolutely different."

His wife said nothing and eyed him strangely. She was sitting far back in the seat and Macomber was sitting forward talking to Wilson who turned sideways talking over the back of the front seat.

"You know, I'd like to try another lion," Macomber said. "I'm really not afraid of them now. After all, what can they do to you?"

"That's it," said Wilson. "Worst one can do is kill you. How does it go? Shakespeare. Damned good. See if I can remember. Oh, damned good. Used to quote it to myself at one time. Let's see. 'By my troth, I care not; a man can die but once; we owe God a death and let it go which way it will he that dies this year is quit for the next.' Damned fine, eh?"

He was very embarrassed, having brought out this thing he had lived by, but he had seen men come of age before and it always moved him. It was not a matter of their twenty-first birthday.

It had taken a strange chance of hunting, a sudden precipitation into action without opportunity for worrying beforehand, to bring this about with Macomber, but regardless of how it had happened it had most certainly happened. Look at the beggar now, Wilson thought. It's that some of them stay little boys so long, Wilson thought. Sometimes all their lives. Their figures stay boyish when they're fifty. The great American boy-men. Damned strange people. But he liked this Macomber now. Damned strange fellow. Probably meant the end of cuckoldry too. Well, that would be a damned good thing. Damned good thing. Beggar had probably been afraid all his life. Don't know what started it. But over now. Hadn't had time to be afraid with the buff. That and being angry too. Motor car too. Motor cars made it familiar. Be a damn fire eater now. He'd seen it in the war work the same way. More of a change than any loss of virginity. Fear gone like an operation. Something else grew in its place. Main thing a man had. Made him into a man. Women knew it too. No bloody fear.

From the far corner of the seat Margaret Macomber looked at the two of them. There was no change in Wilson. She saw Wilson as she had seen him the day before when she had first realized what his great talent was. But she saw the change in Francis Macomber now.

"Do you have that feeling of happiness about what's going to happen?" Macomber asked, still exploring his new wealth.

"You're not supposed to mention it," Wilson said, looking in the other's face. "Much more fashionable to say you're scared. Mind you, you'll be scared too, plenty of times."

"But you *have* a feeling of happiness about action to come?"

"Yes," said Wilson. "There's that. Doesn't do to talk too much about all this. Talk the whole thing away. No pleasure in anything if you mouth it up too much."

"You're both talking rot," said Margot. "Just because you've chased some helpless animals in a motor car you talk like heroes."

"Sorry," said Wilson. "I have been gassing too much." She's worried about it already, he thought.

"If you don't know what we're talking about why not keep out of it?" Macomber asked his wife.

"You've gotten awfully brave, awfully suddenly," his wife said contemptuously, but her contempt was not secure. She was very afraid of something.

Macomber laughed, a very natural hearty laugh. "You know I *have*," he said. "I really have."

"Isn't it sort of late?" Margot said bitterly. Because she had done the best she could for many years back and the way they were together now was no one person's fault.

"Not for me," said Macomber.

Margot said nothing but sat back in the corner of the seat.

"Do you think we've given him time enough?" Macomber asked Wilson cheerfully.

"We might have a look," Wilson said. "Have you any solids left?"

"The gun-bearer has some."

Wilson called in Swahili and the older gun-bearer, who was skinning out one of the heads, straightened up, pulled a box of solids out of his pocket and brought them over to Macomber, who filled his magazine and put the remaining shells in his pocket.

"You might as well shoot the Springfield," Wilson said. "You're used to it. We'll leave the Mannlicher in the car with the Memsahib. Your gun-bearer can carry your heavy gun. I've this damned cannon. Now let me tell you about them."

He had saved this until the last because he did not want to worry Macomber. "When a buff comes he comes with his head high and thrust straight out. The boss of the horns covers any sort of a brain shot. The only shot is straight into the nose. The only other shot is into his chest or, if you're to one side, into the neck or the shoulders. After they've been hit once they take a hell of a lot of killing. Don't try anything fancy. Take the easiest shot there is. They've finished skinning out that head now. Should we get started?"

He called to the gun-bearers, who came up wiping their hands, and the older one got into the back.

"I'll only take Kongoni," Wilson said. "The other can watch to keep the birds away."

As the car moved slowly across the open space toward the island of brushy trees that ran in a tongue of foliage along a dry water course that cut the open swale, Macomber felt his heart pounding and his mouth was dry again, but it was excitement, not fear.

"Here's where he went in," Wilson said. Then to the gun-bearer in Swahili, "Take the blood spoor."

The car was parallel to the patch of bush. Macomber, Wilson and the gun-bearer got down. Macomber, looking back, saw his wife, with the rifle by her side, looking at him. He waved to her and she did not wave back.

The brush was very thick ahead and the ground was dry. The middle-aged gun-bearer was sweating heavily and Wilson had his hat down over his eyes and his red neck showed just ahead of Macomber. Suddenly the gun-bearer said something in Swahili to Wilson and ran forward.

"He's dead in there," Wilson said. "Good work," and he turned to grip Macomber's hand and as they shook hands, grinning at each other, the gun-bearer shouted wildly and they saw him coming out of the bush sideways, fast as a crab, and the bull coming, nose out, mouth tight closed, blood dripping, massive head straight out, coming in a charge, his little pig eyes bloodshot as he looked at them. Wilson, who was ahead was kneeling shooting, and Macomber, as he fired, unhearing his shot in the roaring of Wilson's gun, saw fragments like slate burst from the huge boss of the horns, and the head jerked, he shot again at the wide nostrils and saw the horns jolt again and fragments fly, and he did not see Wilson now and, aiming carefully, shot again with the buffalo's huge bulk almost on him and his rifle almost level with the oncoming head, nose cut, and he could see the little wicked eyes and the head started to lower and he felt a sudden white-hot, blinding flash explode inside his head and that was all he ever felt.

Wilson had ducked to one side to get in a shoulder shot. Macomber had stood solid and shot for the nose, shooting a touch high each time and hitting the heavy horns, splintering and chipping them like hitting a slate roof, and Mrs. Macomber, in the car, had shot at the buffalo with the 6.5 Mannlicher as it seemed about to gore Macomber and had hit her husband about two inches up and a little to one side of the base of his skull.

Francis Macomber lay now face down, not two yards from where the buffalo lay on his side and his wife knelt over him with Wilson beside her.

"I wouldn't turn him over," Wilson said.

The woman was crying hysterically.

"I'd get back in the car," Wilson said. "Where's the rifle?"

She shook her head, her face contorted. The gun-bearer picked up the rifle.

"Leave it as it is," said Wilson. Then, "Go get Abdulla so that he may witness the manner of the accident."

He knelt down, took a handkerchief from his pocket, and spread it over Francis Macomber's crew-cropped head where it lay. The blood sank into the dry, loose earth.

Wilson stood up and saw the buffalo on his side, his legs out, his thinly-haired belly crawling with ticks. "Hell of a good bull," his brain registered automatically. "A good fifty inches, or better. Better." He called to the driver and told him to spread a blanket over the body and stay by it. Then he walked over to the motor car where the woman sat crying in the corner.

"That was a pretty thing to do," he said in a toneless voice. "He *would* have left you too."

"Stop it," she said.

"Of course it's an accident," he said. "I know that."

"Stop it," she said.

"Don't worry," he said. "There will be a certain amount of unpleasantness but I will have some photographs taken that will be very useful at the inquest. There's the testimony of the gun-bearers and the driver too. You're perfectly all right."

"Stop it," she said.

"There's a hell of a lot to be done," he said. "And I'll have to send a

truck off to the lake to wireless for a plane to take the three of us into
Nairobi. Why didn't you poison him? That's what they do in England."

"Stop it. Stop it. Stop it," the woman cried.

Wilson looked at her with his flat blue eyes.

"I'm through now," he said. "I was a little angry. I'd begun to like
your husband."

"Oh, please stop it," she said. "Please, please stop it."

"That's better," Wilson said. "Please is much better. Now I'll stop."

FOR FURTHER CONSIDERATION

The conflict of this story rests on how each of the three principal
characters handles decisions, that is, how each faces and makes decisions, and how each in turn handles the consequences of these decisions.
What important choices does each character make? What kinds of essential values and self-concepts do these choices reveal?

John Barth (1930–   )

*Barth wanted to be a jazz musician, but he instead became one of
America's dominant writers. A product of Maryland and Johns Hopkins
University, he now teaches at the State University in Buffalo, New York.
His writing often explores responses to the existential dilemma, and the
situations, characters, and issues of his works reveal him as a master
satirist. The selection which follows is from his novel* End of the Road.

The Remobilization of Jacob Horner

In September it was time to see the Doctor again: I drove out to the
Remobilization Farm one morning during the first week of the month.
Because the weather was fine, a number of the Doctor's other patients,
quite old men and women, were taking the air, seated in their wheel chairs
or in the ancient cane chairs along the porch. As usual, they greeted me a
little suspiciously with their eyes; visitors of any sort, but particularly of
my age, were rare at the farm, and were not welcomed. Ignoring their
stony glances, I went inside to pay my respects to Mrs. Dockey, the
receptionist-nurse. I found her in consultation with the Doctor himself.

"Good day, Horner," the Doctor beamed.

"Good morning, sir. Good morning, Mrs. Dockey."

That large, masculine woman nodded shortly without speaking—
her custom—and the Doctor told me to wait for him in the Progress and
Advice Room, which, along with the dining room, the kitchen, the
reception room, the bathroom, and the Treatment Room, constituted the
first floor of the old frame house. Upstairs the partitions between the

original bedrooms had been removed to form two dormitories, one for the men and one for the women. The Doctor had his own small bedroom upstairs, too, and there were two bathrooms. I did not know at that time where Mrs. Dockey slept, or whether she slept at the farm at all. She was a most uncommunicative woman.

I had first met the Doctor quite by chance on the morning of March 17, 1951, in what passes for the grand concourse of the Pennsylvania Railroad Station in Baltimore. It happened to be the day after my twenty-eighth birthday, and I was sitting on one of the benches in the station with my suitcase beside me. I was in an unusual condition: I couldn't move. On the previous day I had checked out of my room in an establishment on St. Paul and 33rd Streets owned by the university. I had roomed there since September of the year before, when, halfheartedly, I matriculated as a graduate student and began work on the degree that I was scheduled to complete the following June.

But on March 16, my birthday, with my oral examination passed but my master's thesis not even begun, I packed my suitcase and left the room to take a trip somewhere. Because I have learned not to be much interested in causes and biographies, I shall ascribe this romantic move to simple birthday despondency, a phenomenon sufficiently familiar to enough people so that I need not explain it further. Birthday despondency, let us say, had reminded me that I had no self-convincing reason for continuing for a moment longer to do any of the things that I happened to be doing with myself as of seven o'clock on the evening of March 16, 1951. I had thirty dollars and some change in my pocket: when my suitcase was filled I hailed a taxi, went to Pennsylvania Station, and stood in the ticket line.

"Yes?" said the ticket agent when my turn came.

"Ah—this will sound theatrical to you," I said, with some embarrassment, "but I have thirty dollars or so to take a trip on. Would you mind telling me some of the places I could ride to from here, for, say, twenty dollars?"

The man showed no surprise at my request. He gave me an understanding if unsympathetic look and consulted some sort of rate scales.

"You can go to Cincinnati, Ohio," he declared. "You can go to Crestline, Ohio. And let's see, now—you can go to Dayton, Ohio. Or Lima, Ohio. That's a nice town. I have some of my wife's people up around Lima, Ohio. Want to go there?"

"Cincinnati, Ohio," I repeated, unconvinced. "Crestline, Ohio; Dayton, Ohio; and Lima, Ohio. Thank you very much. I'll make up my mind and come back."

So I left the ticket window and took a seat on one of the benches in the middle of the concourse to make up my mind. And it was there that I simply ran out of motives, as a car runs out of gas. There was no reason go to Cincinnati, Ohio. There was no reason to go to Crestline, Ohio. Or

Dayton, Ohio; or Lima, Ohio. There was no reason, either, to go back to the apartment hotel, or for that matter to go anywhere. There was no reason to do anything. My eyes, as the German classicist Winckelmann said inaccurately of the eyes of Greek statues, were sightless, gazing on eternity, fixed on ultimacy, and when that is the case there is no reason to do anything—even to change the focus of one's eyes. Which is perhaps why the statues stand still. It is the malady *cosmopsis*, the cosmic view, that afflicted me. When one has it, one is frozen like the bullfrog when the hunter's light strikes him full in the eyes, only with *cosmopsis* there is no hunter, and no quick hand to terminate the moment—there's only the light.

Shortsighted animals all around me hurried in and out of doors leading down to the tracks; trains arrived and departed. Women, children, salesmen, soldiers, and redcaps hurried across the concourse toward immediate destinations, but I sat immobile on the bench. After a while Cincinnati, Crestline, Dayton, and Lima dropped from my mind, and their place was taken by that test-pattern of my consciousness, *Pepsi-Cola hits the spot,* intoned with silent oracularity. But it, too, petered away into the void, and nothing appeared in its stead.

If you look like a vagrant it is difficult to occupy a train-station bench all night, even in a busy terminal, but if you are reasonably well-dressed, have a suitcase at your side, and sit erect, policemen and railroad employees will not disturb you. I was sitting in the same place, in the same position, when the sun stuck the grimy station windows next morning, and in the nature of the case I suppose I would have remained thus indefinitely, but about nine o'clock a small, dapper fellow in his fifties stepped in front of me and stared directly into my eyes. He was bald, dark-eyed, and dignified, a Negro, and wore a graying mustache and a trim tweed suit to match. The fact that I did not stir even the pupils of my eyes under his gaze is an index to my condition, for ordinarily I find it next to impossible to return the stare of a stranger.

"Weren't you sitting here like this last night?" he asked me sharply. I did not reply. He came close, bent his face down toward mine, and moved an upthrust finger back and forth about two inches from my eyes. But my eyes did not follow his finger. He stepped back and regarded me critically, then snapped his fingers almost on the point of my nose. I blinked involuntarily, although my head did not jerk back.

"Ah," he said, satisfied, and regarded me again. "Does this happen to you often, young man?"

Perhaps because of the brisk assuredness of his voice, the *no* welled up in me like a belch. And I realized as soon as I deliberately held my tongue (there being in the last analysis no reason to answer his question at all) that as of that moment I was artificially prolonging what had been a genuine physical immobility. Not to choose at all is unthinkable: what I had done before was simply choose not to act, since I had been at rest when the situation arose. Now, however, it was harder—"more of a choice," so to speak—to hold my tongue than to croak out something that filled my mouth, and so after a moment I said, "No."

Then, of course, the trance was broken. I was embarrassed, and rose stiffly from the bench to leave.

"Where will you go?" my examiner asked with a smile.

"What?" I frowned at him. "Oh—get a bus home, I guess. See you around."

"Wait." His voice was mild, but entirely commanding. "Won't you have coffee with me? I'm a physician, and I'd be interested in discussing your case."

"I don't have any case," I said awkwardly. "I was just—sitting there for a minute or so."

"No. I saw you there last night at ten o'clock when I came in from New York," the Doctor said. "You were sitting in the same position. You *were* paralyzed, weren't you?"

I laughed. "Well, if you want to call it that, but there's nothing wrong with me. I don't know what came over me."

"Of course you don't, but I do. My specialty is various sorts of physical immobility. You're lucky I came by this morning."

"Oh, you don't understand—"

"I brought you out of it, didn't I?" he said cheerfully. "Here." He took a fifty-cent piece from his pocket and handed it to me and I accepted it before I realized what he'd done. "I can't go into that lounge over there. Go get two cups of coffee for us and we'll sit here a minute and decide what to do."

"No, listen, I—"

"Why not?" He laughed. "Go on, now. I'll wait here."

Why not, indeed?

"I have my own money," I protested lamely, offering him his fifty-cent piece back, but he waved me away and lit a cigar.

"Now, hurry up," he ordered around the cigar. "Move fast, or you might get stuck again. Don't think of anything but the coffee I've asked you to get."

"All right." I turned and walked with dignity toward the lounge, just off the concourse.

"Fast!" The Doctor laughed behind me. I flushed, and quickened my step.

While I waited for the coffee I tried to feel the curiosity about my invalidity and my rescuer that it seemed appropriate I should feel, but I was too weary in mind and body to wonder at anything. I do not mean to suggest that my condition had been unpleasant—it was entirely anesthetic in its advanced stage, and even a little bit pleasant in its inception—but it was fatiguing, as an overlong sleep is fatiguing, and one had the same reluctance to throw it off that he has to get out of bed when he has slept around the clock. Indeed, as the Doctor had warned (it was at this time, not knowing my benefactor's name, that I began to think of him with a capital D), to slip back into immobility at the coffee counter would have been extremely easy: I felt my mind begin to settle into rigidity, and only the clerk's peremptory, "Thirty cents, please," brought me back to action—luckily, because the Doctor could not have entered the white lounge to help me. I paid the clerk and took the paper cups of coffee back to the bench.

"Good," the Doctor said. "Sit down."

I hesitated. I was standing directly in front of him.

"Here!" he laughed. "On this side!"

I sat where ordered and we sipped our coffee. I rather expected to be asked questions about myself, but the Doctor ignored me.

"Thanks for the coffee," I said. He glanced at me impassibly for a moment, as though I were a hitherto silent parrot who had suddenly blurted a brief piece of nonsense, and then he returned his attention to the crowd in the station.

"I have one or two calls to make before we catch the bus," he announced without looking at me. "Won't take long. I wanted to see if you were still here before I left town."

"What do you mean, catch the bus?"

"You'll have to come over to the farm—my Remobilization Farm near Wicomico—for a day or so, for observation," he explained coldly. "You don't have anything else to do, do you?"

"Well, I should get back to the university, I guess. I'm a student."

"Oh!" He chuckled. "Might as well forget about that for a while. You can come back in a few days if you want to."

"Say, you know, really, I think you must have a misconception about what was wrong with me a while ago. I'm not a paralytic. It's all just silly. I'll explain it to you if you want to hear it."

"No, you needn't bother. No offense intended, but the things you think are important probably aren't even relevant. I'm never very curious about my patients' histories. Rather not hear them, in fact—just clutters things up. It doesn't much matter what caused it anyhow, does it?" He grinned. "My farm's like a nunnery in that respect—I never bother about why my patients come there. Forget about causes; I'm no psychoanalyst."

"But that's what I mean, sir." I explained, laughing uncomfortably. "There's nothing physically wrong with me."

"Except that you couldn't move," the Doctor said. "What's your name?"

"Jacob Horner. I'm a graduate student up at Johns Hopkins—"

"Ah, ah," he warned. "No biography, Jacob Horner." He finished his coffee and stood up. "Come on, now, we'll get a cab. Bring your suitcase along."

"Oh, wait, now!"

"Yes?"

I fumbled for protests: the thing was absurd. "Well—this is absurd."

"Yes. So?"

I hesitated, blinking, wetting my lips.

"Think, think!" the Doctor said brusquely.

My mind raced like a car engine when the clutch is disengaged. There was no answer.

"Well, I—are you sure it's all right?" I asked, not knowing what my question signified.

The Doctor made a short, derisive sound (a sort of "Huf!") and turned away. I shook my head—at the same moment aware that I was watching myself act bewildered—and then fetched up my suitcase and followed after him, out to the line of taxicabs at the curb.

Thus began my *alliance* with the Doctor. He stopped first at an establishment on North Howard Street, to order two wheel chairs, three pairs of crutches, and certain other apparatus for the farm, and then at a pharmaceutical supply house on South Paca Street, where he also gave some sort of order. Then we went to the bus terminal and took the bus to the Eastern Shore. The Doctor's Mercury station wagon was parked at the Wicomico bus depot; he drove to the little settlement of Vineland, about three miles south of Wicomico, turned off into a secondary road, and finally drove up a long, winding dirt lane to the Remobilization Farm, an aged but white-painted clapboard house in a clump of oaks on a knoll overlooking a creek. The patients on the porch, senile men and women, welcomed the Doctor with querulous enthusiasm, and he returned their greeting. Me they regarded with open suspicion, if not hostility, but the Doctor made no explanation of my presence; for that matter, I should have been hard put to explain it myself.

Inside, I was introduced to the muscular Mrs. Dockey and taken to the Progress and Advice Room for my first interview. I waited alone in that clean room—which, though bare, was not really clinical-looking—for some ten minutes, and then the Doctor entered and took his seat very much in front of me. He had donned a white medical-looking jacket and appeared entirely official and competent.

"I'll make a few things clear very quickly, Jacob," he said, leaning forward with his hands on his knees and rolling his cigar around in his mouth between sentences. "The farm, as you can see, is designed for the treatment of paralytics. Most of my patients are old people, but you mustn't infer from that that this is a nursing home for the aged. Perhaps you noticed when we drove up that my patients like me. They do. It has happened several times in the past that for one reason or another I have seen fit to change the location of the farm. Once it was outside of Troy, New York; another time near Fond du Lac, Wisconsin; another time near Biloxi, Mississippi. And we've been other places, too. Nearly all the patients I have on the farm now have been with me at least since Fond du Lac, and if I should have to move tomorrow to Helena, Montana, or The Rockaways, most of them would go with me, and not because they haven't anywhere else to go. But don't think I have an equal love for them. They're just more or less interesting problems in immobility, for which I find it satisfying to work out therapies. I tell this to you, but not to them, because your problem is such that this information is harmless. And for that matter, you've no way of knowing whether anything I've said or will say is the truth, or just a part of my general therapy for you. You can't even tell whether your doubt in this matter is an honestly founded doubt or just a part of your treatment: access to the truth, Jacob, even belief that there is such a thing, is itself therapeutic or antitherapeutic, depending on the problem. The reality of your problem is all that you can be sure of."

"Yes, sir."

"Why do you say that?" the Doctor asked.

"Say what?"

" 'Yes, sir.' Why do you say 'Yes, sir'?"

"Oh—I was just acknowledging what you said before."

"Acknowledging the truth of what I said or merely the fact that I said it?"

"Well," I hesitated, flustered. "I don't know, sir."

"You don't know whether to say you were acknowledging the truth of my statements, when actually you weren't, or to say you were simply acknowledging that I said something, at the risk of offending me by the implication that you don't agree with any of it. Eh?"

"Oh, I agree with *some* of it," I assured him.

"What parts of it do you agree with? Which statements?" the Doctor asked.

"I don't know: I guess—" I searched my mind hastily to remember even one thing that he'd said. He regarded my floundering for a minute and then went on as if the interruption hadn't occurred.

"Agapotherapy—devotion-therapy—is often useful with older patients," he said. "One of the things that work toward restoring their mobility is devotion to some figure, a doctor or other kind of administrator. It keeps their allegiances from becoming divided. For that reason I'd move the farm occasionally even if other circumstances didn't make it desirable. It does them good to decide to follow me. Agapotherapy is one small therapy in a great number, some consecutive, some simultaneous, which are exercised on the patients. No two patients have the same schedule of therapies, because no two people are ever paralyzed in the same way. The authors of medical textbooks," he added with some contempt, "like everyone else, can reach generality only by ignoring enough particularity. They speak of paralysis, and the treatment of paralytics, as though one read the textbook and then followed the rules for getting paralyzed properly. There is no such thing as *paralysis*, Jacob. There is only paralyzed Jacob Horner. And I don't treat paralysis: I schedule therapies to mobilize John Doe or Jacob Horner, as the case may be. That's why I ignore you when you say you aren't paralyzed like the people out on the porch are paralyzed. I don't treat your paralysis; I treat paralyzed you. Please don't say 'Yes, sir.' "

The urge to acknowledge is an almost irresistible habit, but I managed to sit silent and not even nod.

"There are several things wrong with you, I think. I daresay you don't know the seating capacity of the Cleveland Municipal Stadium, do you?"

"What?"

The Doctor did not smile. "You suggest that my question is absurd, when you have no grounds for knowing whether it is or not—you obviously heard me and understood me. Probably you want to delay my learning that you *don't* know the seating capacity of Cleveland Municipal Stadium, since your vanity would be ruffled if the question *weren't* absurd, and even if it were. It makes no difference whether it is or not, Jacob Horner: it's a question asked you by your Doctor. Now, is there any ultimate reason why the Cleveland Stadium shouldn't seat fifty-seven thousand, four hundred, eighty-eight people?"

"None that I can think of." I grinned.

"Don't pretend to be amused. Of course there's not. Is there any reason why it shouldn't seat eighty-eight thousand, four hundred, seventy-five people?"

"No, sir."

"Indeed not. Then as far as Reason is concerned, its seating capacity could be almost anything. Logic will never give you the answer to my question. Only Knowledge of the World will answer it. There's no ultimate reason at all why the Cleveland Stadium should seat exactly seventy-three thousand, eight hundred and eleven people, but it happens that it does. There's no reason in the long run why Italy shouldn't be shaped like a sausage instead of a boot, but that doesn't happen to be the case. *The world is everything that is the case,* and what the case is, is not a matter of logic. If you don't simply *know* how many people can sit in the Cleveland Municipal Stadium, you have no real reason for choosing one number over another, assuming you can make a choice at all—do you understand? But if you have some Knowledge of the World you may be able to say 'Seventy-three thousand, eight hundred and eleven,' just like that. No choice is involved."

"Well," I said, "you'd still have to choose whether to answer the question or not, or whether to answer it correctly, even if you knew the right answer, wouldn't you?"

The Doctor's tranquil stare told me my question was somewhat silly, though it seemed reasonable enough to me.

"One of the things you'll have to do," he said dryly, "is buy a copy of the *World Almanac* for 1951 and begin to study it scrupulously. This is intended as a discipline, and you'll have to pursue it diligently, perhaps for a number of years. Informational Therapy is one of a number of therapies we'll have to initiate at once."

I shook my head and chuckled genially. "Do all your patients memorize the *World Almanac*, Doctor?"

I might as well not have spoken.

"Mrs. Dockey will show you to your bed," the Doctor said, rising to go. "I'll speak to you again presently." At the door he stopped and added,

"One, perhaps two of the older men may attempt familiarities with you at night up in the dormitory. They're on Sexual Therapy. But unless you're accustomed to that sort of thing I don't think you should accept their advances. You should keep your life as uncomplicated as possible, at least for a while. Reject them gently, and they'll go back to each other."

There was little I could say. After a while Mrs. Dockey showed me my bed in the men's dormitory. I was not introduced to my roommates, nor did I introduce myself. In fact, during the three days that I remained at the farm not a dozen words were exchanged between us. When I left they were uniformly glad to see me go.

The doctor spent two or three one-hour sessions with me each day. He asked me virtually nothing about myself; the conversations consisted mostly of harangues against the medical profession for its stupidity in matters of paralysis, and imputations that my condition was the result of defective character and intelligence.

"You claim to be unable to choose in many situations," he said once. "Well, I claim that that inability is only theoretically inherent in situations when there's no chooser. Given a particular chooser, it's unthinkable. So, since the inability *was* displayed in your case, the fault lies not in the situation but in the fact that there was no chooser. Choosing is existence: to the extent that you don't choose, you don't exist. Now, everything we do must be oriented toward choice and action. It doesn't matter whether this action is more or less reasonable than inaction; the point is that it is its opposite."

"But why should anyone prefer it?" I asked.

"There's no reason why you should prefer it, and no reason why you shouldn't. One is a patient simply because he chooses a condition that only therapy can bring him to, not because one condition is inherently better than another. My therapies for a while will be directed toward making you conscious of your existence. It doesn't matter whether you act constructively or even consistently, so long as you act. It doesn't matter to the case whether your character is admirable or not, so long as you think you have one."

"I don't understand why you should choose to treat anyone, Doctor," I said.

"That's my business, not yours."

And so it went. I was charged, directly or indirectly, with everything from intellectual dishonesty and vanity to nonexistence. If I protested, the Doctor observed that my protests indicated my belief in the truth of his statements. If I only listened glumly, he observed that my glumness indicated my belief in the truth of his statements.

"All right, then," I said at last, giving up. "Everything you say is true, all of it is the truth."

The Doctor listened calmly. "You don't know what you're talking about," he said. "There's no such thing as truth as you conceive it."

These apparently pointless interviews did not constitute my only activity at the farm. Before every meal all the patients were made to perform various calisthenics under the direction of Mrs. Dockey. For the older patients these were usually very simple—perhaps a mere nodding of the head or flexing of the arms—although some of the old folks could execute really surprising feats: one gentleman in his seventies was an excellent rope climber, and two old ladies turned agile somersaults. For each patient Mrs. Dockey prescribed different activities; my own special prescription was to keep some sort of visible motion going all the time. If nothing else, I was constrained to keep a finger wiggling or a foot tapping, say, during mealtimes, when more involved movements would have made eating difficult. And I was told to rock from side to side in my bed all night long: not an unreasonable request, as it happened, for I did this habitually anyhow, even in my sleep—a habit carried over from childhood.

"Motion! Motion!" the Doctor would say, almost exalted. "You must be always *conscious* of motion!"

There were special diets and, for many patients, special drugs. I learned of Nutritional Therapy, Medicinal Therapy, Surgical Therapy, Dynamic Therapy, Informational Therapy, Conversational Therapy, Sexual Therapy, Devotional Therapy, Occupational and Preoccupational Therapy, Virtue and Vice Therapy, Theotherapy and Antheotherapy— and, later, Mythotherapy, Philosophical Therapy, Scriptotherapy, and many, many other therapies practiced in various combinations and sequences by the patients. Everything, to the Doctor, was either therapeutic, antitherapeutic, or irrelevant. He was a kind of superpragmatist.

At the end of my last session—it had been decided that I was to return to Baltimore experimentally, to see whether and how soon my immobility might recur—the Doctor gave me some parting instructions.

"It would not be well in your particular case to believe in God," he said. "Religion will only make you despondent. But until we work out something for you it will be useful to subscribe to some philosophy. Why don't you read Sartre and become an existentialist? It will keep you moving until we find something more suitable for you. Study the *World Almanac:* it is to be your breviary for a while. Take a day job, preferably factory work, but not so simple that you are able to think coherently while working. Something involving sequential operations would be nice. Go out in the evenings; play cards with people. I don't recommend buying a television set just yet. Exercise frequently. Take long walks, but always to a previously determined destination; and when you get there, walk right home again, briskly. And move out of your present quarters; the association is unhealthy for you. Don't get married or have love affairs yet, even if you aren't courageous enough to hire prostitutes. Above all, act impulsively; don't let yourself get stuck between alternatives, or you're lost. You're not that strong. If the alternatives are side by side, choose the one on the left; if they're consecutive in time, choose the earlier. If neither of these applies, choose the alternative whose name begins with the earlier letter of the alphabet. These are the principles of Sinistrality, Antecedence, and Alphabetical Priority—there are others, and they're arbitrary, but useful. Good-by."

"Good-by, Doctor," I said, and prepared to leave.

"If you have another attack and manage to recover from it, contact me as soon as you can. If nothing happens, come back in three months. My services will cost you ten dollars a visit—no charge for this one. I have a limited interest in your case, Jacob, and in the vacuum you have for a self. That *is* your case. Remember, keep moving all the time. Be *engagé.* Join things."

I left, somewhat dazed, and took the bus back to Baltimore. There, out of it all, I had a chance to attempt to decide what I thought of the Doctor, the Remobilization Farm, the endless list of therapies, and my own position. One thing seemed fairly clear: the Doctor was operating either outside the law or on its fringes. Sexual Therapy, to name only one thing, could scarcely be sanctioned by the American Medical Association. This doubtless was the reason for the farm's frequent relocation. It was also apparent that he was a crank—though perhaps not an ineffective one—and one wondered whether he had any sort of license to practice medicine at all. Because—his rationalizations aside—I was so clearly different from his other patients, I could only assume that he had some sort of special interest in my case: perhaps he was a frustrated psychoanalyst. At worst he was some combination of quack and prophet running a semilegitimate rest home for senile eccentrics; and yet one couldn't easily laugh off his forcefulness, and his insights frequently struck home. As a matter of fact, I was unable to make any judgment one way or the other about him or the farm or the therapies.

A most extraordinary doctor. Although I kept telling myself that I was just going along with the joke, I actually did move to East Chase Street; I took a job as an assembler on the line of the Chevrolet factory out on Broening Highway, where I operated an air wrench that belted leaf springs on the left side of Chevrolet chasses, and I joined the UAW. I read Sartre, but had difficulty deciding how to apply him to specific situations. (How did existentialism help one decide whether to carry one's lunch to work or buy it in the factory cafeteria? I had no head for philosophy.) I played poker with my fellow assemblers, took walks from Chase Street down to the waterfront and back, and attended B movies. Temperamentally I was already pretty much of an atheist most of the time, and the proscription of women was a small burden, for I was not, as a rule, heavily sexed. I applied Sinistrality, Antecedence, and Alphabetical Priority religiously (though in some instances I found it hard to decide which of those devices best fitted the situation). And every quarter for the next two years I drove over to the Remobilization Farm for advice. It would be idle for me to speculate further on why I assented to this curious alliance, which more often than not was insulting to me—I presume that anyone interested in causes will have found plenty to pick from by now in this account.

I left myself sitting in the Progress and Advice Room, I believe, in September of 1953, waiting for the Doctor. My mood on this morning was an unusual one; as a rule I was almost "weatherless" the moment I entered the farmhouse, and I suppose that weatherlessness is the ideal condition for receiving advice, but on this morning, although I felt unemotional, I was not without weather. I felt dry, clear, and competent, for some reason or other—quite sharp and not a bit humble. In meteorological terms, my weather was *sec supérieur.*

"How are you these days, Horner?" the Doctor asked as he entered the room.

"Just fine, Doctor," I replied breezily. "How's yourself?"

The Doctor took his seat, spread his knees, and regarded me critically, not answering my question.

"Have you begun teaching yet?"

"Nope. Start next week. Two sections of grammar and two of composition."

"Ah." He rolled his cigar around in his mouth. He was studying me, not what I said. "You shouldn't be teaching composition."

"Can't have everything," I said cheerfully, stretching my legs out under his chair and clasping my hands behind my head. "It was that or nothing, so I took it."

The Doctor observed the position of my legs and arms.

"Who is this confident fellow you've befriended?" he asked. "One of the other teachers? He's terribly sure of himself!"

I blushed: it occurred to me that I was imitating one of my office mates, an exuberant teacher of history. "Why do you say I'm imitating somebody?"

"I didn't," the Doctor smiled. "I only asked who was the forceful fellow you've obviously met."

"None of your business, sir."

"Oh, my. Very good. It's a pity you can't take over that manner consistently—you'd never need my services again! But you're not stable enough for that yet, Jacob. Besides, you couldn't act like him when you're in his company, could you? Anyway I'm pleased to see you assuming a role. You do it, evidently, in order to face up to me: a character like your friend's would never allow itself to be insulted by some crank with his string of implausible therapies, eh?"

"That's right, Doctor," I said, but much of the fire had gone out of me under his analysis.

"This indicates to me that you're ready for Mythotherapy, since you seem to be already practicing it without knowing it, and therapeutically, too. But it's best you be aware of what you're doing, so that you won't break down through ignorance. Some time ago I told you to become an existentialist. Did you read Sartre?"

"Some things. Frankly I really didn't get to be an existentialist."

"No? Well, no matter now. Mythotherapy is based on two assumptions: that human existence precedes human essence, if either of the two terms really signifies anything; and that a man is free not only to choose his own essence but to change it at will. Those are both good existentialist premises, and whether they're true or false is of no concern to us—they're *useful* in your case."

He went on to explain Mythotherapy.

"In life," he said, "there are no essentially major or minor characters. To that extent, all fiction and biography, and most historiography, is a lie. Everyone is necessarily the hero of his own life story. Suppose you're an usher in a wedding. From the groom's viewpoint he's the major character; the others play supporting parts, even the bride. From your viewpoint, though, the wedding is a minor episode in the very interesting history of *your* life, and the bride and groom both are minor figures. What you've done is choose to *play the part* of a minor character: it can be pleasant for you to *pretend to be* less important than you know you are, as Odysseus does when he disguises as a swineherd. And every member of the congregation at the wedding sees himself as the major character, condescending to witness the spectacle. So in this sense fiction isn't a lie at all, but a true representation of the distortion that everyone makes of life.

"Now, not only are we the heroes of our own life stories—we're the ones who conceive the story, and give other people the essences of minor characters. But since no man's life story as a rule is ever one story with a coherent plot, we're always reconceiving just the sort of hero we are, and consequently just the sort of minor roles the other people are supposed to play. This is generally true. If any man displays almost the same character day in and day out, all day long, it's either because he has no imagination, like an actor who can play only one role, or because he has an imagination so comprehensive that he sees each particular situation of his life as an episode in some grand over-all plot, and can so distort the situations that the same type of hero can deal with them all. But this is most unusual.

"This kind of role-assigning is mythmaking, and when it's done consciously or unconsciously for the purpose of aggrandizing or protecting your ego—and it's probably done for this purpose all the time—it becomes Mythotherapy. Here's the point: an immobility such as you experienced that time in Penn Station is possible only to a person who for some reason or other has ceased to participate in Mythotherapy. At that time on the bench you were neither a major nor a minor character: you were no character at all. It's because this has happened once that it's necessary for me to explain to you something that comes quite naturally to everyone else. It's like teaching a paralytic how to walk again.

"I've said you're too unstable to play any one part all the time— you're also too unimaginative—so for you these crises had better be met by changing scripts as often as necessary. This should come naturally to you; the important thing for you is to realize what you're doing so you won't get caught without a script, or with the wrong script in a given situation. You did quite well, for example, for a beginner, to walk in here so confidently and almost arrogantly a while ago, and assign me the role of a quack. But you must be able to change masks at once if by some means or other I'm able to make the one you walked in with untenable. Perhaps—I'm just suggesting an offhand possibility—you could change to thinking of me as The Sagacious Old Mentor, a kind of Machiavellian Nestor, say, and yourself as The Ingenuous But Promising Young Protégé, a young Alexander, who someday will put all these teachings into practice and far outshine the master. Do you get the idea? Or—this is repugnant, but it could be used as a last resort—The Silently Indignant Young Man, who tolerates the ravings of a Senile Crank but who will leave this house unsullied by them. I call this repugnant because if you ever used it you'd cut yourself off from much that you haven't learned yet.

"It's extremely important that you learn to assume these masks wholeheartedly. Don't think there's anything behind them: *ego* means *I*, and *I* means *ego*, and the ego by definition is a mask. Where there's no ego—this is you on the bench—there's no *I*. If you sometimes have the feeling that your mask is *insincere*—impossible word!—it's only because one of your masks is incompatible with another. You mustn't put on two at a time. There's a source of conflict; and conflict between masks, like absence of masks, is a source of immobility. The more sharply you can dramatize your situation and define your own role and everybody else's role, the safer you'll be. It doesn't matter in Mythotherapy for paralytics whether your role is major or minor, as long as it's clearly conceived, but in the nature of things it'll normally always be major. Now say something."

I could not.

"Say something!" the Doctor ordered. "Move! Take a role!"

I tried hard to think of one, but I could not.

"Damn you!" the Doctor cried. He kicked back his chair and leaped upon me, throwing me to the floor and pounding me roughly.

"Hey!" I hollered, entirely startled by his attack. "Cut it out! What the hell!" I struggled with him, and being both larger and stronger than he, soon had him off me. We stood facing each other warily, panting from the exertion.

"You watch that stuff!" I said belligerently. "I could make plenty of trouble for you if I wanted to, I'll bet!"

"Anything wrong?" asked Mrs. Dockey, sticking her head into the room. I would not want to tangle with her.

"No, not now." The Doctor smiled, brushing the knees of his white trousers. "A little Pugilistic Therapy for Jacob Horner. No trouble." She closed the door.

"Now, shall we continue our talk?" he asked me, his eyes twinkling. "You were speaking in a manly way about making trouble."

But I was no longer in a mood to go along with the whole ridiculous business. I'd had enough of the old lunatic for this quarter.

"Or perhaps you've had enough of The Old Crank for today, eh?"

"What would the sheriff in Wicomico think of this farm?" I grumbled. "Suppose the police were sent out to investigate Sexual Therapy?"

The Doctor was unruffled by my threats.

"Do you intend to send them?" he asked pleasantly.

"Do you think I wouldn't?"

"I've no idea," he said, still undisturbed.

"Do you dare me to?"

This question, for some reason or other, visibly upset him: he looked at me sharply.

"Indeed I do not," he said at once. "I'm sure you're quite able to do it. I'm sorry if my tactic for mobilizing you just then made you angry. I did it with all good intent. You *were* paralyzed again, you know."

"You and your paralysis!" I sneered.

"You *have* had enough for today, Horner!" the Doctor said. He too was angry now. "Get out! I hope you get paralyzed driving sixty miles ar hour on your way home!" He raised his voice. "Get out of here, you damned moron!"

His obviously genuine anger immediately removed mine, which after the first instant had of course been only a novel mask.

"I'm sorry, Doctor," I said. "I won't lose my temper again."

We exchanged smiles.

"Why not?" He laughed. "It's both therapeutic and pleasant to lose your temper in certain situations." He relit his cigar, which had been dropped during our scuffle. "Two interesting things were demonstrated in the past few minutes, Jacob Horner. I can't tell you about them until your next visit. Good-by, now. Don't forget to pay Mrs. Dockey."

Out he strode, cool as could be, and a few moments later out strode I: A Trifle Shaken. But Sure Of My Strength.

FOR FURTHER CONSIDERATION

Barth questions the motives people have for doing anything. He asks, "If all is absurd, pointless, meaningless, then why act at all?" He then provides at least one answer to that question in the therapy Jacob receives. What is that answer? Compare Jacob's inability to act to Francis Macomber's encounters with choices in Hemingway's "The Short Happy Life of Francis Macomber."

Albert Camus (1913–1960)

Camus grew up in Algeria, drifted into journalism and the theater, and became a key figure in the French Resistance movement in World War II. His success as a newspaperman was followed by international acceptance of his plays and fiction, culminating in a Nobel Prize for Literature in 1957.

Camus' picture of people in a meaningless universe facing ultimate absurdity made him the leading apologist of existentialism, a philosophi-cal stance often easier to grasp in the context of a human situation or story than in a philosophical explanation. Camus was teaching in an Algerian private school when France (and Algeria) fell to Germany in 1940. His protagonist in "The Guest" is a nonpartisan in the midst of the bitter and terror-filled civil war that plagued Algeria in the 1950s and 1960s. He faces the dilemma of a mortal choice in a situation that for him is otherwise meaningless.

The Guest

The schoolteacher watched the two men climb toward his place. One was on horseback, the other on foot. They hadn't yet reached the steep grade leading to his hillside school. They were making slow progress in the snow and over the stones of the immense stretch of high, desolate plateau. From time to time the horse stumbled. Its hoofs couldn't yet be heard where the schoolteacher was standing, but he could see the steamy breath coming from its nostrils. At least one of the men knew the region. They were following the trail that had disappeared several days before under the dirty white blanket of snow. The schoolteacher calculated that they would not reach the top of the hill for another half hour. It was cold. He went into the schoolhouse to get his sweater.

He crossed the empty, frigid schoolroom. On the blackboard, the four rivers of France, traced with chalk of four different colors, had been flowing toward their estuaries for the past three days. Heavy snows had come in mid-October after eight months of drought, and without the transition of rain, and his twenty or so pupils, who lived in the villages scattered over the plateau, had been staying home. They had to wait for better weather. Daru now heated only the single room that constituted his lodging. It adjoined the classroom and also gave onto the plateau, to the east. One of his windows, like the classroom's, opened to the south. On that side, the schoolhouse was only a few kilometers from where the plateau began to slope toward the south. In clear weather you could see the violet mass of the mountain range with its opening to the desert.

Feeling a little warmer, Daru returned to the window from which he had first noticed the two men. He could no longer see them. This meant that they had begun to come up the steep rise. The sky was less overcast; the snow had stopped falling during the night. The morning had risen with a murky light that scarcely grew brighter as the clouds lifted. Now, at two in the afternoon, it seemed as if the day were just beginning. Yet this was better than the three previous days, when the heavy snow was falling in unrelieved darkness and the shifting winds rattled the double door of the classroom. Daru had then waited out the storm, spending long hours in his room and leaving it only to go down into the lean-to in order to feed the chickens and get some coal. Fortunately, the delivery truck from Tadjid, the nearest village to the north, had brought his supplies two days before the tempest. The truck would return in forty-eight hours.

Actually he had enough to sit out a siege. His small room was cluttered with bags of wheat which the authorities had left with him for distribution to those of his pupils whose families were victims of the drought. Misfortune had struck all the families, since they were all poor. Daru planned to give out a daily ration to the children. He knew that they had gone without food during these bad days. Perhaps one of the fathers or one of the big brothers would come before dark and he could let them have the wheat. They simply had to be carried over to the next harvest. There was no alternative. Shiploads of wheat were now arriving from France, and the worst was over. But it would be hard to forget that famine, those ragged ghosts drifting in the sunlight, the plateau burned month after month, the earth literally scorched and gradually shriveling up, every stone splintering into dust underfoot. The sheep had died then by the thousands; also a few men here and there, sometimes without anyone's knowing.

Witnessing such poverty, this man who lived like a monk in his remote schoolhouse, content with the little he had and with his rugged life, had felt like a lord with his whitewashed walls, narrow cot, crude bookshelves, his well, and his modest weekly supply of food and water. Then suddenly the snow, without warning, without the relief of rain. The region was like that, cruel to live in even had it not been for its people, who did not make things easier either. But Daru was born here. Anywhere else he felt like an exile.

He went outside and crossed the terrace. The two men were now halfway up the slope. He recognized the one on horseback—it was Balducci, an old gendarme. Daru had known him for a long time. Balducci was leading an Arab at the end of a rope. The man was walking behind him, his hands tied and his head bowed. The gendarme waved a greeting to which Daru didn't respond, totally absorbed as he was in looking at the Arab. The prisoner was dressed in a loose, faded overgarment called a *djellabah*; he had sandals on his feet but he also wore heavy, raw-wool socks; his head was covered with a *chèche*, a narrow, short scarf twisted into a turban. The two men were approaching. Balducci had reined in his animal so as not to pull too hard on the rope, thus avoiding hurting the Arab. The group was advancing slowly.

When they were within earshot, Balducci shouted, "Did the three kilometers from El Ameur in one hour!" Daru didn't answer. He stood there, short and square in his thick sweater, and watched them climb. Not once did the Arab raise his head.

"Hello," said Daru when they reached the terrace. "Come in and warm up." Balducci dismounted with difficulty; he didn't let go of the rope. He smiled at the schoolteacher from under his bristling mustache. His small dark eyes, deep-set under his tanned forehead, and his mouth surrounded by wrinkles, made him look stern and determined. Daru took the bridle, led the horse to the shed, and returned to the two men who were now waiting for him in the schoolhouse. He took them to his room. "I'm going to heat the classroom," he said. "We'll be more comfortable there."

When he entered his room again, Balducci was on the couch. He had undone the rope which had tied him to the Arab. The Arab was now squatting near the stove. His hands still bound, the *chèche* pushed back on his head, he was looking in the direction of the window. Daru noticed at first only his enormous lips, full, smooth, almost Negroid. He noticed that his nose was thin. His eyes were black and feverish. The raised *chèche* covered a stubborn brow, and the man's whole face, weathered and somewhat discolored with the cold, had an anxious and rebellious look, which struck Daru when the Arab, turning his face toward him, looked him straight in the eyes. "Go into the other room," the schoolteacher said. "I'll make you some mint tea."

"Thanks," said Balducci. "What a job I've got! Can't wait to retire." And addressing his prisoner in Arabic: "Come along, you." The Arab got up and, holding his tied-up wrists in front of him, slowly walked to the classroom.

With the tea Daru brought a chair. But Balducci had enthroned himself in the front on a pupil's table, and the Arab was squatting against the teacher's platform facing the stove, which was between the desk and the window. Offering the glass of tea to the prisoner, Daru hesitated when he saw his bound hands. "Could you perhaps untie him?"

"Sure," said Balducci. "That was only for the trip." And he started to get to his feet. But Daru placed the glass on the floor and knelt down beside the Arab; without saying anything the Arab watched him with his feverish eyes as he untied his hands. He rubbed his freed swollen wrists against each other, lifted the glass of tea, and drank the scalding liquid in eager little sips.

"Well," said Daru to the gendarme, "where will you be going now?"

Balducci withdrew his mustache from the tea. "We stay here, son."

"Odd schoolchildren! Are you staying the night?"

"No. I'm going back to El Ameur. And you will hand over this fellow at Tinguit. The police there know he's on his way."

Balducci looked at Daru with a friendly little smile.

"What kind of story is this?" said the schoolteacher. "Are you pulling my leg?"

"No, son. Those are the orders."

"Orders? But I'm not . . ." Daru hesitated; he didn't want to offend the old Corsican. "I mean, that's not my occupation."

"How's that? . . . You know that doesn't mean anything nowadays. In wartime people are called upon to do all kinds of jobs."

"Then I'll wait for a declaration of war."

Balducci nodded.

"All right. But these are the orders and they concern you too. It appears that things are brewing. There's talk of a coming revolt. We are, so to speak, mobilized."

Daru continued to look determined.

"Listen, son," said Balducci, "I like you a lot, you must know that. There are only about a dozen of us in El Ameur to patrol the territory of the entire department—that's not many, small though the department is, and I have to get back there. They told me to hand this 'zebra' over to you and return in a hurry. Back there he couldn't be guarded safely. His village was up in arms, they wanted to get him out. So you must take him to Tinguit. Do it in the daytime. It's only about twenty kilometers from here; that shouldn't strain a vigorous fellow like you. After that you can forget the whole thing. You can then come back to your kids and to your serene life."

They heard the horse snorting and stamping the ground on the other side of the wall. Daru looked out the window. The weather was certainly clearing, and it was lighter now over the snow-covered plateau. When all the snow had melted, the sun would dominate again and scorch the fields of stone once more. For days the unchanging sky would keep shedding its dry light over the desolate expanse, where there was nothing to suggest the existence of man.

Turning to Balducci, Daru said, "But tell me, what has he done?" And before the gendarme opened his mouth to answer, he asked, "Does he speak French?"

"A little. We looked for him for a month, but they were hiding him. He killed his cousin."

"Is he against us?"

"I don't think so. But you can't be sure."

"Why did he kill him?"

"A family squabble, I think. It seemed one owed some grain to the other. It's not clear. In short, he killed his cousin with a blow of the billhook. You know, like a sheep, *zic!*"

Balducci made the gesture of striking with a blade across his throat, and the Arab, his attention attracted, looked at him uneasily. Daru felt a sudden wrath against this man, against all men and their sordid malice, their endless hatreds, their lust for blood.

But the kettle was purring on the stove. He served Balducci more tea, hesitated, then served the Arab a second time; again the prisoner drank avidly. His raised arms drew the *djellabah* half open, and the schoolteacher noticed his chest, thin and muscular.

"Thanks, son," Balducci said. "And now I'm off."

He got up and went over to the Arab, taking a small rope from his pocket.

"What are you doing?" Daru asked bluntly.

Balducci, nonplused, showed him the rope.

"You don't need to do it."

The old gendarme hesitated.

"All right, have it your way. I suppose you're armed?"

"I have my hunting gun."

"Where?"

"In my trunk."

"You ought to keep it near your bed."

"Why? I have nothing to fear."

"You're mad, son! If they stage a rebellion, no one will be safe—we'll all be in the same boat."

"I'll defend myself. I'll have time to see them coming."

Balducci began to laugh, then suddenly the mustache again covered his white teeth.

"You'll have time, you say? Fine. And I say you have always been a little cracked. But that's why I like you; my son was like that."

At the same time he pulled out his revolver and placed it on the desk.

"Keep it, I don't need two weapons from here to El Ameur."

The revolver sparkled against the black paint of the table. When the gendarme turned toward him, the schoolteacher smelled the odor of leather and horses.

"Listen, Balducci," Daru said suddenly, "all this disgusts me, and worst of all this specimen of yours. But I won't hand him over. I'll fight, yes, if it's necessary. But not that."

The old gendarme stood in front of him and looked at him severely.

"You are acting like a fool," he said slowly. "I don't like it either. You don't get used to putting a rope on a man, even after years of doing it, and you're even, yes, ashamed. But you can't let them do as they please."

"I won't hand him over," Daru repeated.

"It's an order, son, and I'm telling you this again."

"I understand. Repeat to them what I've said to you: I won't hand him over."

Balducci made an apparent effort to weigh the matter. He looked at the Arab and at Daru. At last he came to a decision.

"No, I won't tell them anything. If you want to stand against us, do as you please; I'll not denounce you. I have an order to deliver the prisoner; I'm doing so. Now you'll sign this paper for me."

"There's no need to do that. I'll not deny that you left him with me."

"Don't be difficult with me. I know you'll tell the truth. You are known here, and you are a man. But you must sign, that's the rule."

Daru opened his drawer, took out a small, square bottle of purple ink, the red wooden penholder with the "sergeant-major" penpoint that he used for tracing models of penmanship, and he signed. The gendarme folded the paper carefully and put it into his billfold. Then he moved toward the door.

"I'll see you off," Daru said.

"No," said Balducci. "It's no use being polite. You have offended me."

He looked at the Arab, motionless in the same spot, sniffed with vexation, and turned away toward the door. "Good-by, son," he said. The door slammed behind him. Balducci suddenly loomed outside the window and then disappeared. His footsteps were muffled by the snow. The horse stirred on the other side of the wall and the chickens fluttered in fright. A moment later Balducci passed again in front of the window, pulling the horse by the bridle. He walked toward the slope without turning around and disappeared from sight with the horse following him. A large stone could be heard softly bouncing down.

Daru returned to the prisoner, who hadn't stirred, never taking his eyes off him. "Wait," the schoolteacher said in Arabic and went toward the adjoining room. As he was crossing the threshold, he thought of something, went to the desk, picked up the revolver and stuck it in his pocket. Then, without looking back, he went into his room.

For some time he remained stretched out on his couch, watching the sky gradually close in, and listening to the silence. It was this silence that had disturbed him during the first days here, after the war. He had asked for a position in the little town at the bottom of the foothills that separate the desert from the high plateau. It is there that the rock walls, green and black to the north, pink and lavender to the south, mark the frontier of eternal summer. He had instead been given a position farther north, on the plateau itself. At first the solitude and the stillness had been hard for him on this barren land inhabited only by stones. Here and there furrows suggested cultivation, but they had been dug only to locate a certain kind of stone good for construction. People plowed here only to harvest rocks. Occasionally the thin soil blown into the hollows would be scraped up to enrich the earth of meager village gardens. But that was all—nothing but stones covering three quarters of the region. Towns sprang up here, flourished, then disappeared; men passed through, loved one another or were at each other's throats, then died. In this desolation, neither he nor his guest mattered. And yet, Daru knew that outside this desert neither he nor the other could really have lived.

He got up. No noise came from the classroom. He was amazed at the frank joy that came over him at the mere thought that the Arab might have fled and that he would be alone again, with no decision to make. But the prisoner was there. He had merely stretched out between the stove and the desk. His eyes were open, and he was staring at the ceiling. In this position, his thick lips were particularly noticeable; they gave him a sullen look.

"Come," Daru said. The Arab got up and followed him. In his room the schoolteacher pointed to a chair near the table at the window. The Arab sat down without taking his eyes off Daru.

"Are you hungry?"

"Yes," the prisoner said.

Daru set two places. He took flour and oil, kneaded a flat cake in a plate, and lighted the butane stove. While the cake was frying, he went to the shed for some cheese, eggs, dates, and condensed milk. When the cake was done, he put it on the windowsill to cool, heated some condensed milk diluted with water and, lastly, began to beat up the eggs for an omelette. His arm brushed against the revolver stuck in his right pocket. He put the bowl down, went into the classroom, and put the revolver in his desk drawer. He came back to the room. Night was falling. He turned on the light, and served the Arab. "Eat," he said. The Arab broke off a piece of the flat cake, lifted it avidly to his mouth, but stopped short.

"And you?" he said.

"After you. Then I'll eat."

The thick lips opened slightly. The Arab hesitated, then bit into the cake without further ado.

The meal over, the Arab looked at the schoolteacher. "Are you . . . the judge?"

"No. I'm keeping you until tomorrow."

"Why do you sit down to eat with me?"

"I'm hungry."

The Arab fell silent. Daru got up and left the room. He brought back a folding bed from the shed, set it up between the table and the stove, perpendicular to his own bed. From a large suitcase in the corner, serving as a shelf for school folders, he took two blankets and spread them on the camp bed. This done, he felt at loose ends, and sat down on his bed. There was nothing more to do or to prepare. He had to look at this man. He gazed at him, trying to imagine that face transported with rage. He was unable to. He saw only his gloomy yet shining eyes and the coarse mouth.

"Why did you kill him?" he asked in a voice whose hostile tone surprised him.

The Arab lowered his eyes.

"He ran away. I ran after him."

He looked up at Daru again and his eyes bore an expression of miserable questioning. "Now what will they do to me?"

"Are you afraid?"

The Arab stiffened, and looked away.

"Are you sorry?"

The Arab looked at him openmouthed. Obviously he did not understand. Daru was becoming irritated. At the same time he felt clumsy and ill at ease, with his big body wedged between the two beds.

"Lie down there," he said impatiently. "That's your bed."

The Arab did not move. He called out to Daru:

"Listen!"

The schoolteacher looked at him.

"Is the gendarme coming back tomorrow?"

"I don't know."

"Are you coming with us?"

"I don't know. Why?"

The prisoner got up and stretched out on top of the blankets, his feet toward the window. The light from the electric bulb shone straight into his eyes and he closed them at once.

"Why?" Daru repeated, standing beside the bed.

The Arab opened his eyes under the blinding light and looked at him, trying hard not to blink.

"Come with us," he said.

In the middle of the night Daru was still awake. He had lain down on his bed after undressing completely—he was used to sleeping naked. But now when he realized that he had no clothes on him, he was uneasy. He did not feel safe and was tempted to dress again. Then he shrugged the matter off; after all, he had been through such things before, and if attacked he could break his adversary in two. He observed the Arab from his bed, lying there on his back, still motionless, with his eyes closed against the harsh light. When Daru put out the light, the darkness seemed to thicken all at once. The night grew vivid in the window, the starless sky stirring gently. The schoolteacher could soon distinguish the stretched-out body in front of him. The Arab remained motionless, but his eyes seemed open now. A light wind prowled around the schoolhouse. It would probably chase away the clouds and the sun would return tomorrow.

The wind increased during the night. The hens fluttered a bit and then quieted down. The Arab turned over on his side with his back to Daru. Daru thought he heard him moan. He kept listening to that breathing, so close to him, and brooded, unable to fall asleep. This presence, here in the room where he had been sleeping alone for a long year, disturbed him. But it disturbed him also because it imposed on him a certain kind of brotherhood he knew well—but which he rejected in the present circumstances—the brotherhood of men sharing the same room, such as soldiers or prisoners, when they begin to feel a strange bond. Having shed their armor with their civilian clothes, they are able to gather every evening, despite their differences, in the ancient community of hope and exhaustion. But Daru shook himself; he didn't like such foolish musings, and he had to get some sleep.

Still later, however, when the Arab stirred about almost imperceptibly, the schoolteacher was still awake. When the prisoner moved a second time, he stiffened, on the alert. The Arab slowly raised himself on his arms, almost with the motion of a sleepwalker. Sitting up on his bed, he waited, motionless, without turning his head toward Daru, as if he were listening with all his attention. Daru did not move, though it had just occurred to him that the revolver was still in his desk drawer. It would be better to act right away. Yet he continued to observe the prisoner, who, with the same smooth and soundless motion lowered his feet to the floor, waited again, then began slowly to stand up. Daru was going to call out to him, when the Arab began to walk, in a natural but uncannily silent way. He went toward the back door leading into the shed. He lifted the latch with precaution and went out, pulling the door behind him, without shutting it. Daru had not stirred. "He's escaping," he merely thought. "Good riddance!" Yet he kept his ear cocked. The hens were not fluttering—he must therefore be on the plateau. A faint sound of water reached him, and he didn't understand what it was until the Arab again stood framed in the doorway, closed the door carefully, and came back to bed without a sound. Then Daru turned his back to him and fell asleep. Later, in his deep sleep, he seemed to hear stealthy steps around the schoolhouse. "I'm dreaming, I'm dreaming!" he repeated to himself. And he went on sleeping.

When he awoke, the sky was clear; the loosely fitting window let in a stream of cold and pure air. The Arab was asleep, curled up under the blankets now, his mouth open, completely relaxed. But when Daru shook him, he jumped with terror, staring wildly at Daru without recognizing him and with such an expression of panic that the schoolteacher drew back. "Don't be afraid. It's me. You must get up and have something to eat." The Arab nodded his head and said yes. He was calm again but his expression was vacant and listless.

The coffee was ready. They drank it, both seated on the folding bed and munching their pieces of flat cake. Then Daru led the Arab to the shed and showed him the faucet where he washed. He went back into the room, folded up the blankets and the bed, made his own bed, and put the room in order. Then he went out onto the terrace through the classroom. The sun was already rising in the blue sky; a soft and radiant light was bathing the barren plateau. On the slope the snow was melting here and there. The stones were about to reappear. Crouched on the edge of the plateau, the schoolteacher contemplated the arid expanse. He thought of Balducci. He had hurt the man's feelings, he had sent him off brusquely, seeming indifferent to his predicament. He could still hear the tone of the gendarme's good-by, and, without knowing the reason for it, he felt strangely hollow and vulnerable. At that moment, from the other side of the schoolhouse, he heard the prisoner cough. Daru listened to him almost despite himself, and then, furious, he flung a pebble, sending it whistling through the air before it sank into the snow. The stupid crime the man had committed revolted him, but to hand him over was dishonorable—the mere thought of it made him fume with indignation. And he cursed both his own people who had sent him this Arab and the Arab himself who had had the nerve to kill but had not known how to escape. Daru got up, walked in a circle over the terrace, stood stock-still for a moment, then went back to the schoolhouse.

The Arab, bending over the cement floor of the shed, was washing his teeth with two fingers. Daru looked at him, then said, "Come." He returned to his room, walking ahead of the prisoner. He put on a hunting jacket over his sweater and pulled on his walking shoes. He stood up and waited for the Arab to get into his *chèche* and sandals. They walked into the classroom and the schoolteacher pointed to the exit. "Go," he said. The other didn't move. "I'm coming with you," said Daru. The Arab went out. Daru returned to his room, where he made a package of pieces of rusk, some dates, and sugar. Back in the classroom, before leaving, he hesitated a second in front of his desk, then crossed the school threshold and locked the door.

"We go this way," he said, and started out eastward, followed by the prisoner. When they were but a short distance from the schoolhouse, he thought he heard a slight sound behind him. He retraced his steps and inspected the grounds around the building; there was no one there. The Arab watched him without seeming to understand. "Let's go," Daru said.

They walked for an hour then rested beside a jagged limestone. The snow was melting ever faster, with the sun sucking up the puddles at once and rapidly clearing the plateau, which gradually dried and vibrated like the air itself. When they resumed walking, the newly bared ground rang under their feet. Now and then a bird rent the air in front of them with a joyful cry. Daru drank in the fresh morning radiance with deep breaths. A kind of exaltation rose in him before the familiar vast expanse, almost all of it yellow now under the vault of blue sky. They walked another hour, descending toward the south. They reached a sort of flat-topped elevation covered with crumbling rock. From there the plateau sloped eastward, toward a low plain with a few sparse trees. To the south it sloped toward masses of rock, which gave the landscape a chaotic look.

Daru scanned both directions. There was nothing but the sky on the horizon—there was no sign of man. He turned to the Arab, who was staring at him blankly. Daru held out the parcel to him. "Take it," he said, "they're dates, bread, and sugar—they'll last you for two days. Here are a thousand francs too." The Arab took the parcel and the money; he held them at chest level, as if he didn't know what to do with what had just been given him. "Now look," the schoolteacher said, pointing east, "that's the way to Tinguit. It's a two hours' walk. The administration and the police are at Tinguit—they're expecting you." The Arab looked in the direction in which Daru was pointing, still holding the parcel and the money against his chest. Daru took him by the arm and turned him, not gently, toward the south. At the foot of the elevation on which they were standing, the faint markings of a path could be discerned. "That's the trail across the plateau. In a day's distance from here you'll find pasturelands and the first nomads. They'll welcome you and give you shelter, as is their custom."

The Arab had now turned toward Daru, his face expressing a sort of panic. "Listen," he said.

Daru shook his head, "No, don't speak. I'm going to leave you now." He turned away, took two long strides in the direction of the school, looked around hesitantly at the motionless Arab, and started off again. For a few minutes he heard nothing but his own footsteps against the cold earth, and he did not turn his head. A moment later, however, he turned around. The Arab was still standing there, on the crest of the hill, his arms hanging at his sides now, and he was looking at the schoolteacher. Daru felt a lump in his throat. But he swore, waved his arm with impatience, and started off again. After walking some distance, he again stopped and looked. There was no one on the hill now.

Daru hesitated. The sun was quite high in the sky and was beginning to beat down on his head. He retraced his steps, at first somewhat uncertainly, then with determination. By the time he reached the little hill his body was streaming with sweat. He climbed it as fast as he could and stopped, out of breath, at the top. The fields of rock to the south were clearly outlined against the blue sky, but on the plain to the east a heat-haze was already rising. And in that light haze, Daru, with heavy heart, made out the Arab walking slowly along the road to prison.

A little later, standing in front of the classroom window, the schoolteacher was watching the clear light rise over the whole plateau, but he hardly saw it. Behind him on the blackboard, across the winding French rivers, stretched the words written with chalk, which he had just read: "You handed over our brother. You will pay for this." Daru looked at the sky, the plateau, and beyond, at the invisible regions stretching all the way to the sea. In this vast land he had so loved, he was alone.

FOR FURTHER CONSIDERATION

Believing in none of the causes that the outside world presses upon him, Daru faces an absurd but mortal choice. He attempts to let the prisoner make the choice for him, only to discover that not to choose is to choose, and that one cannot escape from the consequences of absurd choices. What does Camus suggest about the impact on the self of pointlessness and absurdity? When one values nothing, what does it do to the nature of choice?

Woody Allen (1935–   )

Like many great comics, Allen began as someone else's comedy writer. Next it was pieces in The New Yorker, *then films, comic fantasies that arrived to flabbergast us—one after another. In response to the thesis that "God is dead," he here asks quite naturally, "Who done it?"*

Mr. Big

I was sitting in my office, cleaning the debris out of my thirty-eight and wondering where my next case was coming from. I like being a private eye, and even though once in a while I've had my gums massaged with an automobile jack, the sweet smell of greenbacks makes it all worth it. Not to mention the dames, which are a minor preoccupation of mine that I rank just ahead of breathing. That's why, when the door to my office swung open and a long-haired blonde named Heather Butkiss came striding in and told me she was a nudie model and needed my help, my salivary glands shifted into third. She wore a short skirt and a tight sweater and her figure described a set of parabolas that could cause cardiac arrest in a yak.

"What can I do for you, sugar?"

"I want you to find someone for me."

"Missing person? Have you tried the police?"

"Not exactly, Mr. Lupowitz."

"Call me Kaiser, sugar. All right, so what's the scam?"

"God."

"God?"

"That's right, God. The Creator, the Underlying Principle, the First Cause of Things, the All Encompassing. I want you to find Him for me."

I've had some fruit cakes up in the office before, but when they're built like she was, you listened.

"Why?"

"That's my business, Kaiser. You just find Him."

"I'm sorry, sugar. You got the wrong boy."

"But why?"

"Unless I know all the facts," I said, rising.

"O.K., O.K.," she said, biting her lower lip. She straightened the seam of her stocking, which was strictly for my benefit, but I wasn't buying any at the moment.

"Let's have it on the line, sugar."

"Well, the truth is—I'm not really a nudie model."

"No?"

"No. My name is not Heather Butkiss, either. It's Claire Rosensweig and I'm a student at Vassar. Philosophy major. History of Western Thought and all that. I have a paper due January. On Western religion. All the other kids in the course will hand in speculative papers. But I want to *know*. Professor Grebanier said if anyone finds out for sure, they're a cinch to pass the course. And my dad's promised me a Mercedes if I get straight A's."

I opened a deck of Luckies and a pack of gum and had one of each. Her story was beginning to interest me. Spoiled coed. High IQ and a body I wanted to know better.

"What does God look like?"

"I've never seen him."

"Well, how do you know He exists?"

"That's for you to find out."

"Oh, great. Then you don't know what he looks like? Or where to begin looking?"

"No. Not really. Although I suspect he's everywhere. In the air, in every flower, in you and I—and in this chair."

"Uh huh." So she was a pantheist. I made a mental note of it and said I'd give her case a try—for a hundred bucks a day, expenses, and a dinner date. She smiled and okayed the deal. We rode down in the elevator together. Outside it was getting dark. Maybe God did exist and maybe He didn't, but somewhere in that city there were sure a lot of guys who were going to try and keep me from finding out.

My first lead was Rabbi Itzhak Wiseman, a local cleric who owed me a favor for finding out who was rubbing pork on his hat. I knew something was wrong when I spoke to him because he was scared. Real scared.

"Of course there's a you-know-what, but I'm not even allowed to say His name or He'll strike me dead, which I could never understand why someone is so touchy about having his name said."

"You ever see Him?"

"Me? Are you kidding? I'm lucky I get to see my grandchildren."

"Then how do you know He exists?"

"How do I know? What kind of question is that? Could I get a suit like this for fourteen dollars if there was no one up there? Here, feel a gabardine—how can you doubt?"

"You got nothing more to go on?"

"Hey—what's the Old Testament? Chopped liver? How do you think Moses got the Israelites out of Egypt? With a smile and a tap dance? Believe me, you don't part the Red Sea with some gismo from Korvette's. It takes power."

"So he's tough, eh?"

"Yes. Very tough. You'd think with all that success he'd be a lot sweeter."

"How come you know so much?"

"Because we're the chosen people. He takes best care of us of all His children, which I'd also like to someday discuss with Him."

"What do you pay Him for being chosen?"

"Don't ask."

So that's how it was. The Jews were into God for a lot. It was the old protection racket. Take care of them in return for a price. And from the way Rabbi Wiseman was talking, He soaked them plenty. I got into a cab and made it over to Danny's Billiards on Tenth Avenue. The manager was a slimy little guy I didn't like.

"Chicago Phil here?"

"Who wants to know?"

I grabbed him by the lapels and took some skin at the same time.

"What, punk?"

"In the back," he said, with a change of attitude.

Chicago Phil. Forger, bank robber, strong-arm man, and avowed atheist.

"The guy never existed, Kaiser. This is the straight dope. It's a big hype. There's no Mr. Big. It's a syndicate. Mostly Sicilian. It's international. But there is no actual head. Except maybe the Pope."

"I want to meet the Pope."

"It can be arranged," he said, winking.

"Does the name Claire Rosensweig mean anything to you?"

"No."

"Heather Butkiss?"

"Oh, wait a minute. Sure. She's that peroxide job with the bazooms from Radcliffe."

"Radcliffe? She told me Vassar."

"Well, she's lying. She's a teacher at Radcliffe. She was mixed up with a philosopher for a while."

"Pantheist?"

"No. Empiricist, as I remember. Bad guy. Completely rejected Hegel or any dialectical methodology."

"One of those."

"Yeah. He used to be a drummer with a jazz trio. Then he got hooked on Logical Positivism. When that didn't work, he tried Pragmatism. Last I heard he stole a lot of money to take a course in Schopenhauer at Columbia. The mob would like to find him—or get their hands on his textbooks so they can resell them."

"Thanks, Phil."

"Take it from me, Kaiser. There's no one out there. It's a void. I couldn't pass all those bad checks or screw society the way I do if for one second I was able to recognize any authentic sense of Being. The universe is strictly phenomenological. Nothing's eternal. It's all meaningless."

"Who won the fifth at Aqueduct?"

"Santa Baby."

I had a beer at O'Rourke's and tried to add it all up, but it made no sense at all. Socrates was a suicide—or so they said. Christ was murdered. Nietzsche went nuts. If there was someone out there, He sure as hell didn't want anybody to know it. And why was Claire Rosensweig lying about Vassar? Could Descartes have been right? Was the universe dualistic? Or did Kant hit it on the head when he postulated the existence of God on moral grounds?

That night I had dinner with Claire. Ten minutes after the check came, we were in the sack and, brother, you can have your Western thought. She went through the kind of gymnastics that would have won first prize in the Tia Juana Olympics. After, she lay on the pillow next to me, her long blond hair sprawling. Our naked bodies still intertwined. I was smoking and staring at the ceiling.

"Claire, what if Kierkegaard's right?"

"You mean?"

"If you can never really *know*. Only have faith."

"That's absurd."

"Don't be so rational."

"Nobody's being rational, Kaiser." She lit a cigarette. "Just don't get ontological. Not now. I couldn't bear it if you were ontological with me."

She was upset. I leaned over and kissed her, and the phone rang. She got it.

"It's for you."

The voice on the other end was Sergeant Reed of Homicide.

"You still looking for God?"

"Yeah."

"An all-powerful Being? Great Oneness, Creator of the Universe? First Cause of All Things?"

"That's right."

"Somebody with that description just showed up at the morgue. You better get down here right away."

"It was Him all right, and from the looks of Him it was a professional job.

"He was dead when they brought Him in."

"Where'd you find Him?"

"A warehouse on Delancey Street."

"Any clues?"

"It's the work of an existentialist. We're sure of that."

"How can you tell?"

"Haphazard way how it was done. Doesn't seem to be any system followed. Impulse."

"A crime of passion?"

"You got it. Which means you're a suspect, Kaiser."

"Why me?"

"Everybody down at headquarters knows how you feel about Jaspers."

"That doesn't make me a killer."

"Not yet, but you're a suspect."

Outside on the street I sucked air into my lungs and tried to clear my head. I took a cab over to Newark and got out and walked a block to Giordino's Italian Restaurant. There, at a back table, was His Holiness. It was the Pope, all right. Sitting with two guys I had seen in half a dozen police line-ups.

"Sit down," he said, looking up from his fettucine. He held out a ring. I gave him my toothiest smile, but didn't kiss it. It bothered him and I was glad. Point for me.

"Would you like some fettucine?"

"No thanks, Holiness. But you go ahead."

Nothing? Not even a salad?"

"I just ate."

"Suit yourself, but they make a great Roquefort dressing here. Not like at the Vatican, where you can't get a decent meal."

"I'll come right to the point, Pontiff. I'm looking for God."

"You came to the right person."

"Then He does exist? They all found this very amusing and laughed. The hood next to me said, "Oh, that's funny. Bright boy wants to know if He exists."

I shifted my chair to get comfortable and brought the leg down on his little toe. "Sorry." But he was steaming.

"Sure He exists, Lupowitz, but I'm the only one that communicates with him. He speaks only through me."

"Why you, pal?"

"Because I got the red suit."

"This get-up?"

"Don't knock it. Every morning I rise, put on this red suit, and suddenly I'm a big cheese. It's all in the suit. I mean, face it, if I went around in slacks and a sports jacket, I couldn't get arrested religion-wise."

"Then it's a hype. There's no God."

"I don't know. But what's the difference? The money's good."

"You ever worry the laundry won't get your red suit back on time and you'll be like the rest of us?"

"I use the special one-day service. I figure it's worth the extra few cents to be safe."

"Name Claire Rosensweig mean anything to you?"

"Sure. She's in the science department at Bryn Mawr."

"Science, you say? Thanks."

"For what?"

"The answer, Pontiff." I grabbed a cab and shot over the George Washington Bridge. On the way I stopped at my office and did some fast checking. Driving to Claire's apartment, I put the pieces together, and for the first time they fit. When I got there she was in a diaphanous peignoir and something seemed to be troubling her.

"God is dead. The police were here. They're looking for you. They think an existentialist did it."

"No, sugar. It was you."

"What? Don't make jokes, Kaiser."

"It was you that did it."

"What are you saying?"

"You, baby. Not Heather Butkiss or Claire Rosensweig, but Doctor Ellen Shepherd."

"How did you know my name?"

"Professor of physics at Bryn Mawr. The youngest one ever to head a department there. At the midwinter Hop you get stuck on a jazz musician who's heavily into philosophy. He's married, but that doesn't stop you. A couple of nights in the hay and it feels like love. But it doesn't work out because something comes between you. God. Y'see, sugar, he believed, or wanted to, but you, with your pretty little scientific mind, had to have absolute certainty."

"No, Kaiser, I swear."

"So you pretend to study philosophy because that gives you a chance to eliminate certain obstacles. You get rid of Socrates easy enough, but Descartes takes over, so you use Spinoza to get rid of Descartes, but when Kant doesn't come through you have to get rid of him too."

"You don't know what you're saying."

"You made mincemeat out of Leibnitz, but that wasn't good enough for you because you knew if anybody believed Pascal you were dead, so he had to be gotten rid of too, but that's where you made your mistake because you trusted Martin Buber. Except, sugar, he was soft. He believed in God, so you had to get rid of God yourself."

"Kaiser, you're mad!"

"No, baby. You posed as a pantheist and that gave you access to Him—*if* He existed, which he did. He went with you to Shelby's party and when Jason wasn't looking, you killed Him."

"Who the hell are Shelby and Jason?"

"What's the difference? Life's absurd now anyway."

"Kaiser," she said, suddenly trembling. "You wouldn't turn me in?"

"Oh yes, baby. When the Supreme Being gets knocked off, *somebody's* got to take the rap."

"Oh, Kaiser, we could go away together. Just the two of us. We could forget about philosophy. Settle down and maybe get into semantics."

"Sorry, sugar. It's no dice."

She was all tears now as she started lowering the shoulder straps of her peignoir and I was standing there suddenly with a naked Venus whose whole body seemed to be saying, Take me—I'm yours. A Venus whose right hand tousled my hair while her left hand had picked up a forty-five and was holding it behind my back. I let go with a slug from my thirty-eight before she could pull the trigger, and she dropped her gun and doubled over in disbelief.

"How could you, Kaiser?"

She was fading fast, but I managed to get it in, in time.

"The manifestation of the universe as a complex idea unto itself as opposed to being in or outside the true Being of itself is inherently a conceptual nothingness or Nothingness in relation to any abstract form of existing or to exist or having existed in perpetuity and not subject to laws of physicality or motion or ideas relating to non-matter or the lack of objective Being or subjective otherness."

It was a subtle concept but I think she understood before she died.

FOR FURTHER CONSIDERATION

For so brief a story, Woody Allen manages to spread irreverence on pretty generally everything. List the concepts, institutions, and people that the author satirizes. Are the form and plot of the story themselves parodies? If so, of what? What is the difference between satire and parody?

Kurt Vonnegut, Jr. (1922–   )

Except for the shelter of a meat freezer, Vonnegut would have gone up in smoke with the city of Dresden when it was annihilated by Allied fire bombs in World War II. This critical event during his tenure as a prisoner of war has in turn provided the grist for much of the fiction that has made him a leading popular novelist. His humor is black and whimsical, and his love for humanity is clear in his mistrust of technology.

What appears in the "Barnhouse Effect" as an idea in a science fiction yarn has now acquired substantial scientific basis in recent Soviet and American research into psychokinesis (PK). Fictional or real, the philosophical/moral problems at issue in the story become more perplexing as humanity's ability to control life and matter increases.

Report on the Barnhouse Effect

Let me begin by saying that I don't know any more about where Professor Arthur Barnhouse is hiding than anyone else does. Save for one short, enigmatic message left in my mailbox on Christmas Eve, I have not heard from him since his disappearance a year and a half ago.

What's more, readers of this article will be disappointed if they expect to learn how *they* can bring about the so-called "Barnhouse Effect." If I were able and willing to give away that secret, I would certainly be something more important than a psychology instructor.

I have been urged to write this report because I did research under the professor's direction and because I was the first to learn of his astonishing discovery. But while I was his student I was never entrusted with knowledge of how the mental forces could be released and directed. He was unwilling to trust anyone with that information.

I would like to point out that the term "Barnhouse Effect" is a creation of the popular press, and was never used by Professor Barnhouse. The name he chose for the phenomenon was *"dynamopsychism,"* or *force of the mind.*

I cannot believe that there is a civilized person yet to be convinced that such a force exists, what with its destructive effects on display in every national capital. I think humanity has always had an inkling that this sort of force does exist. It has been common knowledge that some people are luckier than others with inanimate objects like dice. What Professor Barnhouse did was to show that such "luck" was a measurable force, which in his case could be enormous.

By my calculations, the professor was about fifty-five times more powerful than a Nagasaki-type atomic bomb at the time he went into hiding. He was not bluffing when, on the eve of "Operation Brainstorm," he told General Honus Barker: "Sitting here at the dinner table, I'm pretty sure I can flatten anything on earth—from Joe Louis to the Great Wall of China."

There is an understandable tendency to look upon Professor Barnhouse as a supernatural visitation. The First Church of Barnhouse in Los Angeles has a congregation numbering in the thousands. He is godlike in neither appearance nor intellect. The man who disarms the world is single, shorter than the average American male, stout, and averse to exercise. His I.Q. is 143, which is good but certainly not sensational. He is quite mortal, about to celebrate his fortieth birthday, and in good health. If he is alone now, the isolation won't bother him too much. He was quiet and shy when I knew him, and seemed to find more companionship in books and music than in his associations at the college.

Neither he nor his powers fall outside the sphere of Nature. His dynamopsychic radiations are subject to many known physical laws that apply in the field of radio. Hardly a person has not now heard the snarl of "Barnhouse static" on his home receiver. The radiations are affected by sunspots and variations in the ionosphere.

However, they differ from ordinary broadcast waves in several important ways. Their total energy can be brought to bear on any single point the professor chooses, and that energy is undiminished by distance. As a weapon, then, dynamopsychism has an impressive advantage over bacteria and atomic bombs, beyond the fact that it costs nothing to use: it enables the professor to single out critical individuals and objects instead of slaughtering whole populations in the process of maintaining international equilibrium.

As General Honus Barker told the House Military Affairs Committee: "Until someone finds Barnhouse, there is no defense against the Barnhouse Effect." Efforts to "jam" or block the radiations have failed. Premier Slezak could have saved himself the fantastic expense of his "Barnhouseproof" shelter. Despite the shelter's twelve-foot-thick lead armor, the premier has been floored twice while in it.

There is talk of screening the population for men potentially as powerful dynamopsychically as the professor. Senator Warren Foust demanded funds for this purpose last month, with the passionate declaration: "He who rules the Barnhouse Effect rules the world!" Commissar Kropotnik said much the same thing, so another costly armaments race, with a new twist, has begun.

This race at least has its comical aspects. The world's best gamblers are being coddled by governments like so many nuclear physicists. There may be several hundred persons with dynamopsychic talent on earth, myself included. But, without knowledge of the professor's technique, they can never be anything but dice-table despots. With the secret, it would probably take them ten years to become dangerous weapons. It took the professor that long. He who rules the Barnhouse Effect is Barnhouse and will be for some time.

Popularly, the "Age of Barnhouse" is said to have begun a year and a half ago, on the day of Operation Brainstorm That was when dynamopsychism became significant politically. Actually, the phenomenon was discovered in May, 1942, shortly after the professor turned down a direct commission in the Army and enlisted as an artillery private. Like X-rays and vulcanized rubber, dynamopsychism was discovered by accident.

From time to time Private Barnhouse was invited to take part in games of chance by his barrack mates. He knew nothing about the games, and usually begged off. But one evening, out of social grace, he agreed to shoot craps. It was terrible or wonderful that he played, depending upon whether or not you like the world as it now is.

"Shoot sevens, Pop," someone said.

So "Pop" shot sevens—ten in a row to bankrupt the barracks. He retired to his bunk and, as a mathematical exercise, calculated the odds against his feat on the back of a laundry slip. His chances of doing it, he found, were one in almost ten million! Bewildered, he borrowed a pair of dice from the man in the bunk next to his. He tried to roll sevens again, but got only the usual assortment of numbers. He lay back for a moment, then resumed his toying with the dice. He rolled ten more sevens in a row.

He might have dismissed the phenomenon with a low whistle. But the professor instead mulled over the circumstances surrounding his two lucky streaks. There was one single factor in common: on both occasions, *the same thought train had flashed through his mind just before he threw the dice.* It was that thought train which aligned the professor's brain cells into what has since become the most powerful weapon on earth.

The soldier in the next bunk gave dynamopsychism its first token of respect. In an understatement certain to bring wry smiles to the faces of the world's dejected demagogues, the soldier said, "You're hotter'n a two-dollar pistol, Pop." Professor Barnhouse was all of that. The dice that did his bidding weighed but a few grams, so the forces involved were minute; but the unmistakable fact that there were such forces was earth-shaking.

Professional caution kept him from revealing his discovery immediately. He wanted more facts and a body of theory to go with them. Later, when the atomic bomb was dropped on Hiroshima, it was fear that made him hold his peace. At no time were his experiments, as Premier Slezak called them, "a bourgeois plot to shackle the true democracies of the world." The professor didn't know where they were leading.

In time, he came to recognize another startling feature of dynamopsychism: *its strength increased with use.* Within six months, he was able to govern dice thrown by men the length of a barracks distant. By the time of his discharge in 1945, he could knock bricks loose from chimneys three miles away.

Charges that Professor Barnhouse could have won the last war in a minute, but did not care to do so, are perfectly senseless. When the war ended, he had the range and power of a 37-millimeter cannon, perhaps— certainly no more. His dynamopsychic powers graduated from the small-arms class only after his discharge and return to Wyandotte College.

I enrolled in the Wyandotte Graduate School two years after the professor had rejoined the faculty. By chance, he was assigned as my thesis adviser. I was unhappy about the assignment, for the professor was, in the eyes of both colleagues and students, a somewhat ridiculous figure. He missed classes or had lapses of memory during lectures. When I arrived, in fact, his shortcomings had passed from the ridiculous to the intolerable.

"We're assigning you to Barnhouse as a sort of temporary thing," the dean of social studies told me. He looked apologetic and perplexed. "Brilliant man, Barnhouse, I guess. Difficult to know since his return, perhaps, but his work before the war brought a great deal of credit to our little school."

When I reported to the professor's laboratory for the first time, what I saw was more distressing than the gossip. Every surface in the room was covered with dust; books and apparatus had not been disturbed for months. The professor sat napping at his desk when I entered. The only signs of recent activity were three overflowing ashtrays, a pair of scissors, and a morning paper with several items clipped from its front page.

As he raised his head to look at me, I saw that his eyes were clouded with fatigue. "Hi," he said, "just can't seem to get my sleeping done at night." He lighted a cigarette, his hands trembling slightly. "You the young man I'm supposed to help with a thesis?"

"Yes, sir," I said. In minutes he converted my misgivings to alarm.

"You an overseas veteran?" he asked.

"Yes, sir."

"Not much left over there, is there?" He frowned. "Enjoy the last war?"

"No, sir."

"Look like another war to you?"

"Kind of, sir."

"What can be done about it?"

I shrugged. "Looks pretty hopeless."

He peered at me intently. "Know anything about international law, the U.N., and all that?"

"Only what I pick up from the papers."

"Same here," he sighed. He showed me a fat scrapbook packed with newspaper clippings. "Never used to pay any attention to international politics. Now I study them the way I used to study rats in mazes. Everybody tells me the same thing—'Looks hopeless.'"

"Nothing short of a miracle—" I began.

"Believe in magic?" he asked sharply. The professor fished two dice from his vest pocket. "I will try to roll twos," he said. He rolled twos three times in a row. "One chance in about 47,000 of that happening. There's a miracle for you." He beamed for an instant, then brought the interview to an end, remarking that he had a class which had begun ten minutes ago.

He was not quick to take me into his confidence, and he said no more about his trick with the dice. I assumed they were loaded, and forgot about them. He set me the task of watching male rats cross electrified metal strips to get to food or female rats—an experiment that had been done to everyone's satisfaction in the nineteen-thirties. As though the pointlessness of my work were not bad enough, the professor annoyed me further with irrelevant questions. His favorites were: "Think we should have dropped the atomic bomb on Hiroshima?" and "Think every new piece of scientific information is a good thing for humanity?"

However, I did not feel put upon for long. "Give those poor animals a holiday," he said one morning, after I had been with him only a month. "I wish you'd help me look into a more interesting problem—namely, my sanity."

I returned the rats to their cages.

"What you must do is simple," he said, speaking softly. "Watch the inkwell on my desk. If you see nothing happen to it, say so, and I'll go quietly—relieved, I might add—to the nearest sanitarium."

I nodded uncertainly.

He locked the laboratory door and drew the blinds, so that we were in twilight for a moment. "I'm odd, I know," he said. "It's fear of myself that's made me odd."

"I've found you somewhat eccentric, perhaps, but certainly not—"

"If nothing happens to that inkwell, 'crazy as a bedbug' is the only description of me that will do," he interrupted, turning on the overhead lights. His eyes narrowed. "To give you an idea of how crazy, I'll tell you what's been running through my mind when I should have been sleeping. I think maybe I can save the world. I think maybe I can make every nation a *have* nation, and do away with war for good. I think maybe I can clear roads through jungles, irrigate deserts, build dams overnight."

"Yes, sir."

"Watch the inkwell!"

Dutifully and fearfully I watched. A high-pitched humming seemed to come from the inkwell; then it began to vibrate alarmingly, and finally to bound about the top of the desk, making two noisy circuits. It stopped, hummed again, glowed red, then popped in splinters with a blue-green flash.

Perhaps my hair stood on end. The professor laughed gently. "Magnets?" I managed to say at last.

"Wish to heaven it were magnets," he murmured. It was then that he told me of dynamopsychism. He knew only that there was such a force; he could not explain it. "It's me and me alone—and it's awful."

"I'd say it was amazing and wonderful!" I cried.

"If all I could do was make inkwells dance, I'd be tickled silly with the whole business." He shrugged disconsolately. "But I'm no toy, my boy. If you like, we can drive around the neighborhood, and I'll show you what I mean." He told me about pulverized boulders, shattered oaks, and abandoned farm buildings demolished within a fifty-mile radius of the campus. "Did every bit of it sitting right here, just thinking—not even thinking hard."

He scratched his head nervously. "I have never dared to concentrate as hard as I can for fear of the damage I might do. I'm to the point where a mere whim is a blockbuster." There was a depressing pause. "Up until a few days ago, I've thought it best to keep my secret for fear of what use it might be put to," he continued. "Now I realize that I haven't any more right to it than a man has a right to own an atomic bomb."

He fumbled through a heap of papers. "This says about all that needs to be said, I think." He handed me a draft of a letter to the Secretary of State.

Dear Sir:

I have discovered a new force which costs nothing to use, and which is probably more important than atomic energy. I should like to see it used most

effectively in the cause of peace, and am, therefore, requesting your advice
as to how this might best be done.

Yours truly,
A. Barnhouse.

"I have no idea what will happen next," said the professor.

There followed three months of perpetual nightmare, wherein the
nation's political and military great came at all hours to watch the
professor's tricks.

We were quartered in an old mansion near Charlottesville, Virginia,
to which we had been whisked five days after the letter was mailed.
Surrounded by barbed wire and twenty guards, we were labeled "Project
Wishing Well," and were classified as Top Secret.

For companionship we had General Honus Barker and the State
Department's William K. Cuthrell. For the professor's talk of peace-
through-plenty they had indulgent smiles and much discourse on practical measures and realistic thinking. So treated, the professor, who had
at first been almost meek, progressed in a matter of weeks toward stubbornness.

He had agreed to reveal the thought train by means of which he
aligned his mind into a dynamopsychic transmitter. But, under Cuthrell's
and Barker's nagging to do so, he began to hedge. At first he declared that
the information could be passed on simply by word of mouth. Later he
said that it would have to be written up in a long report. Finally, at dinner
one night, just after General Barker had read the secret orders for
Operation Brainstorm, the professor announced, "The report may take as
long as five years to write." He looked fiercely at the general. "Maybe
twenty."

The dismay occasioned by this flat announcement was offset somewhat by the exciting anticipation of Operation Brainstorm. The general
was in a holiday mood. "The target ships are on their way to the Caroline
Islands at this very moment," he declared ecstatically. "One hundred and
twenty of them! At the same time, ten V-2s are being readied for firing in
New Mexico, and fifty radio-controlled jet bombers are being equipped
for a mock attack on the Aleutians. Just think of it!" Happily he reviewed
his orders. "At exactly 1100 hours next Wednesday, I will give you the
order to *concentrate*; and you, professor, will think as hard as you can
about sinking the target ships, destroying the V-2s before they hit the
ground, and knocking down the bombers before they reach the Aleutians!
Think you can handle it?"

The professor turned gray and closed his eyes. "As I told you before,
my friend, I don't know what I can do." He added bitterly, "As for this
Operation Brainstorm, I was never consulted about it, and it strikes me as
childish and insanely expensive."

General Barker bridled. "Sir," he said, "your field is psychology, and
I wouldn't presume to give you advice in that field. Mine is national

defense. I have had thirty years of experience and success, Professor, and I'll ask you not to criticize my judgment."

The professor appealed to Mr. Cuthrell. "Look," he pleaded, "isn't it war and military matters we're all trying to get rid of? Wouldn't it be a whole lot more significant and lots cheaper for me to try moving cloud masses into drought areas, and things like that? I admit I know next to nothing about international politics, but it seems reasonable to suppose that nobody would want to fight wars if there were enough of everything to go around. Mr. Cuthrell, I'd like to try running generators where there isn't any coal or water power, irrigating deserts, and so on. Why, you could figure out what each country needs to make the most of its resources, and I could give it to them without costing American taxpayers a penny."

"Eternal vigilance is the price of freedom," said the general heavily.

Mr. Cuthrell threw the general a look of mild distaste. "Unfortunately, the general is right in his own way," he said. "I wish to heaven the world were ready for ideals like yours, but it simply isn't. We aren't surrounded by brothers, but by enemies. It isn't a lack of food or resources that has us on the brink of war—it's a struggle for power. Who's going to be in charge of the world, our kind of people or theirs?"

The professor nodded in reluctant agreement and arose from the table: "I beg your pardon, gentlemen. You are, after all, better qualified to judge what is best for the country. I'll do whatever you say." He turned to me. "Don't forget to wind the restricted clock and put the confidential cat out," he said gloomily, and ascended the stairs to his bedroom.

For reasons of national security, Operation Brainstorm was carried on without the knowledge of the American citizenry which was paying the bill. The observers, technicians, and military men involved in the activity knew that a test was under way—a test of what, they had no idea. Only thirty-seven key men, myself included, knew what was afoot.

In Virginia, the day for Operation Brainstorm was unseasonably cool. Inside a log fire crackled in the fireplace, and the flames were reflected in the polished metal cabinets that lined the living room. All that remained of the room's lovely old furniture was a Victorian love seat, set squarely in the center of the floor, facing three television receivers. One long bench had been brought in for the ten of us privileged to watch. The television screens showed, from left to right, the stretch of desert which was the rocket target, the guinea-pig fleet, and a section of the Aleutian sky through which the radio-controlled bomber formation would roar.

Ninety minutes before H-hour the radios announced that the rockets were ready, that the observation ships had backed away to what was thought to be a safe distance, and that the bombers were on their way. The small Virginia audience lined up on the bench in order of rank, smoked a great deal, and said little. Professor Barnhouse was in his bedroom. General Barker bustled about the house like a woman preparing Thanksgiving dinner for twenty.

At ten minutes before H-hour the general came in, shepherding the professor before him. The professor was comfortably attired in sneakers, gray flannels, a blue sweater, and a white shirt open at the neck. The two of them sat side by side on the love seat. The general was rigid and perspiring; the professor was cheerful. He looked at each of the screens, lighted a cigarette and settled back.

"Bombers sighted!" cried the Aleutian observers.

"Rockets away!" barked the New Mexico radio operator.

All of us looked quickly at the big electric clock over the mantel, while the professor, a half-smile on his face, continued to watch the television sets. In hollow tones, the general counted away the seconds remaining. "Five . . . four . . . three . . . two . . . one . . . *Concentrate!*"

Professor Barnhouse closed his eyes, pursed his lips, and stroked his temples. He held the position for a minute. The television images were scrambled, and the radio signals were drowned in the din of Barnhouse static. The professor sighed, opened his eyes, and smiled confidently.

"Did you give it everything you had?" asked the general dubiously.

"I was wide open," the professor replied.

The television images pulled themselves together, and mingled cries of amazement came over the radios tuned to the observers. The Aleutian sky was streaked with the smoke trails of bombers screaming down in flames. Simultaneously, there appeared high over the rocket target a cluster of white puffs, followed by faint thunder.

General Barker shook his head happily. "By George!" he crowed. "Well, sir, by George, by George, by George!"

"Look!" shouted the admiral seated next to me. "The fleet—it wasn't touched!"

"The guns seem to be drooping," said Mr. Cuthrell.

We left the bench and clustered about the television sets to examine the damage more closely. What Mr. Cuthrell had said was true. The ships' guns curved downward, their muzzles resting on the steel decks. We in Virginia were making such a hullabaloo that it was impossible to hear the radio reports. We were so engrossed, in fact, that we didn't miss the professor until two short snarls of Barnhouse static shocked us into sudden silence. The radios went dead.

We looked around apprehensively. The professor was gone. A harassed guard threw open the front door from the outside to yell that the professor had escaped. He brandished his pistol in the direction of the gates, which hung open, limp and twisted. In the distance, a speeding government station wagon topped a ridge and dropped from sight into the valley beyond. The air was filled with choking smoke, for every vehicle on the grounds was ablaze. Pursuit was impossible.

"What in God's name got into him?" bellowed the general.

Mr. Cuthrell, who had rushed out onto the front porch, now slouched back into the room, reading a penciled note as he came. He thrust the note into my hands. "The good man left this billet-doux under the door knocker. Perhaps our young friend here will be kind enough to read it to you gentlemen, while I take a restful walk through the woods."

"Gentlemen," I read aloud, *"As the first superweapon with a conscience, I am removing myself from your national defense stockpile. Setting a new precedent in the behavior of ordnance, I have humane reasons for going off. A. Barnhouse."*

Since that day, of course, the professor has been systematically destroying the world's armaments, until there is now little with which to equip an army other than rocks and sharp sticks. His activities haven't exactly resulted in peace, but have, rather, precipitated a bloodless and entertaining sort of war that might be called the "War of the Tattletales." Every nation is flooded with enemy agents whose sole mission is to locate military equipment, which is promptly wrecked when it is brought to the professor's attention in the press.

Just as every day brings news of more armaments pulverized by dynamopsychism, so has it brought rumors of the professor's whereabouts. During last week alone, three publications carried articles proving variously that he was hiding in an Inca ruin in the Andes, in the sewers of Paris, and in the unexplored lower chambers of Carlsbad Caverns. Knowing the man, I am inclined to regard such hiding places as unnecessarily romantic and uncomfortable. While there are numerous persons eager to kill him, there must be millions who would care for him and hide him. I like to think that he is in the home of such a person.

One thing is certain: at this writing, Professor Barnhouse is not dead. Barnhouse static jammed broadcasts not ten minutes ago. In the eighteen months since his disappearance, he has been reported dead some half-dozen times. Each report has stemmed from the death of an unidentified man resembling the professor, during a period free of the static. The first three reports were followed at once by renewed talk of rearmament and recourse to war. The saber-rattlers have learned how imprudent premature celebrations of the professor's demise can be.

Many a stouthearted patriot has found himself prone in the tangled bunting and timbers of a smashed reviewing stand, seconds after having announced that the arch-tyranny of Barnhouse was at an end. But those who would make war if they could, in every country in the world, wait in sullen silence for what must come—the passing of Professor Barnhouse.

To ask how much longer the professor will live is to ask how much longer we must wait for the blessings of another world war. He is of short-lived stock: his mother lived to be fifty-three, his father to be forty-nine; and the life-spans of his grandparents on both sides were of the same order. He might be expected to live, then, for perhaps fifteen years more, if he can remain hidden from his enemies. When one considers the number and vigor of these enemies, however, fifteen years seems an extraordinary length of time, which might better be revised to fifteen days, hours, or minutes.

The professor knows that he cannot live much longer. I say this because of the message left in my mailbox on Christmas Eve. Unsigned, typewritten on a soiled scrap of paper, the note consisted of ten sentences. The first nine of these, each a bewildering tangle of psychological jargon and references to obscure texts, made no sense to me at first reading. The tenth, unlike the rest, was simply constructed and contained no large words—but its irrational content made it the most puzzling and bizarre sentence of all. I nearly threw the note away, thinking it a colleague's warped notion of a practical joke. For some reason, though, I added it to the clutter on top of my desk, which included, among other momentos, the professor's dice.

It took me several weeks to realize that the message really meant something, that the first nine sentences, when unsnarled, could be taken as instructions. The tenth still told me nothing. It was only last night that I discovered how it fitted in with the rest. The sentence appeared in my thoughts last night, while I was toying absently with the professor's dice.

I promised to have this report on its way to the publishers today. In view of what has happened, I am obliged to break that promise, or release the report incomplete. The delay will not be a long one, for one of the few blessings accorded a bachelor like myself is the ability to move quickly from one abode to another, or from one way of life to another. What property I want to take with me can be packed in a few hours. Fortunately, I am not without substantial private means, which may take as long as a week to realize in liquid and anonymous form. When this is done, I shall mail the report.

I have just returned from a visit to my doctor, who tells me my health is excellent. I am young, and, with any luck at all, I shall live to a ripe old age indeed, for my family on both sides is noted for longevity.

Briefly, I propose to vanish.

Sooner or later, Professor Barnhouse must die. But long before then I shall be ready. So, to the saber-rattlers of today—and even, I hope, of tomorrow—I say: Be advised. Barnhouse will die. But not the Barnhouse Effect.

Last night, I tried once more to follow the oblique instructions on the scrap of paper. I took the professor's dice, and then, with the last nightmarish sentence flitting through my mind, I rolled fifty consecutive sevens.

Good-by.

FOR FURTHER CONSIDERATION

Psychokinesis, the phenomenon Vonnegut describes in this story, has been the subject of intense study and experimentation in the last few years, particularly in the Soviet Union, where reports state that several people have been trained to actually move small objects by concentrating on them mentally. Vonnegut suggests the frightening military implications of this ability. What moral, psychological, and other implications may exist if humans can be trained to move objects psychokinetically? What might such a power do to a human personality?

William Faulkner (1897–1962)

Faulkner was encouraged to write by Sherwood Anderson, and from his early years as a hungry writer working any and all jobs to support himself, he developed into a dominant voice in American and international letters. His examinations of violence, sexual influences, and life in the South won him the National Book Award, the Pulitzer Prize, and the Nobel Prize. His uses of point of view, his rambling eloquence, and his concern with controversial subjects broadened the acceptable limits of fiction. His works on the fictional Snopes family traced the decline and decay of the antebellum South, demonstrating his immense versatility as a writer.

In "A Rose for Emily" Faulkner uses his talents for suspense and social comment to weave a tale of the degeneration that lies beneath the outward grace and beauty of the South.

A Rose for Emily

When Miss Emily Grierson died, our whole town went to her funeral: the men through a sort of respectful affection for a fallen monument, the women mostly out of curiosity to see the inside of her house, which no one save an old manservant—a combined gardner and cook—had seen in at least ten years.

It was a big, squarish frame house that had once been white, decorated with cupolas and spires and scrolled balconies in the heavily lightsome style of the seventies, set on what had once been our most select street. But garages and cotton gins had encroached and obliterated even the august names of that neighborhood; only Miss Emily's house was left, lifting its stubborn and coquettish decay above the cotton wagons and the gasoline pumps—an eyesore among eyesores. And now Miss Emily had gone to join the representatives of those august names where they lay in the cedar-bemused cemetery among the ranked and anonymous graves of Union and Confederate soldiers who fell at the battle of Jefferson.

Alive, Miss Emily had been a tradition, a duty, and a care; a sort of hereditary obligation upon the town, dating from that day in 1894 when Colonel Sartoris, the mayor—he who fathered the edict that no Negro woman should appear on the streets without an apron—remitted her taxes, the dispensation dating from the death of her father on into perpetuity. Not that Miss Emily would have accepted charity. Colonel Sartoris invented an involved tale to the effect that Miss Emily's father had loaned money to the town, which the town, as a matter of business,

preferred this way of repaying. Only a man of Colonel Sartoris' generation and thought could have invented it, and only a woman could have
believed it.

When the next generation, with its more modern ideas, became
mayors and aldermen, this arrangement created some little dissatisfac-
tion. On the first of the year they mailed her a tax notice. February came,
and there was no reply. They wrote her a formal letter, asking her to call
at the sheriff's office at her convenience. A week later the mayor wrote
her himself, offering to call or to send his car for her, and received in reply
a note on paper of an archaic shape, in a thin, flowing calligraphy in faded
ink, to the effect that she no longer went out at all. The tax notice was also
enclosed, without comment.

They called a special meeting of the Board of Aldermen. A deputa-
tion waited upon her, knocked at the door through which no visitor had
passed since she ceased giving china-painting lessons eight or ten years
earlier. They were admitted by the old Negro into a dim hall from which a
stairway mounted into still more shadow. It smelled of dust and disuse—a
close, dank smell. The Negro led them into the parlor. It was furnished in
heavy, leather-covered furniture. When the Negro opened the blinds of
one window, they could see that the leather was cracked; and when they
sat down, a faint dust rose sluggishly about their thighs, spinning with
slow motes in the single sun-ray. On a tarnished gilt easel before the
fireplace stood a crayon portrait of Miss Emily's father.

They rose when she entered—a small, fat woman in black, with a thin
gold chain descending to her waist and vanishing into her belt, leaning on
an ebony cane with a tarnished gold head. Her skeleton was small and
spare; perhaps that was why what would have been merely plumpness in
another was obesity in her. She looked bloated, like a body long
submerged in motionless water, and of that pallid hue. Her eyes, lost in
the fatty ridges of her face, looked like two small pieces of coal pressed
into a lump of dough as they moved from one face to another while the
visitors stated their errand.

She did not ask them to sit. She just stood in the door and listened
quietly until the spokesman came to a stumbling halt. Then they could
hear the invisible watch ticking at the end of the gold chain.

Her voice was dry and cold. "I have no taxes in Jefferson. Colonel
Sartoris explained it to me. Perhaps one of you can gain access to the city
records and satisfy yourselves."

"But we have. We are the city authorities, Miss Emily. Didn't you get
a notice from the sheriff, signed by him?"

"I received a paper, yes," Miss Emily said. "Perhaps he considers
himself the sheriff . . . I have no taxes in Jefferson."

"But there is nothing on the books to show that, you see. We must go
by the—"

"See Colonel Sartoris. I have no taxes in Jefferson."

"But, Miss Emily—"

"See Colonel Sartoris." (Colonel Sartoris had been dead almost ten

years.) "I have no taxes in Jefferson. Tobe!" The Negro appeared. "Show
these gentlemen out."

So she vanquished them, horse and foot, just as she had vanquished
their fathers thirty years before about the smell. That was two years after
her father's death and a short time after her sweetheart—the one we
believed would marry her—had deserted her. After her father's death she
went out very little; after her sweetheart went away, people hardly saw
her at all. A few of the ladies had the temerity to call, but were not
received, and the only sign of life about the place was the Negro man—a
young man then—going in and out with a market basket.

"Just as if a man—any man—could keep a kitchen properly," the
ladies said; so they were not surprised when the smell developed. It was
another link between the gross, teeming world and the high and mighty
Griersons.

A neighbor, a woman, complained to the mayor, Judge Stevens,
eighty years old.

"But what will you have me do about it, madam?" he said.

"Why, send her word to stop it," the woman said. "Isn't there a
law?"

I'm sure that won't be necessary," Judge Stevens said. "It's probably
just a snake or a rat that nigger of hers killed in the yard. I'll speak to him
about it."

The next day he received two more complaints, one from a man who
came in diffident deprecation. "We really must do something about it,
Judge. I'd be the last one in the world to bother Miss Emily, but we've got
to do something." That night the Board of Aldermen met—three gray-
beards and one younger man, a member of the rising generation.

"It's simple enough," he said. "Send her word to have her place
cleaned up. Give her a certain time to do it in, and if she don't . . ."

"Dammit, sir," Judge Stevens said, "will you accuse a lady to her
face of smelling bad?"

So the next night, after midnight, four men crossed Miss Emily's
lawn and slunk about the house like burglars, sniffing along the base of the
brickwork and at the cellar openings while one of them performed a
regular sowing motion with his hand out of a sack slung from his shoulder.
They broke open the cellar door and sprinkled lime there, and in all the
outbuildings. As they recrossed the lawn, a window that had been dark
was lighted and Miss Emily sat in it, the light behind her, and her upright
torso motionless as that of an idol. They crept quietly across the lawn and
into the shadow of the locusts that lined the street. After a week or two
the smell went away.

That was when people had begun to feel really sorry for her. People
in our town, remembering how old lady Wyatt, her great-aunt, had gone
completely crazy at last, believed that the Griersons held themselves a
little too high for what they really were. None of the young men were
quite good enough to Miss Emily and such. We had long thought of them

as a tableau; Miss Emily a slender figure in white in the background, her father a spraddled silhouette in the foreground, his back to her and clutching a horsewhip, the two of them framed by the back-flung front door. So when she got to be thirty and was still single, we were not pleased exactly, but vindicated; even with insanity in the family she wouldn't have turned down all of her chances if they had really materialized.

When her father died, it got about that the house was all that was left to her; and in a way, people were glad. At last they could pity Miss Emily. Being left alone, and a pauper, she had become humanized. Now she too would know the old thrill and the old despair of a penny more or less.

The day after his death all the ladies prepared to call at the house and offer condolence and aid, as is our custom. Miss Emily met them at the door, dressed as usual and with no trace of grief on her face. She told them that her father was not dead. She did that for three days, with the ministers calling on her, and the doctors, trying to persuade her to let them dispose of the body. Just as they were about to resort to law and force, she broke down, and they buried her father quickly.

We did not say she was crazy then. We believed she had to do that. We remembered all the young men her father had driven away, and we knew that with nothing left, she would have to cling to that which had robbed her, as people will.

She was sick for a long time. When we saw her again, her hair was cut short, making her look like a girl, with a vague resemblance to those angels in colored church windows—sort of tragic and serene.

The town had just let the contracts for paving the sidewalks, and in the summer after her father's death they began the work. The construction company came with niggers and mules and machinery, and a foreman named Homer Barron, a Yankee—a big, dark, ready man, with a big voice and eyes lighter than his face. The little boys would follow in groups to hear him cuss the niggers, and the niggers singing in time to the rise and fall of picks. Pretty soon he knew everybody in town. Whenever you heard a lot of laughing anywhere about the square, Homer Barron would be in the center of the group. Presently we began to see him and Miss Emily on Sunday afternoons driving in the yellow-wheeled buggy and the matched team of bays from the livery stable.

At first we were glad that Miss Emily would have an interest, because the ladies all said, "Of course a Grierson would not think seriously of a Northerner, a day laborer." But there were still others, older people, who said that even grief could not cause a real lady to forget *noblesse oblige*—without calling it *noblesse oblige*. They just said, "Poor Emily. Her kinsfolk should come to her." She had some kin in Alabama; but years ago her father had fallen out with them over the estate of old lady Wyatt, the crazy woman, and there was no communication between the two families. They had not even been represented at the funeral.

And as soon as the old people said, "Poor Emily," the whispering began. "Do you suppose it's really so?" they said to one another. "Of course it is. What else could . . ." This behind their hands; rustling of craned silk and satin behind jalousies closed upon the sun of Sunday afternoon as the thin, swift clop-clop-clop of the matched team passed: "Poor Emily."

She carried her head high enough—even when we believed that she was fallen. It was as if she demanded more than ever the recognition of her dignity as the last Grierson; as if it had wanted that touch of earthiness to reaffirm her imperviousness. Like when she bought the rat poison, the arsenic. That was over a year after they had begun to say "Poor Emily," and while the two female cousins were visiting her.

"I want some poison," she said to the druggist. She was over thirty then, still a slight woman, though thinner than usual, with cold, haughty black eyes in a face the flesh of which was strained across the temples and about the eye-sockets as you imagine a lighthousekeeper's face ought to look. "I want some poison," she said.

"Yes, Miss Emily. What kind? For rats and such? I'd recom—"

"I want the best you have. I don't care what kind."

The druggist named several. "They'll kill anything up to an elephant. But what you want is—"

"Arsenic," Miss Emily said. "Is that a good one?"

"Is . . . arsenic? Yes, ma'am. But what you want—"

"I want arsenic."

The druggist looked down at her. She looked back at him, erect, her face like a strained flag. "Why, of course," the druggist said. "If that's what you want. But the law requires you to tell what you are going to use it for."

Miss Emily just stared at him, her head tilted back in order to look him eye for eye, until he looked away and went and got the arsenic and wrapped it up. The Negro delivery boy brought her the package; the druggist didn't come back. When she opened the package at home there was written on the box, under the skull and bones: "For rats."

So the next day we all said, "She will kill herself"; and we said it would be the best thing. When she had first begun to be seen with Homer Barron, we had said, "She will marry him." Then we said, "She will persuade him yet," because Homer himself had remarked—he liked men, and it was known that he drank with the younger men in the Elks' Club—that he was not a marrying man. Later we said, "Poor Emily" behind the jalousies as they passed on Sunday afternoon in the glittering buggy, Miss Emily with her head high and Homer Barron with his hat cocked and a cigar in his teeth, reins and whip in a yellow glove.

Then some of the ladies began to say that it was a disgrace to the town and a bad example to the young people. The men did not want to interfere, but at last the ladies forced the Baptist minister—Miss Emily's people were Episcopal—to call upon her. He would never divulge what happened during that interview, but he refused to go back again. The next

Sunday they again drove about the streets, and the following day the minister's wife wrote to Miss Emily's relations in Alabama.

So she had blood-kin under her roof again and we sat back to watch developments. At first nothing happened. Then we were sure that they were to be married. We learned that Miss Emily had been to the jeweler's and ordered a man's toilet set in silver, with the letters H. B. on each piece. Two days later we learned that she had bought a complete outfit of men's clothing, including a nightshirt, and we said, "They are married." We were really glad. We were glad because the two female cousins were even more Grierson than Miss Emily had ever been.

So we were not surprised when Homer Barron—the streets had been finished some time since—was gone. We were a little disappointed that there was not a public blowing-off, but we believed that he had gone on to prepare for Miss Emily's coming, or to give her a chance to get rid of the cousins. (By that time it was a cabal, and we were all Miss Emily's allies to help circumvent the cousins.) Sure enough, after another week they departed. And, as we had expected all along, within three days Homer Barron was back in town. A neighbor saw the Negro man admit him at the kitchen door at dusk one evening.

And that was the last we saw of Homer Barron. And of Miss Emily for some time. The Negro man went in and out with the market basket, but the front door remained closed. Now and then we would see her at a window for a moment, as the men did that night when they sprinkled the lime, but for almost six months she did not appear on the streets. Then we knew that this was to be expected too; as if that quality of her father which had thwarted her woman's life so many times had been too virulent and too furious to die.

When we next saw Miss Emily, she had grown fat and her hair was turning gray. During the next few years it grew grayer and grayer until it attained an even pepper-and-salt iron gray, when it ceased turning. Up to the day of her death at seventy-four it was still that vigorous iron-gray, like the hair of an active man.

From that time on her front door remained closed, save for a period of six or seven years, when she was about forty, during which she gave lessons in china-painting. She fitted up a studio in one of the downstairs rooms, where the daughters and granddaughters of Colonel Sartoris' contemporaries were sent to her with the same regularity and in the same spirit that they were sent to church on Sundays with a twenty-five cent piece for the collection plate. Meanwhile her taxes had been remitted.

Then the newer generation became the backbone and the spirit of the town, and the painting pupils grew up and fell away and did not send their children to her with boxes of color and tedious brushes and pictures cut from the ladies' magazines. The front door closed upon the last one and remained closed for good. When the town got free postal delivery, Miss Emily alone refused to let them fasten the metal numbers above her door and attach a mailbox to it. She would not listen to them.

Daily, monthly, yearly we watched the Negro grow grayer and more stooped, going in and out with the market basket. Each December we sent her a tax notice, which would be returned by the post office a week later, unclaimed. Now and then we would see her in one of the downstairs windows—she had evidently shut up the top floor of the house—like the carven torso of an idol in a niche, looking or not looking at us, we could never tell which. Thus she passed from generation to generation—dear, inescapable, impervious, tranquil, and perverse.

And so she died. Fell ill in the house filled with dust and shadows, with only a doddering Negro man to wait on her. We did not even know she was sick; we had long since given up trying to get any information from the Negro. He talked to no one, probably not even to her, for his voice had grown harsh and rusty, as if from disuse.

She died in one of the downstairs rooms, in a heavy walnut bed with a curtain, her gray head propped on a pillow yellow and moldy with age and lack of sunlight.

The Negro met the first of the ladies at the front door and let them in, with their hushed, sibilant voices and their quick, curious glances, and then he disappeared. He walked right through the house and out the back and was not seen again.

The two female cousins came at once. They held the funeral on the second day, with the town coming to look at Miss Emily beneath a mass of bought flowers, with the crayon face of her father musing profoundly above the bier and the ladies sibilant and macabre; and the very old men—some in their brushed Confederate uniforms—on the porch and the lawn, talking of Miss Emily as if she had been a contemporary of theirs, believing that they had danced with her and courted her perhaps, confusing time with its mathematical progression, as the old do, to whom all the past is not a diminishing road but, instead, a huge meadow which no winter ever quite touches, divided from them now by the narrow bottle-neck of the most recent decade of years.

Already we knew that there was one room in that region above stairs which no one had seen in forty years, and which would have to be forced. They waited until Miss Emily was decently in the ground before they opened it.

The violence of breaking down the door seemed to fill this room with pervading dust. A thin, acrid pall as of the tomb seemed to lie everywhere upon this room decked and furnished as for a bridal: upon the valence curtains of faded rose color, upon the rose-shaded lights, upon the dressing table, upon the delicate array of crystal and the man's toilet things backed with tarnished silver, silver so tarnished that the monogram was obscured. Among them lay a collar and tie, as if they had just been removed, which, lifted, left upon the surface a pale crescent in the dust. Upon a chair hung the suit, carefully folded; beneath it the two mute shoes and the discarded socks.

The man himself lay in the bed.

For a long while we just stood there, looking down at the profound and fleshless grin. The body had apparently once lain in the attitude of an embrace, but now the long sleep that outlasts love, that conquers even the grimace of love, had cuckolded him. What was left of him, rotted beneath what was left of the nightshirt, had become inextricable from the bed in which he lay; and upon him and upon the pillow beside him lay that even coating of the patient and biding dust.

Then we noticed that in the second pillow was the indentation of a head. One of us lifted something from it, and leaning forward, that faint and invisible dust dry and acrid in the nostrils, we saw a long strand of iron-gray hair.

FOR FURTHER CONSIDERATION

What does "A Rose for Emily" suggest about the strength of pride and social convention in shaping the behavior of Miss Emily? Of the townspeople? What links exist between the setting of the story and the suspense?

Flannery O'Connor (1925–1965)

If death had not claimed her early, Flannery O'Connor might well have been recognized as the best of America's short story writers. A native of Savannah, Georgia, and a strong Catholic, her interest in the mores and quirks of Bible Belt personalities led her to produce superb character studies.

A Good Man Is Hard to Find

The grandmother didn't want to go to Florida. She wanted to visit some of her connections in east Tennessee and she was seizing at every chance to change Bailey's mind. Bailey was the son she lived with, her only boy. He was sitting on the edge of his chair at the table, bent over the orange sports section of the *Journal*. "Now look here, Bailey," she said, "see here, read this," and she stood with one hand on her thin hip and the other rattling the newspaper at his bald head. "Here this fellow that calls himself The Misfit is aloose from the Federal Pen and headed toward Florida and you read here what it says he did to these people. Just you read it. I wouldn't take my children in any direction with a criminal like that aloose in it. I couldn't answer to my conscience if I did."

Bailey didn't look up from his reading so she wheeled around then and faced the children's mother, a young woman in slacks, whose face was as broad and innocent as a cabbage and was tied around with a green head-kerchief that had two points on the top like rabbit's ears. She was sitting on the sofa, feeding the baby his apricots out of a jar. "The children have been to Florida before," the old lady said. "You all ought to take them somewhere else for a change so they would see different parts of the world and be broad. They never have been to east Tennessee."

The children's mother didn't seem to hear her but the eight-year-old boy, John Wesley, a stocky child with glasses, said, "If you don't want to go to Florida, why dontcha stay at home?" He and the little girl, June Star, were reading the funny papers on the floor.

"She wouldn't stay at home to be queen for a day," June Star said without raising her yellow head.

"Yes and what would you do if this fellow, The Misfit, caught you?" the grandmother asked.

"I'd smack his face," John Wesley said.

"She wouldn't stay at home for a million bucks," June Star said. "Afraid she'd miss something. She has to go everywhere we go."

"All right, Miss," the grandmother said. "Just remember that the next time you want me to curl your hair."

June Star said her hair was naturally curly.

The next morning the grandmother was the first one in the car, ready to go. She had her big black valise that looked like the head of a hippopotamus in one corner, and underneath it she was hiding a basket with Pitty Sing, the cat, in it. She didn't intend for the cat to be left alone in the house for three days because he would miss her too much and she was afraid he might brush against one of the gas burners and accidentally asphyxiate himself. Her son, Bailey, didn't like to arrive at a motel with a cat.

She sat in the middle of the back seat with John Wesley and June Star on either side of her. Bailey and the children's mother and the baby sat in front and they left Atlanta at eight forty-five with the mileage on the car at 55890. The grandmother wrote this down because she thought it would be interesting to say how many miles they had been when they got back. It took them twenty minutes to reach the outskirts of the city.

The old lady settled herself comfortably, removing her white cotton gloves and putting them up with her purse on the shelf in front of the back window. The children's mother still had on slacks and still had her head tied up in a green kerchief, but the grandmother had on a navy blue straw sailor hat with a bunch of white violets on the brim and a navy blue dress with a small white dot in the print. Her collars and cuffs were white organdy trimmed with lace and at her neckline she had pinned a purple spray of cloth violets containing a sachet. In case of an accident, anyone seeing her dead on the highway would know at once that she was a lady.

She said she thought it was going to be a good day for driving, neither too hot nor too cold, and she cautioned Bailey that the speed limit was fifty-five miles an hour and that the patrolmen hid themselves behind billboards and small clumps of trees and sped out after you before you had a chance to slow down. She pointed out interesting details of the scenery: Stone Mountain; the blue granite that in some places came up to both sides of the highway; the brilliant red clay banks slightly streaked with purple; and the various crops that made rows of green lace-work on the ground. The trees were full of silver-white sunlight and the meanest of them sparkled. The children were reading comic magazines and their mother had gone back to sleep.

"Let's go through Georgia fast so we won't have to look at it much," John Wesley said.

"If I were a little boy," said the grandmother, "I wouldn't talk about my native state that way. Tennessee has the mountains and Georgia has the hills."

"Tennessee is just a hillbilly dumping ground," John Wesley said, "and Georgia is a lousy state too."

"You said it," June Star said.

"In my time," said the grandmother, folding her thin veined fingers, "children were more respectful of their native states and their parents and everything else. People did right then. Oh look at the cute little pickaninny!" she said and pointed to a Negro child standing in the door of a shack. "Wouldn't that make a picture, now?" she asked and they all turned and looked at the little Negro out of the back window. He waved.

"He didn't have any britches on," June Star said.

"He probably didn't have any," the grandmother explained. "Little niggers in the country don't have things like we do. If I could paint, I'd paint that picture," she said.

The children exchanged comic books.

The grandmother offered to hold the baby and the children's mother passed him over the front seat to her. She set him on her knee and bounced him and told him about the things they were passing. She rolled her eyes and screwed up her mouth and stuck her leathery thin face into his smooth bland one. Occasionally he gave her a faraway smile. They passed a large cotton field with five or six graves fenced in the middle of it, like a small island. "Look at the graveyard!" the grandmother said, pointing it out. "That was the old family burying ground. That belonged to the plantation."

"Where's the plantation?" John Wesley asked.

"Gone With the Wind," said the grandmother. "Ha. Ha."

When the children finished all the comic books they had brought, they opened the lunch and ate it. The grandmother ate a peanut butter sandwich and an olive and would not let the children throw the box and the paper napkins out the window. When there was nothing else to do they played a game by choosing a cloud and making the other two guess what shape it suggested. John Wesley took one the shape of a cow and June Star guessed a cow and John Wesley said, no, an automobile, and June Star said he didn't play fair, and they began to slap each other over the grandmother.

The grandmother said she would tell them a story if they would keep quiet. When she told a story, she rolled her eyes and waved her head and was very dramatic. She said once when she was a maiden lady she had been courted by a Mr. Edgar Atkins Teagarden from Jasper, Georgia. She

said he was a very good-looking man and a gentleman and that he brought
her a watermelon every Saturday afternoon with his initials cut in it, E. A.
T. Well, one Saturday, she said, Mr. Teagarden brought the watermelon
and there was nobody at home and he left it on the front porch and
returned in his buggy to Jasper, but she never got the watermelon, she
said, because a nigger boy ate it when he saw the initials, E. A. T.! This
story tickled John Wesley's funny bone and he giggled and giggled but
June Star didn't think it was any good. She said she wouldn't marry a man
that just brought her a watermelon on Saturday. The grandmother said
she would have done well to marry Mr. Teagarden because he was a
gentleman and had bought Coca-Cola stock when it first came out and that
he had died only a few years ago, a very wealthy man.

They stopped at The Tower for barbecued sandwiches. The Tower
was a part stucco and part wood filling station and dance hall set in a
clearing outside of Timothy. A fat man named Red Sammy Butts ran it
and there were signs stuck here and there on the building and for miles up
and down the highway saying, TRY RED SAMMY'S FAMOUS BARBE-
CUE. NONE LIKE FAMOUS RED SAMMY'S! RED SAM! THE FAT
BOY WITH THE HAPPY LAUGH. A VETERAN! RED SAMMY'S
YOUR MAN!

Red Sammy was lying on the bare ground outside The Tower with his
head under a truck while a gray monkey about a foot high, chained to a
small chinaberry tree, chattered nearby. The monkey sprang back into the
tree and got on the highest limb as soon as he saw the children jump out of
the car and run toward him.

Inside, The Tower was a long dark room with a counter at one end
and tables at the other and dancing space in the middle. They all sat down
at a board table next to the nickelodeon and Red Sam's wife, a tall
burnt-brown woman with hair and eyes lighter than her skin, came and
took their order. The children's mother put a dime in the machine and
played "The Tennessee Waltz," and the grandmother said that tune
always made her want to dance. She asked Bailey if he would like to
dance but he only glared at her. He didn't have a naturally sunny
disposition like she did and trips made him nervous. The grandmother's
brown eyes were very bright. She swayed her head from side to side and
pretended she was dancing in her chair. June Star said play something she
could tap to so the children's mother put in another dime and played a fast
number and June Star stepped out onto the dance floor and did her tap
routine.

"Ain't she cute?" Red Sam's wife said, leaning over the counter.
"Would you like to come be my little girl?"

"No I certainly wouldn't," June Star said. "I wouldn't live in a
broken-down place like this for a million bucks!" and she ran back to the
table.

"Ain't she cute?" the woman repeated, stretching her mouth politely.

"Arn't you ashamed?" hissed the grandmother.

Red Sam came in and told his wife to quit lounging on the counter and hurry up with these people's order. His khaki trousers reached just to his hip bones and his stomach hung over them like a sack of meal swaying under his shirt. He came over and sat down at a table nearby and let out a combination sigh and yodel. "You can't win," he said. "You can't win," and he wiped his sweating red face off with a gray handkerchief. "These days you don't know who to trust," he said. "Ain't that the truth?"

"People are certainly not nice like they used to be," said the grandmother.

"Two fellers come in here last week," Red Sammy said, "driving a Chrysler. It was a old beat-up car but it was a good one and these boys looked all right to me. Said they worked at the mill and you know I let them fellers charge the gas they bought? Now why did I do that?"

"Because you're a good man!" the grandmother said at once.

"Yes'm, I suppose so," Red Sam said as if he were struck with this answer.

His wife brought the orders, carrying the five plates all at once without a tray, two in each hand and one balanced on her arm. "It isn't a soul in this green world of God's that you can trust," she said. "And I don't count nobody out of that, not nobody," she repeated, looking at Red Sammy.

"Did you read about that criminal, The Misfit, that's escaped?" asked the grandmother.

"I wouldn't be a bit surprised if he didn't attact this place right here," said the woman. "If he hears about it being here, I wouldn't be none surprised to see him. If he hears it's two cent in the cash register, I wouldn't be a tall surprised if he . . ."

"That'll do," Red Sam said. "Go bring these people their Co'-Colas," and the woman went off to get the rest of the order.

"A good man is hard to find," Red Sammy said. "Everything is getting terrible. I remember the day you could go off and leave your screen door unlatched. Not no more."

He and the grandmother discussed better times. The old lady said that in her opinion Europe was entirely to blame for the way things were now. She said the way Europe acted you would think we were made of money and Red Sam said it was no use talking about it, she was exactly right. The children ran outside into the white sunlight and looked at the monkey in the lacy chinaberry tree. He was busy catching fleas on himself and biting each one carefully between his teeth as if it were a delicacy.

They drove off again into the hot afternoon. The grandmother took cat naps and woke up every few minutes with her own snoring. Outside of Toombsboro she woke up and recalled an old plantation that she had visited in this neighborhood once when she was a young lady. She said the house had six white columns across the front and that there was an avenue of oaks leading up to it and two little wooden trellis arbors on either side in front where you sat down with your suitor after a stroll in the garden. She recalled exactly which road to turn off to get to it. She knew that Bailey would not be willing to lose any time looking at an old house, but the more she talked about it, the more she wanted to see it once again and find out if the little twin arbors were still standing. "There was a secret panel in this house," she said craftily, not telling the truth but wishing that she were, "and the story went that all the family silver was hidden in it when Sherman came through but it was never found . . ."

"Hey!" John Wesley said. "Let's go see it! We'll find it! We'll poke all the woodwork and find it! Who lives there? Where do you turn off at? Hey Pop, can't we turn off there?"

"We never have seen a house with a secret panel!" June Star shrieked. "Let's go to the house with the secret panel! Hey Pop, can't we go see the house with the secret panel!"

"It's not far from here, I know," the grandmother said. "It wouldn't take over twenty minutes."

Bailey was looking straight ahead. His jaw was as rigid as a horseshoe. "No." he said.

The children began to yell and scream that they wanted to see the house with the secret panel. John Wesley kicked the back of the front seat and June Star hung over her mother's shoulder and whined desperately into her ear that they never had any fun even on their vacation, that they could never do what THEY wanted to do. The baby began to scream and John Wesley kicked the back of the seat so hard that his father could feel the blows in his kidney.

"All right!" he shouted and drew the car to a stop at the side of the road. "Will you all shut up? Will you all just shut up for one second? If you don't shut up, we won't go anywhere."

"It would be very educational for them," the grandmother murmured.

"All right," Bailey said, "but get this: this is the only time we're going to stop for anything like this. This is the one and only time."

"The dirt road that you have to turn down is about a mile back," the grandmother directed. "I marked it when we passed."

"A dirt road," Bailey groaned.

After they had turned around and were headed toward the dirt road, the grandmother recalled other points about the house, the beautiful glass over the front doorway and the candle-lamp in the hall. John Wesley said that the secret panel was probably in the fireplace.

"You can't go inside this house," Bailey said. "You don't know who lives there."

"While you all talk to the people in front, I'll run around behind and get in a window," John Wesley suggested.

"We'll all stay in the car," his mother said.

They turned onto the dirt road and the car raced roughly along in a swirl of pink dust. The grandmother recalled the times when there were no paved roads and thirty miles was a day's journey. The dirt road was hilly and there were sudden washes in it and sharp curves on dangerous embankments. All at once they would be on a hill, looking down over the blue tops of trees for miles around, then the next minute, they would be in a red depression with the dust-coated trees looking down on them.

"This place had better turn up in a minute," Bailey said, "or I'm going to turn around."

The road looked as if no one had traveled on it in months.

"Its not much farther," the grandmother said and just as she said it, a horrible thought came to her. The thought was so embarrassing that she turned red in the face and her eyes dilated and her feet jumped up, upsetting her valise in the corner. The instant the valise moved, the newspaper top she had over the basket under it rose with a snarl and Pitty Sing, the cat, sprang onto Bailey's shoulder.

The children were thrown to the floor and their mother, clutching the baby, was thrown into the front seat. The car turned over once and landed right-side up in a gulch off the side of the road. Bailey remained in the driver's seat with the cat—gray-striped with a broad white face and an orange nose—clinging to his neck like a caterpillar.

As soon as the children saw they could move their arms and legs, they scrambled out of the car, shouting, "We've had an ACCIDENT!" The grandmother was curled up under the dashboard, hoping she was injured so that Bailey's wrath would not come down on her all at once. The horrible thought she had had before the accident was that the house she had remembered so vividly was not in Georgia but in Tennessee.

Bailey removed the cat from his neck with both hands and flung it out the window against the side of a pine tree. Then he got out of the car and started looking for the children's mother. She was sitting against the side of the red gutted ditch, holding the screaming baby, but she only had a cut down her face and a broken shoulder. "We've had an ACCIDENT!" the children screamed in a frenzy of delight.

"But nobody's killed," June Star said with disappointment as the grandmother limped out of the car, her hat still pinned to her head but the broken front brim standing up at a jaunty angle and the violet spray hanging off the side. They all sat down in the ditch, except the children, to recover from the shock. They were all shaking.

"Maybe a car will come along," said the children's mother hoarsely.

"I believe I have injured an organ," said the grandmother, pressing her side, but no one answered her. Bailey's teeth were chattering. He had on a yellow sport shirt with bright blue parrots designed in it and his face was as yellow as the shirt. The grandmother decided that she would not mention that the house was in Tennessee.

The road was about ten feet above and they could see only the tops of the trees on the other side of it. Behind the ditch they were sitting in there were more woods, tall and dark and deep. In a few minutes they saw a car some distance away on top of a hill, coming slowly as if the occupants were watching them. The grandmother stood up and waved both arms dramatically to attract their attention. The car continued to come on slowly, disappeared around a bend and appeared again, moving even slower, on top of the hill they had gone over. It was a big black battered hearse-like automobile. There were three men in it.

It came to a stop just over them and for some minutes, the driver looked down with a steady expressionless gaze to where they were sitting, and didn't speak. Then he turned his head and muttered something to the other two and they got out. One was a fat boy in black trousers and a red sweat shirt with a silver stallion embossed on the front of it. He moved around on the right side of them and stood staring, his mouth partly open in a kind of loose grin. The other had on khaki pants and a blue striped coat and a gray hat pulled down very low, hiding most of his face. He came around slowly on the left side. Neither spoke.

The driver got out of the car and stood by the side of it, looking down at them. He was an older man than the other two. His hair was just beginning to gray and he wore silver-rimmed spectacles that gave him a scholarly look. He had a long creased face and didn't have on any shirt or undershirt. He had on blue jeans that were too tight for him and was holding a black hat and a gun. The two boys also had guns.

"We've had an ACCIDENT!" the children screamed.

The grandmother had the peculiar feeling that the bespectacled man was someone she knew. His face was as familiar to her as if she had known him all her life but she could not recall who he was. He moved away from the car and began to come down the embankment, placing his feet carefully so that he wouldn't slip. He had on tan and white shoes and no socks, and his ankles were red and thin. "Good afternoon," he said. "I see you all had you a little spill."

"We turned over twice!" said the grandmother.

"Oncet," he corrected. "We seen it happen. Try their car and see will it run, Hiram," he said quietly to the boy with the gray hat.

"What you got that gun for?" John Wesley asked. "Watcha gonna do with that gun?"

"Lady," the man said to the children's mother, "would you mind calling them children to sit down by you? Children make me nervous. I want all you all to sit down right together there where you're at."

"What are you telling US what to do for?" June Star asked.

Behind them the line of woods gaped like a dark open mouth. "Come here," said their mother.

"Look here now," Bailey began suddenly, "we're in a predicament! We're in . . ."

The grandmother shrieked. She scrambled to her feet and stood staring. "You're The Misfit!" she said. "I recognized you at once!"

"Yes'm," the man said, smiling slightly as if he were pleased in spite of himself to be known, "but it would have been better for all of you, lady, if you hadn't of reckernized me."

Bailey turned his head sharply and said something to his mother that shocked even the children. The old lady began to cry and The Misfit reddened.

"Lady," he said, "don't you get upset. Sometimes a man says things he don't mean. I don't reckon he meant to talk to you thataway."

"You wouldn't shoot a lady, would you?" the grandmother said and removed a clean handkerchief from her cuff and began to slap at her eyes with it.

The Misfit pointed the toe of his shoe into the ground and made a little hole and then covered it up again. "I would hate to have to," he said.

"Listen," the grandmother almost screamed, "I know you're a good man. You don't look a bit like you have common blood. I know you must come from nice people!"

"Yes mam," he said, "finest people in the world." When he smiled he showed a row of strong white teeth. "God never made a finer woman than my mother and my daddy's heart was pure gold." he said. The boy with the red sweat shirt had come around behind them and was standing with his gun at his hip. The Misfit squatted down on the ground. "Watch them children, Bobby Lee," he said. "You know they make me nervous." He looked at the six of them huddled together in front of him and he seemed to be embarrassed as if he couldn't think of anything to say. "Ain't a cloud in the sky," he remarked, looking up at it. "Don't see no sun but don't see no cloud neither."

"Yes, it's a beautiful day," said the grandmother. "Listen," she said, "you shouldn't call yourself The Misfit because I know you're a good man at heart. I can just look at you and tell."

"Hush!" Bailey yelled. "Hush! Everybody shut up and let me handle this!" He was squatting in the position of a runner about to sprint forward but he didn't move.

"I pre-chate that, lady," The Misfit said and drew a little circle in the ground with the butt of his gun.

"It'll take a half a hour to fix this here car," Hiram called, looking over the raised hood of it.

"Well, first you and Bobby Lee get him and that little boy to step over yonder with you," The Misfit said, pointing to Bailey and John Wesley. "The boys want to ast you something," he said to Bailey. "Would you mind stepping back in them woods there with them?"

"Listen," Bailey began, "we're in a terrible predicament! Nobody realizes what this is," and his voice cracked. His eyes were as blue and intense as the parrots in his shirt and he remained perfectly still.

The grandmother reached up to adjust her hat brim as if she were going to the woods with him but it came off in her hand. She stood staring at it and after a second she let it fall on the ground. Hiram pulled Bailey up by the arm as if he were assisting an old man. John Wesley caught hold of his father's hand and Bobby Lee followed. They went off toward the woods and just as they reached the dark edge, Bailey turned and supporting himself against a gray naked pine trunk, he shouted, "I'll be back in a minute, Mamma, wait on me!"

"Come back this instant!" his mother shrilled but they all disappeared into the woods.

"Bailey Boy!" the grandmother called in a tragic voice but she found she was looking at The Misfit squatting on the ground in front of her. "I just know you're a good man," she said desperately. "You're not a bit common!"

"Nome, I ain't a good man," The Misfit said after a second as if he had considered her statement carefully, "but I ain't the worst in the world neither. My daddy said I was a different breed of dog from my brothers and sisters. 'You know,' Daddy said, 'it's some that can live their whole life out without asking about it and it's others has to know why it is, and this boy is one of the latters. He's going to be into everything!'" He put on his black hat and looked up suddenly and then away deep into the woods as if he were embarrassed again. "I'm sorry I don't have on a shirt before you ladies," he said, hunching his shoulders slightly. "We buried our clothes that we had on when we escaped and we're just making do until we can get better. We borrowed these from some folks we met," he explained.

That's perfectly all right," the grandmother said. "Maybe Bailey has an extra shirt in his suitcase."

"I'll look and see terrectly," The Misfit said.

"Where are they taking him?" the children's mother screamed.

"Daddy was a card himself," The Misfit said. "You couldn't put anything over on him. He never got in trouble with the Authorities though. Just had the knack of handling them."

"You could be honest too if you'd only try," said the grandmother. "Think how wonderful it would be to settle down and live a comfortable life and not have to think about somebody chasing you all the time."

The Misfit kept scratching in the ground with the butt of his gun as if he were thinking about it. "Yes'm, somebody is always after you," he murmured.

The grandmother noticed how thin his shoulder blades were just behind his hat because she was standing up looking down on him. "Do you ever pray?" she asked.

He shook his head. All she saw was the black hat wiggle between his shoulder blades. "Nome," he said.

There was a pistol shot from the woods, followed closely by another. Then silence. The old lady's head jerked around. She could hear the wind move through the tree tops like a long satisfied insuck of breath. "Bailey Boy!" she called.

"I was a gospel singer for a while," The Misfit said. "I been most everything. Been in the arm service, both land and sea, at home and abroad, been twict married, been an undertaker, been with the railroads, plowed Mother Earth, been in a tornado, seen a man burnt alive oncet," and he looked up at the children's mother and the little girl who were sitting close together, their faces white and their eyes glassy; "I even seen a woman flogged," he said.

"Pray, pray," the grandmother began, "pray, pray . . . ."

"I never was a bad boy that I remember of," The Misfit said in an almost dreamy voice, "but somewheres along the line I done something wrong and got sent to the penitentiary. I was buried alive," and he looked up and held her attention to him by a steady stare.

"That's when you should have started to pray," she said. "What did you do to get sent to the penitentiary that first time?"

"Turn to the right, it was a wall," The Misfit said, looking up again at the cloudless sky. "Turn to the left, it was a wall. Look up it was a ceiling, look down it was a floor. I forget what I done, lady. I set there, trying to remember what it was I done and I ain't recalled it to this day. Oncet in a while, I would think it was coming to me, but it never come."

"Maybe they put you in by mistake," the old lady said vaguely.

"Nome," he said. "It wasn't no mistake. They had the papers on me."

"You must have stolen something," she said.

The Misfit sneered slightly. "Nobody had nothing I wanted," he said. "It was a head-doctor at the penitentiary said what I had done was kill my daddy but I known that for a lie. My daddy died in nineteen ought nineteen of the epidemic flu and I never had a thing to do with it. He was buried in the Mount Hopewell Baptist churchyard and you can go there and see for yourself."

"If you would pray," the old lady said, "Jesus would help you."

"That's right," The Misfit said.

"Well then, why don't you pray?" she asked trembling with delight suddenly.

"I don't want no hep," he said. "I'm doing all right by myself."

Bobby Lee and Hiram came ambling back from the woods. Bobby Lee was dragging a yellow shirt with bright blue parrots in it.

"Thow me that shirt, Bobby Lee," The Misfit said. The shirt came flying at him and landed on his shoulder and he put it on. The grandmother couldn't name what the shirt reminded her of. "No, lady," The Misfit said while he was buttoning it up, "I found out the crime don't matter. You can do one thing or you can do another, kill a man or take a tire off his car, because sooner or later you're going to forget what it was you done and just be punished for it."

The children's mother had begun to make heaving noises as if she couldn't get her breath. "Lady," he asked, "Would you and that little girl like to step off yonder with Bobby Lee and Hiram and join your husband?"

"Yes, thank you," the mother said faintly. Her left arm dangled helplessly and she was holding the baby, who had gone to sleep, in the other. "Hep that lady up, Hiram," The Misfit said as she struggled to climb out of the ditch, "and Bobby Lee, you hold onto that little girl's hand."

"I don't want to hold hands with him," June Star said. "He reminds me of a pig."

The fat boy blushed and laughed and caught her by the arm and pulled her off into the woods after Hiram and her mother.

Alone with The Misfit, the grandmother found that she had lost her voice. There was not a cloud in the sky nor any sun. There was nothing around her but woods. She wanted to tell him that he must pray. She opened and closed her mouth several times before anything came out. Finally she found herself saying, "Jesus. Jesus," meaning, Jesus will help you, but the way she was saying it, it sounded as if she might be cursing.

"Yes'm," The Misfit said as if he agreed. "Jesus thrown everything off balance. It was the same case with Him as with me except He hadn't committed any crime and they could prove I had committed one because they had the papers on me. Of course," he said, "they never shown me my papers. That's why I sign myself now. I said long ago, you get you a signature and sign everything you do and keep a copy of it. Then you'll know what you done and you can hold up the crime to the punishment and see do they match and in the end you'll have something to prove you ain't been treated right. I call myself The Misfit," he said, "because I can't make what all I done wrong fit what all I gone through in punishment."

There was a piercing scream from the woods, followed closely by a pistol report. "Does it seem right to you, lady, that one is punished a heap and another ain't punished at all?"

"Jesus!" the old lady cried. "You've got good blood! I know you wouldn't shoot a lady! I know you come from nice people! Pray! Jesus, you ought not to shoot a lady. I'll give you all the money I've got!"

"Lady," The Misfit said, looking beyond her far into the woods, "there never was a body that give the undertaker a tip."

There were two more pistol reports and the grandmother raised her head like a parched old turkey hen crying for water and called, "Bailey Boy, Bailey Boy!" as if her heart would break.

"Jesus was the only One that ever raised the dead," The Misfit continued, "and He shouldn't have done it. He thrown everything off balance. If He did what He said, then it's nothing for you to do but throw away everything and follow Him, and if He didn't, then it's nothing for you to do but enjoy the few minutes you got left the best way you can—by killing somebody or burning down his house or doing some other meanness to him. No pleasure but meanness," he said and his voice had become almost a snarl.

"Maybe He didn't raise the dead," the old lady mumbled, not knowing what she was saying and feeling so dizzy that she sank down in the ditch with her legs twisted under her.

"I wasn't there so I can't say He didn't," The Misfit said. "I wisht I had been there," he said, hitting the ground with his fist. "It ain't right I wasn't there because if I had of been there I would of known. Listen lady," he said in a high voice, "if I had of been there I would of known and I wouldn't be like I am now." His voice seemed about to crack and the grandmother's head cleared for an instant. She saw the man's face twisted close to her own as if he were going to cry and she murmured, "Why you're one of my babies. You're one of my own children!" She reached out and touched him on the shoulder. The Misfit sprang back as if a snake had bitten him and shot her three times through the chest. Then he put his gun down on the ground and took off his glasses and began to clean them.

Hiram and Bobby Lee returned from the woods and stood over the ditch, looking down at the grandmother who half sat and half lay in a puddle of blood with her legs crossed under her like a child's and her face smiling up at the cloudless sky.

Without his glasses, The Misfit's eyes were red-rimmed and pale and defenseless-looking. "Take her off and throw her where you thrown the others," he said, picking up the cat that was rubbing itself against his leg.

"She was a talker, wasn't she?" Bobby Lee said, sliding down the ditch with a yodel.

"She would of been a good woman," The Misfit said, "if it had been somebody there to shoot her every minute of her life."

"Some fun!" Bobby Lee said.

"Shut up, Bobby Lee," The Misfit said. "It's no real pleasure in life."

FOR FURTHER CONSIDERATION

Characterization in fiction is often the product of dialogue (what a character says, how he or she says it, the responses of others to that person), of externals (clothes, size, age, possessions), and of the character's actions. How does the author go about developing the character of the grandmother? To what extent does the grandmother bring about what befalls the family?

Nathaniel Hawthorne (1804–1864)

Of those who shaped American literature, none stands out more prominently than Hawthorne, romantic, symbolist, explorer of the human heart. Descended from Puritan ancestors, one of whom had presided at the Salem witch trials, Hawthorne tried life in the famed socialist commune at Brooke Farm and later spent a substantial part of his life in two politically appointed jobs, one at a Customs House and the other as United States Consul in Liverpool, England.

Hawthorne employs symbols to suggest layers of meaning, and he adroitly interweaves a sensitivity for complex human feelings with a powerful yet graceful style. His fiction often pursues deep moral issues and psychological stresses bred of guilt. He was known as a careful rewriter, and he shared the fellowship of other writers such as Longfellow and Melville.

Young Goodman Brown

Young Goodman Brown came forth at sunset into the street at Salem village; but put his head back, after crossing the threshold, to exchange a parting kiss with his young wife. And Faith, as the wife was aptly named, thrust her own pretty head into the street, letting the wind play with the pink ribbons of her cap while she called to Goodman Brown.

"Dearest heart," whispered she, softly and rather sadly, when her lips were close to his ear, "prithee put off your journey until sunrise and sleep in your own bed tonight. A lone woman is troubled with such dreams and such thoughts that she's afeard of herself sometimes. Pray tarry with me this night, dear husband, of all nights in the year."

"My love and my Faith," replied young Goodman Brown, "of all nights in the year, this one night must I tarry away from thee. My journey, as thou callest it, forth and back again, must needs be done 'twixt now and sunrise. What, my sweet, pretty wife, dost thou doubt me already, and we but three months married?"

"Then God bless you!" said Faith, with the pink ribbons; "and may you find all well when you come back."

"Amen!" cried Goodman Brown. "Say thy prayers, dear Faith, and go to bed at dusk, and no harm will come to thee."

So they parted; and the young man pursued his way until, being about to turn the corner by the meeting-house, he looked back and saw the head of Faith still peeping after him with a melancholy air, in spite of her pink ribbons.

"Poor little Faith!" thought he, for his heart smote him. "What a wretch am I to leave her on such an errand! She talks of dreams, too. Methought as she spoke there was trouble in her face, as if a dream had warned her what work is to be done tonight. But no, no; 't would kill her to think it. Well, she's a blessed angel on earth; and after this one night I'll cling to her skirts and follow her to heaven."

With this excellent resolve for the future, Goodman Brown felt himself justified in making more haste on his present evil purpose. He had taken a dreary road, darkened by all the gloomiest trees of the forest, which barely stood aside to let the narrow path creep through, and closed immediately behind. It was all as lonely as could be; and there is this peculiarity in such a solitude, that the traveller knows not who may be concealed by the innumerable trunks and the thick boughs overhead; so that with lonely footsteps he may yet be passing through an unseen multitude.

"There may be a devilish Indian behind every tree," said Goodman Brown to himself; and he glanced fearfully behind him as he added, "What if the devil himself should be at my very elbow!"

His head being turned back, he passed a crook of the road, and, looking forward again, beheld the figure of a man, in grave and decent attire, seated at the foot of an old tree. He arose at Goodman Brown's approach and walked onward side by side with him.

"You are late, Goodman Brown," said he. "The clock of the Old South was striking as I came through Boston, and that is full fifteen minutes agone."

"Faith kept me back a while," replied the young man, with a tremor in his voice, caused by the sudden appearance of his companion, though not wholly unexpected.

It was not deep dusk in the forest, and deepest in that part of it where these two were journeying. As nearly as could be discerned, the second traveller was about fifty years old, apparently in the same rank of life as Goodman Brown, and bearing a considerable resemblance to him, though perhaps more in expression than features. Still they might have been taken for father and son. And yet, though the elder person was as simply clad as the younger, and as simple in manner too, he had an indescribable air of one who knew the world, and who would not have felt abashed at the governor's dinner table or in King William's court, were it possible that his affairs should call him thither. But the only thing about him that could be fixed upon as remarkable was his staff, which bore the likeness of a great black snake, so curiously wrought that it might almost be seen to twist and wriggle itself like a living serpent. This, of course, must have been an ocular deception, assisted by the uncertain light.

"Come, Goodman Brown," cried his fellow-traveller, "this is a dull pace for the beginning of a journey. Take my staff, if you are so soon weary."

"Friend," said the other, exchanging his slow pace for a full stop, "having kept covenant by meeting thee here, it is my purpose now to return whence I came. I have scruples touching the matter thou wot'st of."

"Sayest thou so?" replied he of the serpent, smiling apart. "Let us walk on, nevertheless, reasoning as we go; and if I convince thee not thou shalt turn back. We are but a little way in the forest yet."

"Too far! too far!" exclaimed the goodman, unconsciously resuming his walk. "My father never went into the woods on such an errand, nor his father before him. We have been a race of honest men and good Christians since the days of the martyrs; and shall I be the first of the name of Brown that ever took his path and kept—"

"Such company, thou wouldst say," observed the elder person, interpreting his pause. "Well said, Goodman Brown! I have been as well acquainted with your family as with ever a one among the Puritans; and that's no trifle to say. I helped your grandfather, the constable, when he lashed the Quaker woman so smartly through the streets of Salem; and it was I that brought your father a pitch-pine knot, kindled at my own hearth, to set fire to an Indian village, in King Philip's war. They were my good friends, both; and many a pleasant walk have we had along this path, and returned merrily after midnight. I would fain be friends with you for their sake."

"If it be as thou sayest," replied Goodman Brown, "I marvel they never spoke of these matters; or, verily, I marvel not, seeing that the least rumor of the sort would have driven them from New England.

We are a people of prayer, and good works to boot, and abide no such wickedness."

"Wickedness or not," said the traveller with the twisted staff, "I have a very general acquaintance here in New England. The deacons of many a church have drunk the communion wine with me; the selectmen of divers towns make me their chairman; and a majority of the Great and General Court are firm supporters of my interest. The governor and I, too— But these are state secrets."

"Can this be so?" cried Goodman Brown, with a stare of amazement at his undisturbed companion. "Howbeit, I have nothing to do with the governor and council; they have their own ways, and are no rule for a simple husbandman like me. But, were I to go on with thee, how should I meet the eye of that good old man, our minister, at Salem village? Oh, his voice would make me tremble both Sabbath day and lecture day."

Thus far the elder traveller had listened with due gravity; but now burst into a fit of irrepressible mirth, shaking himself so violently that his snake-like staff actually seemed to wriggle in sympathy.

"Ha! ha! ha!" shouted he again and again; then composing himself, "Well, go on, Goodman Brown, go on; but, prithee, don't kill me with laughing."

"Well, then, to end the matter at once," said Goodman Brown, considerably nettled, "there is my wife, Faith. It would break her dear little heart; and I'd rather break my own."

"Nay, if that be the case," answered the other, "e'en go thy ways, Goodman Brown. I would not for twenty old women like the one hobbling before us that Faith should come to any harm."

As he spoke he pointed his staff at a female figure on the path, in whom Goodman Brown recognized a very pious and exemplary dame, who had taught him his catechism in youth, and was still his moral and spiritual adviser, jointly with the minister and Deacon Gookin.

"A marvel, truly, that Goody Cloyse should be so far in the wilderness at nightfall," said he. "But with your leave, friend, I shall take a cut through the woods until we have left this Christian woman behind. Being a stranger to you, she might ask whom I was consorting with and whither I was going."

"Be it so," said his fellow-traveller. "Betake you to the woods, and let me keep the path."

Accordingly the young man turned aside, but took care to watch his companion, who advanced softly along the road until he had come within a staff's length of the old dame. She, meanwhile, was making the best of her way, with singular speed for so aged a woman, and mumbling some indistinct words—a prayer, doubtless—as she went. The traveller put forth his staff and touched her withered neck with what seemed the serpent's tail.

"The devil!" screamed the pious old lady.

"Then Goody Cloyse knows her old friend?" observed the traveller, confronting her and leaning on his writhing stick.

"Ah, forsooth, and is it your worship indeed?" cried the good dame. "Yea, truly is it, and in the very image of my old gossip, Goodman Brown, the grandfather of the silly fellow that now is. But—would your worship believe it?—my broomstick hath strangely disappeared, stolen, as I suspect, by that unhanged witch, Goody Cory, and that, too, when I was all anointed with the juice of smallage, and cinquefoil, and wolf's bane—"

"Mingled with fine wheat and the fat of a new-born babe," said the shape of Old Goodman Brown.

"Ah, your worship knows the recipe," cried the old lady, cackling aloud. "So, as I was saying, being all ready for the meeting, and no horse to ride on, I made up my mind to foot it; for they tell me there is a nice young man to be taken into communion tonight. But now your good worship will lend me your arm, and we shall be there in a twinkling."

"That can hardly be," answered her friend. "I may not spare you my arm, Goody Cloyse; but here is my staff, if you will."

So saying, he threw it down at her feet, where, perhaps, it assumed life, being one of the rods which its owner had formerly lent to the Egyptian magi. Of this face, however, Goodman Brown could not take cognizance. He had cast up his eyes in astonishment, and, looking down again, beheld neither Goody Cloyse nor the serpentine staff, but his fellow-traveller alone, who waited for him as calmly as if nothing had happened.

That old woman taught me my catechism," said the young man; and there was a world of meaning in this simple comment.

They continued to walk onward, while the elder traveller exhorted his companion to make good speed and persevere in the path, discoursing so aptly that his arguments seemed rather to spring up in the bosom of his auditor than to be suggested by himself. As they went, he plucked a branch of maple to serve for a walking stick, and began to strip it of the twigs and little boughs, which were wet with evening dew. The moment his fingers touched them they became strangely withered and dried up as with a week's sunshine. Thus the pair proceeded, at a good free pace, until suddenly, in a gloomy hollow of the road, Goodman Brown sat himself down on the stump of a tree and refused to go any farther.

"Friend," said he, stubbornly, "my mind is made up. Not another step will I budge on this errand. What if a wretched old woman do choose to go to the devil when I thought she was going to heaven: is that any reason why I should quit my dear Faith and go after her?"

"You will think better of this by and by," said his acquaintance, composedly. "Sit here and rest yourself a while; and when you feel like moving again, there is my staff to help you along."

Without more words, he threw his companion the maple stick, and was as speedily out of sight as if he had vanished into the deepening gloom. The young man sat a few moments by the roadside, applauding himself greatly, and thinking with how clear a conscience he should meet the minister in his morning walk, nor shrink from the eye of good old Deacon Gookin. And what calm sleep would be his that very night, which was to have been spent so wickedly, but so purely and sweetly now, in the arms of Faith! Amidst these pleasant and praiseworthy meditations, Goodman Brown heard the tramp of horses along the road, and deemed it advisable to conceal himself within the verge of the forest, conscious of the guilty purpose that had brought him thither, though now so happily turned from it.

On came the hoof tramps and the voices of the riders, two grave old voices, conversing soberly as they drew near. These mingled sounds appeared to pass along the road, within a few yards of the young man's hiding-place; but, owing doubtless to the depth of the gloom at that particular spot, neither the travellers nor their steeds were visible. Though their figures brushed the small boughs by the wayside, it could not be seen that they intercepted, even for a moment, the faint gleam from the strip of bright sky athwart which they must have passed. Goodman Brown alternately crouched and stood on tiptoe, pulling aside the branches and thrusting forth his head as far as he durst without discerning so much as a shadow. It vexed him the more, because he could have sworn, were such a thing possible, that he recognized the voices of the minister and Deacon Gookin, jogging along quietly, as they were wont to do, when bound to some ordination or ecclesiastical council. While yet within hearing, one of the riders stopped to pluck a switch.

"Of the two, reverend sir," said the voice like the deacon's, "I had rather miss an ordination dinner than tonight's meeting. They tell me that some of our community are to be here from Falmouth and beyond, and others from Connecticut and Rhode Island, besides several of the Indian powwows, who, after their fashion, know almost as much deviltry as the best of us. Moreover, there is a goodly young woman to be taken into communion."

"Mighty well, Deacon Gookin!" replied the solemn old tones of the minister. "Spur up, or we shall be late. Nothing can be done, you know, until I get on the ground."

The hoofs clattered again; and the voices, talking so strangely in the empty air, passed on through the forest, where no church had ever been gathered or solitary Christian prayed. Whither, then, could these holy men be journeying so deep into the heathen wilderness? Young Goodman Brown caught hold of a tree for support, being ready to sink down on the ground, faint and overburdened with the heavy sickness of his heart. He looked up to the sky, doubting whether there really was a heaven above him. Yet there was the blue arch, and the stars brightening in it.

"With heaven above and Faith below, I will yet stand firm against the devil!" cried Goodman Brown.

While he still gazed upward into the deep arch of the firmament and had lifted his hands to pray, a cloud, though no wind was stirring, hurried across the zenith and hid the brightening stars. The blue sky was still visible, except directly overhead, where this black mass of cloud was sweeping swiftly northward. Aloft in the air, as if from the depths of the cloud, came a confused and doubtful sound of voices. Once the listener fancied that he could distinguish the accents of towns-people of his own, men and women, both pious and ungodly, many of whom he had met at the communion table, and had seen others rioting at the tavern. The next moment, so indistinct were the sounds, he doubted whether he had heard aught but the murmur of the old forest, whispering without a wind. Then came a stronger swell of those familiar tones, heard daily in the sunshine at Salem village, but never until now from a cloud of night. There was one voice of a young woman, uttering lamentations, yet with an uncertain sorrow, and entreating for some favor, which, perhaps, it would grieve her to obtain; and all the unseen multitude, both saints and sinners, seemed to encourage her onward.

"Faith!" shouted Goodman Brown, in a voice of agony and despera-tion; and the echoes of the forest mocked him, crying, "Faith! Faith!" as if bewildered wretches were seeking her all through the wilderness.

The cry of grief, rage, and terror was yet piercing the night, when the unhappy husband held his breath for a response. There was a scream, drowned immediately in a louder murmur of voices, fading into far-off laughter, as the dark cloud swept away, leaving the clear and silent sky above Goodman Brown. But something fluttered lightly down through the air and caught on the branch of a tree. The young man seized it, and beheld a pink ribbon.

"My Faith is gone!" cried he, after one stupefied moment. "There is no good on earth; and sin is but a name. Come, devil; for to thee is this world given."

And, maddened with despair, so that he laughed loud and long, did Goodman Brown grasp his staff and set forth again, at such a rate that he seemed to fly along the forest path rather than to walk or run. The road grew wilder and drearier and more faintly traced, and vanished at length, leaving him in the heart of the dark wilderness, still rushing onward with the instinct that guides mortal man to evil. The whole forest was peopled with frightful sounds—the creaking of the trees, the howling of wild beasts, and the yell of Indians; while sometimes the wind tolled like a distant church bell, and sometimes gave a broad roar around the traveller, as if all Nature were laughing him to scorn. But he was himself the chief horror of the scene, and shrank not from its other horrors.

"Ha! ha! ha!" roared Goodman Brown when the wind laughed at him. "Let us hear which will laugh loudest. Think not to frighten me with your deviltry. Come witch, come wizard, come Indian powwow, come devil himself, and here comes Goodman Brown. You may as well fear him as he fear you."

In truth, all through the haunted forest there could be nothing more frightful than the figure of Goodman Brown. On he flew among the black pines, brandishing his staff with frenzied gestures, now giving vent to an inspiration of horrid blasphemy, and now shouting forth such laughter as set all the echoes of the forest laughing like demons around him. The fiend in his own shape is less hideous than when he rages in the breast of man. Thus sped the demoniac on his course, until, quivering among the trees, he saw a red light before him, as when the felled trunks and branches of a clearing have been set on fire, and throw up their lurid blaze against the sky, at the hour of midnight. He paused, in a lull of the tempest that had driven him onward, and heard the swell of what seemed a hymn, rolling solemnly from a distance with the weight of many voices. He knew the tune; it was a familiar one in the choir of the village meeting-house. The verse died heavily away, and was lengthened by a chorus, not of human voices, but of all the sounds of the benighted wilderness pealing in awful harmony together. Goodman Brown cried out, and his cry was lost to his own ear by its unison with the cry of the desert.

In the interval of silence he stole forward until the light glared full upon his eyes. At one extremity of an open space, hemmed in by the dark wall of the forest, arose a rock, bearing some rude, natural resemblance either to an altar or a pulpit, and surrounded by four blazing pines, their tops aflame, their stems untouched, like candles at an evening meeting. The mass of foliage that had overgrown the summit of the rock was all on fire, blazing high into the night and fitfully illuminating the whole field. Each pendent twig and leafy festoon was in a blaze. As the red light arose and fell, a numerous congregation alternately shone forth, then disappeared in shadow, and again grew, as it were, out of the darkness, peopling the heart of the solitary woods at once.

"A grave and dark-clad company," quoth Goodman Brown.

In truth they were such. Among them, quivering to and fro between gloom and splendor, appeared faces that would be seen next day at the council board of the province, and others which, Sabbath after Sabbath, looked devoutly heavenward, and benignantly over the crowded pews, from the holiest pulpits in the land. Some affirm that the lady of the governor was there. At least there were high dames well known to her, and wives of honored husbands, and widows, a great multitude, and ancient maidens, all of excellent repute, and fair young girls, who trembled lest their mothers should espy them. Either the sudden gleams of light flashing over the obscure field bedazzled Goodman Brown, or he recognized a score of the church members of Salem village famous for their especial sanctity. Good old Deacon Gookin had arrived, and waited at the skirts of that venerable saint, his revered pastor. But, irreverently consorting with these grave, reputable, and pious people, these elders of the church, these chaste dames and dewy virgins, there were men of dissolute lives and women of spotted fame, wretches given over to all mean and filthy vice, and suspected even of horrid crimes. It was strange to see that the good shrank not from the wicked, nor were the sinners abashed by the saints. Scattered also among their pale-faced enemies were the Indian priests, or powwows, who had often scared their native forest with more hideous incantations than any known to English witchcraft.

"But where is Faith?" thought Goodman Brown; and, as hope came into his heart, he trembled.

Another verse of the hymn arose, a slow and mournful strain, such as the pious love, but joined to words which expressed all that our nature can conceive of sin, and darkly hinted at far more. Unfathomable to mere mortals is the lore of fiends. Verse after verse was sung; and still the chorus of the desert swelled between like the deepest tone of a mighty organ; and with the final peal of that dreadful anthem there came a sound, as if the roaring wind, the rushing streams, the howling beasts, and every other voice of the unconcerted wilderness were mingling and according with the voice of guilty man in homage to the prince of all. The four blazing pines threw up a loftier flame, and obscurely discovered shapes and visages of horror on the smoke wreaths above the impious assembly. At the same moment the fire on the rock shot redly forth and formed a glowing arch above its base, where now appeared a figure. With reverence be it spoken, the figure bore no slight similitude, both in garb and manner, to some grave divine of the New England churches.

"Bring forth the converts!" cried a voice that echoed through the field and rolled into the forest.

At the word, Goodman Brown stepped forth from the shadow of the trees and approached the congregation, with whom he felt a loathful brotherhood by the sympathy of all that was wicked in his heart. He could have well-nigh sworn that the shape of his own dead father beckoned him to advance, looking downward from a smoke wreath, while a woman, with dim features of despair, threw out her hand to warn him back. Was it his mother? But he had no power to retreat one step, nor to resist, even in thought, when the minister and good old Deacon Gookin seized his arms and led him to the blazing rock. Thither came also the slender form of a veiled female, led between Goody Cloyse, that pious teacher of the catechism, and Martha Carrier, who had received the devil's promise to be queen of hell. A rampant hag was she. And there stood the proselytes beneath the canopy of fire.

"Welcome, my children," said the dark figure, "to the communion of your race. Ye have found thus young your nature and your destiny. My children, look behind you!"

They turned; and flashing forth, as it were, in a sheet of flame, the fiend worshippers were seen; the smile of welcome gleamed darkly on every visage.

"There," resumed the sable form, "are all whom ye have reverenced from youth. Ye deemed them holier than yourselves, and shrank from your own sin, contrasting it with their lives of righteousness and prayerful aspirations heavenward. Yet here are they all in my worshipping assembly. This night it shall be granted you to know their secret deeds: how hoary-bearded elders of the church have whispered wanton words to the young maids of their households; how many a woman, eager for widows' weeds, has given her husband a drink at bedtime and let him sleep his last sleep in her bosom; how beardless youths have made haste to inherit their fathers' wealth; and how fair damsels—blush not, sweet ones—have dug little graves in the garden, and bidden me, the sole guest to an infant's funeral. By the sympathy of your human hearts for sin ye shall scent out all the places—whether in church, bedchamber, street, field, or forest—where crime has been committed, and shall exult to behold the whole earth one stain of guilt, one mighty blood spot. Far more than this. It shall be yours to penetrate, in every bosom, the deep mystery of sin, the fountain of all wicked arts, and which inexhaustible supplies more evil impulses than human power—than my power at its utmost—can make manifest in deeds. And now, my children, look upon each other."

They did so; and, by the blaze of the hell-kindled torches, the wretched man beheld his Faith, and the wife her husband, trembling before that unhallowed altar.

"Lo, there ye stand, my children," said the figure, in a deep and solemn tone, almost sad with its despairing awfulness, as if his once angelic nature could yet mourn for our miserable race. "Depending upon one another's hearts, ye had still hoped that virtue were not all a dream. Now are ye undeceived. Evil is the nature of mankind. Evil must be your only happiness. Welcome again, my children, to the communion of your race."

"Welcome," repeated the fiend worshippers, in one cry of despair and triumph.

And there they stood, the only pair, as it seemed, who were yet hesitating on the verge of wickedness in this dark world. A basin was hollowed, naturally, in the rock. Did it contain water, reddened by the lurid light? or was it blood? or, perchance, a liquid flame? Herein did the shape of evil dip his hand and prepare to lay the mark of baptism upon their foreheads, that they might be partakers of the mystery of sin, more conscious of the secret guilt of others, both in deed and thought, than they could now be of their own. The husband cast one look at his pale wife, and Faith at him. What polluted wretches would the next glance show them to each other, shuddering alike at what they disclosed and what they saw!

"Faith! Faith!" cried the husband, "look up to heaven, and resist the wicked one."

Whether Faith obeyed he knew not. Hardly had he spoken when he found himself amid calm night and solitude, listening to a roar of the wind which died heavily away through the forest. He staggered against the rock, and felt it chill and damp; while a hanging twig, that had been all on fire, besprinkled his cheek with the coldest dew.

The next morning young Goodman Brown came slowly into the street of Salem village, staring around him like a bewildered man. The good old minister was taking a walk along the graveyard to get an appetite for breakfast and meditate his sermon, and bestowed a blessing, as he passed, on Goodman Brown. He shrank from the venerable saint as if to avoid an anathema. Old Deacon Gookin was at domestic worship, and the holy words of his prayer were heard through the open window. "What God doth the wizard pray to?" quoth Goodman Brown. Goody Cloyse, that excellent old Christian, stood in the early sunshine at her own lattice, catechizing a little girl who had brought her a pint of morning's milk.

Goodman Brown snatched away the child as from the grasp of the field himself. Turning the corner by the meeting house, he spied the head of Faith, with the pink ribbons, gazing anxiously forth, and bursting into such joy at sight of him that she skipped along the street and almost kissed her husband before the whole village. But Goodman Brown looked sternly and sadly into her face, and passed on without a greeting.

Had Goodman Brown fallen asleep in the forest and only dreamed a wild dream of a witch-meeting?

Be it so if you will; but, alas! it was a dream of evil omen for young Goodman Brown. A stern, a sad, a darkly meditative, a distrustful, if not a desperate man did he become from the night of that fearful dream. On the Sabbath day, when the congregation were singing a holy psalm, he could not listen because an anthem of sin rushed loudly upon his ear and drowned all the blessed strain. When the minister spoke from the pulpit with power and fervid eloquence, and, with his hand on the open Bible, of the sacred truths of our religion, and of saint-like lives and triumphant deaths, and of future bliss or misery unutterable, then did Goodman Brown turn pale, dreading lest the roof should thunder down upon the gray blasphemer and his hearers. Often, waking suddenly at midnight, he shrank from the bosom of Faith; and at morning or eventide, when the family knelt down at prayer, he scowled and muttered to himself, and gazed sternly at his wife, and turned away. And when he had lived long, and was borne to his grave a hoary corpse, followed by Faith, an aged woman, and children and grandchildren, a goodly procession, besides neighbors not a few, they carved no hopeful verse upon his tombstone, for his dying hour was gloom.

FOR FURTHER CONSIDERATION

Observers have long cited the allegorical nature of "Young Goodman Brown," that is, that the story and many of the people, events, and objects in it act as symbols for concepts, forces, and values beyond the context of the story. What allegorical value do you find in the names of the hero and his wife? The staff of the traveler Brown meets in the forest? The pink ribbons? The town versus the forest?

In their impact on his attitude toward his fellow man, does it matter whether Goodman Brown's experiences in the forest were real or merely imagined? What does Hawthorne suggest about the individual's need for faith? The impact of doubt?

Richard Brautigan (1935–   )

*Hip. Whimsical. Stretching a metaphor to the point where it may bust. A
funny, sensitive commentator on contemporary values. Life as seen by an
intellectual bumpkin. For further adventures, begin with his* Trout Fishing
in America *and move on to* The Pill versus the Springhill Mining
Disaster.

The Kool-Aid Wino

When I was a child I had a friend who became a Kool-Aid wino as the
result of a rupture. He was a member of a very large and poor German
family. All the older children in the family had to work in the fields during
the summer, picking beans for two-and-one-half cents a pound to keep the
family going. Everyone worked except my friend who couldn't because
he was ruptured. There was no money for an operation. There wasn't
even enough money to buy him a truss. So he stayed home and became a
Kool-Aid wino.

One morning in August I went over to his house. He was still in bed.
He looked up at me from underneath a tattered revolution of old blankets.
He had never slept under a sheet in his life.

"Did you bring the nickel you promised?" he asked.

"Yeah," I said. "It's here in my pocket."

"Good."

He hopped out of bed and he was already dressed. He had told me
once that he never took off his clothes when he went to bed.

"Why bother?" he had said. "You're only going to get up, anyway.
Be prepared for it. You're not fooling anyone by taking your clothes off
when you go to bed."

He went into the kitchen, stepping around the littlest children, whose
wet diapers were in various stages of anarchy. He made his breakfast: a
slice of homemade bread covered with Karo syrup and peanut butter.

"Let's go," he said.

We left the house with him still eating the sandwich. The store was
three blocks away, on the other side of a field covered with heavy yellow
grass. There were many pheasants in the field. Fat with summer they
barely flew away when we came up to them.

"Hello," said the grocer. He was bald with a red birthmark on his
head. The birthmark looked just like an old car parked on his head. He
automatically reached for a package of grape Kool-Aid and put it on the
counter.

"Five cents."

"He's got it," my friend said.

I reached into my pocket and gave the nickel to the grocer. He nodded and the old red car wobbled back and forth on the road as if the driver were having an epileptic seizure.

We left.

My friend led the way across the field. One of the pheasants didn't even bother to fly. He ran across the field in front of us like a feathered pig.

When we got back to my friend's house the ceremony began. To him the making of Kool-Aid was a romance and a ceremony. It had to be performed in an exact manner and with dignity.

First he got a gallon jar and we went around to the side of the house where the water spigot thrust itself out of the ground like the finger of a saint, surrounded by a mud puddle.

He opened the Kool-Aid and dumped it into the jar. Putting the jar under the spigot, he turned the water on. The water spit, splashed and guzzled out of the spigot.

He was careful to see that the jar did not overflow and the precious Kool-Aid spill out onto the ground. When the jar was full he turned the water off with a sudden but delicate motion like a famous brain surgeon removing a disordered portion of the imagination. Then he screwed the lid tightly onto the top of the jar and gave it a good shake.

The first part of the ceremony was over.

Like the inspired priest of an exotic cult, he had performed the first part of the ceremony well.

His mother came around the side of the house and said in a voice filled with sand and string, "When are you going to do the dishes? . . . Huh?"

"Soon," he said.

"Well, you better," she said.

When she left, it was as if she had never been there at all. The second part of the ceremony began with him carrying the jar very carefully to an abandoned chicken house in the back. "The dishes can wait," he said to me. Bertrand Russell could not have stated it better.

He opened the chicken house door and we went in. The place was littered with half-rotten comic books. They were like fruit under a tree. In the corner was an old mattress and beside the mattress were four quart jars. He took the gallon jar over to them, and filled them carefully not spilling a drop. He screwed their caps on tightly and was now ready for a day's drinking.

You're supposed to make only two quarts of Kool-Aid from a package, but he always made a gallon, so his Kool-Aid was a mere shadow of its desired potency. And you're supposed to add a cup of sugar to every package of Kool-Aid, but he never put any sugar in his Kool-Aid because there wasn't any sugar to put in it.

He created his own Kool-Aid reality and was able to illuminate himself by it.

FOR FURTHER CONSIDERATION

Brautigan offers the reader a series of progressively outrageous metaphors. Review what he compares with the old red car, a feathered pig, the
finger of a saint, fruit under a tree. What does he suggest with the lines
" 'The dishes can wait,' he said to me. Bertrand Russell could not have
stated it better"? How does the metaphoric progression of the story
prepare the reader for the flight of fancy required in the last line?

Part Two

POETRY

"Every Word Was Once A Poem"

Ralph Waldo Emerson

Readers sophisticated and unsophisticated may both find value in the brief introductory poetry regimen recommended here. Before immersing yourself in the fine poems which follow, you might try these three simple steps. First read slowly Archibald MacLeish's extraordinary poem "Ars Poetica" and give some thought to the attributes of poetry he suggests there. Next, read in Part IV John Ciardi's excellent essay "The Act of Language," wherein you will discover one of the more lucid explanations of poetry ever authored. And finally read again "Ars Poetica," this time applying what Ciardi discusses in his essay and recognizing that just as we learn best from the act itself in learning to sail a boat, we learn best to enjoy the experience of poetry from reading poetry, not from reading about it. In being exposed to the finest of poetic sensibilities, the reader must inevitably experience some of the joy poetry offers and be lured further on.

Briefly, a reader of poems has several things to remember.

1 Never approach a poem with a long face. For all its serious-

ness, poetry contains a most unpredictable and vibrant kind of life. It exists essentially to provide enjoyment, and to approach a poem with the demeanor of an undertaker, or with any other predetermined stance, will defeat much of the opportunity for that enjoyment. If you will bring an open mind, your full attention, and a willing imagination, your encounters with poetry will prove full ones.

2   Economy operates as a ruling principle in poetry. Good poets make every word count, and more, they understand what happens in the chemistry of putting one word next to another. Note, then, that as a poet frequently abandons the abundance of words and the grammar and syntax of prose, he or she instead creates a highly intense language experience by using words sparely, spending each one carefully. This intensity results in part from the poet's close control of rhythm, emphasis, metaphor, tone and other elements. It also results from a talent for communicating in a powerful way the reality or feeling that underlies the words, while still giving us cause to enjoy simply the play of the words themselves. Observe if you can, then, the subtle link that exists between the economy with words that we find in poetry and the potential of a poem to provide a reader with a glimpse of a realm that we only occasionally recognize, the reality we use words to represent.

3   Poetry calls on a reader's senses, all of them. Have yours at the ready—nose, touch, eyes, and ears—use them when the poem calls on them. The best readers can often *hear* a poem as they read it.

4   Just as we cannot separate the dancer from the dance, we cannot separate the *how* of poetry from the *what*. You may be asked, for example, to speak of imagery, rhyme, or some other poetic element as if it existed independently of the way it appears in a certain poem. Remember that such separations are most often only learning exercises aimed at developing familiarity with the conventions of poetry. No one can separate what the poet says from how he or she says it, for form and content remain irrevocably bonded. They are the same thing, to be experienced or felt simultaneously, and in their interplay lies the joy of a poem.

5   Metaphor sits at the heart of poetry. It is the comparison of unlike things, the description of one thing in terms of another that allows the reader to see in a larger sense the oneness of life. That oneness has much to do with the mysterious power of poetry to let us glimpse the spark of truth and to feel the flood of warmth that accompanies such glimpses.

6   A reader should not expect a poem to *mean* anything. It simply provides an experience, and the reader must determine if some kind of significance accompanies that experience. Oddly enough, however, we often find such significance in poetry—that is, meaning for our personal lives, so much so that we are sometimes left wordless by the experience of a poem.

Finally, observe the recurrence of the central theme of self in the selections offered here and the various ways that poetry leads to self. Because poets must explore their inner worlds to produce their art, we find in poetry the quintessential self, the deepest feelings, and spiritual center of sensitive human beings. As we encounter these revelations, we often discover that the experience calls things out of our own subconscious realms—emotions, unconventional ideas, imaginings otherwise locked inside. Beyond providing a look into the innermost promptings of the poet and allowing us to adventure into our selves in responding to a poem, poetry unites us with the poet and with other readers of the poem in a shared experience. Thus a poem lets us overcome our separate worlds, although each reader may remain in fact alone. And last, many poems allow us to forge beyond common sense, beyond senses conditioned to see things as the consensus would have us see them. In this forging we communicate with our own uniqueness and sense in a special way the nature of the identity that matters most, the one within.

William Shakespeare (1564–1616)

Shakespeare spent most of his working life in London writing and producing drama and performing as an actor in the Lord Chamberlain's theatrical company. In the tragedies, comedies, and poetry that he wrote between 1590 and 1612, he demonstrated a genius that established him as probably the greatest writer in Western history. He combined remarkable psychological insight with an ability to unify thought, motivation, action, and language.

As for the recurring rumor that his works may have been written by Jonson, Marlow, or another poet-playwright, H. L. Mencken summed it up best when he said, "Shakespeare's works were written either by Shakespeare or by someone else with the same name."

Thematically Shakespeare's poems speak often of the relentlessness of time and of the enduring value of love.

SONNET 18

Shall I Compare Thee to a Summer's Day?

Shall I compare thee to a summer's day?
Thou are more lovely and more temperate;
Rough winds do shake the darling buds of May,
And summer's lease hath all too short a date;
Sometime too hot the eye of heaven shines,   5
And often is his gold complexion dimmed;
And every fair from fair sometimes declines,
By chance, or nature's changing course untrimmed.
But thy eternal summer shall not fade,
Nor lose possession of that fair thou owest,   10
Nor shall death brag thou wander'st in his shade
When in eternal lines to time thou growest:
So long as men can breathe, or eyes can see,
So long lives this, and this gives life to thee.

SONNET 29

When, in Disgrace With Fortune and Men's Eyes

When, in disgrace with Fortune and men's eyes,
I all alone beweep my outcast state,
And trouble deaf heaven with my bootless cries,

And look upon myself and curse my fate,
Wishing me like to one more rich in hope,   5
Featured like him, like him with friends possessed,
Desiring this man's art, and that man's scope,
With what I most enjoy contented least;
Yet in these thoughts myself almost despising,
Haply I think on thee, and then my state,   10
Like to the lark at break of day arising
From sullen earth, sings hymns at heaven's gate;
For thy sweet love rememb'red such wealth brings
That then I scorn to change my state with kings.

SONNET 30

When to the Sessions of Sweet Silent Thought

When to the sessions of sweet silent thought
I summon up remembrance of things past,
I sigh the lack of many a thing I sought,
And with old woes new wail my dear time's waste:
Then can I drown an eye, unused to flow,   5
For precious friends hid in death's dateless night,
And weep afresh love's long since cancelled woe,
And moan the expense of many a vanished sight:
Then can I grieve at grievances foregone,
And heavily from woe to woe tell o'er   10
The sad account of fore-bemoaned moan,
Which I new pay as if not paid before.
     But if the while I think on thee, dear friend,
     All losses are restored and sorrows end.

SONNET 73

That Time of Year Thou Mayst in Me Behold

That time of year thou mayst in me behold
When yellow leaves, or none, or few, do hang
Upon those boughs which shake against the cold,
Bare ruined choirs, where late the sweet birds sang.
In me thou see'st the twilight of such day   5
As after sunset fadeth in the west,
Which by and by black night doth take away,

Death's second self that seals up all in rest.
In me thou see'st the glowing of such fire,
That on the ashes of his youth doth lie,   10
As the death-bed, whereon it must expire
Consumed with that which it was nourished by.
    This thou perceiv'st, which makes thy love more strong
    To love that well, which thou must leave ere long.

FOR FURTHER CONSIDERATION

In "Sonnet 73" how is one metaphor extended to the next? What do the
basic metaphors in each of the three quatrains have in common? From
one quatrain to the next, does the succession of metaphors move from
general to particular or particular to general?
    In what way does the rhyme scheme serve the statement of this
poem?

John Donne (1572–1631)

*A Catholic in anti-Catholic England, Donne searched his soul, then
converted to Anglicanism at the age of twenty-one. After he had eloped
with his patron's young niece and thereby lost a possible post in the royal
court, James I appointed him to the clergy in 1615. As Dean of St. Paul's,
he rapidly earned a reputation as a superb speaker and metaphysician and
became quite well known. He circulated his poetry, however, only privately
during his life. It is said he preached his own funeral sermon several days
before his death.*

    *Donne clearly saw parallels between passions of the flesh and a
passion for God. Where his love poems abound with wit, candor, and
delicate metaphors, they share with his other poems an intensity that
leaves readers feeling they have glimpsed the most private, spiritual side of
the man.*

A Valediction: Forbidding Mourning

As virtuous men passe mildly away,
   And whisper to their soules, to goe,
Whilst some of their sad friends doe say,
   The breath goes now, and some say, no:

So let us melt, and make no noise,   5
   No teare-floods, nor sigh-tempests move,
T'were prophanation of our joyes
   To tell the layetie our love.

Moving of th'earth brings harmes and feares,
   Men reckon what it did and meant,   10
But trepidation of the spheares,
   Though greater farre, is innocent.

Dull sublunary lovers love
   (Whose soule is sense) cannot admit
Absence, because it doth remove   15
   Those things which elemented it.

But we by a love, so much refin'd,
   That our selves know not what it is,
Inter-assured of the mind,
   Care lesse, eyes, lips, and hands to misse.   20

Our two soules therefore, which are one,
   Though I must goe, endure not yet
A breach, but an expansion,
   Like gold to airy thinnesse beate.

If they be two, they are two so   25
   As stiffe twin compasses are two,
Thy soule the fixt foot, makes no show
   To move, but doth, if th'other doe.

And though it in the center sit,
   Yet when the other far doth rome,   30
It leanes, and hearkens after it,
   And growes erect, as that comes home.

Such wilt thou be to mee, who must
   Like th'other foot, obliquely runne;
Thy firmnes drawes my circle just,   35
   And makes me end, where I begunne.

The Canonization

For Godsake hold your tongue, and let me love,
   Or chide my palsy, or my gout,
My five gray hairs, or ruin'd fortune flout,
   With wealth your state, your mind with arts improve,
      Take you a course, get you a place,   5
      Observe his honor, or his grace,
Or the King's reall, or his stamped face
   Contemplate, what you will, approve,
      So you will let me love.

Alas, Alas, who's injur'd by my love?   10
   What merchants' ships have my sighs drown'd?

Who says my tears have overflow'd his ground?
  When did my colds a forward spring remove
    When did the heats which my veins fill
      Add one more to the plaguy bill?   15

Soldiers find wars, and lawyers find out still
  Litigious men, which quarrels move,
  Though she and I do love.

Call us what you will, we are made such by love;
  Call her one, me another fly,   20
We are tapers too, and at our own cost die,
  And we in us find the eagle and the dove.
    The phoenix riddle hath more wit
      By us, we two being one, are it.
So, to one neutral thing both sexes fit,   25
  We die and rise the same, and prove
  Mysterious by this love.

We can die by it, if not live by love,
  And if unfit for tombs and hearse
Our legend be, it will be fit for verse;   30
  And if no piece of chronicle we prove,
    We'll build in sonnets pretty rooms;
    As well a well wrought urn becomes
The greatest ashes, as half-acre tombs,
  And by these hymns, all shall approve   35
  Us *Canoniz'd* for Love:

And thus invoke us; You whom reverend love
  Made one another's hermitage;
You, to whom love was peace, that now is rage;
  Who did the whole world's soul contract, and drove   40
    Into the glasses of your eyes
    (So made such mirrors, and such spies,
That they did all to you epitomize,)
  Countries, towns, Courts: Beg from above
  A pattern of your love!   45

The Ecstasy

Where, like a pillow on a bed,
  A pregnant bank swelled up to rest
The violet's reclining head,
  Sat we two, one another's best.

Our hands were firmly cemented   5
  With a fast balm, which thence did spring;
Our eye-beams twisted, and did thread

Our eyes upon one double string;
So to entergraft our hands, as yet
 Was all the means to make us one,   10
And pictures in our eyes to get
 Was all our propagation.
As, 'twixt two equal armies, fate
 Suspends uncertain victory,
Our souls, which to advance their state   15
 Were gone out, hung 'twixt her and me.
And whilst our souls negotiate there,
 We like sepulchral statues lay;
All day, the same our postures were,
 And we said nothing, all the day.   20
If any, so by love refined
 That he soul's language understood,
And by good love were grown all mind,
 Within convenient distance stood,
He, though he knew not which soul spake,   25
 Because both meant, both spake the same,
Might thence a new concoction take
 And part far purer than he came.
This ecstasy doth unperplex,
 We said, and tell us what we love: 30
We see by this it was not sex,
 We see we saw not what did move;
But as all several souls contain
 Mixture of things, they know not what,
Love these mixed souls doth mix again   35
 And makes both one, each this and that.
A single violet transplant,
 The strength, the color, and the size,
All which before was poor and scant,
 Redoubles still, and multiplies.   40
When love with one another so
 Interinanimates two souls,
That abler soul, which thence doth flow,
 Defects of loneliness controls.
We then, who are this new soul, know   45
 Of what we are composed, and made,
For the atomies of which we grow
 Are souls, whom no change can invade.
But O alas! so long, so far,
 Our bodies why do we forbear?   50
They are ours, though they are not we; we are
 The intelligences, they the spheres.
We owe them thanks, because they thus
 Did us, to us, at first convey,

Yielded their forces, sense, to us,   55
  Nor are dross to us, but allay.
On man heaven's influence works not so,
  But that it first imprints the air;
So soul into the soul may flow,
  Though it to body first repair.   60
As our blood labors to beget
  Spirits, as like souls as it can,
Because such fingers need to knit
  That subtle knot, which makes us man,
So must pure lovers' souls descend   65
  To affections, and to faculties,
Which sense may reach and apprehend;
  Else a great prince in prison lies.
To our bodies turn we then, that so
  Weak men on love revealed may look;   70
Love's mysteries in souls do grow,
  But yet the body is his book.
And if some lover, such as we,
  Have heard this dialogue of one,
Let him still mark us, he shall see   75
  Small change when we're to bodies gone.

Song: Go and Catch a Falling Star

Go and catch a falling star,
  Get with child a mandrake root,
Tell me where all past years are,
  Or who cleft the devil's foot,
Teach me to hear mermaids singing,   5
Or to keep off envy's stinging,
     And find
     What wind
Serves to advance an honest mind.

If thou beest born to strange sights,   10
  Things invisible to see,
Ride ten thousand days and nights,
  Till age snow white hairs on thee.
Thou, when thou return'st, wilt tell me
All strange wonders that befell thee,   15
     And swear
     No where
Lives a woman true and fair.

If thou find'st one, let me know:
  Such a pilgrimage were sweet;   20

Yet do not; I would not go,
   Though at next door we might meet.
Though she were true when you met her,
And last till you write your letter,
      Yet she   25
      Will be
False, ere I come, to two or three.

HOLY SONNET 10

Death Be Not Proud

Death be not proud, though some have called thee
Mighty and dreadful, for, thou art not so;
For, those whom thou think'st thou dost overthrow,
Die not, poor death, nor yet canst thou kill me.
From rest and sleep, which but thy pictures be,   5
Much pleasure; then from thee, much more must flow,
And soonest our best men with thee do go,
Rest of their bones, and soul's delivery.
Thou art slave to Fate, Chance, kings, and desperate men,
And dost with poison, war, and sickness dwell,   10
And poppy, or charms can make us sleep as well,
And better than thy stroke; why swell'st thou then?
One short sleep past, we wake eternally,
And death shall be no more; death, thou shalt die.

FOR FURTHER CONSIDERATION

This poem sustains an *apostrophe* (that is, a personification addressed
directly—as if spoken to) throughout. Describe the elements of this
apostrophe. What ironies does Donne suggest in the personification of
death? Compare the impact of rhyme in this poem with its impact in
Shakespeare's "Sonnet 73."

Andrew Marvell (1621–1678)

*Marvell managed to straddle the political fence during the Cromwell
interregnum in seventeenth-century England, and later became an assistant to the blind poet at court, Milton. After the Stuart Restoration, he
became a Member of Parliament and was repeatedly reelected. Marvell's
poetry presents the wit, vigor, paradox, and highly intellectual use of poetic
devices that we now associate with the metaphysical poets.*

To His Coy Mistress

Had we but world enough, and time,
This coyness, Lady, were no crime.
We would sit down, and think which way
To walk, and pass our long love's day.
Thou by the Indian Ganges' side   5
Should'st rubies find: I by the tide
Of Humber would complain. I would
Love you ten years before the Flood:
And you should, if you please, refuse
Till the Conversion of the Jews.   10
My vegetable love should grow
Vaster than empires, and more slow.
An hundred years should go to praise
Thine eyes, and on thy forehead gaze;
Two hundred to adore each breast: 15
But thirty thousand to the rest:
An age at least to every part,
And the last age should show your heart.
For, Lady, you deserve this state;
Nor would I love at lower rate.   20
   But at my back I always hear
Time's winged chariot hurrying near:
And yonder all before us lie
Deserts of vast eternity.
Thy beauty shall no more be found;   25
Nor, in thy marble vault, shall sound
My echoing song: then worms shall try
That long preserved virginity:
And your quaint honor turn to dust;
And into ashes all my lust.   30
The grave's a fine and private place,
But none I think do there embrace.
   Now therefore, while the youthful hue
Sits on thy skin like morning dew,
And while thy willing soul transpires   35
At every pore with instant fires,
Now let us sport us while we may;
And now, like am'rous birds of prey,
Rather at once our time devour,
Than languish in his slow-chapt° power.   40
Let us roll all our strength, and all
Our sweetness, up into one ball:

°Chewed slowly.

And tear our pleasures with rough strife,
Thorough the iron gates of life.
Thus, though we cannot make our sun   45
Stand still, yet we will make him run.

Robert Herrick (1591–1674)

*Once an apprentice goldsmith, Herrick rose to a substantial position as a
Royalist Anglican clergyman during the reigns of the early Stuart kings.
His prodigious production (over 1,400 poems) suggests a spirit steeped in
metaphor, and his poems reflect a mind that delighted in the play of words.
Although he never married, he did not allow his role in the church to
subdue his sensuality, as these two poems illustrate.*

Delight in Disorder

A sweet disorder in the dress
Kindles in clothes a wantonness:
A lawn about the shoulders thrown
Into a fine distraction:
An erring lace, which here and there   5
Enthralls the crimson stomacher:
A cuff neglectful, and thereby
Ribbons to flow confusedly:
A winning wave (deserving note)
In the tempestuous petticoat: 10
A careless shoestring, in whose tie
I see a wild civility:
Does more bewitch me than when art
Is too precise in every part.

Upon Julia's Clothes

Whenas in silks my Julia goes,
Then, then (methinks) how sweetly flows
That liquefaction of her clothes.

Next, when I cast my eyes and see
That brave vibration each way free,   5
O how that glittering taketh me!

William Blake (1757–1827)

Although he had no formal schooling, Blake learned early in life to draw the fantastic figures and places that appeared to him in visions. A painter, engraver, book illustrator, and political dissident, he lived in his own world of mysticism and abstraction. His poems suggest the high value of innocence and the importance of recognizing that opposites in life, things which appear to be antagonistic, in actuality exist as part of a union or common flow.

London

I wander thro' each charter'd street,
Near where the charter'd Thames does flow,
And mark in every face I meet
Marks of weakness, marks of woe.

In every cry of every Man,   5
In every Infant's cry of fear,
In every voice: in every ban,
The mind-forg'd manacles I hear.

How the Chimney-sweeper's cry
Every blackening Church appalls;   10
And the hapless Soldier's sigh
Runs in blood down Palace walls.

But most thro' midnight streets I hear
How the youthful Harlot's curse
Blasts the new born Infant's tear,   15
And blights with plagues the Marriage hearse.

FOR FURTHER CONSIDERATION

Blake's use of meter lends certain words a special emphasis. Which words receive this emphasis? What have these words in common? Describe the tone established by the words receiving this stress. Cite the places where the poet creates special effects with uses of sound.

The Sick Rose

O Rose, thou art sick!
The invisible worm
That flies in the night,
In the howling storm,

Has found out thy bed   5

Of crimson joy:
And his dark secret love
Does thy life destroy.

The Tyger

Tyger! Tyger! burning bright
In the forests of the night,
What immortal hand or eye
Could frame thy fearful symmetry?

In what distant deeps or skies   5
Burnt the fire of thine eyes?
On what wings dare he aspire?
What the hand dare sieze the fire?

And what shoulder & what art,
Could twist the sinews of thy heart?   10
And when thy heart began to beat,
What dread hand? & what dread feet?

What the hammer? what the chain?
In what furnace was thy brain?
What the anvil? what dread grasp   15
Dare its deadly terrors clasp?

When the stars threw down their spears,
And water'd heaven with their tears,
Did he smile his work to see?
Did he who made the Lamb make thee?   20

Tyger! Tyger! burning bright
In the forests of the night,
What immortal hand or eye
Dare frame thy fearful symmetry?

John Keats (1795–1820)

Keats was a very intense man, poor but generous, and always thoughtful toward his brothers and his sister. His short life is a study of frustration and tragedy. His fever for poetry caused him to forsake medical training to become a poet. He could not marry the girl he loved because of his poverty, and he soon realized he was dying of tuberculosis. One of the most famous poets in the English language, he was a complete failure in his lifetime.

Keats' passion for Greek legends was generated when he first saw the famous Elgin Marbles in the British Museum, after which he wrote "Ode on a Grecian Urn." His poetry often appeals physically to the senses, and it reflects his deep belief that "Beauty is truth, truth beauty."

On First Looking into Chapman's Homer

Much have I travelled in the realms of gold,
And many goodly states and kingdoms seen;
Round many western islands have I been
Which bards in fealty to Apollo hold.
Oft of one wide expanse had I been told   5
That deep-browed Homer ruled as his demesne;
Yet did I never breathe its pure serene
Till I heard Chapman speak out loud and bold:

Then felt I like some watcher of the skies
When a new planet swims into his ken;   10
Or like stout Cortez when with eagle eyes
He stared at the Pacific—and all his men
Looked at each other with a wild surmise—
Silent, upon a peak in Darien.

To Autumn

Seasons of mists and mellow fruitfulness,
    Close bosom-friend of the maturing sun;
Conspiring with him how to load and bless
    With fruit the vines that round the thatch-eaves run;
To bend with apples the moss'd cottage trees,   5
    And fill all fruit with ripeness to the core;
        To swell the gourd, and plump the hazel shells
    With a sweet kernel; to set budding more,
And still more, later flowers for the bees,
Until they think warm days will never cease,   10
        For Summer has o'er-brimmed their clammy cells.

Who hath not seen thee oft amid thy store?
    Sometimes whoever seeks abroad may find
Thee sitting careless on a granary floor,
    Thy hair soft-lifted by the winnowing wind;   15
Or on a half-reap'd furrow sound asleep,
    Drows'd with the fume of poppies, while they hook
        Spares the next swath and all its twinèd flowers:

And sometimes like a gleaner thou dost keep
　　Steady thy laden head across a brook;   20
　　Or by a cider-press, with patient look,
　　　Thou watchest the last oozings hours by hours.

Where are the songs of Spring? Aye, where are they?
　　Think not of them, thou hast thy music too,—
While barrèd clouds bloom the soft-dying day,   25
　　And touch the stubble-plains with rosy hue;
Then in a wailful choir the small gnats mourn
　　Among the river sallows, borne aloft
　　　Or sinking as the light wind lives or dies;
And full-grown lambs loud bleat from hilly bourn;   30
　　Hedge-crickets sing; and now with treble soft
The red-breast whistles from a garden-croft;
　　And gathering swallows twitter in the skies.

FOR FURTHER CONSIDERATION

Like Donne in "Holy Sonnet 10," Keats uses a basic sustained metaphor throughout this poem. What is it? What kind of imagery dominates in each of the three stanzas? What particular poetic device emphasizing sound appears in line 22?

Ode on Melancholy

No, no, go not to Lethe, neither twist
　　Wolfs-bane, tight-rooted, for its poisonous wine;
Nor suffer thy pale forehead to be kiss'd
　　By nightshade, ruby grape of Proserpine;
Make not your rosary of yew-berries,   5
　　Nor let the beetle, nor the death-moth be
　　　Your mournful Psyche, nor the downy owl
A partner in your sorrow's mysteries;
　　For shade to shade will come too drowsily,
　　　And drown the wakeful anguish of the soul.   10

But when the melancholy fit shall fall
　　Sudden from heaven like a weeping cloud,
That fosters the droop-headed flowers all,
　　And hides the green hill in an April shroud;
Then glut thy sorrow on a morning rose,   15
　　Or on the rainbow of the salt sand-wave,
　　　Or on the wealth of globèd peonies;
Or if thy mistress some rich anger shows,
　　Emprison her soft hand, and let her rave,
　　　And feed deep, deep upon her peerless eyes.   20

She dwells with Beauty—Beauty that must die;
   And Joy, whose hand is ever at his lips
Bidding adieu; and aching Pleasure nigh,
   Turning to poison while the bee-mouth sips:
Ay, in the very temple of Delight   25
   Veil'd Melancholy has her sovran shrine,
     Though seen of none save him whose strenuous
       tongue
   Can burst Joy's grape against his palate fine;
His soul shall taste the sadness of her might,
     And be among her cloudy trophies hung.   30

Ode on a Grecian Urn

Thou still unravished bride of quietness,
   Thou foster-child of silence and slow time,
Sylvan historian, who canst thus express
   A flowery tale more sweetly than our rhyme;
What leaf-fringed legend haunts about thy shape   5
   Of deities or mortals, or of both,
     In Tempe or the dales of Arcady?
What men or gods are these? What maidens loth?
   What mad pursuit? What struggle to escape?
     What pipes and timbrels? What wild ecstasy?   10

Heard melodies are sweet, but those unheard
   Are sweeter; therefore, ye soft pipes, play on;
Not to the sensual ear, but, more endeared,
   Pipe to the spirit ditties of no tone:

Fair youth, beneath the trees, thou canst not leave   15
   Thy song, nor ever can those trees be bare;
   Bold Lover, never never canst thou kiss,
Though winning near the goal—yet, do not grieve;
   She cannot fade, though thou hast not thy bliss,
     For ever wilt thou love, and she be fair!   20

Ah, happy, happy boughs! that cannot shed
   Your leaves, nor ever bid the Spring adieu;
And, happy melodist unwearièd,
   For ever piping songs for ever new;
More happy love! more happy, happy love!   25
   For ever warm and still to be enjoyed,
     For ever panting, and for ever young;
All breathing human passion far above,
   That leaves a heart high-sorrowful and cloyed,
     A burning forehead, and a parching tongue.   30

Who are these coming to the sacrifice?
　　To what green altar, O mysterious priest,
Lead'st thou that heifer lowing at the skies,
　　And all her silken flanks with garlands dressed?
What little town by river or sea shore,   35
　　Or mountain-built with peaceful citadel,
　　　Is emptied of its folk, this pious morn?
And, little town, thy streets for evermore
　　Will silent be; and not a soul, to tell
　　　Why thou art desolate, can e'er return.   40

O Attic shape! Fair attitude! with brede
　　Of marble men and maidens overwrought,
With forest branches and the trodden weed;
　　Thou, silent form, dost tease us out of thought
As doth eternity: Cold Pastoral!   45
　　When old age shall this generation waste,
　　　Thou shalt remain, in midst of other woe
Than ours, a friend to man, to whom thou say'st,
　　"Beauty is truth, truth beauty,"—that is all
　　　Ye know on earth, and all ye need to know.   50

Robert Browning (1812–1889)

*Browning had the good fortune to be educated at home by a thoughtful
father and a succession of tutors amid the thousands of volumes in his
family's library. His frame of reference was immense; in fact, it in-
truded into his longer poems to the point of distraction. His courtship of
and marriage to Elizabeth Barrett made him a partner in one of the most
celebrated love matches in history. He distinguished himself best with his
shorter dramatic monologues, where the reader may find a whole personality and a whole story in one brief encounter with the speaker.*

My Last Duchess

FERRARA

That's my last Duchess painted on the wall,
Looking as if she were alive. I call
That piece a wonder, now: Frà Pandolf's hands
Worked busily a day, and there she stands.
Will't please you sit and look at her? I said   5
"Frà Pandolf" by design, for never read
Strangers like you that pictured countenance,

The depth and passion of its earnest glance,
But to myself they turned (since none puts by
The curtain I have drawn for you, but I)   10
And seemed as they would ask me, if they durst,
How such a glance came there; so, not the first
Are you to turn and ask thus. Sir, 'twas not
Her husband's presence only, called that spot
Of joy into the Duchess' cheek: perhaps   15
Frà Pandolf chanced to say "Her mantle laps
Over my Lady's wrist too much," or "Paint
Must never hope to reproduce the faint
Half-flush that dies along her throat;" such stuff
Was courtesy, she thought, and cause enough   20
For calling up that spot of joy. She had
A heart—how shall I say?—too soon made glad,
Too easily impressed; she liked whate'er
She looked on, and her looks went everywhere.
Sir, 'twas all one! My favour at her breast,   25
The dropping of the daylight in the West,
The bough of cherries some officious fool
Broke in the orchard for her, the white mule
She rode with round the terrace—all and each
Would draw from her alike the approving speech,   30
Or blush, at least. She thanked men,—good! but thanked
Somehow—I know not how—as if she ranked
My gift of a nine-hundred-years-old name
With anybody's gift. Who'd stoop to blame
This sort of trifling? Even had you skill   35
In speech—(which I have not)—to make your will
Quite clear to such an one, and say, "Just this
Or that in you disgusts me; here you miss,
Or there exceed the mark"—and if she let
Herself be lessoned so, nor plainly set   40
Her wits to yours, forsooth, and made excuse,
—E'en then would be some stooping, and I choose
Never to stoop. Oh, sir, she smiled, no doubt,
Whene'er I passed her; but who passed without
Much the same smile? This grew; I gave commands;   45
Then all smiles stopped together. There she stands
As if alive. Will't please you rise? We'll meet
The company below, then. I repeat,
The Count your Master's known munificence
Is ample warrant that no just pretence   50
Of mine for dowry will be disallowed;
Though his fair daughter's self, as I avowed
At starting, is my object. Nay, we'll go

Together down, sir. Notice Neptune, though,
Taming a sea-horse, thought a rarity,   55
Which Claus of Innsbruck cast in bronze for me.

FOR FURTHER CONSIDERATION

What is it that enrages the speaker in this poem? Why is the use of
dramatic monologue essential in this poem?

Alfred Lord Tennyson (1809–1892)

*Trained at home by a father who worshipped the classics, Tennyson
produced an epic poem of 6,000 lines at the age of eight. By fifteen he had
won prizes for his plays and poetry, and by twenty-one he was committed
to a poet's life. His poetry committed him to relative poverty as well,
forcing him to defer marriage until he became Poet Laureate of England
at forty-one. He was then recognized as the dominant poet of his time in
England, often read poetry to Queen Victoria, and late in life became a
peer of the realm.*

    *A handsome but basically unhappy man, Tennyson produced poetry
sometimes dense and pedantic and sometimes (like the poems which
follow) open, insightful, and dramatic.*

Ulysses

It little profits that an idle king,
By this still hearth, among these barren crags,
Matched with an aged wife, I mete and dole
Unequal laws unto a savage race,
That hoard, and sleep, and feed, and know not me.   5
I cannot rest from travel; I will drink
Life to the lees. All times I have enjoyed
Greatly, have suffered greatly, both with those
That loved me, and alone; on shore, and when
Through scudding drifts the rainy Hyades   10
Vexed the dim sea. I am become a name;
For always roaming with a hungry heart
Much have I seen and known—cities of men
And manners, climates, councils, governments,
Myself not least, but honoured of them all—   15
And drunk delight of battle with my peers,
Far on the ringing plains of windy Troy.
I am a part of all that I have met;
Yet all experience is an arch wherethrough

Gleams that untraveled world whose margin fades 20
Forever and forever when I move.
How dull it is to pause, to make an end,
To rust unburnished, not to shine in use!
As though to breathe were life! Life piled on life
Were all too little, and of one to me 25
Little remains; but every hour is saved
From that eternal silence, something more,
A bringer of new things; and vile it were
For some three suns to store and hoard myself,
And this grey spirit yearning in desire 30
To follow knowledge like a sinking star,
Beyond the utmost bound of human thought.
     This is my son, mine own Telemachus,
To whom I leave the scepter and the isle—
Well-loved of me, discerning to fulfill 35
This labour, by slow prudence to make mild
A rugged people, and through soft degrees
Subdue them to the useful and the good.
Most blameless is he, centered in the sphere
Of common duties, decent not to fail 40
In offices of tenderness, and pay
Meet adoration to my household gods,
When I am gone. He works his work, I mine.
     There lies the port; the vessel puffs her sail;
There gloom the dark, broad seas. My mariners, 45
Souls that have toiled, and wrought, and thought with me—
That ever with a frolic welcome took
The thunder and the sunshine, and opposed
Free hearts, free foreheads—you and I are old;
Old age hath yet his honour and his toil. 50
Death closes all; but something ere the end,
Some work of noble note, may yet be done,
Not unbecoming men that strove with gods.
The lights begin to twinkle from the rocks;
The long day wanes; the slow moon climbs; the deep 55
Moans round with many voices. Come, my friends,
'Tis not too late to seek a newer world.
Push off, and sitting well in order smite
The sounding furrows; for my purpose holds
To sail beyond the sunset, and the baths 60
Of all the western stars, until I die.
It may be that the gulfs will wash us down;
It may be we shall touch the Happy Isles,
And see the great Achilles, whom we knew.
Though much is taken, much abides; and though 65
We are not now that strength which in old days

Moved earth and heaven, that which we are, we are—
One equal temper of heroic hearts,
Made weak by time and fate, but strong in will
To strive, to seek, to find, and not to yield.   70

FOR FURTHER CONSIDERATION

After fighting at the siege of Troy, Ulysses spent ten wildly adventurous
years attempting to reach home. As he speaks in this poem, what feelings
does he express about the virtues of home versus the lure of adventure?
What sound device appears in line 46? What part does time play in this
poem, and where do references to time appear?

The Eagle

He clasps the crag with crooked hands;
Close to the sun in lonely lands,
Ring'd with the azure world, he stands.

The wrinkled sea beneath him crawls;
He watches from his mountain walls,   5
And like a thunderbolt he falls.

William Butler Yeats (1865–1939)

*A lifelong poet, Yeats was also a notable playwright, scholar, mystic, and
politician. His poetry is remarkable for the way it combines economy,
lyricism, and imagery. The poems which follow—interwoven as they are
with classical allusions and striking images—demonstrate his devotion to
mythology and history.*

The Second Coming

Turning and turning in the widening gyre
The falcon cannot hear the falconer;
Things fall apart; the centre cannot hold;
Mere anarchy is loosed upon the world,
The blood-dimmed tide is loosed, and everywhere   5
The ceremony of innocence is drowned;
The best lack all conviction, while the worst
Are full of passionate intensity.

Surely some revelation is at hand;

Surely the Second Coming is at hand.   10
The Second Coming! Hardly are those words out
When a vast image out of *Spiritus Mundi*
Troubles my sight: somewhere in sands of the desert
A shape with lion body and the head of a man,
A gaze blank and pitiless as the sun,   15
Is moving its slow thighs, while all about it
Reel shadows of the indignant desert birds.

Sailing to Byzantium

I

That is no country for old men. The young
In one another's arms, birds in the trees
—Those dying generations—at their song,
The salmon-falls, the mackerel-crowded seas,
Fish, flesh, or fowl, commend all summer long   5
Whatever is begotten, born, and dies.
Caught in that sensual music all neglect
Monuments of unageing intellect.

II

An aged man is but a paltry thing,
A tattered coat upon a stick, unless   10
Soul clap its hands and sing, and louder sing
For every tatter in its mortal dress,
Nor is there singing school but studying
Monuments of its own magnificence;
And therefore I have sailed the seas and come   15
To the holy city of Byzantium.

III

O sages standing in God's holy fire
As in the gold mosaic of a wall,
Come from the holy fire, perne in a gyre,
And be the singing-masters of my soul.   20
Consume my heart away; sick with desire
And fastened to a dying animal
It knows not what its is; and gather me
Into the artifice of eternity.

IV

Once out of nature I shall never take   25
My bodily form from any natural thing,
But such a form as Grecian goldsmiths make
Of hammered gold and gold enamelling

To keep a drowsy Emperor awake;
Or set upon a golden bough to sing   30
To lords and ladies of Byzantium
Of what is past, or passing, or to come.

Leda and the Swan

A sudden blow: the great wings beating still
Above the staggering girl, her thighs caressed
By the dark webs, her nape caught in his bill,
He holds her helpless breast upon his breast.

How can those terrified vague fingers push   5
The feathered glory from her loosening thighs?
And how can body, laid in that white rush,
But feel the strange heart beating where it lies?

A shudder in the loins engenders there
The broken wall, the burning roof and tower   10
And Agamemnon dead.
                           Being so caught up,
So mastered by the brute blood of the air,
Did she put on his knowledge with his power
Before the indifferent beak could let her drop?

Walt Whitman (1819–1892)

*After working as a teacher and an undistinguished newsman until age
thirty-six, Whitman revolutionized American poetry in 1855 with* Leaves
of Grass, *a series of wild, overflowing poems that often oddly approximate
prose. When his book called down showers of critical abuse, Whitman
responded resolutely with anonymous reviews praising his own genius.
Successive editions eventually won him a large following and bore out his
self-estimates. He distinguished himself by helping the wounded during the
Civil War and became the best known of America's nineteenth-century free
thinkers.*

*Whitman was one of a kind, a restless, unrestrained but basically
lonely man who did much to free poetry from its nineteenth-century
propriety. He offers what his spiritual father, Emerson, called
"incomparable things said incomparably well"—individualism, freedom,
pantheism, and a wash of words that lifts readers and carries them along.
His poems seize the joy and sorrow that sensing, feeling, and thinking bring
to life, and he expresses these things "with original energy."*

Song of Myself

I celebrate myself, and sing myself,
And what I assume you shall assume,
For every atom belonging to me as good belongs to you.

I loafe and invite my soul,
I lean and loafe at my ease observing a spear of summer
    grass.   5

My tongue, every atom of my blood, form'd from this
    soil, this air,
Born here of parents born here from parents the same,
    and their parents the same,
I, now thirty-seven years old in perfect health begin,
Hoping to cease not till death.

Creeds and schools in abeyance,   10
Retiring back a while sufficed at what they are, but never
    forgotten,
I harbor for good or bad, I permit to speak at every
    hazard,
Nature without check with original energy.

A child said *What is the grass*? fetching it to me with full
    hands,
How could I answer the child? I do not know what it is
    any more than he.   15

I guess it must be the flag of my disposition, out of
    hopeful green stuff woven.

Or I guess it is the handkerchief of the Lord,
A scented gift and remembrancer designedly dropt,
Bearing the owner's name someway in the corners, that
    we may see and remark, and say *Whose*?

Or I guess the grass is itself a child, the produced babe of
    the vegetation.   20

Or I guess it is a uniform hieroglyphic,
And it means, Sprouting alike in broad zones and narrow
    zones,
Growing among black folks as among white,
Kanuck, Tuckahoe, Congressman, Cuff, I give them the
    same, I receive them the same.

And now it seems to me the beautiful uncut hair of
    graves.   25

Tenderly will I use you curling grass,

It may be you transpire from the breasts of young men,
It may be if I had known them I would have loved them,
It may be you are from old people, or from offspring
        taken soon out of their mothers' laps.
And here you are the mothers' laps.   30

This grass is very dark to be from the white heads of old
        mothers,
Darker than the colorless beards of old men,
Dark to come from under the faint red roofs of mouths.

O I perceive after all so many uttering tongues,
And I perceive they do not come from the roofs of
        mouths for nothing.   35

I wish I could translate the hints about the dead young
        men and women,
And the hints about old men and mothers, and the
        offspring taken soon out of their laps.

What do you think has become of the young and old
        men?
And what do you think has become of the women and
        children?
They are alive and well somewhere,   40
The smallest sprout shows there is really no death,
And if ever there was it led forward life, and does not
        wait at the end to arrest it,
And ceas'd the moment life appear'd.

All goes onward and outward, nothing collapses,
And to die is different from what any one supposed, and
        luckier.   45

FOR FURTHER CONSIDERATION

In "Song of Myself," what reasons does Whitman offer to support his
remark that "to die is different from what any one supposed, and
luckier"? How does he prepare the reader to accept these reasons? How
is line 3 of the poem linked to his attitude toward death? How many
different metaphors deal with grass in this poem? What is the cumulative
impact of these various grass images?

Song of the Open Road

I think heroic deeds were all conceiv'd in the open air,
        and all free poems also,

I think I could stop here myself and do miracles,

I think whatever I shall meet on the road I shall like, and
     whoever beholds me shall like me,
I think whoever I see must be happy.

From this hour I ordain myself loos'd of limits and
     imaginary lines,   5
Going where I list, my own master total and absolute,
Listening to others, considering well what they say,
Pausing, searching, receiving, contemplating,
Gently, but with undeniable will, divesting myself of the
     holds that would hold me.

I inhale great draughts of space,   10
The east and the west are mine, and the north and the
     south are mine.

I am larger, better than I thought,
I did not know I held so much goodness.

A Noiseless Patient Spider

A noiseless patient spider,
I mark'd where on a little promontory it stood isolated,
Mark'd how to explore the vacant vast surrounding,
It launch'd forth filament, filament, filament, out of itself,
Ever unreeling them, ever tirelessly speeding them.   5

And you O my soul where you stand,
Surrounded, detached, in measureless oceans of space,
Ceaselessly musing, venturing, throwing, seeking the
     spheres to connect them,
Till the bridge you will need be form'd, till the ductile
     anchor hold,
Till the gossamer thread you fling catch somewhere, O my
     soul.   10

Out of the Cradle Endlessly Rocking

Out of the cradle endlessly rocking,
Out of the mockingbird's throat, the musical shuttle,
Out of the Ninth-month midnight,
Over the sterile sands and the fields beyond, where the
     child leaving his bed wandered alone, bareheaded,
     barefoot,
Down from the showered halo,   5
Up from the mystic play of shadows twining and twisting
     as if they were alive,

Out from the patches of briers and blackberries,
From the memories of the bird that chanted to me,
From your memories sad brother, from the fitful risings
    and fallings I heard,
From under that yellow half-moon late-risen and swollen
    as if with tears,   10
From those beginning notes of yearning and love there in
    the mist,
From the thousand responses of my heart never to cease,
From the myriad thence-aroused words,
From the word stronger and more delicious than any,
From such as now they start the scene revisiting,   15
As a flock, twittering, rising or overhead passing,
Borne hither, ere all eludes me, hurriedly,

A man, yet by these tears a little boy again,
Throwing myself on the sand, confronting the waves,
I, chanter of pains and joys, uniter of here and hereafter,   20
Taking all hints to use them, but swiftly leaping beyond
    them,
A reminiscence sing.

Emily Dickinson (1830–1886)

After a happy, outgoing childhood, followed by an obscure, thwarted romance, Emily Dickinson became a recluse. She committed her loneliness, her sensitivity, and her fantasies to paper in some 1,750 poems, only seven of which were ever published in her lifetime. Themes of time, death, nature, and love appear in verse marked by its economy and originality of metaphor.

Because I Could Not Stop for Death

Because I could not stop for Death,
He kindly stopped for me;
The carriage held but just ourselves
And Immortality.
We slowly drove, he knew no haste,   5

And I had put away
My labor, and my leisure too,
For his civility.

We passed the school where children played

At wrestling in a ring;   10
We passed the fields of gazing grain,
We passed the setting sun.

We paused before a house that seemed
A swelling of the ground;
The roof was scarcely visible,   15
The cornice but a mound.

Since then 'tis centuries; but each
Feels shorter than the day
I first surmised the horses' heads
Were toward eternity.   20

My Life Closed Twice

My life closed twice before its close;
   It yet remains to see
If Immortality unveil
   A third event to me,

So huge, so hopeless to conceive,   5
   As these that twice befell.
Parting is all we know of heaven,
   And all we need of hell.

I Taste a Liquor Never Brewed

I taste a liquor never brewed,
From tankards scooped in pearl;
Not all the vats upon the Rhine
Yield such an alcohol!

Inebriate of air am I,   5
And debauchee of dew,
Reeling, through endless summer days,
From inns of molten blue.

When landlords turn the drunken bee
Out of the foxglove's door,   10
When butterflies renounce their drams,
I shall but drink the more!

Till seraphs swing their snowy hats,
And saints to windows run,
To see the little tippler   15
Leaning against the sun!

I Heard a Fly Buzz When I Died

I heard a fly buzz when I died;
  The stillness round my form
Was like the stillness in the air
  Between the heaves of storm.

The eyes beside had wrung them dry,   5
  And breaths were gathering sure
For that last onset, when the king
  Be witnessed in his power.

I willed my keepsakes, signed away
  What portion of me I   10
Could make assignable,—and then
  There interposed a fly,

With blue, uncertain, stumbling buzz,
  Between the light and me;
And then the windows failed, and then   15
  I could not see to see.

Edwin Arlington Robinson (1869–1935)

A very popular poet in the early twentieth century, Robinson won three Pulitzer Prizes for his dark and sometimes whimsical investigations of the human psyche. His work is filled with irony and suggests, as he put it, that "The world is a hell of a place, but the universe is a fine thing."

Miniver Cheevy

Miniver Cheevy, child of scorn,
  Grew lean while he assailed the seasons;
He wept that he was ever born,
  And he had reasons.

Miniver loved the days of old   5
  When swords were bright and steeds were prancing;
The vision of a warrior bold
  Would set him dancing.

Miniver sighed for what was not,
  And dreamed, and rested from his labors;   10
He dreamed of Thebes and Camelot,
  And Priam's neighbors.

Miniver mourned the ripe renown

That made so many a name so fragrant;
He mourned Romance, now on the town,   15
   And Art, a vagrant.

Miniver loved the Medici,
   Albeit he had never seen one;
He would have sinned incessantly
   Could he have been one.   20

Miniver cursed the commonplace
   And eyed a khaki suit with loathing;
He missed the mediæval grace
   Of iron clothing.

Miniver scorned the gold he sought,   25
   But sore annoyed was he without it;
Miniver thought, and thought, and thought,
   And thought about it.

Miniver Cheevy, born too late,
   Scratched his head and kept on thinking;   30
Miniver coughed, and called it fate,
   And kept on drinking.

FOR FURTHER CONSIDERATION

What impact does the shortened meter of the last line of each stanza have
on the last word of each stanza? How would you describe the tone
Robinson achieves in this poem? Is the tone compatible with the
statement of the poem? Which words and poetic devices contribute most
substantially to this tone?

Richard Cory

Whenever Richard Cory went down town,
We people on the pavement looked at him:
He was a gentleman from sole to crown,
Clean favored, and imperially slim.

And he was always quietly arrayed,   5
And he was always human when he talked;
But still he fluttered pulses when he said,
"Good-morning," and he glittered when he walked.

And he was rich—yes, richer than a king—
And admirably schooled in every grace: 10
In fine, we thought that he was everything
To make us wish that we were in his place.

So on we worked, and waited for the light,
And went without the meat, and cursed the bread;
And Richard Cory, one calm summer night,
Went home and put a bullet through his head.   15

T. S. Eliot (1888–1965)

*A Nobel Prize winner and America's most famous literary expatriate, Eliot
ranks among the most intellectual of twentieth-century poets. After prep
school in New England and college at Harvard, he tried teaching and bank
clerking before becoming a successful London publisher. A very proper
man himself, Eliot eloquently pictured the boredom, timidity, and ugliness
of modern civilization as signs of a life that has lost its purpose. His
allusions range from nursery rhymes to classical references that can tax
the best of scholars. His images, his ironic air of disillusionment, and his
interest in human conscience suggest the soulless character of modern
urban life.*

The Waste Land

I. The Burial of the Dead

April is the cruellest month, breeding
Lilacs out of the dead land, mixing
Memory and desire, stirring
Dull roots with spring rain.
Winter kept us warm, covering   5
Earth in forgetful snow, feeding
A little life with dried tubers.
Summer surprised us, coming over the Starnbergersee
With a shower of rain; we stopped in the colonnade,
And went on in sunlight, into the Hofgarten,   10
And drank coffee, and talked for an hour.
Bin gar keine Russin, stamm' aus Litauen, echt deutsch.
And when we were children, staying at the arch-duke's,
My cousin's, he took me out on a sled,
And I was frightened. He said, Marie,   15
Marie, hold on tight. And down we went.
In the mountains, there you feel free.
I read, much of the night, and go south in the winter.

What are the roots that clutch, what branches grow
Out of this stony rubbish? Son of man,   20

You cannot say, or guess, for you know only
A heap of broken images, where the sun beats,
And the dead tree gives no shelter, the cricket no relief,
And the dry stone no sound of water. Only
There is shadow under this red rock,   25
(Come in under the shadow of this red rock),
And I will show you something different from either
Your shadow at morning striding behind you
Or your shadow at evening rising to meet you;
I will show you fear in a handful of dust.   30
      Frisch weht der Wind
      Der Heimat zu
      Mein Irisch Kind,
      Wo weilest du?
'You gave me hyacinths first a year ago;   35
'They called me the hyacinth girl.'
—Yet when we came back, late, from the hyacinth garden,
Your arms full, and your hair wet, I could not
Speak, and my eyes failed, I was neither
Living nor dead, and I knew nothing,   40
Looking into the heart of light, the silence.
Oed' und leer das Meer.

Madame Sosostris, famous clairvoyante,
Had a bad cold, nevertheless
Is known to be the wisest woman in Europe,   45
With a wicked pack of cards. Here, said she,
Is your card, the drowned Phoenician Sailor,
(Those are pearls that were his eyes. Look!)
Here is Belladonna, the Lady of the Rocks,
The lady of situations.   50
Here is the man with three staves, and here the Wheel,
And here is the one-eyed merchant, and this card,
Which is blank, is something he carries on his back,
Which I am forbidden to see. I do not find
The Hanged Man. Fear death by water.   55
I see crowds of people, walking round in a ring.
Thank you. If you see dear Mrs. Equitone,
Tell her I bring the horoscope myself:
One must be so careful these days.

Unreal City,   60
Under the brown fog of a winter dawn,
A crowd flowed over London Bridge, so many,
I had not thought death had undone so many.
Sighs, short and infrequent, were exhaled,
And each man fixed his eyes before his feet.   65
Flowed up the hill and down King William Street,

To where Saint Mary Woolnoth kept the hours
With a dead sound on the final stroke of nine.
There I saw one I knew, and stopped him, crying: 'Stetson!
'You who were with me in the ships at Mylae!   70
'That corpse you planted last year in your garden,
'Has it begun to sprout? Will it bloom this year?
'Or has the sudden frost disturbed its bed?
'O keep the Dog far hence, that's friend to men,
'Or with his nails he'll dig it up again!   75
'You! hypocrite lecteur!—mon semblable,—mon frère!'

II. A Game of Chess

The Chair sat she in, like a burnished throne,
Glowed on the marble, where the glass
Held up by standards wrought with fruited vines
From which a golden Cupidon peeped out   80
(Another hid his eyes behind his wing)
Doubled the flames of sevenbranched candelabra
Reflecting light upon the table as
The glitter of her jewels rose to meet it,
From satin cases poured in rich profusion.   85
In vials of ivory and coloured glass
Unstoppered, lurked her strange synthetic perfumes,
Unguent, powdered, or liquid—troubled, confused
And drowned the sense in odours; stirred by the air
That freshened from the window, these ascended   90
In fattening the prolonged candle-flames,
Flung their smoke into the laquearia,
Stirring the pattern on the coffered ceiling.
Huge sea-wood fed with copper
Burned green and orange, framed by the coloured stone,   95
In which sad light a carvèd dolphin swam.
Above the antique mantel was displayed
As though a window gave upon the sylvan scene
The change of Philomel, by the barbarous king
So rudely forced; yet there the nightingale   100
Filled all the desert with inviolable voice
And still she cried, and still the world pursues,
'Jug Jug' to dirty ears.
And other withered stumps of time
Were told upon the walls; staring forms   105
Leaned out, leaning, hushing the room enclosed.
Footsteps shuffled on the stair.
Under the firelight, under the brush, her hair

Spread out in fiery points
Glowed into words, then would be savagely still.   110

'My nerves are bad to-night. Yes, bad. Stay with me.
'Speak to me. Why do you never speak. Speak.
    'What are you thinking of? What thinking? What?
'I never know what you are thinking. Think.'

I think we are in rats' alley   115
Where the dead men lost their bones.

'What is that noise?'
                    The wind under the door.
'What is that noise now? What is the wind doing?
                    Nothing again nothing.   120
                                                        'Do
'You know nothing? Do you see nothing? Do you remember
'Nothing?'
        I remember
Those are pearls that were his eyes.   125
'Are you alive, or not? Is there nothing in your head?'
                                                        But

O O O O that Shakespeherian Rag—
It's so elegant
So intelligent   130
'What shall I do now? What shall I do?'
'I shall rush out as I am, and walk the street
'With my hair down, so. What shall we do tomorrow?
'What shall we ever do?'
                    The hot water at ten.   135
And if it rains, a closed car at four.
And we shall play a game of chess,
Pressing lidless eyes and waiting for a knock upon the door.

When Lil's husband got demobbed, I said—
I didn't mince my words, I said to her myself,   140
HURRY UP PLEASE ITS TIME
Now Albert's coming back, make yourself a bit smart.
He'll want to know what you have done with that money he gave
    you
To get yourself some teeth. He did, I was there.
You have them all out, Lil, and get a nice set,   145
He said, I swear, I can't bear to look at you.
And no more can't I, I said, and think of poor Albert,
He's been in the army four years, he wants a good time,
And if you don't give it him, there's others will, I said.
Oh is there, she said. Something o' that, I said.   150
Then I'll know who to thank, she said, and give me a straight
    look.

HURRY UP PLEASE ITS TIME
If you don't like it you can get on with it, I said.
Others can pick and choose if you can't.
But if Albert makes off, it won't be for lack of telling.   155
You ought to be ashamed, I said, to look so antique.
(And her only thirty-one.)
I can't help it, she said, pulling a long face,
It's them pills I took, to bring it off, she said.
(She's had five already, and nearly died of young George.)   160
The chemist said it would be all right, but I've never been
      the same.

You *are* a proper fool, I said.
Well, if Albert won't leave you alone, there it is, I said,
What you get married for if you don't want children?
HURRY UP PLEASE ITS TIME   165
Well, that Sunday Albert was home, they had a hot gammon,
And they asked me in to dinner, to get the beauty of it hot—
HURRY UP PLEASE ITS TIME
HURRY UP PLEASE ITS TIME
Goonight Bill. Goonight Lou. Goonight May. Goonight.   170
Ta ta. Goonight. Goonight.
Good night, ladies, good night, sweet ladies, good night,
      good night.

III. The Fire Sermon

The river's tent is broken; the last fingers of leaf
Clutch and sink into the wet bank. The wind
Crosses the brown land, unheard. The nymphs are departed.   175
Sweet Thames, run softly, till I end my song.
The river bears no empty bottles, sandwich papers,
Silk handkerchiefs, cardboard boxes, cigarette ends
Or other testimony of summer nights. The nymphs are
      departed.
And their friends, the loitering heirs of City directors;   180
Departed, have left no addresses.
By the waters of Leman I sat down and wept . . .
Sweet Thames, run softly till I end my song,
Sweet Thames, run softly, for I speak not loud or long.
But at my back in a cold blast I hear   185
The rattle of the bones, and chuckle spread from ear to ear.
A rat crept softly through the vegetation
Dragging its slimy belly on the bank
While I was fishing in the dull canal

On a winter evening round behind the gashouse 190
Musing upon the king my brother's wreck
And on the king my father's death before him.
White bodies naked on the low damp ground
And bones cast in a little low dry garret,
Rattled by the rat's foot only, year to year. 195
But at my back from time to time I hear
The sound of horns and motors, which shall bring
Sweeney to Mrs. Porter in the spring.
O the moon shone bright on Mrs. Porter
And on her daughter 200
They wash their feet in soda water
Et o ces voix d'enfants, chantant dans la coupole!

Twit twit twit
Jug jug jug jug jug jug
So rudely forc'd. 205
Tereu

Unreal City
Under the brown fog of a winter noon
Mr. Eugenides, the Smyrna merchant
Unshaven, with a pocket full of currants 210
C.i.f. London: documents at sight,
Asked me in demotic French
To luncheon at the Cannon Street Hotel
Followed by a weekend at the Metropole.

At the violet hour, when the eyes and back 215
Turn upward from the desk, when the human engine waits
Like a taxi throbbing waiting,
I Tiresias, though blind, throbbing between two lives,
Old man with wrinkled female breasts, can see
At the violet hour, the evening hour that strives 220
Homeward, and brings the sailor home from sea,
The typist home at teatime, clears her breakfast, lights
Her stove, and lays out food in tins.
Out of the window perilously spread
Her drying combinations touched by the sun's last rays, 225
On the divan are piled (at night her bed)
Stockings, slippers, camisoles, and stays.
I Tiresias, old man with wrinkled dugs
Perceived the scene, and foretold the rest—
I too awaited the expected guest. 230
He, the young man carbuncular, arrives,
A small house agent's clerk, with one bold stare,
One of the low on whom assurance sits

As a silk hat on a Bradford millionaire.
The time is now propitious, as he guesses,   235
The meal is ended, she is bored and tired,
Endeavours to engage her in caresses
Which still are unreproved, if undesired.
Flushed and decided, he assaults at once;
Exploring hands encounter no defence;   240
His vanity requires no response,
And makes a welcome of indifference.
(And I Tiresias have foresuffered all
Enacted on this same divan or bed;
I who have sat by Thebes below the wall   245
And walked among the lowest of the dead.)
Bestows one final patronising kiss,
And gropes his way, finding the stairs unlit . . .

She turns and looks a moment in the glass,
Hardly aware of her departed lover;   250
Her brain allows one half-formed thought to pass:
'Well now that's done: and I'm glad it's over.'
When lovely woman stoops to folly and
Paces about her room again, alone,
She smoothes her hair with automatic hand,   255
And puts a record on the gramophone.

'This music crept by me upon the waters'
And along the Strand, up Queen Victoria Street.
O City city, I can sometimes hear
Beside a public bar in Lower Thames Street,   260
The pleasant whining of a mandoline
And a clatter and a chatter from within
Where fishmen lounge at noon: where the walls
Of Magnus Martyr hold
Inexplicable splendour of Ionian white and gold.   265

      The river sweats
      Oil and tar
      The barges drift
      With the turning tide
      Red sails   270
      Wide
      To leeward, swing on the heavy spar.
      The barges wash
      Drifting logs
      Down Greenwich reach   275
      Past the Isle of Dogs.
          Weialala leia
          Wallala leialala

Elizabeth and Leicester
Beating oars   280
The stern was formed
A gilded shell
Red and gold
The brisk swell
Rippled both shores   285
Southwest wind
Carried down stream

The peal of bells
White towers
    Weialala leia   290
    Wallala leialala

'Trams and dusty trees.
Highbury bore me. Richmond and Kew
Undid me. By Richmond I raised my knees
Supine on the floor of a narrow canoe.'   295
'My feet are at Moorgate, and my heart
Under my feet. After the event
He wept. He promised "a new start."
I made no comment. What should I resent?'

'On Margate Sands.   300
I can connect
Nothing with nothing.
The broken fingernails of dirty hands.
My people humble people who expect
Nothing.'   305
    la la

To Carthage then I came

Burning burning burning burning
O Lord Thou pluckest me out
O Lord Thou pluckest   310

burning

IV. *Death by Water*

Phlebas the Phoenician, a fortnight dead,
Forgot the cry of gulls, and the deep sea swell
And the profit and loss.
    A current under sea   315
Picked his bones in whispers. As he rose and fell
He passed the stages of his age and youth

Entering the whirlpool.
        Gentile or Jew
O you who turn the wheel and look to windward,   320
Consider Phlebas, who was once handsome and tall as you.

V. *What the Thunder Said*

After the torchlight red on sweaty faces
After the frosty silence in the gardens
After the agony in stony places
The shouting and the crying   325
Prison and palace and reverberation
Of thunder of spring over distant mountains
He who was living is now dead
We who were living are now dying
With a little patience   330

Here is no water but only rock
Rock and no water and the sandy road
The road winding above among the mountains
which are mountains of rock without water
If there were water we should stop and drink   335
Amongst the rock one cannot stop or think
Sweat is dry and feet are in the sand
If there were only water amongst the rock
Dead mountain mouth of carious teeth that cannot spit
Here one can neither stand nor lie nor sit   340
There is not even silence in the mountains
But dry sterile thunder without rain
There is not even solitude in the mountains
But red sullen faces sneer and snarl
From doors of mudcracked houses   345
                    If there were water
   And no rock
   If there were rock
   And also water
   And water   350
   A spring
   A pool among the rock
   If there were the sound of water only
   Not the cicada
   And dry grass singing   355
   But sound of water over a rock
   Where the hermit-thrush sings in the pine trees
   Drip drop drip drop drop drop drop
   But there is no water

Who is the third who walks always beside you?   360
When I count, there are only you and I together
But when I look ahead up the white road
There is always another one walking beside you
Gliding wrapt in a brown mantle, hooded
I do not know whether a man or a woman   365
—But who is that on the other side of you?

What is that sound high in the air
Murmur of maternal lamentation
Who are those hooded hordes swarming
Over endless plains, stumbling in cracked earth   370
Ringed by the flat horizon only
What is the city over the mountains
Cracks and reforms and bursts in the violet air
Falling towers
Jerusalem Athens Alexandria   375
Vienna London
Unreal

A woman drew her long black hair out tight
And fiddled whisper music on those strings
And bats with baby faces in the violet light   380
Whistled, and beat their wings
And crawled head downward down a blackened wall
And upside down in air were towers
Tolling reminiscent bells, that kept the hours
And voices singing out of empty cisterns and exhausted wells   385

In this decayed hole among the mountains
In the faint moonlight, the grass is singing
Over the tumbled graves, about the chapel
There is the empty chapel, only the wind's home.
It has no windows, and the door swings,   390
Dry bones can harm no one.
Only a cock stood on the rooftree
Co co rico co co rico
In a flash of lightning. Then a damp gust
Bringing rain   395

Ganga was sunken, and the limp leaves
Waited for rain, while the black clouds
Gathered far distant, over Himavant.
The jungle crouched, humped in silence.
Then spoke the thunder   400
DA
Datta: what have we given?
My friend, blood shaking my heart
The awful daring of a moment's surrender

Which an age of prudence can never retract   405
By this, and this only, we have existed
Which is not to be found in our obituaries
Or in memories draped by the beneficent spider
Or under seals broken by the lean solicitor
In our empty rooms   410
DA
Dayadhvam: I have heard the key
Turn in the door once and turn once only
We think of the key, each in his prison   415
Thinking of the key, each confirms a prison
Only at nightfall, aethereal rumours
Revive for a moment a broken Coriolanus
DA
Damyata: The boat responded
Gaily, to the hand expert with sail and oar   420
The sea was calm, your heart would have responded
Gaily, when invited, beating obedient
To controlling hands

              I sat upon the shore
Fishing, with the arid plain behind me   425
Shall I at least set my lands in order?
London Bridge is falling down falling down falling down
Poi s'ascose nel foco che gli affina
Quando fiam uti chelidon—O swallow swallow
Le Prince d'Aquitaine à la tour abolie   430
These fragments I have shored against my ruins
Why then Ile fit you. Hieronymo's mad againe.
Datta. Dayadhvam. Damyata.
             Shantih   shantih   shantih

FOR FURTHER CONSIDERATION

The Waste Land ranks among the most challenging poems ever written, for to grasp its complex of allusions and metaphor, the reader must give the poem intense scrutiny and substantial scholarly research. But the casual reader need not despair, for at any level of approach the poem is still highly rewarding, its statement and theme proving readily accessible.

    What does the title of the poem suggest about modern civilization? What passages in the poem support your explanation of the title? Where in the poem does the poet express a consciousness of the discontinuity and fragmentation that characterize modern life? What classical and historical allusions do you find in the poem?

The Love Song of J. Alfred Prufrock

S'io credesse che mia risposta fosse
A persona che mai tornasse al mondo,
Questa fiamma staria senza piu scosse.
Ma perciocche giammai di questo fondo
Non torno vivo alcun, s'i'odo il vero,
Senza tema d'infamia ti rispondo.

Let us go then, you and I,
When the evening is spread out against the sky
Like a patient etherised upon a table;
Let us go, through certain half-deserted streets,
The muttering retreats   5
Of restless nights in one-night cheap hotels
And sawdust restaurants with oyster-shells:
Streets that follow like a tedious argument
Of insidious intent
To lead you to an overwhelming question. . . .   10
Oh, do not ask, "What is it?"
Let us go and make our visit.

In the room the women come and go
Talking of Michelangelo.

The yellow fog that rubs its back upon the window-panes,   15
The yellow smoke that rubs its muzzle on the window-panes,
Licked its tongue into the corners of the evening,
Lingered upon the pools that stand in drains,
Let fall upon its back the soot that falls from chimneys,
Slipped by the terrace, made a sudden leap,   20
And seeing that it was a soft October night,
Curled once about the house, and fell asleep.

And indeed there will be time
For the yellow smoke that slides along the street,
Rubbing its back upon the window-panes;   25
There will be time, there will be time
To prepare a face to meet the faces that you meet;
There will be time to murder and create,
And time for all the works and days of hands
That lift and drop a question on your plate;   30
Time for you and time for me,
And time yet for a hundred indecisions,
And for a hundred visions and revisions,
Before the taking of a toast and tea.

In the room the women come and go   35
Talking of Michelangelo.

And indeed there will be time
To wonder, "Do I dare?" and, "Do I dare?"
Time to turn back and descend the stair,
With a bald spot in the middle of my hair—   40
(They will say: "How his hair is growing thin!")
My morning coat, my collar mounting firmly to the chin,
My necktie rich and modest, but asserted by a simple pin—
(They will say: "But how his arms and legs are thin!")
Do I dare   45
Disturb the universe?
In a minute there is time
For decisions and revisions which a minute will reverse.

For I have known them all already, known them all:
Have known the evenings, mornings, afternoons,   50
I have measured out of my life with coffee spoons;
I know the voices dying with a dying fall
Beneath the music from a farther room.
   So how should I presume?

And I have known the eyes already, known them all—   55
The eyes that fix you in a formulated phrase,
And when I am formulated, sprawling on a pin,
When I am pinned and wriggling on the wall,
Then how should I begin
To spit out all the butt-ends of my days and ways?   60
   And how should I presume?

And I have known the arms already, known them all—
Arms that are braceleted and white and bare
(But in the lamplight, downed with light brown hair!)
Is it perfume from a dress   65
That makes me so digress?
Arms that lie along a table, or wrap about a shawl,
   And should I then presume?
   And how should I begin?
                    ·   ·   ·   ·

Shall I say, I have gone at dusk through narrow streets   70
And watched the smoke that rises from the pipes
Of lonely men in shirt-sleeves, leaning out of windows? . . .

I should have been a pair of ragged claws
Scuttling across the floors of silent seas.
                    ·   ·   ·   ·

And the afternoon, the evening, sleeps so peacefully!   75
Smoothed by long fingers,
Asleep . . . tired . . . or it malingers,
Stretched on the floor, here beside you and me.
Should I, after tea and cakes and ices,

Have the strength to force the moment to its crisis?   80
But though I have wept and fasted, wept and prayed,
Though I have seen my head (grown slightly bald) brought in
    upon a platter,
I am no prophet—and here's no great matter;
I have seen the moment of my greatness flicker,
And I have seen the eternal Footman hold my coat, and snicker,   85
And in short, I was afraid.

And would it have been worth it, after all,
After the cups, the marmalade, the tea,
Among the porcelain, among some talk of you and me,
Would it have been worth while,   90
To have bitten off the matter with a smile,
To have squeezed the universe into a ball
To roll it toward some overwhelming question,
To say: "I am Lazarus, come from the dead,
Come back to tell you all, I shall tell you all"—   95
If one, settling a pillow by her head,
    Should say: "That is not what I meant at all.
    That is not it, at all."

And would it have been worth it, after all,
Would it have been worth while,   100
After the sunsets and the dooryards and the sprinkled streets,
After the novels, after the teacups, after the skirts that trail
    along the floor—
And this, and so much more?—
It is impossible to say just what I mean!
But as if a magic lantern threw the nerves in patterns on a
    screen: 105
Would it have been worth while
If one, settling a pillow or throwing off a shawl,
And turning toward the window, should say:
    "That is not it at all,
    That is not what I meant, at all."   110

No! I am not Prince Hamlet, nor was meant to be;
Am an attendant lord, one that will do
To swell a progress, start a scene or two,
Advise the prince; no doubt, an easy tool,
Deferential, glad to be of use,   115
Politic, cautious, and meticulous;
Full of high sentence, but a bit obtuse;
At times, indeed, almost ridiculous—
Almost, at times, the Fool.

I grow old . . . I grow old . . .   120

I shall wear the bottoms of my trousers rolled.

Shall I part my hair behind? Do I dare to eat a peach?
I shall wear white flannel trousers, and walk upon the beach.
I have heard the mermaids singing, each to each.

I do not think that they will sing to me.   125

I have seen them riding seaward on the waves
Combine the white hair of the waves blown back
When the wind blows the water white and black.

We have lingered in the chambers of the sea
By sea-girls wreathed with seaweed red and brown   130
Till human voices wake us, and we drown.

Robert Frost (1874–1963)

Frost struggled for twenty years to establish himself as a poet, drifting in and out of college, running an egg farm, and teaching. Finally he risked all by selling his house and using the money to take his family to England, where in a year he produced two books that won him recognition. He returned toAmerica to farm again, but moved into lecturing as his fame developed; eventually he held a number of writer-in-residence chairs at major universities. He won a Pulitzer Prize, was awarded over thirty honorary degrees, and became perhaps the best loved poet in the country. The understatement, economy, and outward simplicity of his poems combine with subtlety, sustained metaphor, and an appealing, earthy philosophy.

Mending Wall

Something there is that doesn't love a wall,
That sends the frozen ground swell under it,
And spills the upper boulders in the sun;
And makes gaps even two can pass abreast.
The work of hunters is another thing: 5
I have come after them and made repair
Where they have left not one stone on a stone,
But they would have the rabbit out of hiding,
To please the yelping dogs. The gaps I mean,
No one has seen them made or heard them made,   10
But at spring mending time we find them there.
I let my neighbor know beyond the hill;
And on a day we meet to walk the line
And set the wall between us once again.

We keep the wall between us as we go.   15
To each the boulders that have fallen to each.
And some are loaves and some so nearly balls
We have to use a spell to make them balance:
"Stay where you are until our backs are turned!"
We wear our fingers rough with handling them.   20
Oh, just another kind of outdoor game,
One on a side. It comes to little more:
There where it is we do not need the wall:
He is all pine and I am apple orchard.
My apple trees will never get across   25
And eat the cones under his pines, I tell him.
He only says, "Good fences make good neighbors."
Spring is the mischief in me, and I wonder
If I could put a notion in his head:
"*Why* do they make good neighbors? Isn't it   30
Where there are cows? But here there are no cows.
Before I built a wall I'd ask to know
What I was walling in or walling out,
And to whom I was like to give offense.
Something there is that doesn't love a wall,   35
That wants it down." I could say "Elves" to him,
But it's not elves exactly, and I'd rather
He said it for himself. I see him there
Bringing a stone grasped firmly by the top
In each hand, like an old-stone savage armed.   40
He moves in darkness as it seems to me,
Not of woods only and the shade of trees.
He will not go behind his father's saying,
And he likes having thought of it so well
He says again, "Good fences make good neighbors."   45

FOR FURTHER CONSIDERATION

How is the basic sustained metaphor of the *wall* assisted by irony in the
poem? Where does irony appear? In what ways is the wall symbolic?

Birches

When I see birches bend to left and right
Across the lines of straighter darker trees,
I like to think some boy's been swinging them.
But swinging doesn't bend them down to stay.
Ice storms do that. Often you must have seen them   5
Loaded with ice a sunny winter morning
After a rain. They click upon themselves

As the breeze rises, and turn many-colored
As the stir cracks and crazes their enamel.
Soon the sun's warmth makes them shed crystal shells   10
Shattering and avalanching on the snow crust—
Such heaps of broken glass to sweep away
You'd think the inner dome of heaven had fallen.
They are dragged to the withered bracken by the load,
And they seem not to break; though once they are bowed   15
So low for long, they never right themselves:
You may see their trunks arching in the woods
Years afterwards, trailing their leaves on the ground
Like girls on hands and knees that throw their hair
Before them over their heads to dry in the sun.   20
But I was going to say when Truth broke in
With all her matter-of-fact about the ice storm
I should prefer to have some boy bend them
As he went out and in to fetch the cows—
Some boy too far from town to learn baseball,   25
Whose only play was what he found himself,
Summer or winter, and could play alone.
One by one he subdued his father's trees
By riding them down over and over again
Until he took the stiffness out of them.   30
And not one but hung limp, not one was left
For him to conquer. He learned all there was
To learn about not launching out too soon
And so not carrying the tree away
Clear to the ground. He always kept his poise   35
To the top branches, climbing carefully
With the same pains you use to fill a cup
Up to the brim, and even above the brim.
Then he flung outward, feet first, with a swish,
Kicking his way down through the air to the ground.   40
So was I once myself a swinger of birches,
And so I dream of going back to be.
It's when I'm weary of considerations,
And life is too much like a pathless wood
Where your face burns and tickles with the cobwebs   45
Broken across it, and one eye is weeping
From a twig's having lashed across it open.
I'd like to get away from earth awhile
And then come back to it and begin over.
May no fate willfully misunderstand me   50
And half grant what I wish and snatch me away
Not to return. Earth's the right place for love:
I don't know where it's likely to go better.
I'd like to go by climbing a birch tree,

And climb black branches up a snow-white trunk   55
Toward heaven, till the tree could bear no more,
But dipped its top and set me down again.
That would be good both going and coming back.
One could do worse than be a swinger of birches.

The Road Not Taken

Two roads diverged in a yellow wood,
And sorry I could not travel both
And be one traveler, long I stood
And looked down one as far as I could
To where it bent in the undergrowth;   5

Then took the other, as just as fair,
And having perhaps the better claim,
Because it was grassy and wanted wear;
Though as for that the passing there
Had worn them really about the same,   10

And both that morning equally lay
In leaves no step had trodden black.
Oh, I kept the first for another day!
Yet knowing how way leads on to way,
I doubted if I should ever come back.   15

I shall be telling this with a sigh
Somewhere ages and ages hence:
Two roads diverged in a wood, and I—
I took the one less traveled by,
And that has made all the difference.   20

Stopping by Woods on a Snowy Evening

Whose woods these are I think I know.
His house is in the village though;
He will not see me stopping here
To watch his woods fill up with snow.

My little horse must think it queer   5
To stop without a farmhouse near
Between the woods and frozen lake
The darkest evening of the year.

He gives his harness bells a shake
To ask if there is some mistake.   10

The only other sound's the sweep
Of easy wind and downy flake.

The woods are lovely, dark and deep.
But I have promises to keep,
And miles to go before I sleep,   15
And miles to go before I sleep.

Wallace Stevens (1879–1955)

People who think of lawyers or business people as somehow the opposite of poets should think again. Stevens received his law degree at Harvard and after practicing briefly in New York City, became the vice president of a large insurance company, a position he held for many years while quietly producing superb poetry. The strength of the images and the wit in his works won him a Pulitzer Prize in 1955.

Peter Quince at the Clavier

I
Just as my fingers on these keys
Make music, so the selfsame sounds
On my spirit make a music, too.

Music is feeling, then, not sound;
And thus it is that what I feel,   5
Here in this room, desiring you,

Thinking of your blue-shadowed silk,
Is music. It is like the strain
Waked in the elders by Susanna.

Of a green evening, clear and warm,   10
She bathed in her still garden, while
The red-eyed elders watching, felt

The basses of their beings throb
In witching chords, and their thin blood
Pulse pizzicati of Hosanna.   15

II
In the green water, clear and warm,
Susanna lay.
She searched
The touch of springs,
And found   20
Concealed imaginings.

She sighed,
For so much melody.

Upon the bank, she stood
In the cool   25
Of spent emotions.
She felt, among the leaves,
The dew
Of old devotions.

She walked upon the grass,   30
Still quavering.
The winds were like her maids,
On timid feet,
Fetching her woven scarves,
Yet wavering.   35

A breath upon her hand
Muted the night.
She turned—
A cymbal crashed,
And roaring horns.   40

III
Soon, with a noise like tambourines,
Came her attendant Byzantines.

They wondered why Susanna cried
Against the elders by her side;

And as they whispered, the refrain   45
Was like a willow swept by rain

Anon, their lamps' uplifted flame
Revealed Susanna and her shame.

And then, the simpering Byzantines
Fled, with a noise like tambourines.   50

IV
Beauty is momentary in the mind—
The fitful tracing of a portal;
But in the flesh it is immortal.

The body dies; the body's beauty lives.
So evenings die, in their green going,   55
A wave, interminably flowing.
So gardens die, their meek breath scenting
The cowl of winter, done repenting.
So maidens die, to the auroral
Celebration of a maiden's choral.   60

Susanna's music touched the bawdy strings
Of those white elders; but, escaping,
Left only Death's ironic scraping.
Now, in its immortality, it plays
On the clear viol of her memory,   65
And makes a constant sacrament of praise.

W. H. Auden (1907–1973)

*Auden ranks with Eliot and a handful of others who have dominated
English poetry in the twentieth century. A satirical touch appears often in
his work, as does a grasp of humanity caught up in the uncontrollable
whirl of civilization. After an early period as a Marxist, he moved deeply
into Catholicism. Auden was born in England, became a United States
citizen, taught and lectured in America, and eventually retired to Europe,
where he finished his days.*

The Unknown Citizen

*(To JS/07/M378
This Marble Monument
Is Erected by the State)*

He was found by the Bureau of Statistics to be
One against whom there was no official complaint,
And all the reports on his conduct agree
That, in the modern sense of an old-fashioned word, he was
          a saint,
For in everything he did he served the Greater
          Community.   5
Except for the War till the day he retired
He worked in a factory and never got fired,
But satisfied his employers, Fudge Motors Inc.
Yet he wasn't a scab or odd in his views,
For his Union reports that he paid his dues,   10
(Our report on his Union shows it was sound)
And our Social Psychology workers found
That he was popular with his mates and liked a drink.
The Press are convinced that he bought a paper every day
And that his reactions to advertisements were normal in
          every way.   15
Policies taken out in his name prove that he was fully
          insured,

And his Health-card shows he was once in hospital but left
    it cured.
Both Producers Research and High-Grade Living declare
He was fully sensible to the advantages of the Instalment
    Plan
And had everything necessary to the Modern Man,   20
A phonograph, a radio, a car and a frigidaire.
Our researchers into Public Opinion are content
That he held the proper opinions for the time of year;
When there was peace, he was for peace; when there was
    war, he went.
He was married and added five children to the population,   25
Which our Eugenist says was the right number for a parent
    of his generation,
And our teachers report that he never interfered with their
    education.
Was he free? Was he happy? The question is absurd:
Had anything been wrong, we should certainly have heard.

FOR FURTHER CONSIDERATION

Auden makes a strong comment on the encroachment of science,
technology, and specialization on the individual's privacy and sense of
self. How does the poet's use of capital letters affect the value of the
words capitalized? The poem begins with an ironic title, and the irony
builds from there. Cite examples of irony in the poem. How does the
absence of figurative language or metaphor affect the statement of this
poem?

Musée des Beaux Arts

About suffering they were never wrong,
The Old Masters: how well they understood
Its human position; how it takes place
While someone else is eating or opening a window or just
    walking dully along;
How, when the aged are reverently, passionately waiting   5
For the miraculous birth, there always must be
Children who did not specially want it to happen, skating
On a pond at the edge of the wood:
They never forgot
That even the dreadful martyrdom must run its course   10

Anyhow in a corner, some untidy spot

Where the dogs go on with their doggy life and the
    torturer's horse
Scratches its innocent behind on a tree.

In Brueghel's *Icarus*, for instance: how everything turns away
Quite leisurely from the disaster; the ploughman may   15
Have heard the splash, the forsaken cry,
But for him it was not an important failure; the sun shone
As it had to on the white legs disappearing into the green
Water; and the expensive delicate ship that must have seen
Something amazing, a boy falling out of the sky,   20
Had somewhere to get to and sailed calmly on.

Theodore Roethke (1908–1963)

The encouragement of writers such as W. H. Auden, Edith Sitwell, and William Carlos Williams helped the young Roethke move into the realm of internationally recognized poets. Although he hated both high school and college, he spent most of his life as a college teacher. His explorations of beauty in the ordinary and his striking metaphors won him the Pulitzer Prize.

Elegy for Jane
My Student, Thrown by a Horse

I remember the neckcurls, limp and damp as tendrils;
And her quick look, a sidelong pickerel smile;
And how, once startled into talk, the light syllables leaped for her,
And she balanced in the delight of her thought,
A wren, happy, tail into the wind,   5
Her song trembling the twigs and small branches.
The shade sang with her;
The leaves, their whispers turned to kissing;
And the mold sang in the bleached valleys under the rose.

Oh, when she was sad, she cast herself down into such a pure depth, 10
Even a father could not find her:
Scraping her cheek against straw;
Stirring the clearest water.

My sparrow, you are not here,
Waiting like a fern, making a spiny shadow.   15
The sides of wet stones cannot console me,
Nor the moss, wound with the last light.

If only I could nudge you from this sleep,

My maimed darling, my skittery pigeon.
Over this damp grave I speak the words of my love: 20
I, with no rights in this matter,
Neither father nor lover.

I Knew a Woman

I knew a woman, lovely in her bones,
When small birds sighed, she would sigh back at them;
Ah, when she moved, she moved more ways than one:
The shapes a bright container can contain!
Of her choice virtues only gods should speak,   5
Or English poets who grew up on Greek
(I'd have them sing in chorus, cheek to cheek).

How well her wishes went! She stroked my chin,
She taught me Turn, and Counter-turn, and Stand;
She taught me Touch, that undulant white skin;   10
I nibbled meekly from her proffered hand;
She was the sickle; I, poor I, the rake,
Coming behind her for her pretty sake
(But what prodigious mowing we did make).

Loves like a gander, and adores a goose: 15
Her full lips pursed, the errant note to seize;
She played it quick, she played it light and loose;
My eyes, they dazzled at her flowing knees;
Her several parts could keep a pure repose,
Or one hip quiver with a mobile nose   20
(She moved in circles, and those circles moved)

Let seed be grass, and grass turn into hay:
I'm martyr to a motion not my own;
What's freedom for? To know eternity.
I swear she cast a shadow white as stone.   25
But who would count eternity in days?
These old bones live to learn her wanton ways:
(I measure time by how a body sways).

FOR FURTHER CONSIDERATION

What examples of metaphoric language appear in the poem? To how
many different things is this woman compared? How does Roethke go
about establishing the good-humored tone?

My Papa's Waltz

The whiskey on your breath
Could make a small boy dizzy;
But I hung on like death:
Such waltzing was not easy.

We romped until the pans   5
Slid from the kitchen shelf;
My mother's countenance
Could not unfrown itself.

The hand that held my wrist
Was battered on one knuckle;   10
At every step you missed
My right ear scraped a buckle.

You beat time on my head
With a palm caked hard by dirt,
Then waltzed me off to bed   15
Still clinging to your shirt.

Dolor

I have known the inexorable sadness of pencils,
Neat in their boxes, dolor of pad and paper-weight,
All the misery of manilla folders and mucilage,
Desolation in immaculate public places,
Lonely reception room, lavatory, switchboard,   5
The unalterable pathos of basin and pitcher.
Ritual of multigraph, paper-clip, comma,
Endless duplication of lives and objects.
And I have seen dust from the walls of institutions,
Finer than flour, alive, more dangerous than silica,   10
Sift, almost invisible, through long afternoons of tedium,
Dropping a fine film on nails and delicate eyebrows,
Glazing the pale hair, the duplicate gray standard faces.

William Carlos Williams (1883–1963)

The special strength of Williams's poetry lies in his incredibly visual metaphors. One has the impression of actually seeing what he suggests with words, then later grasping the significance of the picture conveyed. Williams was a medical doctor who excelled in writing poetry, short stories, and nonfiction. He was a consultant on poetry to the Library of Congress and was awarded numerous honorary degrees and the National Book Award.

The Yachts

contend in a sea which the land partly encloses
shielding them from the too heavy blows
of an ungoverned ocean which when it chooses

tortures the biggest hulls, the best man knows
to pit against its beatings, and sinks them pitilessly.   5
Mothlike in mists, scintillant in the minute

brilliance of cloudless days, with broad bellying sails
they glide to the wind tossing green water
from their sharp prows while over them the crew crawls

ant like, solicitously grooming them, releasing,   10
making fast as they turn, lean far over and having
caught the wind again, side by side, head for the mark.

In a well guarded arena of open water surrounded by
lesser and greater craft which, sycophant, lumbering
and fluttering follow them, they appear youthful, rare   15

as the light of a happy eye, live with the grace
of all that in the mind is feckless, free and
naturally to be desired. Now the sea which holds them

is moody, lapping their glossy sides, as if feeling
for some slightest flaw but fails completely.   20
Today no race. Then the wind comes again. The yachts

move, jockeying for a start, the signal is set and they
are off. Now the waves strike at them but they are too
well made, they slip through, though they take in canvas.

Arms with hands grasping seek to clutch at the prows.   25
Bodies thrown recklessly in the way are cut aside.
It is a sea of faces about them in agony, in despair

until the horror of the race dawns staggering the mind,
the whole sea become an entanglement of watery bodies
lost to the world bearing what they cannot hold. Broken,   30

beaten, desolate, reaching from the dead to be taken up
they cry out, failing, failing! their cries rising
in waves still as the skillful yachts pass over.

FOR FURTHER CONSIDERATION

Two central metaphors appear in this poem. What are they? Review the
imagery in the poem. To what senses do the images in the first six stanzas
appeal? The last five stanzas?

The Red Wheelbarrow

so much depends
upon

a red wheel
barrow

glazed with rain   5
water

beside the white
chickens

Tract

I will teach you my townspeople
how to perform a funeral—
for you have it over a troop
of artists—
unless one should scour the world—   5
you have the ground sense necessary.

See! the hearse leads.
I begin with a design for a hearse.
For Christ's sake not black—
nor white either—and not polished!   10
Let it be weathered—like a farm wagon—
with gilt wheels (this could be
applied fresh at small expense)
or no wheels at all:
a rough dray to drag over the ground.   15

Knock the glass out!
My God—glass, my townspeople!
For what purpose? Is it for the dead
to look out or for us to see

how well he is housed or to see 20
the flowers or the lack of them—
or what?
To keep the rain and snow from him?
He will have a heavier rain soon:
pebbles and dirt and what not. 25
Let there be no glass—
and no upholstery phew!
and no little brass rollers
and small easy wheels on the bottom—
my townspeople what are you thinking of? 30

A rough plain hearse then
with gilt wheels and no top at all.
On this the coffin lies
by its own weight.

        No wreaths please— 35
especially no hothouse flowers.
Some common memento is better,
something he prized and is known by:
his old clothes—a few books perhaps—
God knows what! You realize 40
how we are about these things
my townspeople—
something will be found—anything
even flowers if he had come to that.
So much for the hearse. 45

For heaven's sake though see to the driver!
Take off the silk hat! In fact
that's no place at all for him —
up there unceremoniously
dragging our friend out to his own dignity! 50
Bring him down—bring him down!
Low and inconspicuous! I'd not have him ride
on the wagon at all—damn him—
the undertaker's understrapper!
Let him hold the reins 55
and walk at the side
and inconspicuously too!

Then briefly as to yourselves:
Walk behind—as they do in France,
seventh class, or if you ride 60
Hell take curtains! Go with some show
of inconvenience; sit openly—
to the weather as to grief.
Or do you think you can shut grief in?

What—from us? We who have perhaps   65
nothing to lose? Share with us
share with us—it will be money
in your pockets.
          Go now
I think you are ready.   70

Langston Hughes (1902–1967)

*Hughes won attention for "The Negro Speaks of Rivers" in 1921, and later
he was well received as a professional writer. His poems, short stories,
plays, song lyrics, and essays were among the first to call popular
attention to the roots and the circumstances of black life in America.*

The Negro Speaks of Rivers

I've known rivers:
I've known rivers ancient as the world and older than the
      flow of human blood in human veins.

My soul has grown deep like the rivers.

I bathed in the Euphrates when dawns were young.
I built my hut near the Congo and it lulled me to sleep.   5
I looked upon the Nile and raised the pyramids above it.
I heard the singing of the Mississippi when Abe Lincoln
      went down to New Orleans, and I've seen its
      muddy bosom turn all golden in the sunset.

I've known rivers: 10
Ancient, dusky rivers.

My soul has grown deep like the rivers.

I, Too

I, too, sing America.

I am the darker brother.
They send me to eat in the kitchen
When company comes,
But I laugh,   5
And eat well,
And grow strong.

Tomorrow,

I'll sit at the table
When company comes.   10
Nobody'll dare
Say to me,
"Eat in the kitchen,"
Then.

Besides,   15
They'll see how beautiful I am
And be ashamed—

I, too, am America.

As I Grew Older

It was a long time ago.
I have almost forgotten my dream.
But it was there then,
In front of me,
Bright like a sun—   5
My dream.

And then the wall rose,
Rose slowly,
Slowly,
Between me and my dream.   10
Rose slowly, slowly,
Dimming,
Hiding,
The light of my dream
Rose until it touched the sky—   15
The wall.

Shadow.
I am black.

I lie down in the shadow.
No longer the light of my dream before me,   20
Above me.
Only the thick wall.
Only the shadow.
My hands!
My dark hands!   25
Break through the wall!
Find my dream!
Help me to shatter this darkness,
To smash this night,
To break this shadow   30

Into a thousand lights of sun,
Into a thousand whirling dreams
Of sun!

Archibald MacLeish (1892-   )

*A true Renaissance man: poet, playwright, politician, and diplomat—a
thinker, leader, and man of action. MacLeish directed the very unpoetic
Office of Facts and Figures in World War II and was later Librarian of
Congress, the American delegate to UNESCO, and a college teacher. A
man of immense capability, humanism, and insight, he has won the
Pulitzer Prize and the National Book Award. His play* J.B. *continues to
attract audiences, and the lasting value of his poetry is universally
acknowledged. Of particular note is his command of levels of metaphor, as
the selections which follow demonstrate.*

Ars Poetica

A poem should be palpable and mute
As a globed fruit

Dumb
As old medallions to the thumb

Silent as the sleeve-worn stone   5
Of casement where the moss has grown—

A poem should be wordless
As the flight of birds

       .   .   .   .   .

A poem should be motionless in time
As the moon climbs   10

Leaving, as the moon releases
Twig by twig the night-entangled trees,

Leaving, as the moon behind the winter leaves,
Memory by memory the mind—

A poem should be motionless in time   15
As the moon climbs

       .   .   .   .   .

A poem should be equal to:
Not true

For all the history of grief
An empty doorway and a maple leaf   20

For love
The leaning grasses and two lights above the sea—

A poem should not mean
But be.

FOR FURTHER CONSIDERATION

What does each metaphor contribute to the qualities MacLeish suggests a
poem "should" have? Given the poem's last two lines, does "Ars Poetica"
"mean" or does it "be"? Does the difference between the poem itself and
the admonition in these last lines constitute a paradox? An irony? An
attempt to communicate on several levels?

The End of the World

Quite unexpectedly as Vasserot
The armless ambidextrian was lighting
A match between his great and second toe
And Ralph the lion was engaged in biting
The neck of Madame Sossman while the drum   5
Pointed, and Teeny was about to cough
In waltz time swinging Jocko by the thumb—
Quite unexpectedly the top blew off:

And there, there overhead, there, there, hung over
Those thousands of white faces, those dazed eyes,   10
There in the starless dark the poise, the hover,
There with vast wings across the canceled skies,
There in the sudden blackness the black pall
Of nothing, nothing, nothing—nothing at all.

E. E. Cummings (1894-1962)

Cummings's innovations with typography, punctuation, and word combi-
nations blend beautifully with his raffish wit. A National Book Award
winner, he delighted in puns, double entendre, and the wildest kinds of
metaphors. No better satiric poet has come out of America. Readers
should be sure to read his poems aloud to discover how tightly he weaves
what he says into how he says it.

The Cambridge Ladies

the Cambridge ladies who live in furnished souls
are unbeautiful and have comfortable minds
(also, with the church's protestant blessings
daughters, unscented shapeless spirited)
they believe in Christ and Longfellow, both dead,   5
are invariably interested in so many things—
at the present writing one still finds
delighted fingers knitting for the is it Poles?
perhaps. While permanent faces coyly bandy
scandal of Mrs. N and Professor D   10
. . . . the Cambridge ladies do not care, above
Cambridge if sometimes in its box of
sky lavender and cornerless, the
moon rattles like a fragment of angry candy

O Sweet Spontaneous Earth

O sweet spontaneous
earth how often have
the
doting

        fingers of   5
prurient philosophers pinched
and
poked

thee
, has the naughty thumb   10
of science prodded
thy

     beauty   . how
often have religions taken
thee upon their scraggy knees   15
squeezing and

buffeting thee that thou mightest conceive
gods
      (but
true   20

to the incomparable
couch of death thy
rhythmic

lover

    thou answerest   25

them only with

        spring)

FOR FURTHER CONSIDERATION

Cummings here relies on one of the oldest of metaphors. To what does he compare the earth? What does this poem suggest about the efforts of science, philosophy, and religion? Compare the statement of this poem with that made in Auden's "The Unknown Citizen." Cite the uses of alliteration that Cummings makes.

Next to of Course God

"next to of course god america i
love you land of the pilgrims' and so forth oh
say can you see by the dawn's early my
country 'tis of centuries come and go
and are no more what of it we should worry   5
in every language even deaf and dumb
thy sons acclaim your glorious name by gorry
by jingo by gee by gosh by gum
why talk of beauty what could be more beaut-
iful than these heroic happy dead   10
who rushed like lions to the roaring slaughter
they did not stop to think they died instead
then shall the voice of liberty be mute?"

He spoke. And drank rapidly a glass of water

In Just-Spring

in Just-
spring   when the world is mud-
luscious the little
lame balloonman

whistles   far   and wee   5

and eddieandbill come
running from marbles and
piracies and it's
spring

when the world is puddle-wonderful   10

the queer
old balloonman whistles
far   and   wee
and bettyandisbel come dancing

from hop-scotch and jump-rope and   15

it's
spring
and
    the

         goat-footed   20

balloonMan   whistles
far
and
wee

Anyone Lived in a Pretty How Town

anyone lived in a pretty how town
(with up so floating many bells down)
spring summer autumn winter
he sang his didn't he danced his did.

Women and men (both little and small)   5
cared for anyone not at all
they sowed their isn't they reaped their same
sun moon stars rain

children guessed (but only a few
and down they forgot as up they grew   10
autumn winter spring summer)
that noone loved him more by more

when by now and tree by leaf
she laughed his joy she cried his grief
bird by snow and stir by still   15
anyone's any was all to her

someones married their everyones
laughed their cryings and did their dance
(sleep wake hope and then) they
said their nevers they slept their dream   20

stars rain sun moon
(and only the snow can begin to explain

how children are apt to forget to remember
with up so floating many bells down)

one day anyone died i guess   25
(and noone stooped to kiss his face)
busy folk buried them side by side
little by little and was by was

all by all and deep by deep
and more by more they dream their sleep   30
noone and anyone earth by april
wish by spirit and if by yes.

Women and men (both dong and ding)
summer autumn winter spring
reaped their sowing and went their came   35
sun moon stars rain

Dylan Thomas (1914-1953)

*Thomas died tragically of alcoholism, unable to cope with the fame and
public life that had moved him away from his roots in rural Wales. A poet,
short story writer, and playwright, he felt that his writing should raise
questions rather than answer them, and that immersion in the sound, feel,
and flow of words held tremendous beauty and value. Hence, he liked his
works to be read aloud. Ironically, it was while on tour reading his own
works and lecturing that the eccentric, boisterous, and often painfully
honest writer collapsed and died. The amazing flow and sense of sound in
Thomas's work disguises the lengthy hours he spent in careful rewriting so
that he might achieve these effects.*

The Force That through the Green Fuse

The force that through the green fuse drives the flower
Drives my green age; that blast the roots of trees
Is my destroyer.
And I am dumb to tell the crooked rose
My youth is bent by the same wintry fever.   5

The force that drives the water through the rocks
Drives my red blood; that dries the mouthing streams
Turns mine to wax.
And I am dumb to mouth unto my veins
How at the mountain spring the same mouth sucks.   10

The hand that whirls the water in the pool
Stirs the quicksand; that ropes the blowing wind
Hauls my shroud sail.

And I am dumb to tell the hanging man
How of my clay is made the hangman's lime.   15

The lips of time leech to the fountain head;
Love drips and gathers, but the fallen blood
Shall calm her sores.
And I am dumb to tell a weather's wind
How time has ticked a heaven round the stars.   20

And I am dumb to tell the lover's tomb
How at my sheet goes the same crooked worm.

FOR FURTHER CONSIDERATION

What "force" does the poet refer to? What things are being compared,
associated, or contrasted to establish the metaphors in the poem? Why is
the speaker "dumb" in each instance where he would speak?

Fern Hill

Now as I was young and easy under the apple boughs
About the lilting house and happy as the grass was green,
    The night above the dingle starry,
       Time let me hail and climb
    Golden in the heydays of his eyes,   5
And honoured among wagons I was prince of the apple towns
And once below a time I lordly had the trees and leaves
       Trail with daisies and barley
    Down the rivers of the windfall light.

And as I was green and carefree, famous among the barns   10
About the happy yard and singing as the farm was home,
    In the sun that is young once only,
       Time let me play and be
    Golden in the mercy of his means,
And green and golden I was huntsman and herdsman, the
          calves   15
Sang to my horn, the foxes on the hills barked clear and cold,
      And the sabbath rang slowly
    In the pebbles of the holy streams.

All the sun long it was running, it was lovely, the hay
Fields high as the house, the tunes from the chimneys, it
        was air   20

And playing, lovely and watery
    And fire green as grass.
And nightly under the simple stars
As I rode to sleep the owls were bearing the farm away,
All the moon long I heard, blessed among stables, the night-
        jars   25
    Flying with the ricks, and the horses
        Flashing into the dark.

And then to awake, and the farm, like a wanderer white
With the dew, come back, the cock on his shoulder: it was all
    Shining, it was Adam and maiden,   30
        The sky gathered again
    And the sun grew round that very day.
So it must have been after the birth of the simple light
In the first, spinning place, the spellbound horses walking
        warm
    Out of the whinnying green stable   35
        On to the fields of praise.

And honoured among foxes and pheasants by the gay house
Under the new made clouds and happy as the heart was long,
    In the sun born over and over,
        I ran my heedless ways,   40
    My wishes raced through the house high hay
And nothing I cared, at my sky blue trades, that time allows
In all his tuneful turning so few and such morning songs
    Before the children green and golden
        Follow him out of grace,   45

Nothing I cared, in the lamb white days, that time would
        take me
Up to the swallow thronged loft by the shadow of my hand,
    In the moon that is always rising,
        Nor that riding to sleep
    I should hear him fly with the high fields   50
And wake to the farm forever fled from the childless land.
Oh as I was young and easy in the mercy of his means,
        Time held me green and dying
    Though I sang in my chains like the sea.

Do Not Go Gentle into That Good Night

Do not go gentle into that good night,
Old age should burn and rave at close of day;
Rage, rage against the dying of the light.

Though wise men at their end know dark is right,
Because their words had forked no lightning they   5
Do not go gentle into that good night.

Good men, the last wave by, crying how bright
Their frail deeds might have danced in a green bay,
Rage, rage against the dying of the light.

Wild men who caught and sang the sun in flight,   10
And learn, too late, they grieved it on its way,
Do not go gentle into that good night.

Grave men, near death, who see with blinding sight
Blind eyes could blaze like meteors and be gay,
Rage, rage against the dying of the light.   15

And you, my father, there on the sad height,
Curse, bless, me now with your fierce tears, I pray.
Do not go gentle into that good night.
Rage, rage against the dying of the light.

Sylvia Plath (1932-1963)

*A product of Smith and Harvard and a Fulbright scholar, Sylvia Plath
established herself as a major modern poet before her suicide. Her ability
to convey the shattered self and to close the gap between the external thing
perceived and the perceiver marked her work as unique. She produced a
lone novel entitled* The Bell Jar.

*Plath lived in England, was married to the poet Ted Hughes, and had
two children.*

Daddy

You do not do, you do not do
Any more, black shoe
In which I have lived like a foot
For thirty years, poor and white,
Barely daring to breathe or Achoo.   5

Daddy, I have had to kill you.
You died before I had time—
Marble-heavy, a bag full of God,
Ghastly statue with one grey toe
Big as a Frisco seal   10

And a head in the freakish Atlantic

Where it pours bean green over blue
In the waters off beautiful Nauset.
I used to pray to recover you.
Ach, du.   15

In the German tongue, in the Polish town
Scraped flat by the roller
Of wars, wars, wars.
But the name of the town is common.
My Polack friend   20

Says there are a dozen or two.
So I never could tell where you
Put your foot, your root,
I never could talk to you.
The tongue stuck in my jaw.   25

It stuck in a barb wire snare.
Ich, ich, ich, ich,

I could hardly speak.
I thought every German was you.
And the language obscene   30

An engine, an engine
Chuffing me off like a Jew.
A Jew to Dachau, Auschwitz, Belsen.
I began to talk like a Jew.
I think I may well be a Jew.   35

The snows of the Tyrol, the clear beer of Vienna
Are not very pure or true.
With my gypsy ancestress and my weird luck
And my Taroc pack and my Taroc pack
I may be a bit of a Jew.   40

I have always been scared of *you,*
With your Luftwaffe, your gobbledygoo.
And your neat moustache
And your Aryan eye, bright blue.
Panzer-man, panzer-man, O You—   45

Not God but a swastika
So black no sky could squeak through.
Every woman adores a Fascist,
The boot in the face, the brute
Brute heart of a brute like you.   50

You stand at the blackboard, daddy,
In the picture I have of you,
A cleft in your chin instead of your foot

But no less a devil for that, no not
Any less the black man who   55

Bit my pretty red heart in two.
I was ten when they buried you.
At twenty I tried to die
And get back, back, back to you.
I thought even the bones would do.   60

But they pulled me out of the sack,
And they stuck me together with glue.
And then I knew what to do.
I made a model of you,
A man in black with a Meinkampf look   65

And a love of the rack and the screw.
And I said I do, I do.
So daddy, I'm finally through.
The black telephone's off at the root,
The voices just can't worm through.   70

If I've killed one man, I've killed two—
The vampire who said he was you
And drank my blood for a year,
Seven years, if you want to know.
Daddy, you can lie back now.   75

There's a stake in your fat black heart
And the villagers never liked you.
They are dancing and stamping on you.
They always *knew* it was you.
Daddy, daddy, you bastard, I'm through.   80

The Applicant

First, are you our sort of a person?
Do you wear
A glass eye, false teeth or a crutch,
A brace or a hook,
Rubber breasts or a rubber crotch,   5

Stitches to show something's missing? No, no? Then
How can we give you a thing?
Stop crying.
Open your hand.
Empty? Empty. Here is a hand   10

To fill it and willing
To bring teacups and roll away headaches

And do whatever you tell it.
Will you marry it?
It is guaranteed 15

To thumb shut your eyes at the end
And dissolve of sorrow.
We make new stock from the salt.
I notice you are stark naked.
How about this suit— 20

Black and stiff, but not a bad fit.
Will you marry it?
It is waterproof, shatterproof, proof
Against fire and bombs through the roof.
Believe me, they'll bury you in it. 25

Now your head, excuse me, is empty.
I have the ticket for that.

Come here, sweetie, out of the closet.
Well, what do you think of *that?*
Naked as paper to start 30

But in twenty-five years she'll be silver,
In fifty, gold.
A living doll, everywhere you look.
It can sew, it can cook,
It can talk, talk, talk. 35

It works, there is nothing wrong with it.
You have a hole, it's a poultice.
You have an eye, it's an image.
My boy, it's your last resort.
Will you marry it, marry it, marry it. 40

FOR FURTHER CONSIDERATION

In what ways is the conclusion of the poem linked to each of the first five stanzas? Explain the levels of metaphor operating in the poem. How is one metaphor extended to another?

Philip Larkin (1922-   )

With poetry remarkable for its clarity, careful diction, and comfortable wedding of rhythm and statement, Larkin examines isolation and the self responding to the demands of society. His volumes of poetry and his novels have established him as a versatile and sensitive commentator on the stance of the individual toward what he feels is required of him.

Poetry of Departures

Sometimes you hear, fifth-hand,
As epitaph:
He chucked up everything
And just cleared off,
And always the voice will sound   5
Certain you approve
This audacious, purifying,
Elemental move.

And they are right, I think.
We all hate home   10
And having to be there:
I detest my room,
Its specially-chosen junk,
The good books, the good bed,
And my life, in perfect order: 15
So to hear it said

He walked out on the whole crowd
Leaves me flushed and stirred,
Like *Then she undid her dress*
Or *Take that you bastard;*   20
Surely I can, if he did?
And that helps me stay
Sober and industrious.
But I'd go today,

Yes, swagger the nut-strewn roads,   25
Crouch in the fo'c'sle
Stubbly with goodness, if
It weren't so artificial,
Such a deliberate step backwards
To create an object: 30
Books; china; a life
Reprehensibly perfect.

Gary Snyder (1930-   )

One of the best of America's contemporary poets, Snyder is thoroughly
familiar with Buddhism, fluent in both Japanese and Chinese, and given to
spending time in the woods. His poems demonstrate a willingness to give
his feelings freedom of expression, a quality many seek and more admire.
Snyder has published several volumes of poetry.

Four Poems for Robin

Siwashing It out once in Siuslaw Forest

I slept under   rhododendron
All night   blossoms fell
Shivering on   a sheet of cardboard
Feet stuck   in my pack
Hands deep   in my pockets   5
Barely able   to sleep.
I remembered   when we were in school
Sleeping together   in a big warm bed
We were   the youngest lovers
When we broke up   we were still nineteen.   10
Now our   friends are married
You teach   school back east
I dont mind   living this way
Green hills   the long blue beach
But sometimes   sleeping in the open   15
I think back   when I had you.

A Spring Night in Shokoku-ji

Eight years ago this May
We walked under cherry blossoms
At night in an orchard in Oregon.
All that I wanted then   20
Is forgotten now, but you.
Here in the night
In a garden of the old capital
I feel the trembling ghost of Yugao
I remember your cool body   26
Naked under a summer cotton dress.

An Autumn Morning in Shokoku-ji

Last night watching the Pleiades,
Breath smoking in the moonlight,
Bitter memory like vomit
Choked my throat.   30
I unrolled a sleeping bag
On mats on the porch
Under thick autumn stars.
In dream you appeared
(Three times in nine years)   35

Wild, cold, and accusing.
I woke shamed and angry:
The pointless wars of the heart.
Almost dawn. Venus and Jupiter.
The first time I have   40
Ever seen them close.

December at Yase

You said, that October,
In the tall dry grass by the orchard
When you chose to be free,
"Again someday, maybe ten years."   45

After college I saw you
One time. You were strange.
And I was obsessed with a plan.

Now ten years and more have
Gone by: I've always known
        where you were—   50
I might have gone to you
Hoping to win your love back.
You still are single.

I didn't.
I thought I must make it alone. I   55
Have done that.

Only in dream, like this dawn,
Does the grave, awed intensity
Of our young love
Return to my mind, to my flesh.   60

We had what the others
All crave and seek for;
We left it behind at nineteen.

I feel ancient, as though I had
Lived many lives.   65

And may never now know
If I am a fool
Or have done what my
        karma demands.

José Angel Gutierrez (1949-   )

A modern Chicano poet comments on the sensibilities of growing up Mexican in American culture.

22 Miles . . .

From 22 I see my first 8 weren't.
  Around the 9th, I was called "meskin".
    By the 10th, I knew and believed I was.
      I found out what it meant to know, to believe. .before my 13th.

Through brown eyes, seeing only brown colors and feeling only brown
feelings. . .I saw. . .I felt. . .I hated. . .I cried. . .I tried. . .I didn't understand during these 4.   5
            I rested by just giving up.

While, on the side. . .I realized I BELIEVED in
  white as pretty,
    my being governor,
      blond blue eyed baby Jesus,   10
        cokes and hamburgers,
          equality for all regardless of race, creed, or color,
            Mr. Williams, our banker.
        I had to!
      That was all I had.   15
    Beans and Communism were bad.
        Past the weeds, atop the hill, I looked back.

Pretty people, combed and squeaky clean, on arrowlike roads.
Pregnant girls, ragged brats, swarthy machos, rosary beads,
and friends waddle clumsily over and across hills, each other,   20
mud, cold, and woods on caliche ruts.
At the 19th mile, I fought blindly at everything and anything.
  Not knowing, Not caring about WHY, WHEN, or FOR WHAT.
    I fought. And fought.
      By the 21st, I was tired and tried.   25
        But now. . . . .
I've been told that I am dangerous.
That is because I am good at not being a Mexican.
That is because I know now that I have been cheated.
That is because I hate circumstances and love choices.   30
    You know. . .chorizo tacos y tortillas ARE good, even at school.
  Speaking Spanish is a talent.
Being Mexican IS as good as Rainbo bread.
And without looking back, I know that there are still too many. . .
  brown babies,   35
    pregnant girls,

old 25 year-old women,
    drunks,
        who should have lived but didn't,
            on those caliche ruts.   40

        It is tragic that my problems during these past 21 miles
        were/are/might be. . .
            looking into blue eyes,
            wanting to touch a gringita,
                ashamed of being Mexican,   45
        believing I could not make it at college,
    pretending that I liked my side of town,
    remembering the Alamo,
    speaking Spanish in school bathrooms only,
and knowing that Mexico's prostitutes like Americans better.   50
At 22, my problems are still the same but now I know I am your problem. That farm boys, Mexicans and Negro boys are in Vietnam is but one
thing I think about:

        Crystal City, Texas 78839
        The migrant worker;   55
        The good gringo:

Staying Mexican enough;
Helping;
Looking at the world from the back of a truck.

The stoop labor with high school rings on their fingers;   60
The Anglo cemetery,
Joe the different Mexican,
                Damn.
                Damn.
                Damn.   65

FOR FURTHER CONSIDERATION

The poet has considerable success in emphasizing certain words. What
words receive emphasis, and how does he achieve this emphasis? What,
in turn, do many of these emphasized words contribute to the tone of the
poem? How does the tone of the poem shift at line 51?

Paul Simon (1940-   )

*In one lyric after another Simon has established himself as a poet,
troubador, and social commentator of major importance.*

The Sound of Silence*

Hello darkness my old friend,
I've come to talk with you again,
Because a vision softly creeping,
Left its seeds while I was sleeping
And the vision that was planted in my brain   5
Still remains within the sound of silence.

In restless dreams I walked alone,
Narrow streets of cobble stone
'Neath the halo of a street lamp,
I turned my collar to the cold and damp   10
When my eyes were stabbed by the flash of a neon light
That split the night, and touched the sound of silence.

And in the naked light I saw
Ten thousand people maybe more,
People talking without speaking,   15
People hearing without listening,
People writing songs that voices never share
And no one dares disturb the sound of silence.

"Fools!" said I, "You do not know
Silence like a cancer grows.   20
Hear my words that I might teach you
Take my arms that I might reach you."
But my words like silent raindrops fell
And echoed, in the wells of silence.

And the people bowed and prayed   25
To the neon God they made,
And the sign flashed out its warning
In the words that it was forming,
And the sign said:
    "The words of the prophets are written   30
    on the subway walls and tenement halls"
And whispered in the sounds of silence.

*© 1964 by Paul Simon. Used with the permission of the publisher.

FOR FURTHER CONSIDERATION

What poetic device does Simon employ in his title? In the third stanza a
series of apparent contradictions appear. What comment do lines 15, 16,
and 17 make on human relationships in contemporary civilization? What
links exist between these lines and the last three lines of the poem?

Carole King (1944-   )

A successful songwriter turned performer, King has a particular gift with lyrics of timeless value.

You've Got a Friend*

When you're down and troubled,
And you need some loving care,
And nothing, nothing is going right,
Close your eyes and think of me,
And soon I will be there,   5
To brighten up even your darkest night.

You just call out my name
And you know wherever I am,
I'll come running to see you again.
Winter, spring, summer or fall,   10
All you have to do is call,
And I'll be there,
You've got a friend.
If the sky above you,
Grows dark and full of clouds,   15
And that old north wind begins to blow,
Keep your head together,
And call my name out loud,
Soon you'll hear me knocking at your door.

You just call out my name,   20
And you know wherever I am,
I'll come running to see you.
Winter, spring, summer or fall,
All you have to do is call,
And I'll be there.   25

Ain't it good to know that you've got a friend,
When people can be so cold,
They'll hurt you, and desert you,
And take your soul if you let them,
Oh, but don't you let them.   30

You just call out my name,
And you know wherever I am,
I'll come running to see you again.
Winter, spring, summer or fall,
All you have to do is call,   35
And I'll be there,
You've got a friend.

Bernard Gunther (1930-   )

Gunther is a consultant at the Esalen Institute in Big Sur, California. His experience with gestalt therapy, Yoga, Zen, and sensory awareness combines with his innovative wit to produce poems remarkable for their word play and intellectual delight. He is the author of Sense Relaxation *and* Love View—*both popular books—and has produced films on sensory awareness.*

now
here
this

u
.
is
half
of
us

_____

as
summer
leaves

fall

define myself
in a word

why that's

absurd

Part Three

Drama

To read a play and enjoy it, one must be at once the actors, the director, the playwright, and an intelligent member of the audience, a sizable demand for even the best of imaginations. Nothing can substitute for being present at a dramatic performance, but as long as one brings to a written play a willing imagination, the experience of reading drama holds more creative joy than perhaps that of any other form of literature. For the reader the characters are what he or she wants them to be, and the action, pace, and theme one's own interpretation rather than that of someone else. In this demand for greater responsiveness and creativity, the play reader may also encounter the intensified pleasure of close involvement with the people, actions, and ideas that the playwright offers. An added benefit accrues as well in the opportunity to ruminate — to read, pause for thought, and perhaps reread a particularly striking passage, a joy unavailable in even the best of dramatic performances.

A word about economy in drama. Good poetry usually has few if any extraneous words, and good drama in its own way shares this need for economy. To develop quickly some sense of who a character is and why we should find him or her interesting, a playwright must suggest a great deal with a few words or risk boring us. And given the limited amount of time we will devote to watching (or reading) a play, a playwrite faces the same problem with the conflict and plot, that is, he or she has to capture our attention early and get on with things lest we lose interest. As a result you may expect to discover in good drama considerable connotative value and significance in even the most ordinary dialogue, economy being the ruling principle of dramatic writing.

The three plays in this section present extremely diverse examples of what constitutes drama. *King Oedipus,* an archetypal tragedy, continues to intrigue audiences after thousands of years. *A Thousand Clowns,* on the other hand, has established itself as a rarity in modern comedy in that it continues to draw audiences and laughter a generation after its debut. *In an Oval Office* appears as a new dimension in drama, a slice of contemporary reality written artfully yet unwittingly by its original actors. One may classify it as tragedy, comedy, melodrama, farce, or theater of the absurd depending on one's politics and one's disposition. Its dramatic content, however, remains undisputed, and a reader might do worse than compare the play and the historical events which proceeded from it to the tragic conclusion of *King Oedipus.*

In the dilemma of Oedipus, Sophocles shows us the ingredients of classical tragedy: a good man facing the opposite demands of two ultimate loyalties. In choosing one of these loyalties, he must tragically forsake the other and then discover, as countless men have, that the best and mightiest of struggles may prove hollow and ironic in the face of the contrary operations of Fate.

Herb Gardner's protagonist Murray Burns, in contrast, shows us in *A Thousand Clowns* that despite the play of larger forces—mundane forces such as bureaucracies, the work ethic, the need for acceptance—a blithe spirit or an antihero stands a chance of making it if he abandons the whole game that modern urban civilization seems to require that we play. Murray's abandonment of a numbing, dehumanizing routine inevitably leads him to face a second decision, one which might prove tragic but for the antic disposition and firm grasp of the absurd that he displays.

If drama usually appears as the product of conscious art, we must also occasionally recognize drama in actual human events, in this case in the recorded exchange of powerful men struggling with politically mortal issues. The veracity of White House edited tape transcripts is of little matter; political reality by definition exists as different things to different people. What does matter is that we recognize in *In an Oval Office* one of those occasions where reality has the stuff as well as the form of drama, blurring the distinction between art and reality.

In a way each of us is author, actor, and audience in the drama of *In an Oval Office*—author in our responsibility as electors of the men who govern us, actor in that each of us had a high stake in the outcome of the conflict, and audience in the usual sense of the interested witness who does not feel he or she can affect the outcome of the events witnessed. With three roles instead of one, then, it seems likely that each of us should find in the intrigues of this play an intensity unmatched by conventional drama.

Sophocles (496-405 B.C.)

History suggests that Sophocles's popularity as a writer of tragedies helped him tobecome a political leader during the Periclean Age in Athens. Only seven of his approximately one hundred and twenty plays remain, but his eminence as a playwright, rhetorician, and politician has been well documented. His explorations of pride, fate, and the demands of divided loyalties have made his tragedies timeless.

King Oedipus

DRAMATIS PERSONAE:

OEDIPUS, *King of Thebes*
JOCASTA, *wife of* OEDIPUS
ANTIGONE, *daughter of* OEDIPUS
ISMENE, *daughter of* OEDIPUS
CREON, *brother-in-law of* OEDIPUS
TIRESIAS, *a seer*
A PRIEST
MESSENGERS
A HERDSMAN
CHORUS

Setting: In front of the royal palace in Thebes, a city-state in the highlands of Greece.

OEDIP. Children, descendants of old Cadmus, why do you come before me, why do you carry the branches of suppliants, while the city smokes with incense and murmurs with prayer and lamentation? I would not learn from any mouth but yours, old man, therefore I question you myself. Do you know of anything that I can do and have not done? How can I, being the man I am, being King Oedipus, do other than all I know? I were indeed hard of heart did I not pity such suppliants.

PRIEST Oedipus, King of my country, we who stand before your door are of all ages, some too young to have walked so many miles, some— priests of Zeus such as I—too old. Among us stand the pick of the young men, and behind in the marketplaces the people throng, carrying suppliant branches. We all stand here because the city stumbles towards death, hardly able to raise up its head. A blight has fallen upon the fruitful blossoms of the land, a blight upon flock and field and upon the bed of marriage—plague ravages the city. Oedipus, King, not God but foremost of living men, seeing that when you first came to this town of Thebes you freed us from that harsh singer, the riddling Sphinx, we beseech you, all we suppliants, to find some help; whether you find it by your power as a man, or because, being near the Gods, a God has whispered you. Uplift our State; think upon your fame; your coming brought us luck, be lucky to us still; remember that it is better to rule over men than over a waste place, since neither walled town nor ship is anything if it be empty and no man within it.

OEDIP.   My unhappy children! I know well what need has brought you, what suffering you endure; yet, sufferers though you be there is not a single one whose suffering is as mine—each mourns himself, but my soul mourns the city, myself, and you. It is not therefore as if you came to arouse a sleeping man. No! Be certain that I have wept many tears and searched hither and thither for some remedy. I have already done the only thing that came into my head for all my search. I have sent the son of Menocceus, Creon, my own wife's brother, to the Pythian House of Phoebus, to hear if deed or word of mine may yet deliver this town. I am troubled, for he is a long time away—a longer time than should be—but when he comes I shall not be an honest man unless I do whatever the God commands.

PRIEST   You have spoken at the right time. They have just signalled to us that Creon has arrived.

OEDIP.   O King Apollo, may he bring brighter fortune, for his face is shining!

PRIEST   He brings good news, for he is crowned with bay.

OEDIP.   We shall know soon. Brother-in-law, Menoeceus' son, what news from the God?

CREON   Good news; for pain turns to pleasure when we have set the crooked straight.

OEDIP.   But what is the oracle?—so far the news is neither good nor bad.

CREON   If you would hear it with all these about you, I am ready to speak. Or do we go within?

OEDIP.   Speak before all. The sorrow I endure is less for my own life than these.

CREON   Then, with your leave, I speak. Our lord Phoebus bids me drive out a defiling thing that has been cherished in this land,

OEDIP.   By what purification?

CREON   King Laius was our King before you came to pilot us.

OEDIP.   I know—but not of my own knowledge, for I never saw him.

CREON   He was killed; and the God now bids us revenge it on his murderers, whoever they be.

OEDIP.   Where shall we come upon their track after all these years? Did he meet his death in house or field, at home or in some foreign land?

CREON   In a foreign land: he was journeying to Delphi.

OEDIP.   Did no fellow-traveller see the deed? Was there none there who could be questioned?

CREON   All perished but one man who fled in terror and could tell for certain but one thing of all he had seen.

OEDIP.   One thing might be a clue to many things.

CREON   He said that they were fallen upon by a great troop of robbers.

OEDIP.   What robbers would be so daring unless bribed from here?

CREON   Such things were indeed guessed at, but Laius once dead no avenger arose. We were amid our troubles.

OEDIP.   But when royalty had fallen what troubles could have hindered search?

CREON   The riddling Sphinx put those dark things out of our thoughts— we thought of what had come to our own doors.

OEDIP.   But I will start afresh and make the dark things plain. In doing right by Laius I protect myself, for whoever slew Laius might turn a hand against me. Come, my children, rise up from the altar steps; lift up these suppliant boughs and let all the children of Cadmus be called hither that I may search out everything and find for all happiness or misery as God wills.

PRIEST   May Phoebus, sender of the oracle, come with it and be our saviour and deliverer!

[*The* CHORUS *enters.*]

CHORUS   What message comes to famous Thebes from the Golden House?
What message of disaster from that sweet-throated Zeus?

What monstrous thing our fathers saw do the seasons bring?
Or what that no man ever saw, what new monstrous thing?
Trembling in every limb I raise my loud importunate cry.
And in a sacred terror wait the Delian God's reply.

Apollo chase the God of Death that leads no shouting men
Bears no rattling shield and yet consumes this form with pain
Famine takes what the plague spares, and all the crops are
  lost;
No new life fills the empty place—ghost flits after ghost
To that God-trodden western shore, as flit benighted buds,
Sorrow speaks to sorrow, but no comfort finds in words.

Hurry him from the land of Thebes with a fair wind behind
Out onto that formless deep where not a man can find
Hold for an anchor-fluke, for all is world-enfolding sea;
Master of the thunder-cloud, set the lightning free,
And add the thunder-stone to that and fling them on his head,
For death is all the fashion now, till even Death be dead.

We call against the pallid face of this God-hated God
The springing heel of Artemis in the hunting sandal shod,
The tousel-headed Maenads, blown torch and drunken sound,
The stately Lysian king himself with golden fillet crowned.
And in his hands the golden bow and the stretched golden
  string,
And Bacchus' wine-ensanguined face that all the Maenads
  sing.

OEDIP. You are praying, and it may be that your prayer will be answered; that if you hear my words and do my bidding you may find help out of all your trouble. This is my proclamation, children of Cadmus. Whoever among you knows by what man Laius, son of Labdacus, was killed, must tell all he knows. If he fear for himself and being guilty denounce himself, he shall be in the less danger, suffering no worse thing than banishment. If on the other hand there be one that knows that a foreigner did the deed, let him speak, and I shall give him a reward and my thanks: but if any man keep silent from fear or to screen a friend, hear all what I will do to that man. No one in this land shall speak to him, nor offer sacrifice beside him; but he shall be driven from their homes as if he himself had done the deed. And in this I am the ally of the Pythian God and of the murdered man, and I pray that the murderer's life may, should he be so hidden and screened, drop from him and perish away, whoever he may be, whether he did the deed with others or by himself alone: and on you I lay it to make—so far as man may—these words good, for my sake, and for the God's sake, and for the sake of this land. And even if the God had not spurred us to it, it were a wrong to leave the guilt unpurged, when one so noble, and he your King, had perished; and all have sinned that could have searched it out and did not: and now since it is I who hold the power which he held once, and have his wife for wife—she who would have borne him heirs had he but lived—I take up this cause even as I would were it that of my own father. And if there be any who do not obey me in it, I pray that the Gods send them neither harvest of the earth nor fruit of the womb; but let them be wasted by this plague, or by one more dreadful still. But may all be blessed for ever who hear my words and do my will!

CHORUS   We do not know the murderer, and it were indeed more fitting that Phoebus, who laid the task upon us, should name the man.

OEDIP.   No man can make the Gods speak against their will.

CHORUS   Then I will say what seems the next best thing.

OEDIP.   If there is a third course, show it.

CHORUS   I know that our lord Tiresias is the seer most like to our lord Phoebus, and through him we may unravel all.

OEDIP.   So I was advised by Creon, and twice already have I sent to bring him.

CHORUS   If we lack his help we have nothing but vague and ancient rumors.

OEDIP.   What rumors are they? I would examine every story.

CHORUS   Certain wayfarers were said to have killed the King.

OEDIP.   I know, I know. But who was there that saw it?

CHORUS   If there is such a man, and terror can move him, he will not keep silence when they have told him of your curses.

OEDIP.   He that such a deed did not terrify will not be terrified because of a word.

CHORUS   But there is one who shall convict him. For the blind prophet comes at last—in whom alone of all men the truth lives.

> [*Enter* TIRESIAS, *led by a boy.*]

OEDIP.   Tiresias, master of all knowledge, whatever may be spoken, whatever is unspeakable, whatever omens of earth and sky reveal, the plague is among us, and from that plague, Great Prophet, protect us and save us. Phoebus in answer to our question says that it will not leave us till we have found the murderers of Laius, and driven them into exile or put them to death. Do you therefore neglect neither the voice of birds, nor any other sort of wisdom, but rescue yourself, rescue the State, rescue me, rescue all that are defiled by the deed. For we are in your hands, and what greater task falls to a man than to help other men with all he knows and has?

TIR.   Aye, and what worse task than to be wise and suffer for it? I know this well; it slipped out of mind, or I would never have come.

OEDIP.   What now?

TIR.   Let me go home. You will bear your burden to the end more easily, and I bear mine—if you but give me leave for that.

OEDIP.   Your words are strange and unkind to the State that bred you.

TIR.   I see that you, on your part, keep your lips tight shut, and therefore I have shut mine that I may come to no misfortune.

OEDIP.   For God's love do not turn away—if you have knowledge. We suppliants implore you on our knees.

TIR.   You are fools—I will bring misfortune neither upon you nor upon myself.

OEDIP.   What is this? You know all and will say nothing? You are minded to betray me and Thebes?

TIR.   Why do you ask these things? You will not learn them from me.

OEDIP.   What! Basest of the base! You would enrage the very stones. Will you never speak out? Cannot anything touch you?

TIR.   The future will come of itself though I keep silent.

OEDIP.   Then seeing that come it must, you had best speak out.

TIR.   I will speak no further. Rage if you have a mind to; bring out all the fierceness that is in your heart.

OEDIP.   That will I. I will not spare to speak my thoughts. Listen to what I have to say. It seems to me that you have helped to plot the deed; and, short of doing it with your own hands, have done the deed yourself. Had you eyesight I would declare that you alone had done it.

TIR.   So that is what you say? I charge you to obey the decree that you yourself have made, and from this day out to speak neither to these nor to me. You are the defiler of this land.

OEDIP. So brazen in your impudence? How do you hope to escape punishment?

TIR. I have escaped; my strength is in my truth.

OEDIP. Who taught you this? You never got it by your art.

TIR. You, because you have spurred me to speech against my will.

OEDIP. What speech? Speak it again that I may learn it better.

TIR. You are but tempting me—you understand me well enough.

OEDIP. No; not so that I can say I know it; speak it again.

TIR. I say that you are yourself the murderer that you seek.

OEDIP. You shall rue it for having spoken twice such outrageous words.

TIR. Would you that I say more that you may be still angrier?

OEDIP. Say what you will. I will not let it move me.

TIR. I say that you are living with your next of kin in unimagined shame.

OEDIP. Do you think you can say such things and never smart for it?

TIR. Yes, if there be strength in truth.

OEDIP. There is; yes—for everyone but you. But not for you that are maimed in ear and in eye and in wit.

TIR. You are but a poor wretch flinging taunts that in a little while everyone shall fling at you.

OEDIP. Night, endless night has covered you up so that you can neither hurt me nor any man that looks upon the sun.

TIR. Your doom is not to fall by me. Apollo is enough: it is his business to work out your doom.

OEDIP. Was it Creon that planned this or you yourself?

TIR. Creon is not your enemy; you are your own enemy.

OEDIP.   Power, ability, position, you bear all burdens, and yet what envy you create! Great must that envy be if envy of my power in this town—a power put into my hands unsought—has made trusty Creon, my old friend Creon, secretly long to take that power from me; if he has suborned this scheming juggler, this quack and trickster, this man with eyes for his gains and blindness in his art. Come, come, where did you prove yourself a seer? Why did you say nothing to set the townsmen free when the riddling Sphinx was here? Yet that riddle was not for the first-comer to read; it needed the skill of a seer. And none such had you! Neither found by help of birds, nor straight from any god. No, I came; I silenced her, I the ignorant Oedipus, it was I that found the answer in my mother-wit, untaught by any birds. And it is I that you would pluck out of my place, thinking to stand close to Creon's throne. But you and the plotter of all this shall mourn despite your zeal to purge the land. Were you not an old man, you had already learnt how bold you are and learnt it to your cost.

CHORUS   Both this man's words and yours, Oedipus, have been said in anger. Such words cannot help us here, nor any but those that teach us to obey the oracle.

TIR.   King though you are, the right to answer when attacked belongs to both alike. I am not subject to you, but to Loxias; and therefore I shall never be Creon's subject. And I tell you, since you have taunted me with blindness, that though you have your sight, you cannot see in what misery you stand, nor where you are living, nor with whom, unknowing what you do—for you do not know the stock you come of—you have been your own kin's enemy be they living or be they dead. And one day a mother's curse and father's curse alike shall drive you from this land in dreadful haste with darkness upon those eyes. Therefore, heap your scorn on Creon and on my message if you have a mind to; for no one of living men shall be crushed as you shall be crushed.

OEDIP.   Begone this instant! Away, away! Get you from these doors!

TIR.   I had never come but that you sent for me.

OEDIP.   I did not know you were mad.

TIR.   I may seem mad to you, but your parents thought me sane.

OEDIP.   My parents! Stop! Who was my father?

TIR.   This day shall you know your birth; and it will ruin you.

OEDIP.   What dark words you always speak!

TIR.   But are you not most skillful in the unravelling of dark words?

OEDIP.   You mock me for that which made me great?

TIR.   It was that fortune that undid you.

OEDIP.   What do I care? For I delivered all this town.

TIR.   Then I will go: boy, lead me out of this.

OEDIP.   Yes, let him lead you. You take vexation with you.

TIR.   I will go: but first I will do my errand. For frown though you may you cannot destroy me. The man for whom you look, the man you have been threatening in all the proclamations about the death of Laius, that man is here. He seems, so far as looks go, an alien; yet he shall be found a native Theban and shall nowise be glad of that fortune. A blind man, though now he has his sight; a beggar, though now he is most rich; he shall go forth feeling the ground before him with his stick; so you go in and think on that, and if you find I am in fault say that I have no skill in prophecy.

[TIRESIAS *is led out by the boy.* OEDIPUS *enters the palace.*]
CHORUS   The Delphian rock has spoken out, now must a wicked mind,
Planner of things I dare not speak and of this bloody wrack,
Pray for feet that are as fast as the four hoofs of the wind:
Cloudy Parnassus and the Fates thunder at his back.

That sacred crossing-place of lines upon Parnassus' head,
Lines that have run through North and South, and run through West
   and East,
That navel of the world bids all men search the mountain
   wood,
The solitary cavern, till they have found that infamous beast.

[CREON *enters from the house.*]
CREON   Fellow-citizens, having heard that King Oedipus accuses me of dreadful things, I come in my indignation. Does he think that he has suffered wrong from me in these present troubles, or anything that could lead to wrong, whether in word or deed? How can I live under blame like that? What life would be worth having if by you here, and by my nearest friends, called a traitor through the town?

CHORUS   He said it in anger, and not from his heart out.

CREON   He said it was I put up the seer to speak those falsehoods.

CHORUS   Such things were said.

CREON   And had he his right mind saying it?

CHORUS   I do not know—I do not know what my masters do.

[OEDIPUS *enters.*]

OEDIP.   What brought you here? Have you a face so brazen that you come to my house—you, the proved assassin of its master—the certain robber of my crown? Come, tell me in the face of the gods what cowardice, or folly, did you discover in me that you plotted this? Did you think that I would not see what you were at till you had crept upon me, or seeing it would not ward it off? What madness to seek a throne, having neither friends nor followers!

CREON   Now, listen, hear my answer, and then you may with knowledge judge between us.

OEDIP.   You are plausible, but waste words now that I know you.

CREON   Hear what I have to say. I can explain it all.

OEDIP.   One thing you will not explain away—that you are my enemy.

CREON   You are a fool to imagine that senseless stubbornness sits well upon you.

OEDIP.   And you to imagine that you can wrong a kinsman and escape the penalty.

CREON   That is justly said, I grant you; but what is this wrong that you complain of?

OEDIP.   Did you advise, or not, that I should send for that notorious prophet?

CREON   And I am of the same mind still.

OEDIP.   How long is it, then, since Laius—

CREON   What, what about him?

OEDIP.   Since Laius was killed by an unknown hand?

CREON   That was many years ago.

OEDIP.   Was this prophet at his trade in those days?

CREON   Yes; skilled as now and in equal honor.

OEDIP.   Did he ever speak of me?

CREON   Never certainly when I was within earshot.

OEDIP.   And did you inquire into the murder?

CREON   We did inquire but learnt nothing.

OEDIP.   And why did he not tell out his story then?

CREON   I do not know. When I know nothing I say nothing.

OEDIP.   This much at least you know and can say out.

CREON   What is that? If I know it I will say it.

OEDIP.   That if he had not consulted you he would never have said that it was I who killed Laius.

CREON   You know best what he said; but now, question for question.

OEDIP.   Question your fill—I cannot be proved guilty of that blood.

CREON   Answer me then. Are you not married to my sister?

OEDIP.   That cannot be denied.

CREON   And do you not rule as she does? And with a like power?

OEDIP.   I give her all she asks for.

CREON   And am not I the equal of you both?

OEDIP.   Yes: and that is why you are so false a friend.

CREON   Not so; reason this out as I reason it, and first weigh this: who would prefer to lie awake amid terrors rather than to sleep in peace, granting that his power is equal in both cases? Neither I nor any sober-minded man. You give me what I ask and let me do what I want, but were I King I would have to do things I did not want to do. Is not influence and no trouble with it better than any throne, am I such a fool as to hunger after unprofitable honors? Now all are glad to see me, everyone wishes me well, all that want a favor from you ask speech of me—finding in that their hope. Why should I give up these things and take those? No wise mind is treacherous. I am no contriver of plots, and if another took to them he would not come to me for help. And in proof of this go to the Pythian Oracle, and ask if I have truly told what the gods said: and after that, if you have found that I have plotted with the Soothsayer, take me and kill me; not by the sentence of one mouth only—but of two mouths, yours and my own. But do not condemn me in a corner, upon some fancy and without proof. What right have you to declare a good man bad or a bad good? It is as bad a thing to cast off a true friend as it is for a man to cast away his own life—but you will learn these things with certainty when the time comes; for time alone shows a just man; though a day can show a knave.

CHORUS   King! He has spoken well, he gives himself time to think; a headlong talker does not know what he is saying.

OEDIP.   The plotter is at his work, and I must counterplot headlong, or he will get his ends and I miss mine.

CREON   What will you do then? Drive me from the land?

OEDIP.   Not so; I do not desire your banishment—but your death.

CREON   You are not sane.

OEDIP.   I am sane at least in my own interest.

CREON   You should be in mine also.

OEDIP.   No, for you are false.

CREON   But if you understand nothing?

OEDIP.   Yet I must rule.

CREON   Not if you rule badly.

OEDIP.   Hear him, O Thebes!

CREON   Thebes is for me also, not for you alone.

CHORUS   Cease, princes: I see Jocasta coming out of the house; she comes just in time to quench the quarrel.

[JOCASTA *enters.*]

JOCAS.   Unhappy men! Why have you made this crazy uproar? Are you not ashamed to quarrel about your own affairs when the whole country is in trouble? Go back into the palace, Oedipus, and you Creon, to your own house. Stop making all this noise about some petty thing.

CREON   Your husband is about to kill me—or to drive me from the land of my fathers.

OEDIP.   Yes: for I have convicted him of treachery against me.

CREON   Now may I perish accursed if I have done such a thing!

JOCAS.   For God's love believe it, Oedipus. First, for the sake of his oath, and then for my sake, and for the sake of these people here.

CHORUS   [all]. King, do what she asks.

OEDIP.   What would you have me do?

CHORUS   Not to make a dishonorable charge, with no more evidence than rumor, against a friend who has bound himself with an oath.

OEDIP.   Do you desire my exile or my death?

CHORUS   No, by Helios, by the first of all the gods, may I die abandoned by Heaven and earth if I have that thought! What breaks my heart is that our public griefs should be increased by your quarrels.

OEDIP.   Then let him go, though I am doomed thereby to death or to be thrust dishonored from the land; it is your lips, not his, that move me to compassion; wherever he goes my hatred follows him.

CREON   You are as sullen in yielding as you were vehement in anger, but such natures are their own heaviest burden.

OEDIP.   Why will you not leave me in peace and begone?

CREON   I will go away; what is your hatred to me? In the eyes of all here I am a just man.

[*He goes.*]

CHORUS   Lady, why do you not take your man in to the house?

JOCAS.   I will do so when I have learnt what has happened.

CHORUS   The half of it was blind suspicion bred of talk; the rest the wounds left by injustice.

JOCAS.   It was on both sides?

CHORUS   Yes.

JOCAS.   What was it?

CHORUS   Our land is vexed enough. Let the thing alone now that it is over.

[*Exit leader of* CHORUS.]

JOCAS.   In the name of the gods, King, what put you in this anger?

OEDIP.   I will tell you; for I honor you more than these men do. The cause is Creon and his plots against me.

JOCAS.   Speak on, if you can tell clearly how this quarrel arose.

OEDIP.   He says that I am guilty of the blood of Laius.

JOCAS.   On his own knowledge, or on hearsay?

OEDIP.   He has made a rascal of a seer his mouthpiece.

JOCAS.   Do not fear that there is truth in what he says. Listen to me, and learn to your comfort that nothing born of woman can know what is to come. I will give you proof of that. An oracle came to Laius once, I will not say from Phoebus, but from his ministers, that he was doomed to die by the hand of his own child sprung from him and me. When his child was but three days old, Laius bound its feet together and had it thrown by sure hands upon a trackless mountain; and when Laius was murdered at the place where three highways meet, it was, or so at least the rumor says, by foreign robbers. So Appollo did not bring it about that the child should kill its father, nor did Laius die in the dreadful way he feared by his child's hand. Yet that was how the message of the seers mapped out the future. Pay no attention to such things. What the God would show he will need no help to show it, but bring it to light himself.

OEDIP.   What restlessness of soul, lady, has come upon me since I heard you speak, what a tumult of the mind!

JOCAS.   What is this new anxiety? What has startled you?

OEDIP.   You said that Laius was killed where three highways meet.

JOCAS.   Yes: that was the story.

OEDIP.   And where is the place?

JOCAS.   In Phocis where the road divides branching off to Delphi and to Daulis.

OEDIP.   And when did it happen? How many years ago?

JOCAS. News was published in this town just before you came into power.

OEDIP. O Zeus! What have you planned to do unto me?

JOCAS. He was tall; the silver had just come into his hair; and in shape not greatly unlike to you.

OEDIP. Unhappy that I am! It seems that I have laid a dreadful curse upon myself, and did not know it.

JOCAS. What do you say? I tremble when I look on you, my King.

OEDIP. And I have a misgiving that the seer can see indeed. But I will know it all more clearly; if you tell me one thing more.

JOCAS. Indeed, though I tremble I will answer whatever you ask.

OEDIP. Had he but a small troop with him; or did he travel like a great man with many followers?

JOCAS. There were but five in all—one of them a herald; and there was one carriage with Laius in it.

OEDIP. Alas! It is now clear indeed. Who was it brought the news, lady?

JOCAS. A servant—the one survivor.

OEDIP. Is he by chance in the house now?

JOCAS. No; for when he found you reigning instead of Laius he besought me, his hand clasped in mine, to send him to the fields among the cattle that he might be far from the sight of this town; and I sent him. He was a worthy man for a slave and might have asked a bigger thing.

OEDIP. I would have him return to us without delay.

JOCAS. Oedipus, it is easy. But why do you ask this?

OEDIP. I fear that I have said too much, and therefore I would question him.

JOCAS. He shall come, but I too have a right to know what lies so heavy upon your heart, my King.

OEDIP. Yes: and it shall not be kept from you now that my fear has grown so heavy. Nobody is more to me than you, nobody has the same right to learn my good or evil luck. My father was Polybus of Corinth, my mother the Dorian Merope, and I was held the foremost man in all that town until a thing happened—a thing to startle a man, though not to make him angry as it made me. We were sitting at the table, and a man who had drunk too much cried out that I was not my father's son—and I, though angry, restrained my anger for that day; but the next day went to my father and my mother and questioned them. They were indignant at the taunt and that comforted me—and yet the man's words rankled, for they had spread a rumor through the town. Without consulting my father or my mother I went to Delphi, but Phoebus told me nothing of the thing for which I came, but much of other things—things of sorrow and of terror: that I should live in incest with my mother, and beget a brood that men would shudder to look upon; that I should be my father's murderer. Hearing those words I fled out of Corinth, and from that day have but known where it lies when I have found its direction by the stars. I sought where I might escape those infamous things—the doom that was laid upon me. I came in my flight to that very spot where you tell me this king perished. Now, lady, I will tell you the truth. When I had come close up to those three roads, I came upon a herald, and a man like him you have described seated in a carriage. The man who held the reins and the old man himself would not give me room, but thought to force me from the path, and I struck the driver in my anger. The old man, seeing what I had done, waited till I was passing him and then struck me upon the head. I paid him back in full, for I knocked him out of the carriage with a blow of my stick. He rolled on his back, and after that I killed them all. If this stranger were indeed Laius, is there a more miserable man in the world than the man before you? Is there a man more hated of Heaven? No stranger, no citizen, may receive him into his house, not a soul may speak to him, and no mouth but my own mouth has laid this curse upon me. Am I not wretched? May I be swept from this world before I have endured this doom!

CHORUS   These things, O King, fill us with terror; yet hope till you speak with him that saw the deed, and have learnt all.

OEDIP.   Till I have learnt all, I may hope. I await the man that is coming from the pastures.

JOCAS.   What is it that you hope to learn?

OEDIP.   I will tell you. If his tale agrees with yours, then I am clear.

JOCAS.   What tale of mine?

OEDIP.   He told you that Laius met his death from robbers; if he keeps to that tale now and speaks of several slayers, I am not the slayer. But if he says one lonely wayfarer, then beyond a doubt the scale dips to me.

JOCAS.   Be certain of this much at least, his first tale was of robbers. He cannot revoke that tale—the city heard it and not I alone. Yet, if he should somewhat change his story, King, at least he cannot make the murder of Laius square with prophecy; for Loxias plainly said of Laius that he would die by the hand of my child. That poor innocent did not kill him, for it died before him. Therefore from this out I would not, for all divination can do, so much as look to my right hand or to my left hand, or fear at all.

OEDIP.   You have judged well; and yet for all that, send and bring this peasant to me.

JOCAS.   I will send without delay. I will do all that you would have of me—but let us come into the house.

> [*They go into the house.*]

CHORUS   For this one thing above all I would be praised as a man,
That in my words and my deeds I have kept those laws in
    mind
Olympian Zeus, and that high clear Empyrean,
Fashioned, and not some man or people of mankind,
Even those sacred laws nor age nor sleep can blind.

A man becomes a tyrant out of insolence,
He climbs and climbs, until all people call him great,
He seems upon the summit, and God flings him thence;
Yet an ambitious man may lift up a whole State,
And in his death be blessed, in his life fortunate.

And all men honor such; but should a man forget
The holy images, the Delphian Sibyl's trance,
And the world's navel-stone, and not be punished for it
And seem most fortunate, or even blessed perchance,
Why should we honor the gods, or join the sacred dance?

> [JOCASTA *enters from the palace.*]

JOCAS.   It has come into my head, citizens of Thebes, to visit every altar of the Gods, a wreath in my hand and a dish of incense. For all manner of alarms trouble the soul of Oedipus, who instead of weighing new oracles by old, like a man of sense, is at the mercy of every mouth that speaks terror. Seeing that my words are nothing to him, I cry to you, Lycian Apollo, whose altar is the first I meet: I come, a suppliant, bearing symbols of prayer; O, make us clean, for now we are all afraid, seeing him afraid, even as they who see the helmsman afraid.

[Enter MESSENGER.]

MESS.   May I learn from you, stranger, where is the home of King Oedipus? Or better still, tell me where he himself is, if you know.

CHORUS   This is his house, and he himself, stranger, is within it, and this lady is the mother of his children.

MESS.   Then I call a blessing upon her, seeing what man she has married.

JOCAS.   May God reward those words with a like blessing, stranger! But what have you come to seek or to tell?

MESS.   Good news for your house, Lady, and for your husband.

JOCAS.   What news? From whence have you come?

MESS.   From Corinth, and you will rejoice at the message I am about to give you; yet, maybe, it will grieve you.

JOCAS.   What is it? How can it have this double power?

MESS.   The people of Corinth, they say, will take him for king.

JOCAS.   How then? Is old Polybus no longer on the throne?

MESS.   No. He is in his tomb.

JOCAS.   What do you say? Is Polybus dead, old man?

MESS.   May I drop dead if it is not the truth.

JOCAS.   Away! Hurry to your master with this news, O oracle of the gods, where are you now? This is the man whom Oedipus feared and shunned lest he should murder him, and now this man has died a natural death, and not by the hand of Oedipus.

[Enter OEDIPUS.]

OEDIP.   Jocasta, dearest wife, why have you called me from the house?

JOCAS.   Listen to this man, and judge to what the oracles of the gods have come.

OEDIP.   And he—who may he be? And what news has he?

JOCAS.   He has come from Corinth to tell you that your father, Polybus, is dead.

OEDIP.   How, stranger? Let me have it from your own mouth.

MESS.   If I am to tell the story, the first thing is that he is dead and gone.

OEDIP.   By some sickness or by treachery?

MESS.   A little thing can bring the aged to their rest.

OEDIP.   Ah! He died, it seems, from sickness?

MESS.   Yes; and of old age.

OEDIP.   Alas! Alas! Why, indeed, my wife, should one look to that Pythian seer, or to the birds that scream above our heads? For they would have it that I was doomed to kill my father. And now he is dead—hid already beneath the earth. And here am I—who had no part in it, unless indeed he died from longing for me. If that were so, I may have caused his death; but Polybus has carried the oracles with him into Hades—the oracles as men have understood them—and they are worth nothing.

JOCAS.   Did I not tell you so, long since?

OEDIP.   You did, but fear misled me.

JOCAS.   Put this trouble from you.

OEDIP.   Those bold words would sound better, were not my mother living. But as it is—I have some grounds for fear; yet you have said well.

JOCAS.   Yet your father's death is a sign that all is well.

OEDIP.   I know that: but I fear because of her who lives.

MESS.   Who is this woman who makes you afraid?

OEDIP.   Merope, old man, the wife of Polybus.

MESS.   What is there in her to make you afraid?

OEDIP.   A dreadful oracle sent from Heaven, stranger.

MESS.   Is it a secret, or can you speak it out?

OEDIP.   Loxias said that I was doomed to marry my own mother, and to shed my father's blood. For that reason I fled from my house in Corinth; and I did right, though there is great comfort in familiar faces.

MESS.   Was it indeed for that reason that you went into exile?

OEDIP.   I did not wish, old man, to shed my father's blood.

MESS.   King, have I not freed you from that fear?

OEDIP.   You shall be fittingly rewarded.

MESS.   Indeed, to tell the truth, it was for that I came; to bring you home
and be the better for it—

OEDIP.   No! I will never go to my parents' home.

MESS.   Ah, my son, it is plain enough, you do not know what you do.

OEDIP.   How, old man? For God's love, tell me.

MESS.   If for these reasons you shrink from going home.

OEDIP.   I am afraid lest Phoebus has spoken true.

MESS.   You are afraid of being made guilty through Merope?

OEDIP.   That is my constant fear.

MESS.   A vain fear.

OEDIP.   How so, if I was born of that father and mother?

MESS.   Because they were nothing to you in blood.

OEDIP.   What do you say? Was Polybus not my father?

MESS.   No more nor less than myself.

OEDIP.   How can my father be no more to me than you who are nothing
to me?

MESS.   He did not beget you any more than I.

OEDIP.   No? Then why did he call me his son?

MESS.   He took you as a gift from these hands of mine.

OEDIP.   How could he love so dearly what came from another's hands?

MESS.   He had been childless.

OEDIP.   If I am not your son, where did you get me?

MESS.   In a wooded valley of Cithaeron.

OEDIP.   What brought you wandering there?

MESS.   I was in charge of mountain sheep.

OEDIP.   A shepherd—a wandering, hired man.

MESS.   A hired man who came just in time.

OEDIP.   Just in time—had it come to that?

MESS.   Have not the cords left their marks upon your ankles?

OEDIP.   Yes, that is an old trouble.

MESS.   I took your feet out of the spancel.

OEDIP.   I have had those marks from the cradle.

MESS.   They have given you the name you bear.

OEDIP.   Tell me, for God's sake, was that deed my mother's or my father's?

MESS.   I do not know— he who gave you to me knows more of that than I.

OEDIP.   What? You had me from another? You did not chance on me yourself?

MESS.   No. Another shepherd gave you to me.

OEDIP.   Who was he? Can you tell me who he was?

MESS.   I think that he was said to be of Laius' household.

OEDIP.   The king who ruled this country long ago?

MESS.   The same—the man was herdsman in his service.

OEDIP.   Is he alive, that I might speak with him?

MESS.   You people of this country should know that.

OEDIP.   Is there any one here present who knows the herd he speaks of?

Any one who has seen him in the town pastures? The hour has come when all must be made clear.

CHORUS   I think he is the very herd you sent for but now; Jocasta can tell you better than I.

JOCAS.   Why ask about that man? Why think about him? Why waste a thought on what this man has said? What he has said is of no account.

OEDIP.   What, with a clue like that in my hands and fail to find out my birth?

JOCAS.   For God's sake, if you set any value upon your life, give up this search—my misery is enough.

OEDIP.   Though I be proved the son of a slave, yes, even of three generations of slaves, you cannot be made base-born.

JOCAS.   Yet, hear me, I implore you. Give up this search.

OEDIP.   I will not hear of anything but searching the whole thing out.

JOCAS.   I am only thinking of your good—I have advised you for the best.

OEDIP.   Your advice makes me impatient.

JOCAS.   May you never come to know who you are, unhappy man!

OEDIP.   Go, some one, bring the herdsman here—and let that woman glory in her noble blood.

JOCAS.   Alas, alas, miserable man! Miserable! That is all that I can call you now or for ever.

[*She goes out.*]

CHORUS   Why has the lady gone, Oedipus, in such a transport of despair? Out of this silence will burst a storm of sorrows.

OEDIP.   Let come what will. However lowly my origin I will discover it. That woman, with all a woman's pride, grows red with shame at my base birth. I think myself the child of Good Luck, and that the years are my foster-brothers. Sometimes they have set me up, and sometimes thrown me down, but he that has Good Luck for mother can suffer no dishonor. That is my origin, nothing can change it, so why should I renounce this search into my birth?

CHORUS   Oedipus' nurse, mountain of many a hidden glen,

Behonored among men;
A famous man, deep-thoughted, and his body strong;
Be honored in dance and song.
Who met in the hidden glen? Who let his fancy run
Upon nymph of Helicon?
Lord Pan or Lord Apollo or the mountain lord
By the Bacchantes adored?

OEDIP.   If I, who have never met the man, may venture to say so, I think that the herdsman we await approaches; his venerable age matches with this stranger's, and I recognize as servants of mine those who bring him. But you, if you have seen the man before, will know the man better than I.

CHORUS   Yes. I know the man who is coming; he was indeed in Laius' service, and is still the most trusted of the herdsmen.

OEDIP.   I ask you first, Corinthian stranger, is this the man you mean?

MESS.   He is the very man.

OEDIP.   Look at me, old man! Answer my questions. Were you once in Laius' service?

HERD.   I was: not a bought slave, but reared up in the house.

OEDIP.   What was your work—your manner of life?

HERD.   For the best part of my life I have tended flocks.

OEDIP.   Where, mainly?

HERD.   Cithaeron or its neighborhood.

OEDIP.   Do you remember meeting with this man there?

HERD.   What man do you mean?

OEDIP.   This man. Did you ever meet him?

HERD.   I cannot recall him to mind.

MESS.   No wonder in that, master; but I will bring back his memory. He and I lived side by side upon Cithaeron. I had but one flock and he had two. Three full half-years we lived there, from spring to autumn, and every winter I drove my flock to my own fold, while he drove his to the fold of Laius. Is that right? Was it not so?

HERD.   True enough; though it was long ago.

MESS.   Come, tell me now—do you remember giving me a boy to rear as my own foster-son?

HERD.   What are you saying? Why do you ask me that?

MESS.   Look at that man, my friend, he is the child you gave me.

HERD.   A plague upon you! Cannot you hold your tongue?

OEDIP.   Do not blame him, old man; your own words are more blamable.

HERD.   And how have I offended, master?

OEDIP.   In not telling of that boy he asks of.

HERD.   He speaks from ignorance, and does not know what he is saying.

OEDIP.   If you will not speak with a good grace you shall be made to speak.

HERD.   Do not hurt me for the love of God, I am an old man.

OEDIP.   Some one there, tie his hands behind his back.

HERD.   Alas! Wherefore! What more would you learn?

OEDIP.   Did you give this man the child he speaks of?

HERD.   I did: would I had died that day!

OEDIP.   Well, you may come to that unless you speak the truth.

HERD.   Much more am I lost if I speak it.

OEDIP.   What! Would the fellow make more delay?

HERD.   No, no. I said before that I gave it to him.

OEDIP.   Where did you come by it? Your own child, or another?

HERD.   It was not my own child—I had it from another.

OEDIP.   From any of those here? From what house?

HERD.   Do not ask any more, master; for the love of God do not ask.

OEDIP.   You are lost if I have to question you again.

HERD.   It was a child from the house of Laius.

OEDIP.   A slave? Or one of his own race?

HERD.   Alas! I am on the edge of dreadful words.

OEDIP.   And I of hearing: yet hear I must.

HERD.   It was said to have been his own child. But your lady within can tell you of these things best.

OEDIP.   How? It was she who gave it to you?

HERD.   Yes, King.

OEDIP.   To what end?

HERD.   That I should make away with it.

OEDIP.   Her own child?

HERD.   Yes: from fear of evil prophecies.

OEDIP.   What prophecies?

HERD.   That he should kill his father.

OEDIP.   Why, then, did you give him up to this old man?

HERD.   Through pity, master, believing that he would carry him to whatever land he had himself come from—but he saved him for dreadful misery; for if you are what this man says, you are the most miserable of all men.

OEDIP.   O! O! All brought to pass! All truth! Now O light, may I look my last upon you, having been found accursed in bloodshed, accursed in marriage, and in my coming into the world accursed!

[*He rushes into the palace.*]

CHORUS   What can the shadow-like generations of man attain
But build up a dazzling mockery of delight that under their
     touch dissolves again?
Oedipus seemed blessed, but there is no man blessed amongst
     men.

Oedipus overcame the woman-breasted Fate;
He seemed like a strong tower against Death and first among
    the fortunate;
He sat upon the ancient throne of Thebes, and all men called
    him great.

But, looking for a marriage-bed, he found the bed of his
    birth,
Tilled the field his father had tilled, cast seed into the same
    abounding earth;
Entered through the door that had sent him wailing forth.

Begetter and begot as one! How could that be hid?
What darkness cover up that marriage-bed? Time watches,
    he is eagle-eyed,
And all the works of man are known and every soul is tried.

Would you had never come to Thebes, nor to this house,
Nor riddled with the woman-breasted Fate, beaten off Death
    and succored us,
That I had never raised this song, heartbroken Oedipus!

                        [SECOND MESSENGER *coming from the house.*]
Friends and kinsmen of this house! What deeds must you look upon, what burden of sorrow bear, if true to race you still love the House of Labdacus. For not Ister nor Phasis could wash this house clean, so many misfortunes have been brought upon it, so many has it brought upon itself, and those misfortunes are always the worst that a man brings upon himself.

CHORUS   Great already are the misfortunes of this house, and you bring us a new tale.

S. MESS.   A short tale in the telling: Jocasta, our Queen, is dead.

CHORUS   Alas, miserable woman, how did she die?

S. MESS.   By her own hand. It cannot be as terrible to you as to one that saw it with his eyes, yet so far as words can serve, you shall see it. When she had come into the vestibule, she ran half crazed towards her marriage-bed, clutching at her hair with the fingers of both hands, and once within the chamber dashed the doors together behind her. Then called upon the name of Laius, long since dead, remembering that son who killed the father and upon the mother begot an accursed race. And wailed because of that marriage wherein she had borne a twofold race—husband by husband, children by her child. Then Oedipus with a shriek burst in and running here and there asked for a sword, asked where he would find the wife that was no wife but a mother who had borne his children and himself. Nobody answered him, we all stood dumb; but supernatural power helped him, for, with a dreadful shriek, as though beckoned, he sprang at the double doors, drove them in, burst the bolts out of their sockets, and ran into the room. There we saw the woman hanging in a swinging halter, and with a terrible cry he loosened the halter from her neck. When that unhappiest woman lay stretched upon the ground, we saw another dreadful sight. He dragged the golden brooches from her dress and lifting them struck them upon his eyeballs, crying out, 'You have looked enough upon those you ought never to have looked upon, failed long enough to know those that you should have known; henceforth you shall be dark.' He struck his eyes, not once, but many times, lifting his hands and speaking such or like words. The blood poured down and not with a few slow drops, but all at once over his beard in a dark shower as it were hail.

[*The* CHORUS *wails and he steps further on to the stage.*] Such evils have come forth from the deeds of those two and fallen not on one alone but upon husband and wife. They inherited much happiness, much good fortune; but today, ruin, shame, death, and loud crying, all evils that can be counted up, all, all are theirs.

CHORUS   Is he any quieter?

S. MESS.   He cries for some one to unbar the gates and to show to all the men of Thebes his father's murderer, his mother's—the unholy word must not be spoken. It is his purpose to cast himself out of the land that he may not bring all this house under his curse. But he has not the strength to do it. He must be supported and led away. The curtain is parting; you are going to look upon a sight which even those who shudder must pity.

[*Enter* OEDIPUS.]
OEDIP.   Woe, woe, is me! Miserable, miserable that I am! Where am I? Where am I going? Where am I cast away? Who hears my words?

CHORUS   Cast away indeed, dreadful to the sight of the eye, dreadful to the ear.

OEDIP.   Ah, friend, the only friend left to me, friend still faithful to the blind man! I know that you are there; blind though I am, I recognize your voice.

CHORUS   Where did you get the courage to put out your eyes? What unearthly power drove you to that?

OEDIP.   Apollo, friends, Apollo, but it was my own hand alone, wretched that I am, that quenched these eyes.

CHORUS   You were better dead than blind.

OEDIP.   No, it is better to be blind. What sight is there that could give me joy? How could I have looked into the face of my father when I came among the dead, aye, or on my miserable mother, since against them both I sinned such things that no halter can punish? And what to me this spectacle, town, statue, wall, and what to me this people, since I, thrice wretched, I, noblest of Theban men, have doomed myself to banishment, doomed myself when I commanded all to thrust out the unclean thing?

CHORUS   It had indeed been better if that herdsman had never taken your feet out of the spancel or brought you back to life.

OEDIP.   O three roads, O secret glen; O coppice and narrow way where three roads met; you that drank up the blood I spilt, the blood that was my own, my father's blood: remember what deeds I wrought for you to look upon, and then, when I had come hither, the new deeds that I wrought. O marriagebed that gave me birth and after that gave children to your child, creating an incestuous kindred of fathers, brothers, sons, wives, and mothers. Yes, all the shame and the uncleanness that I have wrought among men.

CHORUS   For all my pity I shudder and turn away.

OEDIP.   Come near, condescend to lay your hands upon a wretched man; listen, do not fear. My plague can touch no man but me. Hide me somewhere out of this land for God's sake, or kill me, or throw me into the sea where you shall never look upon me more.

[*Enter* CREON *and attendants.*]

CHORUS   Here Creon comes at a fit moment; you can ask of him what you will, help or counsel, for he is now in your place. He is King.

OEDIP.   What can I say to him? What can I claim, having been altogether unjust to him?

CREON   I have not come in mockery, Oedipus, nor to reproach you. Lead him in to the house as quickly as you can. Do not let him display his misery before strangers.

OEDIP.   I must obey, but first, since you have come in so noble a spirit, you will hear me.

CREON   Say what you will.

OEDIP.   I know that you will give her that lies within such a tomb as befits your own blood, but there is something more, Creon. My sons are men and can take care of themselves, but my daughters, my two unhappy daughters, that have ever eaten at my own table and shared my food, watch over my daughters, Creon. If it is lawful, let me touch them with my hands. Grant it, Prince, grant it, noble heart. I would believe, could I touch them, that I still saw them.

[ISMENE *and* ANTIGONE *are led in by attendants.*]
But do I hear them sobbing? Has Creon pitied me and sent my children, my darlings? Has he done this?

CREON   Yes, I ordered it, for I know how greatly you have always loved them.

OEDIP.   Then may you be blessed, and may Heaven be kinder to you than it has been to Me! My children, where are you? Come hither—hither—come to the hands of him whose mother was your mother; the hands that put out your father's eyes, nothing, seeing nothing, became your father by her that bore him. I weep when I think of the bitter life that men will make you live, and the days that are to come. Into what company dare you go, to what festival, but that you shall return home from it not sharing in the joys, but bathed in tears? When you are old enough to be married, what man dare face the reproach that must cling to you and to your children? What misery is there lacking? Your father killed his father, he begat you at the spring of his own being, offspring of her that bore him. That is the taunt that would be cast upon you and on the man that you should marry. That man is not alive; my children, you must wither away in barrenness. Ah, son of Menoeceus, listen. Seeing that you are the only father now left to them, for we their parents are lost, both of us lost, do not let them wander in beggary—are they not your own kindred?—do not let them sink down into my misery. No, pity them, seeing them utterly wretched in helpless childhood if you do not protect them. Show me that you promise, generous man, by touching me with your hand.

[CREON *touches him.*]
My children, there is much advice that I would give you were you but old enough to understand, but all I can do now is bid you pray that you may live wherever you are let live, and that your life be happier than your father's.

CREON   Enough of tears. Pass into the house.

OEDIP.   I will obey, though upon conditions.

CREON   Conditions?

OEDIP.   Banish me from this country. I know that nothing can destroy me, for I wait some incredible fate; yet cast me upon Cithaeron, chosen by my father and my mother for my tomb.

CREON   Only the gods can say yes or no to that.

OEDIP.   No, for I am hateful to the gods.

CREON   If that be so you will get your wish the quicker. They will banish that which they hate.

OEDIP.   Are you certain of that?

CREON   I would not say it if I did not mean it.

OEDIP.   Then it is time to lead me within.

CREON   Come, but let your children go.

OEDIP.   No, do not take them from me.

CREON   Do not seek to be master; you won the mastery but could not keep it to the end.

[*He leads* OEDIPUS *into the palace, followed by* ISMENE, ANTIGONE, *and attendants.*]
CHORUS   Make way for Oedipus. All people said,
'That is a fortunate man';
And now what storms are beating on his head!
Call no man fortunate that is not dead.
The dead are free from pain.

FOR FURTHER CONSIDERATION

Oedipus persistently struggles to define his identity, to discover his origins and trace the development of his self. He finds revealed at last a person who has violated strong taboos, and his deepest loyalties at that point stand divided. What opposing loyalties or commitments does Oedipus feel, and which does he choose at the cost of the others? Why is his choice tragic?

Herb Gardner (1934-   )

A successful writer of plays, screenplays, and short stories, Gardner excels with crisp dialogue and explorations of the self in combat with the stress of contemporary civilization.

A Thousand Clowns

ACT ONE

In complete darkness, before the curtain goes up, we hear the voice of Chuckles the Chipmunk.

CHUCKLES' VOICE *(intimately, softly)* Goshes and gollygoods, kidderoonies; now what're all us Chippermunkies gonna play first this mornin'?

CHORUS OF KIDS   Gonna play Chuckle-Chip Dancing.

CHUCKLES' VOICE   And with who?

CHORUS OF KIDS   With you!

CHUCKLES' VOICE *(louder)*   And who is me?

CHORUS OF KIDS *(screaming)* Chuckles the Chippermunkie! Rayyyyyyyyyyyyyyy.

The curtain goes up on this last screaming syllable, revealing MURRAY BURNS' *one-room apartment. The voices of Chuckles and the kids continue but are now coming from an ancient table-model T.V. set at the left. The set is facing away from the audience and is being watched by* NICHOLAS BURNS, *a twelve-year-old. The apartment is on the second floor of a brownstone on the lower West Side of Manhattan. It consists of one large, high-ceilinged room in which borrowed furniture rambles in no meaningful arrangement—some gaudy, some impractical, no matching pieces. It is obvious from* MURRAY BURNS' *apartment that he is a collector, though it is not entirely clear just what he is a collector of. All about the room, on the floor, on the coffee table, on dresser tops, is* MURRAY'S *collection: eighteen broken radios, some with interesting cathedral-style cabinets; over two dozen elaborately disabled clocks of different sizes, some of them on the wall; parts of eight Victrolas, mostly cabinets; a variety of hats, including a Prussian helmet and a deerstalker; a pirate pistol; a bugle; a megaphone; and stacks of magazines and books. It is somehow, though, a very comfortable-looking apartment. There is an alcove at the left, with a small bed, a child's desk and some bookshelves. This is* NICK'S *part of the place and it is very neat, ordered, organized, seeming almost to have nothing to do with the main room. There is a bathroom door at left below the small alcove. Right of the alcove are three large windows and a built-in window seat. A closed venetian blind covers all three windows. At center is a large, comfortable rumpled bed with an elaborate wooden headboard running up the wall almost to the ceiling. The headboard is loaded with clocks, radios, and two lamps. At right is the entrance door to the apartment. To the left of the door are two large office-style filing cabinets in which* MURRAY *keeps some of his clothes, and to the right is a bureau covered with knickknacks on which* MURRAY's *hats are hung. Downstage right is the kitchen door; to the left of it is a desk buried under papers, and built-in bookshelves stuffed with a jumble of books and nonsense. There is a closet to the left of the desk. A Morris chair and an armless swivel chair are on either side of a small table at right and there is a brightly colored beach chair at left in front of the windows.*

AT RISE: *It is eight-thirty on a Monday morning; it is rather dark, the only real light is a scattered haze from the television set. The chorus of kids is now singing the "Chuckles Song."* NICK *watches expressionlessly.*

CHORUS OF KIDS *(singing)*   Who's whitcha at—eight-thirty?
Whose face is so—so dirty?
Who's sparky—who's spunky?
Chip, Chip, Chip, Chip—Chippermunkie!

NICK *(quietly)*   Oh, this is terrible. This is rotten.

CHORUS OF KIDS   Who's always good—for funnin'? Whose scooter-bike—keeps runnin'?

*(*MURRAY *enters from the kitchen carrying a cup of coffee; he is in his mid-thirties. He is wearing shorts and an undershirt and is not quite awake yet.)*

MURRAY *(walking across to the bed)*   Get those kids outa here. *(Sits on the bed.)* Nick, what'd I tell you about bringing your friends in here this early in the morning?

NICK   It's not my friends; it's the T.V.

MURRAY   Play with your friends outside. Get those kids out of here. *(*NICK *turns the set off.* MURRAY *looks over at the front door, waves at it and shouts.)* Good. And none of you kids come back here till this afternoon.

NICK   It wasn't my friends. It was Chuckles the Chipmunk.

MURRAY *(sleepily)*   That's very comforting.

NICK *(brings a pack of cigarettes to* MURRAY*)*   Boy, it's a terrible program now. It was a much better show when you were writing it.

MURRAY   When Sandburg and Faulkner quit, I quit. What kind of a day is it outside?

NICK *(going to the kitchen)*   It's a Monday.

MURRAY   I mean warm or cold or sunny is what I mean.

NICK   I haven't been outside yet.

MURRAY *(he pulls the blind up revealing the windows; there is no change whatever in the lighting, the room remains dark. The windows have no view other than the gray blank wall of the building a few feet opposite)*   Ah, light. *(He leans out of the window, cranes his head around to look up at the sky.)* Can't see a thing. Not a thing. *(Pulls his head back in.)* No matter what time of day or what season, we got a permanent fixture out there; twilight in February.

NICK *(bringing the coffee pot out of the kitchen and filling MURRAY'S cup)*   You better call the weather record like always.

MURRAY   One morning I'll wake up and that damn building'll have fallen down into Seventh Avenue so I can see the weather. *(Picks up the phone; dialing.)* Using a machine to call up another machine. I do not enjoy the company of ghosts. *(Into the phone)* Hello, Weather Lady! Well, I'm just fine, and how is your nasal little self this morning? What's the weather? Uh-huh. That high? And the wind, which way does the wind blow this morning? Ah, good. Uh-huh, all the way to East Point and Block Island. Humidity? Very decent. Whoops, oh, there you go again. You simply *must* learn not to repeat yourself. I keep telling you every morning that once is enough. You'll never learn. *(Hangs up.)* Women seldom sense when they have become boring. *(Goes to the window again, leans out, raises his voice, shouting out of the window.)* Neighbors, I have an announcement for you. I have *never seen* such a collection of dirty windows. Now I want to see you all out there on the fire escape with your Mr. Clean bottles, and let's snap it up . . .

NICK   Gee, Murray, you gotta shout like that every morning?

MURRAY   It clears my head. *(After glancing around clock-filled apartment)* What time is it?

NICK   It's eight-forty.

MURRAY   Well, what're you doing here? Why aren't you in school?

NICK   It's a holiday. It's Irving R. Feldman's birthday, like you said.

MURRAY   Irving R. Feldman's birthday is my own personal national holiday. I did not open it up for the public. He is proprietor of perhaps the most distinguished kosher delicatessen in this neighborhood and as such I hold the day of his birth in reverence.

NICK   You said you weren't going to look for work today because it was Irving R. Feldman's birthday, so I figured I would celebrate too, a little.

MURRAY   Don't kid *me,* Nick, you know you're supposed to be in school. I thought you *liked* that damn genius' school—why the hell—

NICK   Well, I figured I'd better stay home today till you got up. *(Hesitantly)* There's something I gotta discuss with you. See, because it's this special school for big brains they watch you and take notes and make reports and smile at you a lot. And there's this psychologist who talks to you every week, each kid separately. He's the biggest smiler they got up there.

MURRAY   Because you got brains they figure you're nuts.

NICK   Anyway, we had Show and Tell time in Mrs. Zimmerman's class on Monday; and each kid in the class is supposed to tell about some trip he took and show pictures. Well, y'remember when I made you take me with you to the El Bambino Club over on Fifty-second?

MURRAY   Nick . . . you showed and you told.

NICK   Well, it turned out they're very square up at the Revere School. And sometimes in class, when we have our Wednesday Free-Association-Talk Period, I sometimes quote you on different opinions . . .

MURRAY   That wasn't a good idea.

NICK   Well, I didn't know they were such nervous people there. Murray, they're very nervous there. And then there was this composition I wrote in Creative Writing about the advantages of Unemployment Insurance.

MURRAY   Why did you write about that?

NICK   It was just on my mind. Then once they got my record out they started to notice what they call "significant data." Turns out they've been keeping this file on me for a long time, and checking with that Child Welfare place; same place you got those letters from.

MURRAY   I never answer letters from large organizations.

NICK   So, Murray . . . when they come over here, I figure we'd better . . .

MURRAY   When they come over here?

NICK   Yeah, this Child Welfare crowd, they want to take a look at our environment here.

MURRAY   Oh, that's charming. Why didn't you tell me about this before, Nick?

NICK   Well, y'know, the past coupla nights we couldn't get together.

MURRAY   That was unavoidable. You know when I have a lot of work you stay up at Mrs. Myers'.

NICK   *(pointing at the dresser)*   Murray; your work forgot her gloves last night.

MURRAY   That's very bright.

NICK   Anyway, for this Child Welfare crowd, I figure we better set up some kind of story before they get here.

MURRAY   You make it sound like a vice raid.

NICK   I mean, for one thing, you don't even have a job right now.

MURRAY   Look, you want me to put up some kind of front when they get here? O.K., I will. Don't worry, kid. I'll show 'em good.

NICK   I thought maybe you could at least look in the papers for a job, this morning before they get here. So we could tell them about your possibilities.

MURRAY   *(without much conviction)*   I look every day.

NICK   Couldn't I just read you from the *Times* again like last week? While you get dressed?

MURRAY   O.K., read me from the paper. *(He starts to get dressed.)*

NICK   And then, maybe, you'll take a shave?

MURRAY   All right, all right.

NICK *(picking up the Times from the swivel chair)*   This paper is three days old.

MURRAY   So what do you want me to do, bury it? Is it starting to rot or something? Read me from the paper.

NICK   But most of these jobs, somebody must have taken them. Look, I'll go down and get a newer—

MURRAY   We do *not* need a newer paper. All the really important jobs stay forever. Now start on the first page of Help-Wanted-Male and read me from the paper.

NICK   O.K. *(Puts on his glasses; reads aloud.)* "Administ, Exoppty. To ninety dollars." What's that?

MURRAY   Administrative Assistant, excellent opportunity. Nothing. Keep reading.

NICK   But ninety dollars would be ninety dollars more than nothing. Nothing is what you make now.

MURRAY   Have you ever considered being the first twelve-year-old boy in space?

NICK   But, ninety dollars . . .

MURRAY   *You* go be an administ, Exoppty. They *need* men like you. Read further.

NICK *(reading from the paper)*   "Versatile Junior, traffic manager, industrial representative organization. One hundred to one hundred twenty-five dollars. Call Mr. Shiffman."

MURRAY *(picks up the cardboard from his shirt collar and talks into it)*   Hello, Mr. Shiffman? I read your name in the New York *Times,* so I know you must be real. My name is Mandrake the Magician. I am a versatile Junior and I would like to manage your traffic for you. You see, sir, it has long been my ambition to work in a pointless job, with no future and a cretin like you as my boss . . .

NICK   But, Murray, it says "one hundred twenty-five dollars," that's a lot of . . .

MURRAY   Just read the ads. No editorial comment or personal recommendations. When I need your advice, I'll ask for it. Out of the mouths of babes comes drooling.

NICK   You said that last week. Murray, you don't want a job is the whole thing.

MURRAY   Would you just concentrate on being a child? Because I find your imitation of an adult hopelessly inadequate.

NICK   You want to be your own boss, but the trouble with that is you don't pay yourself anything. *(NICK decides that what he has just said is very funny. He laughs.)* Hey—you don't pay yourself anything—that's a good line—I gotta remember that.

MURRAY   That's what *you* said last week.

NICK   Look, Murray. *(He puts the paper down and stands up.)* Can I speak to you man to man?

MURRAY   That was cute about a year ago, buddy, but that line has got to go.

NICK *(takes off his glasses)*   Murray, I am upset. For me as an actual child the way you live in this house and we live is a dangerous thing for my later life when I become an actual person. An unemployed person like you are for so many months is bad for you as the person involved and is definitely bad for me who he lives with in the same house where the rent isn't paid for months sometimes. And I wish you would get a job, Murray. Please.

(MURRAY tries to control himself but cannot hide his laughter; he sees that NICK is offended by this and tries to stop. NICK walks away from him, goes to his alcove.)

MURRAY *(goes to NICK in the alcove)*   Kid, I know. I'm sorry. You're right. You are. This *is* terrible.

NICK   You're not kidding.

MURRAY   Nick.

NICK   Yeah?

MURRAY   Nick, y'know when I said I was looking for work last week? *(Somewhat ashamed)* Well, I went to the movies. Every day. In the afternoon.

NICK   *Murray,* you mean you really . . .

MURRAY   Now don't give me any of that indignant crap. I happen to be admitting something to you, and it is bad enough I should have to discuss my adult problems with a grotesque cherub, without you giving me dirty looks on top of it. Swell crowd in the movies on a weekday working afternoon. Nobody sits next to anybody, everybody there figures that evervbody else is a creep; and *all* of them are right. *(Suddenly smiling, taking* NICK'S *arm, trying to change the subject)* Have you ever been to the top of the Empire State Building?

NICK   Yes. Six times. With you. In November.

MURRAY   Oh, really? Have you ever been to the Statue of Liberty?

NICK   No.

MURRAY   Today is Irving R. Feldman's birthday. We will go to the top of the Statue of Liberty and watch the *Queen Elizabeth* come in, full of those tired, poor, huddled masses yearning to breath free.

NICK   Murray, why did you go to the movies in the middle of the afternoon when you said you were looking for work?

MURRAY   There's a window right in her navel, we will look out and see . . .

NICK   What is it? Were you very tired, or what?

MURRAY*(sits down in his chair)*   See, last week I was going to check with Uncle Arnie and some of the other agents about writing for some of the new T.V. shows. I was on the subway, on my way there, and I got off at Forty-second Street and went to the movies. *(He leans back in his chair, lights a cigarette;* NICK *sits opposite him on the bed.)* There are eleven movie houses on that street, Nick. It is Movieland. It breathes that seductive, carpety, minty air of the inside of movie houses. Almost as irresistible for me as pastrami. Now, there is the big question as you approach the box office, with the sun shining right down the middle of a working day, whether everybody going in is as embarrassed as you are. But once you are past the awkward stage, and have gotten your ticket torn by the old man inside, all doubts just go away. Because it is dark. And inside it is such a scene as to fracture the imagination of even a nut like yourself, Nick, because inside it is lovely and a little damp and nobody can see you, and the dialogue is falling like rain on a roof and you are sitting deep in front of a roaring, color, Cinemascope, stereophonic, nerve-cooling, heart-warming, spine-softening, perfect-happy-ending pic-ture show and it is Peacefulville, U.S.A. There are men there with neat mustaches who have shaved, and shined their shoes and put on a tie even, to come and sit alone in the movies. And there are near-sighted cute pink ladies who eat secret caramels; and very old men who sleep; and the *ushers;* buddy, you are not kidding *these* boys. They know you are not there because you are waiting for a train, or you are on a vacation, or you work a night job. They know you are there to *see* the *movie.* It is the business and the purpose of your day, and these boys give you their sneaky smile to show you that they know. *(Depressed by his own words; quietly, almost to himself)* Now the moral question for me here, is this: When one is faced with life in the bare-assed, job-hunting raw on the one hand, and eleven fifty-cent double features on the other, what is the mature, sensible, and mentally healthy step to take? *(He is slumped in his chair now.)*

NICK *(seeing MURRAY'S depression; softly, with concern)* What's wrong, Murray?

MURRAY *(walks slowly to the window, leans against the wall, looks sadly out of the window; speaks quietly)* I don't know. I'm not sure.

NICK   Hey, Murray, you all right . . .? *(He goes to MURRAY touches his arm. Then smiling suddenly in an attempt to cheer him)* Murray, lets go to the Statue of Liberty.

(MURRAY turns, laughs in agreement, and NICK starts for his jacket while MURRAY puts his binoculars around his neck and begins putting on his jacket. The doorbell rings. NICK looks at MURRAY, then goes to answer it. NICK is holding the front door only part-way open, hesitating to let in two people we now see standing outside in the hall. They are ALBERT AMUNDSON and SANDRA MARKOWITZ. ALBERT, graduate of N.Y.U.'s School of Social Work, is a middle-aged man of twenty-eight, SANDRA, though a pretty girl of twenty-five, wears clothes obviously more suited to a much older woman. ALBERT carries a small briefcase and SANDRA carries two manila file envelopes and a gigantic handbag.)

ALBERT   Hello, young man, I am Mr. Amundson, this is Miss Markowitz. We would like to speak to your uncle.

NICK *(still not opening the door all the way)*   Well, I don't know if . . .

ALBERT   Isn't he in?

MURRAY   Hello.

ALBERT   How do you do, Mr. Burns. Miss Markowitz and I are a Social Service unit assigned to the New York Bureau of Child Welfare. We have been asked by the Bureau to—May we come in?

MURRAY   Certainly.

(NICK *opens the door all the way, letting them both into the main room.*)

ALBERT   We, Miss Markowitz and I, have been asked by the B.C.W. to investigate and examine certain pupils of the Revere School. There is certain information which the school and the city would like to have, regarding young Nicholas.

MURRAY   Sit down, Miss Markowitz, please. Mr. Amundson. I'll just get rid of these things.

(MURRAY *takes pants, shirts, a bugle, a clock, a yoyo, a half-empty bag of peanuts and an ashtray off the chairs, and with one sweeping movement puts all of them on the bed. The three of them take seats around the coffee table,* NICK *standing nervously off to one side.*)

ALBERT   I'd like to explain just why we are here, Mr. Burns . . .

NICK   Would anybody like some coffee?

ALBERT   Why, thank you, Nicholas. Miss Markowitz?

SANDRA   Yes, thank you.

NICK *(whispering to* MURRAY *on his way to the kitchen)*   Watch it.

ALBERT *(smiling politely)*   It might be best, Mr. Burns, for the child if perhaps you sent him downstairs to play or something, while we have our discussion. Your case is . . .

MURRAY   Our "case." I had no idea we were a "case."

ALBERT   We do have a file on certain students at Revere.

MURRAY   So we're on file somewhere. Are we a great big, fat file, or a li'l teeny file?

ALBERT   Due to the fact that you have chosen not to answer our letters and several of our phone calls, there are many areas in which the file is incomplete, several questions—Mr. Burns, it might be better if the child went outside . . .

MURRAY   You gonna talk dirty?

ALBERT   It would be more advisable for the child not to be present, since Miss Markowitz, who will be discussing the psychological area . . . that is, we will be discussing certain matters which . . .

NICK *(from the kitchen).*   Cream and sugar for everybody?

ALBERT *(to the kitchen)*   Yes, Nicholas. *(To* MURRAY *again)* Mr. Burns, it's going to be awkward, with the child present, to . . .

MURRAY *(to* SANDRA*)*   Miss Markowitz, may I know your first name?

SANDRA   Sandra.

MURRAY   And you are the psychologist part of this team, Sandy?

SANDRA   That's right, Mr. Burns.

MURRAY *(to* ALBERT*)*   And you, I take it, are the brawn of the outfit?

ALBERT   Perhaps I should explain. Mr. Burns, that the Social Service teams which serve Revere School are a carefully planned balance of Social Case Worker, such as myself, and Psychological Social Work-er, such as Miss Markowitz, or, actually, *Dr.* Markowitz. *(*NICK *enters from the kitchen with four cups, gives one each to* ALBERT, SANDRA, MURRAY; *keeps one for himself.)* Mr. Burns, it is not easy to define those elements, those influences and problems which go into the make-up of a young boy.

MURRAY   I thought it was just frogs and snails and puppy dogs' tails.

ALBERT *(using once again his polite smile)*   I appreciate the infor-mality with which you approach this meeting, Mr. Burns, but on the more serious side, if I may, Miss Markowitz and I have a few matters . . .

NICK   Is the coffee any good?

ALBERT   Yes, very good. Thank you, Nicholas.

SANDRA   Very nice, Nicholas. *(She sees the cup in* NICK'S *hand, speaks with professional interest.)* Are you drinking coffee, Nicholas? Don't you think it would be better if . . .

NICK   No. Milk. I like to drink it from a cup.

MURRAY *(to* SANDRA, *smiling)*   Now aren't you ashamed of your-self?

ALBERT *(taking a rather large file out of his brief case)* Now, to plunge right in here . . .

MURRAY Sometimes I put his milk in a shot glass. Better for getting him to drink it than adding chocolate syrup.

SANDRA *(firmly)* Mr. Burns, Mr. Amundson and I have several cases to examine today, and we would appreciate a certain amount of cooperation . . .

MURRAY *(to NICK)* East Bronx, Mosholu Parkway.

NICK *(looks at SANDRA, then to MURRAY)* With a couple of years in maybe Massachusetts.

MURRAY No Massachusetts at all. Complete Bronx.

SANDRA I don't understand what . . .

MURRAY *(sitting on the beach chair)* Oh, excuse me. Nick and I are merely testing our sense of voice and accent. Nick insists he's better at it than I am.

SANDRA *(smiling)* As a matter of fact, the Bronx is right, but it's Grand Concourse.

MURRAY The Massachusetts thing, way off, right?

SANDRA Actually I took my graduate work with a professor, a man with a very strong New England accent, who could very well've influenced my speech. Nick is quite right.

NICK *(proudly)* Thank you, lady.

SANDRA You certainly have a fine ear for sound, Nick. Do you and your uncle play many of these sorts of games together?

NICK Oh, yes. We play many wholesome and constructive-type games together.

MURRAY You're a big phony, Nick. Miss Markowitz has beautiful hazel eyes that have read many case histories and are ever watchful, and even clever little boys are not going to snow her. The lady is here for the facts.

ALBERT Quite so, Mr. Burns. But facts alone cannot complete our examination *(He takes out a pen, opens to a blank page in the file.)* We wish to understand . . .

NICK *(to* SANDRA, *showing off for her)*   Jersey City, maybe Newark. And . . . a little bit of Chicago.

MURRAY   Uh-huh. Think you've hit it, Nick.

SANDRA   That's really quite remarkable. Albert—Mr. Amundson *is* from New Jersey, and he went to Chicago University for several . . .

ALBERT *(firmly)*   This is really quite beside the point, Sandra . . .

SANDRA   I just think it's quite remarkable, Albert, the boy's ability to . . .

ALBERT *(purposely interrupting her)*   Suppose I just plunge right in here, before Dr. Markowitz begins her part of the interview . . .

(There is a noise at the front door and ARNOLD BURNS *enters. He is carrying a medium-sized grocery delivery carton filled with a variety of fruit. He makes a rather incongruous delivery boy, in that he is in his early forties and dressed in expensive, distinguished clothes, top coat, and hat. He is* MURRAY'S *older brother, and his agent. It is obvious in the way he enters and automatically sets the delivery carton down on the desk that this is a daily ritual enacted at this same time every day and in this same manner.* MURRAY *does not even look up to greet him and* NICK *makes some casually mumbled greeting in his direction.)*

ARNOLD   The honeydew melon's in season again but not really ripe yet so . . .

(He turns, sees that there are strangers there.)   Oh, sorry. Didn't know you had company . . . *(Turns, goes to the door.)* See you Nick.

NICK   Yeah, see you, Uncle Arnie. *(*ARNOLD *exits.)*

ALBERT *(looking at the door)*   There is somebody else living here with you?

MURRAY   No. That's just my brother Arnold. He brings fruit every morning on his way to the office. He's a fruit nut.

ALBERT   I see here in the file that our research team spoke to your brother; your agent, I believe. We also called the people at your last business address, N.B.C. . . .

MURRAY *(rising)* You really do a lot of that stuff, calling people, going into my personal . . .

ALBERT You've refused for quite some time, Mr. Burns, to answer any of our regular inquiries. We understand that you have been unemployed at this point for nearly five months.

NICK *(to* ALBERT*)* He has an excellent opportunity to be an administrative assistant . . .

ALBERT *(pressing forward)* Other than your activities as free-lance script writer, I understand that you wrote regularly for an N.B.C. program for several years.

MURRAY I was chief writer for Leo Herman, better known as Chuckles the Chipmunk, friend of the young'uns, and seller of Chuckle-Chips, the potato chips your friend 'Chuckles the Chipmunk eats and chuckles over.

ALBERT And the circumstances under which you left the employ of . . .

MURRAY I quit.

ALBERT You felt that this was not the work you . . .

MURRAY I felt that I was not reaching all the boys and girls out there in Televisionland. Actually it was not so much that I wasn't reaching the boys and girls, but the boys and girls were starting to reach *me*. Six months ago, a perfectly adult bartender asked me if I wanted an onion in my martini, and I said, "Gosh n'gollies, you betcha." I knew it was time to quit.

ALBERT May I ask if this is a pattern; that is, in the past, has there been much shifting of position?

MURRAY I *always* take an onion in my martini. This is a constant and unswerving . . .

*(*NICK, *concerned with* MURRAY'S *behavior, goes toward him in an attempt to quiet him down.)*

SANDRA *(firmly, standing)* Mr. Burns. Perhaps you are not aware of just how serious your situation is. This entire matter is a subject of intense interest to the B.C.W. The circumstances of this child's environment, the danger of . . .

ALBERT   Our investigation, Mr. Burns, is the result of what the Bureau considers to be almost an emergency case.

NICK   He just likes to kid around, lady. But, see, we really got a great environment here . . .

MURRAY *(to* NICK*)*   Relax, kid. *(To* ALBERT *and* SANDRA*)* Look, people, I'm sorry. Let's get back to the questions.

SANDRA   Fine. Nick, suppose you and I have a little chat right here.

NICK *(as he sits down next to her)*   Fine. I was gonna suggest that myself.

SANDRA   Nick, I bet you love to come home when you've been out playing and you get tired. You say to yourself, "Gee, I'd like to go home now."

NICK   Sure, right. And I'm happy here. Boy, if you think I'm happy now, you should see me when I'm *really* happy.

MURRAY *(to* SANDRA, *sympathetically)*   He's on to you, honey. You're gonna have to be a lot foxier than that . . .

SANDRA   And I'm sure that you and your uncle have a great deal of fun together.

NICK   It's not *all* laughs.

SANDRA   Oh, I'm sure there are times when the fun stops and you have nice talks and your uncle teaches you things, helps you to . . .

NICK   I can do a great Peter Lorre imitation. Murray taught me.

ALBERT   Nicky, what Miss Markowitz means, is that you and your uncle must sometimes . . .

NICK *(in the voice of Peter Lorre, a rather good imitation)*   You can't hang me . . . I didn't do it, I tell you . . . that's not my knife . . . I am innocent . . . it's all a mistake . . .

*(*MURRAY *beams, smiles proudly during imitation.)*

ALBERT   Nicky, that's not what we meant, we . . .

MURRAY   What's the trouble? That happens to be a very good imitation.

ALBERT   Perhaps; but we are trying to . . .

MURRAY   Can *you* imitate Peter Lorre?

NICK *(confidentially, to* SANDRA*)*   I can do a pretty good James Cagney; I mean it's not fantastic like my Peter Lorre, but it . . .

ALBERT *(raising his voice a bit, somewhat commanding)*   Nicholas, please. Try to pay attention. Now if I may proceed to . . .

SANDRA *(aside, to* ALBERT, *somewhat annoyed with him)*   Albert, if you'll just let me handle this area. *(Then, to* NICK*)* Nick, let's talk about games. O.K.?

NICK   O.K.

SANDRA   Now, what kind of games do you like the best?

NICK   Mostly I like educational games and things like that. Murray gets me to develop my natural inquiring mind.

SANDRA   I wonder, do you have any favorite games or toys you'd like to show me? Some plaything that is just the most favorite one of all?

NICK   I just now threw away my collection of *National Geographics* and other educational-type magazines I had a whole collection of . . .

ALBERT   Nicky, Miss Markowitz is very interested in you and cares about you and everything. And if you brought out some of your favorite toys and playthings for her to see, I'm sure that she'd love them just as much as you do.

NICK   Well, there's Bubbles . . . *(He gets up to get it for them.)*

MURRAY   I don't think you'd be interested in seeing Bubbles . . .

*(*NICK *goes to a cardboard cartoon at the bureau, opens it, and takes out a twenty-four-inch-high plastic statue of a bare-chested hula girl. The statue is in bright colors and has an electric switch as its pedestal.* NICK *places the statue on the table between* ALBERT *and* SANDRA *and turns it on.)*

NICK   Bubbles is what you'd call an electric statue. *(The breasts of the statue light up and continue to blink on and off in spectacular fashion for the next part of the scene.* ALBERT *looks at the statue, begins busily going through the file on his lap.* SANDRA *regards the statue scientifically, professionally.* NICK *smiles proudly over his possession.)* It's got an electric battery timer in there that makes it go on and off like that.

SANDRA   Nick, is this your favorite toy?

NICK   Well, after a while it gets pretty boring. But it's a swell gimmick. There was another one in the store that was even better. . . .

MURRAY   Anybody want orange juice or toast or anything?

SANDRA   Nick, tell me . . . do you like best the fact that the chest of the lady lights up?

NICK   Well, you got to admit, you don't see boobies like that every day. You want to see the effect when the lights are out? When the room is dark?

SANDRA   Tell me, Nick, is *that* what you like best about it, that you can be alone in the dark with it.

NICK   Well, I don't know. But in the dark they really knock your eye out.

(ALBERT is blinking nervously at the blinking lights of the statue.)

ALBERT *(with strenuous calm)*   Perhaps, don't you think we ought to switch it off, turn off the . . .

SANDRA   Nick, does Bubbles, does she in any way, does her face remind you at all of, oh, let me see, your mother, for example?

NICK *(he looks at the face of the statue)*   No. I mean, it's just a doll, it's not a statue of anybody I know. I got it in this store downtown.

SANDRA   Her chest, is that something which . . .

NICK *(smiling broadly)*   It's something all right, isn't it?

SANDRA   When you think of your mother, do you . . .

NICK   I don't think about her much.

SANDRA   But when you *do* think of her, do you remember her face best, or her *hands,* or . . .

NICK   I remember she has this terrific laugh. The kind of laugh that when she laughs it makes you laugh too. Of course, she overdoes that a lot.

SANDRA   I mean, physically, when you think of her, do you, well, when you see Bubbles, and Bubbles goes on and off like that . . .

MURRAY   Sandra, his mother's chest did not light up. Let's get that settled right now; mark it down in the file.

ALBERT *(nervously; pointing at the blinking statue)*   Nicky, I wonder if you would turn those off . . . I mean, turn *it* off, turn her off, unplug it . . .

(MURRAY turns the statue off, puts it back into the box.)

SANDRA   Nicky, when you bought this doll . . .

MURRAY   Sandy, why don't I save you a lot of time. Nick is a fairly bright kid and he knows that girls are *not* boys. Other than that his interest in ladies is confined right now to ones that light up or don't light up.

NICK   I mostly like to read books that are healthy, constructive, and extremely educational for a person.

MURRAY   Don't push it, Nick. He does not have any unusual fixations, Sandy. He is no more abnormally interested in your bust than Mr. Amundson is.

ALBERT   Mr. Burns, it is not necessary to . . .

MURRAY   Of course, I might be wrong about that.

ALBERT   Our interest in that doll . . .

MURRAY   You really *are* interested in that doll, Albert.

ALBERT   Our interest . . .

NICK *(to ALBERT)*   I'll sell it to you for two dollars. That's fifty cents less than I paid for it.

(SANDRA is unable to suppress her amusement and laughs happily.)

ALBERT *(quite annoyed with her)*   Sandra, I fail to see . . .

SANDRA *(controlling herself again, but still smiling)*   It's just that it was funny, Albert.

ALBERT *(taking command)*   Suppose I pursue, then, the psychological part of . . .

SANDRA *(bristling at him)*   Excuse me, Albert, I really do feel it would be better if I were to . . .

MURRAY   Albert, the lady was just laughing because something funny happened. That's actually the best thing to do under the circumstances.

ALBERT   Mr. Burns . . .

MURRAY   How would you all like to go to the Statue of Liberty? I have it on good authority from the Weather Lady that today is a beautiful day.

ALBERT   Is it at all possible, Mr. Burns, for you to stick to the point?

MURRAY   Albert, I bet you'd make Sandy a lot happier if you took her off somewhere once in a while. Doesn't have to be the Statue of Liberty; actually any . . .

ALBERT   My relationship with Dr. Markowitz is of no . . .

MURRAY   Well, there's obviously some relationship. When Nick asked you if you'd have sugar in your coffee before, Albert, you answered for Sandy.

ALBERT   Mr. Burns, this entire interview has reached a point . . .

NICK   I'm going to get my educational books. I left them out on the street.

(He leaves the apartment, his exit unnoticed by the others.)

ALBERT   This entire interview, Mr. Burns, has . . .

SANDRA   Mr. Burns, I . . .

ALBERT   Damn it, Sandra, don't interrupt me!

SANDRA   Albert, for goodness sakes, you . . .

ALBERT *(stands up)*   Sandra, perhaps we . . . *(To* MURRAY*)* Would you excuse us for just a moment, Mr. Burns? I'd like to have a short conference with Sandra . . . Miss . . . *Dr.* Markowitz for a moment. *(She gets up.* ALBERT *and* SANDRA *walk over to the alcove, where* MURRAY *cannot hear them.* MURRAY *starts to peer at them through his binoculars until* ALBERT *turns and looks at him; he then goes to desk and tinkers with clock. Now alone with* SANDRA, ALBERT'S *manner changes somewhat. He speaks more softly and with more warmth, a departure from the stiff, professional manner he uses in dealing with* MURRAY.*) Sandra, what are you *doing,* have we lost all control?

SANDRA   Are you seriously talking to *me* about control?

ALBERT   Dear, I told *you* and I told Dr. Malko. It's much too soon for you to go out on cases. You need another year in the office, behind the lines, I told both of you. You're simply *not* ready.

SANDRA   Really, Albert, you hardly let me get started. I was attempting to deal with the whole child.

ALBERT   Three months out of grad school and you want to go right into the front lines. Not advisable.

SANDRA   *(whispering angrily)*   Don't you think that this is rather stupid and unprofessional? Right here in front of him you decide to have a conference.

ALBERT   A necessity. I am supposedly the leader of our examining team . . .

SANDRA   Oh, *really . . .*

ALBERT   You get too *involved,* Sandra. Each case, you get much too emotionally involved. This is an exploratory visit, we are *scientists,* dear, you lose sight of the . . .

SANDRA   You make me sick today, Albert. This is no way to approach this man's problem. We . . .

ALBERT   *(sighing)*   Oh, fine. That's fine. Well . . . fine . . .

*(*MURRAY, *at the other side of the room, picks up a megaphone.)*

MURRAY   *(through the megaphone)*   How are we doing? *(Puts the megaphone down, comes over to them in the alcove, sits between them; speaks sympathetically.)* I personally don't feel that you're gonna work out your problems with each other. But I'm glad you came to me because I think I can help you. Al, Sandy is not going to respect you because you threaten her. Respect will have to come gradually, naturally, a maturing process . . .

ALBERT   Mr. Burns . . .

MURRAY   Sandy, I bet he's got a file on you.

ALBERT   Mr. Burns, according to the B.C.W., the child's continuance in your home is in serious and immediate doubt. I am trying to encourage your cooperation . . . *(He is making a genuine attempt to speak warmly, understandingly.)* Aren't you at all willing to answer some questions, to give some evidence in your favor for our report, some evidence to support your competency as a guardian? The Board is thoroughly aware that Nicholas is not legally adopted.

MURRAY   He's my nephew. He's staying with me for a while. He's visiting.

ALBERT   How long has he been here?

MURRAY   Seven years.

ALBERT   So you see, the Child Welfare Board has, I assure you, the right to question . . .

MURRAY *(rises, faces* ALBERT *angrily)* You don't assure me of anything, buddy, you make me damn nervous. Do you mean to tell me that four years at N.Y.U. has made you my judge? *(*ALBERT *shrugs, defeated; crosses to Morris chair for his coat, signals* SANDRA *that they are leaving.* MURRAY *goes toward them; speaks quietly, apologetically.)* O.K., all right. What do you want to know? I'll be cooperative.

*(*SANDRA *and* ALBERT *sit down again.)*

ALBERT   Nicholas' father, where is he?

MURRAY   That's not a *where* question. That's a *who* question.

ALBERT   I don't quite . . .

MURRAY   Nick's mother, she didn't quite either.

SANDRA   She is still living . . .

MURRAY   My sister is unquestionably alive.

SANDRA   But her responsibility to the child.

MURRAY   For five years she did everything she could for Nick . . .

but get married. Now that's not easy to understand since she used to get married to *everybody.* But, somehow, having Nick matured her, she felt a responsibility not to get married to just *any*body any more, so she didn't marry Nick's father, nor was she married at the time he was born. You might call Nick a bastard, or "little bastard," depending on how whimsical you feel at the time. Is that the sort of information you wanted? . . . Ah, this situation is the social workers' paradise. What a case history, huh? . . . My sister Elaine showed up here one day with two suitcases, a hatbox, a blue parakeet, a dead gold fish, and a five-year-old child. Three days later she went downstairs to buy a pack of filter-tip cigarettes . . . (MURRAY *shrugs.)* Six years later she returned for the suitcases and the hatbox . . . the parakeet I had given away, the gold fish I had long since flushed down the toilet, and the five-year-old child had, with very little effort, become six years older. When Elaine returned for her luggage I reminded her of the child and the pack of filter-tip cigarettes and suggested that this was perhaps the longest running practical joke in recent history. She was accompanied by a tall chap with sunglasses who was born to be her fifth divorce and who tried to start a small conversation with me. At this point I slapped my sister, Fifth Divorce slugged me, Sister cried, stopped quite suddenly, and then proceeded to explain to me, briefly, her well-practiced theory on the meaning of life, a philosophy falling somewhere to the left of Whoopie. At which point, I remember, I started laughing and then we all laughed and said "good-bye" like people at the end of a long party. That was almost a year ago. And I've still got Nick.

(SANDRA *is obviously sympathetic to this situation, emotionally involved in the story;* ALBERT *continues his cool professionalism, here and there jotting notes in the file.)*

SANDRA   But . . . but I'm sure she must have had *some* concern about Nicholas . . . about the child . . .

MURRAY   His name is not Nicholas. I will admit that he has stayed with that name much longer than the others . . . no, actually he was "Bill" for almost eight months . . .

SANDRA   I'm sure on his birth certificate . . .

MURRAY   Certainly an elusive document. Not having given him a last name, Elaine felt reticent about assigning him a first one. When Nick first came here this presented a real difficulty. Nick answered to nothing whatsoever. Even the parakeet recognized its own name. Nick only knew I was calling him when he was positive there was no one else in the room.

SANDRA *(very much emotionally involved in this now)*   Well, how did you communicate with . . .

MURRAY   I made a deal with him when he was six, up to which time he was known rather casually as Chubby, that he could try out any name he wished, for however long he wished, until his thirteenth birthday, at which point he'd have to decide on a name he liked permanently. He went through a long period of dogs' names when he was still little, Rover and King having a real vogue there for a while. For three months he referred to himself as Big Sam, then there was Little Max, Snoopy, Chip, Rock, Rex, Mike, Marty, Lamont, Chevrolet, Wyatt, Yancy, Fred, Phil, Woodrow, Lefty, The Phantom . . . He received his library card last year in the name of Raphael Sabatini, his Cub Scout membership lists him as Barry Fitzgerald, and only last week a friend of his called asking if Toulouse could come over to his house for dinner. Nick seems to be the one that'll stick, though.

SANDRA   His mother . . .?

MURRAY   His mother, when last heard, was studying mime in Paris, having been given a sort of scholarship by a twenty-two-year-old handbag heir named Myron, who seems to believe strongly in the development of talent and student exchange. Well, I don't believe I've left anything out.

ALBERT   I was not aware that Nick was an O.W. child.

MURRAY   O.W.?

ALBERT   Out of wedlock.

MURRAY   For moment I thought you meant Prisoner of War. I think it's that natural warmth of yours that leads me to misunderstand.

ALBERT   But as concerns the child . . . (*Looks around the room*) Where *is* the child?

SANDRA   You preferred not having him here anyway, Albert.

ALBERT   (*sharply*)   I am perfectly aware, Sandra, of what I *prefer*, and what I do *not* prefer.

SANDRA   (*sharply*)   I don't care for that tone of voice at *all*, Albert.

ALBERT   (*rises, begins to put on his coat; calmly*)   Sandra, I understand perfectly what has happened. We have allowed this man to disturb us and we have *both* gotten a bit upset. Now, I really do feel that it's time we got over to that family problem in Queens. It's there in your file, the Ledbetters, the introverted child. We've really given an unreasonable amount of time to this case. This interview, I'm afraid, Mr. Burns, has reached a point . . .

SANDRA *(attempting to sound authoritative)* Albert, I personally feel that it would not be advisable to leave this particular case, at this point.

ALBERT Sandra, we have done here this morning all we . . .

SANDRA I feel that we have not really given Mr. Burns a chance to . . .

ALBERT Sandra, it's really time we left for Queens . . .

SANDRA *(hands* ALBERT *one of her two file envelopes)* Here's the Ledbetter file, I'm staying here.

ALBERT *(raising his voice a little)* Sandra.

SANDRA I have decided to pursue this case.

ALBERT *(almost shouting)* Sandra, have we lost all professional control?

SANDRA *(angry, flustered)* You just . . . you just go yourself to the Leadbellies . . . you go on to Queens.

ALBERT *(takes her by the arm, gently, but firmly)* May I just talk to you for a moment?

*(*ALBERT *leads* SANDRA *over to the alcove.)*

MURRAY Time out for signals again?

ALBERT *(away from* MURRAY, *now he speaks, softly, less stiffly, though still angry)* What *is* this dear? What has happened to you today? What are you doing?

SANDRA I'm doing what I think is right.

ALBERT I know how you feel, Sandra, but there is no more we can do here.

SANDRA *(emotionally)* I just . . . I just don't understand your behavior when you're on a case. We're supposed to be of some help, he . . .

ALBERT Of course I want to help. But don't forget that the child is the one who needs protection, who needs . . .

SANDRA Are you really going to leave that man here like that?

You're not going to even try to help him or tell him what to do about the Board separating him from the child . . . I mean . . . just so cold.

ALBERT *(takes her hand)*   Dear, you spent much too much time at that graduate school and not enough time in the field. That's your whole trouble. You've got to learn your job, Sandra . . .

SANDRA *(angry, frustrated)*   Oh *really,* is that so? Albert Amundson, don't give me any of that nonsense.

ALBERT *(glancing over at* MURRAY*)*   Please, Sandra . . . dear, this is not the time or the place for . . .

SANDRA *(shouting)*   Graduate school wouldn't have done *you* any harm, Albert, believe *me!* Oh, this is the most terrible thing . . . *(Very close to tears)* You mean . . . you're just going to leave . . .? Do you know what you are . . .? You're a . . . I don't know; . . . but I'll think of something . . .

(ALBERT walks away, leaving her in the alcove, goes into the main room, calmly picks up his briefcase.)

ALBERT *(retaining his control, but just a little shaken. To* MURRAY*)* Mr. Burns . . . You can assume at this point that Miss Markowitz is no longer involved with your case. The Board will be informed that she is no longer involved with this particular case. Her continuing here, to discuss your case . . . at this point . . . is entirely unofficial. You can dismiss any conference . . . that may resume after I leave . . . when I leave here, from your mind. And, regardless of what you think of me . . .

MURRAY   I think you're a dirty O.W.

(Some of SANDRA*'s file papers slip from her hand and fall to the floor.)*

ALBERT   And . . . and do you know what *you* are? *(Readying himself to deliver a crushing insult to* MURRAY*)* Maladjusted! *(Goes to the door, opens it.)* Good afternoon, Mr. Burns. Good afternoon, Sandra.

MURRAY   Good afternoon, Mr. Amundson. Watch out crossing the street.

(ALBERT exits, closing door sharply behind him. SANDRA *stands for a moment in the alcove, then begins to pick up the papers she had dropped on the floor.)*

SANDRA   Mr. Burns . . . *(She is making a very strong attempt to control herself, but she is obviously on the verge of tears. She goes into the main room, begins to collect her things to leave.)* Mr. Burns, I must apologize to you. We . . . we have put you . . . you have been put at a disadvantage this morning. You have been involved in a personal problem that has nothing to do whatsoever with your particular case. It is entirely wrong for me to give you this impression of our . . . of our profession. *(She can no longer control herself and becomes, suddenly, a sort of child. She stands quite still, with her hands at her sides, and cries. It is not loud, hysterical crying, but intermittent and disorganized sobs, squeaks, whines, sniffles and assorted feminine noises which punctuate her speech.)* Do you know what? I just lost my job. This is awful. He's right, you know. I'm not suited to my work. I get too involved. That's what he said and he's right. *(Rummaging through her purse for Kleenex)* Please don't look at me. Do you *have* to stand there? Please go away. Still, he didn't have to talk to me like that. This is the first *week* we've ever gone on cases together. I didn't think he'd behave that way. That was no way. Why don't I ever have any Kleenex? *(He gives her the closest thing at hand to blow her nose in, his undershirt from the bed.)* Thank you. *(She sits down on the bed.)* Do you know that even with two fellowships it still cost me, I mean my parents mostly, it cost them seven thousand two hundred and forty-five dollars for me to go through school. I was the eighth youngest person to graduate in New York State last year and I can't stop crying. Maybe if I hurry, if I took a cab, I could still meet him in Queens.

MURRAY You can't. Queens is closed. It's closed for the season.

SANDRA Do you know what? *(Her crying lets up a bit.)*

MURRAY What?

SANDRA *(with a new burst of sobs)* I hate the Ledbetters.

MURRAY Then I'm sure once I got to know them I'd hate them too.

SANDRA Mr. Burns, you don't understand. Some of the cases I love and some of them I hate, and that's all wrong for my work, but I can't help it. I hate Raymond Ledbetter and he's only nine years old and he makes me sick and I don't give a damn about him.

MURRAY *(pointing to the file on her lap)* You can't like everybody in your portfolio.

SANDRA But some of them I like too much and worry about them all day . . . *(She is making an attempt to control her tears.)* It is an obvious conflict against all professional standards. I didn't like Raymond Ledbetter so I tried to understand him, and now that I understand him I hate him.

MURRAY   I think that's wonderful. Can I get you a cup of coffee?

SANDRA *(she turns to* MURRAY *as if to answer him, but instead bursts into fresh tears)*   He's gone to Queens and I'll never hear from him again. I wrote out what my married name would be after dinner last night on a paper napkin, Mrs. Albert Amundson, to see how it would look. You know what I think I am, I think I'm crazy.

MURRAY   Well, then, I can talk to you.

SANDRA   We were going to get married. It was all planned, Mrs. Albert Amundson on a napkin. You have to understand Albert. He's really a very nice person when he's not on cases. He's a very intelligent man but last month I fell asleep twice while he was talking. I've known him for so long. *(She tries once again to stop crying but the effort only increases her sobs.)* Mr. Burns, don't look at me. Why don't you go away?

MURRAY   But I live here.

SANDRA   I would like everybody to go away.

MURRAY   *(attempting to comfort her)*   Can I get you a pastrami sandwich?

SANDRA   Oh, I don't know you and I'm crying right in front of you. Go away.

MURRAY   Couldn't you just think of this as Show-and-Tell time?

SANDRA *(turning away again, still seated on the bed)*   The minute I got out of school I wanted to go right back inside. *(With a great sob.)* Albert is gone and I just lost my job.

MURRAY *(he walks over to her)*   Now, you're really going to have to stop crying, because I am going out of my mind.

SANDRA   I cry all the time and I laugh in the wrong places in the movies. I am unsuited to my profession and I can't do anything right. Last night I burned an entire chicken and after seven years of school I can't work and I've got no place to go. An entire chicken.

MURRAY   If I do my Peter Lorre imitation, will you stop crying?

SANDRA *(she pokes the file-envelope in her lap)*   Look what I've done, I've cried on one of my files. The ink is running all over the Grumbacher twins . . .

MURRAY *(in the voice of Peter Lorre, a decent imitation)*   It was all a mistake, I didn't stab Mrs. Marmalade . . . it was my knife, but someone else did it, I tell you . . .

SANDRA   That's an awful imitation, Mr. Burns . . .

(She turns away from him and sobs into the bedclothes. He takes the Bubbles statue out of the box, switches it on, places it on the floor near the bed; it starts to blink on and off. Her face peeks out, she sees the blinking statue and puts her face back into the bedclothes, but we hear some giggles mixing with her sobs now, and then overtaking them, until she finally lifts her face and we see that she is laughing.)

MURRAY *(smiling)*   There. Progress. *(He turns off the statue.)* Would you like a cup of coffee, or a pastrami sandwich or something?

SANDRA   No, thank you. *(SANDRA begins to compose herself, she has stopped crying completely and is wiping her eyes with the undershirt he gave her. Then she begins to fold the undershirt neatly, smoothing it out into a nice little square on her lap.)* This is absolutely the most unprofessional experience I have ever had.

MURRAY   People fall into two distinct categories, Miss Markowitz; people who like delicatessen, and people who don't like delicatessen. A man who is not touched by the earthy lyricism of hot pastrami, the pungent fantasy of corned beef, pickles, frankfurters, the great lusty impertinence of good mustard . . . is a man of stone and without heart. Now, Albert is obviously not a lover of delicatessen and you are well rid of him.

(SANDRA is still sitting on the bed, her hands folded neatly in her lap on top of her files and his undershirt.)

SANDRA   What am I going to do? This is an awful day.

MURRAY *(he sits on the swivel chair next to the bed)*   Miss Markowitz, this is a beautiful day and I'll tell you why. My dear, you are really a jolly old girl and you are well rid of Albert. You have been given a rare opportunity to return the unused portion and have your money refunded.

SANDRA   But . . . my work . . . what am I going to . . .

MURRAY   You are a lover, Dr. Markowitz, you are a lover of things and people so you took up work where you could get at as many of them as possible; and it just turned out that there were too many of them and too much that moves you. Damn it, please be glad that it turned out you are not reasonable and sensible. Have all the gratitude you can, that you are capable of embarrassment and joy and are a marathon crier.

SANDRA *(looking directly at him)*   There is a kind of relief that it's gone . . . the job, and even Albert. But I know what it is, it's just irresponsible . . . I don't have the vaguest idea who I am . . .

MURRAY *(he takes her hand)*   It's just there's all these Sandras running around who you never met before, and it's confusing at first, fantastic, like a Chinese fire drill. But god *damn,* isn't it great to find out how many Sandras there are? Like those little cars in the circus, this tiny red car comes out and putters around, suddenly its doors open and out come a thousand clowns, whooping and hollering and raising hell.

SANDRA *(she lets go of his hand in order to pick up the undershirt in her lap)*   What's this?

MURRAY   That's my undershirt. How's about going to the Empire State Building with me?

SANDRA   I'll have that coffee now.

MURRAY   You didn't answer my question. Would you like to visit the Empire State Building?

SANDRA   No, not really.

MURRAY   Well, then how about the zoo?

SANDRA   Not just now.

MURRAY   Well, then will you marry me?

SANDRA   What?

MURRAY   Just a bit of shock treatment there. I have found after long experience that it's the quickest way to get a woman's attention when her mind wanders. Always works.

SANDRA   Mr. Burns . . .

MURRAY   Now that you've cried you can't call me Mr. Burns. Same rule applies to laughing. My name is Murray.

SANDRA   Well, Murray, to sort of return to reality for a minute . . .

MURRAY   I will only go as a tourist.

SANDRA   Murray, you know, you're in trouble with the Child Welfare Board. They could really take Nick away. Murray, there's some things you could try to do . . . to make your case a little stronger . . .

MURRAY   Sandra, do you realize that you are not wearing your shoes?

SANDRA *(she looks down at her bare feet)*   Oh.

(The front door opens and NICK *bursts into the room, laden with books.)*

NICK   Well, here I am with all my favorite books, *Fun in the Rain, The Young Railroader, Great Philosophers, Science for Youth,* a Spanish dictionary. What I did was I left them out in the street when I was playing, and I went down to . . .

MURRAY   Nick, you just killed a month's allowance for nothing. Miss Markowitz isn't even on our case any more.

NICK   I shouldn't have left. You got angry and insulted everybody.

MURRAY   Don't worry about it, Nick, we'll work it out. *(He goes over to the closet for something.)*

NICK *(dropping his books regretfully on the chair)*   Four dollars right out the window. *(To* SANDRA*)* Y'know, I really do read educational books and am encouraged in my home to think.

SANDRA   I'm sure that's true, Nicholas, but I'm not in a position to do you much official good any more.

NICK   We're in real trouble now, right? *(He turns to* MURRAY *who has taken two ukuleles from the closet and is coming toward* NICK*.)* I figured it would happen; you got angry and hollered at everybody.

MURRAY   Nick, we have a guest, a music lover . . . *(He hands the smaller of the two ukuleles to* NICK*.)* We've got to do our song. I am sure it will be requested.

NICK *(protesting, gesturing with his ukulele)*   Murray, stop it . . . we—this is no time to sing songs, Murray . . .

MURRAY *(striking a downbeat on his ukulele)*   Come on, where's your professional attitude?

*(*MURRAY *starts playing "Yes, Sir, That's My Baby" on the ukulele,*

then sings the first line. NICK *turns away at first, shaking his head solemnly at* MURRAY'S *behavior.* MURRAY *goes on with the second line of the song. Reluctantly,* NICK *begins to pick out the melody on his ukulele, then he smiles in spite of himself and sings the third line along with* MURRAY.

They really go into the song now, singing and playing "Yes, Sir, That's My Baby," doing their routine for SANDRA. *She sits in front of them on the bed, smiling, enjoying their act.* NICK *is in the spirit of it now and having a good time. In the middle of the song* NICK *and* MURRAY *do some elaborate soft-shoe dance steps for a few lines, ukuleles held aloft. This is followed by some very fast and intricate two-part ukulele harmony on the last few lines of the song for a big finish.*

SANDRA *applauds.*

MURRAY *and* NICK, *singing and strumming ukes, go into a reprise of the song,* MURRAY *moving forward and sitting down on the bed next to* SANDRA. NICK, *left apart from them now, does a line or two more of the song along with* MURRAY, *then gradually stops.* NICK *considers them both for a moment as* MURRAY *goes on doing the song alone now for* SANDRA. NICK *nods to himself, circles around in front of them and, unnoticed by them, puts his uke down on the window seat, goes to his alcove, gets school briefcase and pajamas from his bed.* MURRAY *is still playing the uke and singing the song to* SANDRA *as* NICK *goes past them on his way to the front door, carrying his stuff.)*

NICK *(pleasantly, to* SANDRA*)*   Nice to meet you, lady. I'll see you around.

MURRAY *(stops singing, turns to* NICK*)*   Where you off to, Nick?

NICK   Gonna leave my stuff up at Mrs. Myers'. *(Opens the door.)* I figure I'll be staying over there tonight.

*(*NICK *exits, waving a pleasant goodbye to* SANDRA, SANDRA *looks at the front door, puzzled; then she looks at* MURRAY, *who resumes the song, singing and strumming the uke.)*

CURTAIN

ACT TWO

Scene: MURRAY'S *apartment, eight* A.M. *the following morning.*
At rise: The phone is ringing loudly on the window seat. MURRAY *enters from the bathroom with his toothbrush in his mouth, grabs the*

phone. The room is as it was at the end of Act One except that there is a six-foot-high folding screen placed around the bed, hiding it from view, and the shades are drawn again on the windows.

MURRAY *(speaks immediately into the phone)* Is this somebody with good news or money? No? Good-bye. *(He hangs up.)* It's always voices like that you hear at eight A.M. Maniacs. *(He pulls up the shade to see what kind of a day it is outside. As usual the lighting of the room changes not at all with the shade up, as before he sees nothing but the blank, grayish wall opposite.)* Crap. *(With a sigh of resignation, he picks up the phone, dials, listens.)* Hello, Weather Lady. I am fine, how are you? What is the weather? Uh-huh . . . uh-huh . . . uh-huh . . . very nice. Only a *chance* of showers? Well, what exactly does that . . . Aw, there she goes again . . . *(He hangs up.)* Chance of showers. *(The phone rings. He picks it up, speaks immediately into it.)* United States Weather Bureau forecast for New York City and vicinity: eight A.M. temperature, sixty-five degrees, somewhat cooler in the suburbs, cloudy later today with a chance of . . . *(Looks incredulously at the phone.)* He hung up. Fool. Probably the most informative phone call he'll make all day. *(He stands, opens the window, leans out, raising his voice, shouting out the window.)* This is your neighbor speaking! Something must be done about your garbage cans in the alley here. It is definitely second-rate garbage! By next week I want to see a better class of garbage, more empty champagne bottles and caviar cans! So let's *snap* it up and get on the *ball!*

(SANDRA's head appears at the top of the screen, like a puppet's head. She is staring blankly at MURRAY, MURRAY steps toward her, she continues to stare blankly at him. Her head suddenly disappears again behind the screen. The screen masks the entire bed and SANDRA from his view, and the view of audience. We hear a rustle of sheets and blankets, silence for a couple of seconds, and then SANDRA's voice; she speaks in a cold, dignified, ladylike voice, only slightly tinged with sleep, impersonal, polite, and distant, like one unintroduced party guest to another.)

SANDRA   Good morning.

MURRAY   Good morning.

SANDRA   How are you this morning?

MURRAY   I am fine this morning. How are you?

SANDRA   I am fine also. Do you have a bathrobe?

MURRAY   Yes, I have a bathrobe.

SANDRA   May I have your bathrobe, please?

MURRAY   I'll give you Nick's. It'll fit you better.

SANDRA   That seems like a good idea.

(He takes NICK'S *bathrobe from the hook in the alcove, tosses it over the top of the screen.)*

MURRAY   There you go.

SANDRA *(her voice from behind the screen is getting even colder)* Thank you. What time is it?

MURRAY   It is eight-fifteen and there is a chance of showers. Did you sleep well?

SANDRA   Yes, how long have you been up?

MURRAY   Little while.

SANDRA   Why didn't you wake me?

MURRAY   Because you were smiling. *(Silence for a moment)* How does the bathrobe fit?

SANDRA   This bathrobe fits fine. *(After a moment.)* Did you happen to see my clothes?

MURRAY *(starts for the bathroom)* They're in the bathroom. Shall I get them?

SANDRA   No, thank you. *(She suddenly pops out from behind the screen and races across the room into the kitchen at right, slamming the kitchen door behind her. We hear her voice from behind the door.)* This isn't the bathroom. This is the kitchen.

MURRAY   If it *was* the bathroom then this would be a very extreme version of an efficiency apartment. *(He goes to the bathroom to get her clothes, brings them with him to the kitchen door. He knocks on the door.)* Here are your clothes. Also toothpaste and toothbrush.

(The kitchen door opens slightly, her hand comes out. He puts the stuff in it, her hand goes back, the door closes again.)

SANDRA   Thank you.

MURRAY   Sandy, is everything all right?

SANDRA   What?

MURRAY   I said, is everything all right?

SANDRA   Yes, I'm using the last of your toothpaste.

MURRAY   That's all right. There's soap by the sink.

SANDRA   I know. I found it.

MURRAY   That's good.

SANDRA   It was right by the sink.

MURRAY   Suppose we broaden this discussion to other matters . . .

SANDRA   I saw the soap when I came in.

(The front door opens and ARNOLD BURNS *enters as he did before, carrying a grocery carton filled with varieties of fruit. He sets it down on the desk.)*

ARNOLD   Morning, Murray.

MURRAY *(without turning to look at him)*   Morning, Arnold.

ARNOLD   Murray, Chuckles called again yesterday. I told him I'd talk to you. And Jimmy Sloan is in from the coast; he's putting a new panel-show package together . . .

MURRAY   Arnold, you have many successful clients . . .

ARNOLD   Murray . . .

MURRAY   With all these successful people around, where are all of our new young failures going to come from?

ARNOLD   Murray, those people I saw here yesterday; they were from the Welfare Board, right? I tried to warn you . . .

MURRAY   Nothing to worry about.

ARNOLD   These Welfare people don't kid around.

MURRAY   Arnold, I don't mind you coming with fruit if you keep quiet, but you bring a word with every apple . . . Everything's fine. You'll be late for the office.

ARNOLD   Is Nick all right?

MURRAY   Fine.

ARNOLD   O.K., good-bye, Murray.

MURRAY   Good-bye, Arnold. *(ARNOLD exits.* MURRAY *talks to the closed kitchen door again.)* There's coffee still in the pot from last night, if you want to heat it up.

SANDRA   I already lit the flame.

MURRAY   Good. The cups are right over the sink. Will you be coming out soon?

SANDRA   I found the cups.

MURRAY   Do you think you will be coming out soon?

SANDRA   Yes, I think so. Cream and sugar in your coffee?

MURRAY   Yes, thank you.

SANDRA   Murray.

MURRAY   Yes.

SANDRA   I'm coming out now.

MURRAY   That's good.

SANDRA   I'm all finished in here so I'm coming out now.

MURRAY   That's very good.

(The kitchen door opens. SANDRA, *dressed neatly, comes out of the kitchen, carrying two cups of coffee and* NICK'S *bathrobe.)*

SANDRA *(pausing at kitchen doorway, smiles politely)*   Well, here I am *(She goes to* MURRAY, *gives him a cup, sits on swivel chair. He sits next to her, on the stool. She takes a sip of coffee, straightens her hair. She is quite reserved, though pleasant; she behaves as though at a tea social.)* You know, yesterday was the first time I've ever been to the Statue of

Liberty. It's funny how you can live in a city for so long and not visit one of its most fascinating sights.

MURRAY   That is funny. *(He sips his coffee.)* This coffee isn't bad, for yesterday's coffee.

SANDRA   I think it's very good, for yesterday's coffee. *(Takes another sip.)* What kind of coffee is it?

MURRAY   I believe it's Chase and Sanborn coffee.

SANDRA   "Good to the last drop," isn't that what they say?

MURRAY   I think that's Maxwell House.

SANDRA   Oh, yes. Maxwell House coffee. "Good to the last drop."

MURRAY   It's Chase and Sanborn that used to have the ad about the ingredients: "Monizalles for mellowness" was one.

SANDRA   They used to sponsor Edgar Bergen and Charlie McCarthy on the radio.

MURRAY   Yes. You're right.

SANDRA   "Monizalles for mellowness." I remember. That's right. *(She finishes her coffee, puts her cup down on the table. Then, after a moment)* I have to leave now.

MURRAY   Oh?

SANDRA   Yes. I'll have to be on my way. *(She stands, takes her pocketbook, puts on her shoes and starts to exit.)*

MURRAY   *(takes her files from the floor, hands them to her)* Don't forget your files.

SANDRA   Oh yes. My files. *(She takes them from him, stands looking at him)* Well, good-bye.

MURRAY   Good-bye, Sandra.

SANDRA   Good-bye. *(She walks out of the apartment, and closes the door behind her. Alone in the apartment now, MURRAY stands for a moment looking at the door. He then runs to open the door; she has had her hand on the outside knob and is dragged into the room as he does so.)*

MURRAY *(laughing, relieved)*   You nut. I was ready to kill you.

SANDRA *(throws her arms around him, drops her bag and files on floor)*   What happened? You didn't say anything. I was waiting for you to say something. Why didn't you say something or kiss me or . . .

MURRAY   I was waiting for *you,* for God's sake. *(He kisses her.)*

SANDRA   I didn't know *what* was going on. *(She kisses him, their arms around each other; he leans away from her for a moment to put his coffee cup on the table.)* Don't let me go . . .

MURRAY   I was just putting my coffee cup down . . .

SANDRA   Don't let me go. *(He holds her tightly again.)* Murray, I thought about it, and I probably love you.

MURRAY   That's very romantic. I probably love you too. You have very small feet. For a minute yesterday, it looked like you only had four toes, and I thought you were a freak. I woke up in the middle of the night and counted them. There are five.

SANDRA   I could have told you that.

MURRAY *(he sits in the swivel chairchair; she is on his lap)*   You knocked down maybe seven boxes of Crackerjacks yesterday. You are twelve years old. You sleep with the blanket under your chin like a napkin. When you started to talk about the coffee before, I was going to throw you out the window except there'd be no place for you to land but the trash can from the Chinese restaurant.

SANDRA   You mean that you live above a Chinese restaurant?

MURRAY   Yes, It's been closed for months, though.

SANDRA   Do you mean that you live above an abandoned Chinese restaurant?

MURRAY   Yes, I do.

SANDRA   That's wonderful. *(She kisses him; jumps up from his lap happily excited about what she has to say. Takes off her jacket and hangs it on the back of the Morris chair.)* I didn't go to work this morning and I simply can't tell you how fantastic that makes me feel. I'm not going to do a *lot* of things any more. *(Picks at the material of her blouse.)* This blouse I'm wearing, my mother picked it out, everybody picks out things for me. She gets all her clothes directly from Louisa May Alcott. *(Picks up the stool, changes its position in the room.)* Well, we've all seen the last of this blouse anyway. Do you realize that I feel more at home here after twenty-four hours than I do in my parents' house after twenty-five years? Of course, we'll have to do something about curtains . . . and I hope you didn't mind about the screen around the bed, I just think it gives such a nice, separate bedroomy effect to that part of the room . . . *(Picks up her bag and files from the floor where she dropped them, puts them in the closet. She is moving in.)* Oh, there are so many wonderful tricks you can try with a one-room apartment, really, if you're willing to use your imagination . . . *(He watches helplessly as she moves happily about the apartment judging it with a decorator's eye.)* I don't care if it sounds silly, Murray, but I was projecting a personality identification with the Statue of Liberty yesterday . . . courageous and free and solid metal . . . *(She kisses him, then continues pacing happily.)* I was here with you last night and I don't give a damn who knows it or what anybody thinks, and that goes for Dr. Malko, Albert, my mother, Aunt Blanche . . . Oh, I'm going to do so many things I've always wanted to do.

MURRAY   For example.

SANDRA   Well . . . I'm not sure right now. And that's marvelous too, I am thoroughly enjoying the idea that I don't know what I'm going to do next. *(Stops pacing.)* Do you have an extra key?

MURRAY   What?

SANDRA   An extra key. Altman's has this terrific curtain sale, thought I'd go and . . .

MURRAY   Well, then I'd better give you some money . . .

SANDRA   No, that's all right. *(Holds out her hand.)* Just the key.

MURRAY   Oh. *(He looks at her blankly for a moment, then reaches into his pocket slowly, finds the key, slowly hands it to her.)*

SANDRA *(snatches up the key, goes on delightedly pacing up and down)*   Murray, did we bring back any Crackerjacks?

MURRAY *(pointing to some packages on the desk)*   Only stuff we brought back was that cleaning equipment. I'll admit this place is a little dirty, but all that stuff just for . . .

(The doorbell rings. SANDRA flinches for a moment, but then smiles and stands firmly.)

SANDRA   You'd better answer it, Murray.

MURRAY   Sandra, would you prefer to . . .

(He indicates the kitchen as a hiding place, but she stands right where she is, refusing to move.)

SANDRA   I've got no reason to hide from anybody.

(MURRAY goes to the front door and opens it halfway, but enough for us to see the visitor, ALBERT AMUNDSON. ALBERT cannot see beyond the door to where SANDRA is standing.)

ALBERT   Good morning, Mr. Burns.

MURRAY   Albert, how are you?

(SANDRA, hearing ALBERT's voice, and realizing who it is, goes immediately into the closet, closing the door behind her.)

ALBERT   May I come in?

MURRAY   Sure.

(MURRAY opens the front door all the way, allowing ALBERT into the main room. MURRAY closes the door, then follows ALBERT into the room. MURRAY smiles to himself when he sees that SANDRA is not there and then glances at the closet door.)

ALBERT   I called you twice this morning, Mr. Burns.

MURRAY   That was you.

ALBERT   That was me. Miss Markowitz did not show up in Queens yesterday.

MURRAY   So?

ALBERT   Her parents are quite upset. I am quite upset. Where is she?

MURRAY   She's hiding in the closet.

ALBERT   We're really all quite anxious to know where she is.

MURRAY   I'm not kidding. She's in the closet.

(ALBERT goes to the closet, opens the door, sees SANDRA, *then closes the door.* ALBERT *comes back to* MURRAY.)*

ALBERT   She *is* in the closet.

MURRAY   I wouldn't lie to you, Albert.

ALBERT   Why is she in the closet?

MURRAY   I don't know. She's got this thing about closets.

ALBERT   That's a very silly thing for her to be in that closet.

MURRAY   Don't knock it till you've tried it. Now, what else can I do for you?

ALBERT   That's a difficult thing for me to believe. I mean, that she's right there in the closet. You are not a person, Mr. Burns, you are an experience.

MURRAY *(goes into the kitchen)*   That's very nice, Albert, I'll have to remember that.

ALBERT   Actually, Dr. Markowitz is not the reason for my visit today. I came here in an official capacity.

MURRAY *(from the kitchen)*   You don't wear an official capacity well, Albert. Coffee?

ALBERT   No, thank you.

*(*MURRAY *brings the pot out, fills the two cups on the table; brings one of the cups of coffee to the closet and hands it through the partly open door.)*

MURRAY *(returns to the table, sits opposite* ALBERT)   What have you got on your mind, Albert?

ALBERT *(sit; begins hesitantly)*   Burns, late yesterday afternoon the Child Welfare Board made a decision on your case. Their decision is based on three months of a thorough study; our interview yesterday is only a small part of the . . . I want you to understand that I am not responsible, personally, for the decision they've reached, I . . .

MURRAY   Relax, Albert, I won't even hold you responsible for the shadow you're throwing on my rug.

ALBERT   For eleven months you have avoided contact with the
Board, made a farce of their inquiries. You are not employed, show no
inclination to gain employment, have absolutely no financial stability . . .

MURRAY   Look, Albert, I . . .

ALBERT   Months of research by the Board and reports by the Revere
School show a severe domestic instability, a libertine self-indulgence, a
whole range of circumstances severely detrimental to the child's
welfare . . .

MURRAY   Look, stop the tap-dancing for a second, Albert; what's
going on, what . . .

ALBERT   It is the Board's decision that you are unfit to be the
guardian of your nephew, and that action be taken this Friday to remove
the child from this home and the deprivation you cause him.

MURRAY   You mean they can really . . . *(Sips his coffee, putting on
an elaborate display of calm, showing no emotion.)* Where'd they get this
routine from, Charles Dickens?

ALBERT   The Board is prepared to find a more stable, permanent
home for your nephew, a family with whom he will live a more
wholesome, normal . . .

MURRAY   Look, Albert, there must be some kind of a hearing or
something, where I'll have a chance to . . .

ALBERT   You will have the opportunity Thursday to state your case
to the Board. If there is some substantial change in your circumstances,
some evidence they're not aware of; if you can demonstrate that you are a
responsible member of society . . .

MURRAY   It's Tuesday; what the hell am I supposed to do in two
days, win the Nobel Peace Prize? They sent you here to tell me this?

ALBERT   No, you were to be informed by the court. But in view of
the confusion which took place here yesterday, for which I consider
myself responsible, I felt it my duty to come here and explain . . .

MURRAY   Buddy, you speak like you write everything down before
you say it.

ALBERT   Yes, I do speak that way, Mr. Burns. I wish that I spoke
more spontaneously. I realize that I lack warmth. I will always appear

foolish in a conversation with a person of your imagination. Please understand, there is no vengeance in my activities here. I love my work, Mr. Burns. I believe that you are a danger to this child. I wish this were not true, because it is obvious that you have considerable affection for your nephew. It is in your face, this feeling. I admire you for your warmth, Mr. Burns, and for the affection the child feels for you. I admire this because I am one for whom children do not easily feel affection. I am not one of the warm people. But your feeling for the child does not mollify the genuinely dangerous emotional climate you have made for him. *(He moves toward* MURRAY.) I wish you could understand this, I would so much rather you understood, could really hear what I have to say. For yours is, I believe, a distorted picture of this world.

MURRAY   Then why don't you send *me* to a foster home?

ALBERT   I was right. You really can't listen to me. You are so sure of your sight. Your villains and heroes are all so terribly clear to you, and I am obviously one of the villains. *(Picks up his briefcase.)* God save you from your vision, Mr. Burns. *(Goes to the front door, opens it.)* Good-bye. (ALBERT *exits.)*

MURRAY   *(stands at the window with his coffee cup in his hand, looking out at gray, blank wall of the building opposite)*   Hey, courageous, free one, you can come out now.

(SANDRA *comes out of closet carrying her coffee cup;* MURRAY *does not look at her.)*

SANDRA   I'm sorry, Murray. I'm really very embarrassed. I don't know what happened. I just ran into the closet. And . . . and once I was in there, I just didn't want to come out. I'm sorry, Murray . . .

MURRAY   Don't be nervous, lady, you're just going through an awkward stage. You're between closets. *(Quietly, calmly)* Look, if Nick has to leave, if he goes, he goes, and my life stays about the same. But it's no good for *him,* see, not for a couple of years, anyway. Right now he's still ashamed of being sharper than everybody else, he could easily turn into another peeled and boiled potato. Are you listening to me?

SANDRA   Yes, of course . . .

MURRAY   Well, make some kind of listening noise then, will you? Wink or nod your head or something.

SANDRA   But, I'm . . .

MURRAY   *(casually; gesturing with his coffee cup)*   Tell you the truth, it's even a little better for me if he goes. I mean, he's a middle-aged kid. When I signed with the network he sat up all night figuring out the fringe benefits and the pension plan. And he started to make lists this year. Lists of everything; subway stops, underwear, what he's gonna do next week. If somebody doesn't watch out he'll start making lists of what he's gonna next year and the next ten years. Hey, suppose they put him in with a whole family of listmakers? *(Angrily)* I didn't spend six years with him so he should turn into a listmaker. He'll learn to know everything before it happens, he'll learn to plan, he'll learn how to be one of the nice dead people. Are you listening?

SANDRA   Of course, I told you, Murray, I . . .

MURRAY   Then stamp your feet or mutter so I'll know you're there, huh? *(Still speaking quite calmly)* I just want him to stay with me till I can be sure he won't turn into Norman Nothing. I want to be sure he'll know when he's chickening out on himself. I want him to get to know exactly the special thing he is or else he won't notice it when it starts to go. I want him to stay awake and know who the phonies are, I want him to know how to holler and put up an argument, I want a little guts to show before I can let him go. I want to be sure he sees all the wild possibilities. I want him to know it's worth all the trouble just to give the world a little goosing when you get the chance. And I want him to know the subtle, sneaky, important reason why he was born a human being and not a chair. *(Pause)* I will be very sorry to see him go. That kid was the best straight man I ever had. He is a laugher, and laughers are rare. I mean, you tell that kid something funny . . . not just any piece of corn, but something funny, and he'll give you your money's worth. It's not just funny jokes he reads, or I tell him, that he laughs at. Not just set-up funny stuff. He sees street jokes, he has the good eye, he sees subway farce and crosstown-bus humor and all the cartoons that people make by being alive. He has a good eye. And I don't want him to leave until I'm certain he'll never be ashamed of it. *(Still quite calmly, unemotionally)* And in addition to that . . . besides that . . . see *(Suddenly; loudly)* Sandy, I don't want him to go. I like having him around here. What should I do, Sandy: Help me out. *(Suddenly slumps forward in his chair, covers his face with his hands; very quietly)* I like when he reads me from the want ads.

SANDRA *(takes his hands)*   Murray, don't worry, we'll do something. I know the Board, their procedure, there's things you can do . . .

MURRAY *(quietly, thoughtfully)*   What I'll do is I'll buy a new suit. The first thing is to get a dignified suit.

SANDRA   If you could get some kind of a job, get your brother to help you.

MURRAY   Right. Right.

SANDRA   Is there something you can get in a hurry?

MURRAY   Sure, one of those suits with the ready-made cuffs . . .

SANDRA   No, I mean a job. If we could just bring some proof of employment to the hearing, Murray, show them how anxious you are to change. We'll show them you want to be reliable.

MURRAY *(brightening)*   Yeah, reliable . . . *(Rises; going toward the phone)* Sandy, we will put on a God-damned show for them. Spectacular reliability; a reliability parade; bands, floats, everything. *(Starts to dial)* Sandy, go to the files and pick me out a tie that is quiet but at the same time projects a mood of inner strength. *(Into the phone)* Arnold Burns' office, please.

SANDRA *(on her way to the file cabinet)*   One quiet tie with a mood of inner strength.

MURRAY *(into the phone)*   Hello, Margot? It's Murray. Oh, well, when Arnie comes in here's what you do. First you tell him to sit down. Then you tell him I want to get a job. When he has recovered sufficiently from that shock, tell him . . . *(Sandra comes to him with a tie.)* Excuse me a second, Margot . . . *(To SANDRA, indicating the tie)* Yes, quiet but with strength. *(SANDRA laughs.)* Sandy, that is the greatest happy laugh I ever heard on a lady. Do that again. *(She laughs again.)* Great. Keep that laugh. I'll need it later. *(Into the phone)* Margot, tell him I'm going downtown to pick up a new suit for myself and a beautiful pineapple for him, call him back in about an hour, O.K.? Thanks, Margot. *(Puts the phone down, goes to get his jacket.)*

SANDRA   Can I come with you? I'd love to buy a suit with you.

MURRAY *(putting on his jacket)*   Better not, Sandy. Gotta move fast. These shoes look O.K.? *(She nods, he takes her hand.)* Look, don't go away.

SANDRA   I won't. *(She kisses him.)*

MURRAY *(goes to the front door; turns to her, smiles)*   Say "Good luck."

SANDRA   Good luck.

MURRAY *(opening the door)*   Now say "You are a magnificent human being."

SANDRA   You are a magnificient human being.

MURRAY *(as he exits)*   I *thought* you'd notice.

*She stands in door and watches him go as the lights fade out quickly. Immediately, as the lights fade, we hear the voice of Chuckles the Chipmunk. (*LEO HERMAN*).*

LEO'S VOICE   Hi there, kidderoonies; there's nothin' more lonelier than a lonely, little looney Chippermunk. So won't ya please come on along with me fer a fun hour, 'cuz that loneliest, littlest, looniest Chippermunk, is *me* . . . Chuckles. *(Lights come up now in* ARNOLD BURNS' *office, later that afternoon. The office is part of a large theatrical agency of which* ARNOLD *is a rather successful member; modern, wood paneling, nonobjective paintings and framed photographs of his clients on the wall, a spectacularly large window behind the desk with a twenty-second-floor skyline view. A large bowl of fruit is on an end table near the door. One of the two phones on* ARNOLD'S *desk is a special speaker-phone, consisting of a small loudspeaker box on the desk which amplifies clearly the voice of whoever is calling. It can also be spoken in from almost any point in the room if one is facing it. As the following scene progresses the speaker-phone is treated by those present as if it were a person in the room, they gesture to it, smile at it.* ARNOLD *is alone in his office, leaning against his desk, listening to the speaker phone, from which we continue to hear the voice of* LEO HERMAN.) God damn it, Arn; that's the intro Murray wrote for me two *years* ago, and it's still lovely, still warm. It's the way the kids know me, the way I say "Hello, kids"; he's a sweetie of a writer.

ARNOLD   That was *last* year he won the sweetie award, Leo.

LEO'S VOICE *(laughs good-naturedly)*   Please excuse my little words. They slip out of my face once in a while. Arn, you got my voice comin' out of that speaker-phone in your office, huh? Comes out like the biggest phony you ever met, right? That's how I sound, don't I? Big phony.

ARNOLD   No, Leo.

LEO'S VOICE   I'm getting sick of myself. Hey, Arn, you figure there's a good chance of Murray comin' back with me on the show?

ARNOLD   Can't guarantee it, Leo; I've sent him to one other appointment today, fairly good offer . . .

LEO'S VOICE   Well, I'm hopin' he comes back with *me*, Arn. Funny bit you being the agent for your own brother—what d'ya call that?

ARNOLD   It's called incest. *(The intercom buzzes;* ARNOLD *picks it up.)* O.K., send him in. *(Into the speaker-phone)* Got a call, fellah; check back with you when Murray shows.

LEO'S VOICE   Right, 'bye now.

(MURRAY enters wearing a new suit and carrying a beautiful pine-apple.)

MURRAY   Good afternoon, Mr. Burns.

ARNOLD   Good afternoon, Mr. Burns. Hey, you really did get a new suit, didn't you? How'd the appointment go with . . .

MURRAY *(putting the pineapple on the desk, gestures around at the office)*   Arnold, every time I see you, the agency's put you on a higher floor. I swear, next time I come you'll be up in a balloon.

ARNOLD   Murray, the appointment . . .

MURRAY   Can't get over this office, Arnie. *(Goes to the window, looks out.)* Twenty-second floor. You can see everything. *(Shocked by something he sees out of the window.)* My God, I don't believe it; it's King Kong. He's sitting on top of the Time-Life Building. He . . . he seems to be crying. Poor gorilla bastard, they shoulda told him they don't make those buildings the way they used to . . .

ARNOLD *(raising his hand in the air)*   Hello, Murray, hello there . . . here we are in my office. Welcome to Tuesday. Now, come *on,* how'd it go with Jimmy Sloan?

MURRAY   He took me to lunch at Steffanos, East Fifty-third. Christ, it's been a coupla years since I hustled around lunchland. There is this crazy hum that I haven't heard for so long, Arnie; eight square yards of idea men, busily having ideas, eating away at their chef's salad like it's Crackerjacks and there's a prize at the bottom.

ARNOLD   And Sloan . . .?

MURRAY *(sitting on the sofa)*   Sloan lunches beautifully, can out-lunch anybody. He used to be a Yes-man but he got himself some guts and now he goes around bravely saying "maybe" to everybody. And a killer, this one, Arnie; notches on his attaché case. Told me this idea he had where I'd be a lovable eccentric on his panel show. This somehow led him very logically to his conception of God, who he says is "probably a really fun guy."

ARNOLD   What'd you tell him about the offer?

MURRAY I told him good-bye. I don't think he noticed when I left; he focuses slightly to the right of you when he talks, just over your shoulder, so if you stay out of range he can't tell that you're gone. Probably thinks I'm still there.

ARNOLD Murray, you told me this morning to get any job I could; Sloan's offer wasn't so bad . . .

MURRAY Sloan is an idiot.

ARNOLD (sitting next to him on the sofa; angrily, firmly) Listen, cookie, I got *news* for you, right now you *need* idiots. You got a bad reputation for quitting jobs; I even had trouble grabbing Sloan for you. Why did you have to go and build your own personal blacklist; why couldn't you just be blacklisted as a Communist like everybody else?

MURRAY Don't worry, Arnie; I figured I'd go back with Chuckles. He's ready to take me back, isn't he?

ARNOLD Yeah, he's ready. I just spoke to him. (Solemnly) Hey, Murray, Leo says he came up to your place last January, a week after you quit him, to talk you into coming back with the show. And right in the middle you went into the kitchen and started singing "Yes, Sir, That's My Baby." Just left him standing there. Your way of saying "good-bye."

MURRAY Well, that was five months ago, Arnie . . .

ARNOLD (attempts to conceal his amusement, then turns to MURRAY, smiling) So, what'd you do with him, just left him standing there? (He laughs.) Like to have been there, seen that, must have been great.

MURRAY Arnie, it was beautiful.

ARNOLD (still laughing) It's about time somebody left Leo Herman standing around talking to himself. (Rubbing his head) I wish to God I didn't enjoy you so much. Crap, I don't do you any good at all. (Then, solemnly again.) Murray, no fun and games with Leo today, understand? He is absolutely *all* we got left before the hearing Thursday.

MURRAY Yes, I understand.

ARNOLD (goes to pick up the phone on the desk) I wish we coulda got something better for you, kid, but there just wasn't any time.

MURRAY Well, Chuckles won't be so bad for a while . . .

ARNOLD No, Murray. (Puts phone down firmly.) Not just for a while. You'll really have to stick with Chuckles. I had our agency lawyer check the facts for me. Most the Board'll give you is a probationary year with Nick; a trial period. The Board's investigators will be checking on you every week . . .

MURRAY   That's charming.

ARNOLD   . . . checking to see if you've still got the job, checking with Leo on your stability, checking up on the change in your home environment.

MURRAY   Sounds like a parole board.

ARNOLD *(into the intercom phone)*   Margot; get me Leo Herman on the speaker-phone here, his home number. Thanks. *(Puts the phone down.)* He's waiting for our call. Look, Murray, maybe he's not the greatest guy in the world; but y'know, he really *likes* you, Murray, he . . .

MURRAY   Yeah. I have a way with animals.

ARNOLD *(pointing at MURRAY)*   That was your last joke for today. *(A click is heard from speaker-phone; ARNOLD turns it on.)* You there, Leo?

LEO'S VOICE   Right, Arn. I'm down here in the basement, in my gymnasium; lot of echoing. Am I coming through, am I coming through O.K.?

ARNOLD   Clearly, Leo. Murray's here.

LEO'S VOICE   Murray! Murray the wonderful wild man; fellah, how are ya?

MURRAY *(takes his hat off, waves hello to the speaker-phone)*   O.K., Leo, how're you doing?

LEO'S VOICE   Oh, you crazy bastard, it's damn good to hear that voice again. You're an old monkey, aren't ya?

MURRAY   You sound about the same too, Leo.

LEO'S VOICE   Not the same. I'm *more impossible* than I used to be. Can you imagine that?

MURRAY   Not easily, Leo; no.

LEO'S VOICE   Murray, I need you, fellah; I need you back with the show. Murr', we'll talk a while now, and then I'll come over to your place tonight, go over some ideas for next week's shows. It'll be great, sweetie . . . Oh, there's that word again. "Sweetie," I said that word again. Oh, am I getting *sick* of myself. Big phony. The truth, fellah, I'm the biggest phony you ever met, right?

MURRAY   Probably, Leo.

LEO'S VOICE. *(after a pause; coldly)*   Probably, he says. There he goes, there goes Murray the old joker, right? You're a jester, right? Some fooler. You can't fool with a scheduled show, Murray; a scheduled show with a tight budget. *(Softly, whispering)* Murray, come closer, tell you a secret . . . *(*MURRAY *comes closer to the box.)* You're gonna hate me for it, but we can't have the same Murray we used to have on the show. Who appreciates a good joke more than anybody? *Me.* But who jokes too much? *(Suddenly louder) You!*

MURRAY   Leo, couldn't we talk about this tonight when we get together . . .

LEO'S VOICE *(softly again)*   It hurt me, Murr', it hurt me what you used to do. When all those thousands of kids wrote in asking for the definition of a chipmunk and you sent back that form letter sayin' a chipmunk was a . . . was a what?

MURRAY   A cute rat.

LEO'S VOICE *(still soft)*   A cute rat; yeah. I remember my skin broke out somethin' terrible. Some jester you are, foolin' around at the script conferences, toolin' around at the studio. Now, we're not gonna have any more of that, are we?

MURRAY *(subservient, apologetic)*   No, we won't, I'm sorry, Leo.

LEO'S VOICE   Because we can't fool with the innocence of children, can we? My God, they believe in the little Chipmunk, don't ask me why; I'm nothing; God, I know that. I've been damned lucky. A person like me should get a grand and a half a week for doin' nothin'. I mean, I'm one of the big no-talents of all time, right?

MURRAY   Right . . . I mean, no, Leo, no.

LEO'S VOICE   Oh, I know it's the truth and I don't kid myself about it. But there'll be no more jokin'; right, Murr'? Because I'll tell you the truth, I can't stand it.

MURRAY   Right, Leo.

LEO'S VOICE *(softly)* Good. Glad we cleared that up. Because my skin breaks out somethin' terrible. *(Up again)* You're the best, Murray, such talent, you know I love ya, don't ya? You old monkey.

MURRAY *(to* ARNOLD*)* Please, tell him we'll talk further tonight, too much of him all at once. . . .

ARNOLD Say, Leo, suppose we . . .

LEO'S VOICE Murray, I want you to put some fifteen-minute fairy tales into the show. You've got your Hans Christian Andersens there, your Grimm Brothers, your Goldilocks, your Sleepin' Beauties, your Gingerbread Men, your Foxy-Loxies, your legends, your folk tales . . . do I reach ya, Murr'?

MURRAY *(quietly)* Yeah, Leo . . .

LEO'S VOICE Now, what I want in those scripts is this, Murray, I want you to give 'em five minutes a action, five minutes a poignancy and then five minutes of the moral message; race-relations thing; world-peace thing; understanding-brings-love thing. I don't know. Shake 'em up a little. Controversy. Angry letters from parents. Kid's show with something to say, get some excitement in the industry, wild . . .

MURRAY *(he leans over very close to speaker-phone; whispers into it)* Hey, Leo, I might show up one day with eleven minutes of poignancy, no action and a twelve-second moral message . . .

ARNOLD Murray, stop it . . .

MURRAY *(shouting into the speaker-phone)* *And then where would we be?*

(There is a pause. No sound comes from the speaker-phone. Then:)

LEO'S VOICE See how he mocks me?Well, I guess there's plenty to mock. Plenty mocking. Sometimes I try to take a cold look at what I am. *(Very soft)* Sweaty Leo jumping around in a funny costume trying to make a buck out of being a chipmunk. The Abominable Snowman in a cute suit. But I'll tell you something, Murray . . . sit down for a minute. *(*MURRAY *is standing;* LEO'S VOICE *is still fairly pleasant.)* Are ya sitting down, Murray?*(*MURRAY *remains standing;* LEO'S VOICE *is suddenly loud, sharp, commanding.)* Murray, sit down! *(*MURRAY *sits down.)* Good. Now I'm gonna tell you a story . . .

MURRAY *(softly, painfully)* Arnold, he's gonna do it again . . . the story . . .

LEO'S VOICE   Murray . . .

MURRAY *(softly, miserably)*   The story I got tattooed to my skull . . .

LEO'S VOICE   On June the third . . .

MURRAY *(hunching over in his chair, looking down at the floor)-* Story number twelve . . . the "Laughter of Children" story . . . again . . .

LEO'S VOICE   I will be forty-two years old . . .

MURRAY *(to* ARNOLD; *painfully, pleading)*   Arnie . . .

LEO'S VOICE And maybe it's the silliest, phoniest, cop–out thing . . .

LEO'S VOICE and MURRAY. *(in unison).*   . . . you ever heard, but the Chipmunk, Chuckles, the little guy I pretend to be, is real to me . . .

LEO'S VOICE . . . as real to me as . . . as this phone in my hand; those children, don't ask me why, God I don't know, but they believe in that little fellah . . . *(*MURRAY *looks up from the floor now and over at the speaker-phone, which is on the other side of the room; his eyes are fixed on it.)* Look, Murr', I do what I can for the cash-monies; but also, and I say it without embarrassment, I just love kids, the laughter of children, and we can't have you foolin' with that, Murr', can't have you jokin' . . . *(*MURRAY *stands up, still looking at the speaker-phone.)* because it's this whole, bright, wild sorta child kinda thing . . . *(*MURRAY *is walking slowly toward the speaker-phone now;* ARNOLD, *watching* MURRAY, *starts to rise from his chair.)* it's this very up feeling, it's all young, and you can't joke with it; the laughter of children; those warm waves, that fresh, open, spontaneous laughter, you can feel it on your face . . .

MURRAY *(picking the speaker-phone up off the desk)* Like a sunburn . . .

LEO'S VOICE   Like a sunburn . . .

ARNOLD   *(coming   toward   MURRAY   as   if   to   stop him)* Murray . . . wait . . .

LEO'S VOICE   And it's a pride thing . . . *(*MURRAY *turns with the speaker-phone held in his hands and drops it into the wastepaper basket next to the desk. He does this calmly.* ARNOLD, *too late to stop him, stands watching, dumbly paralyzed.* LEO, *unaware, goes right on talking, his voice somewhat garbled and echoing from the bottom of the wastepaper basket.)* . . . so then how lovely, how enchanting it is, that I should be paid so well for something I love so much . . . *(Pause)* Say, there's this noise . . . there's this . . . I'm getting this cracking noise on my end here . . . What's happened to the phone?

ARNOLD *(sadly, solemnly; looking down into the basket)*   Leo, you're in a wastepaper basket.

LEO'S VOICE   That you, Murray? . . . There's this crackling noise. . . . I can't hear you. . . . Hello? . . . what's going on? . . .

ARNOLD   Leo, hold it just a minute, I'll get you.

LEO'S VOICE   There's this funny noise. . . . Where'd everybody go? Where is everybody? . . . Hello, Murray . . . hello . . . come back . . . come back . . .

ARNOLD *(fishing amongst the papers in basket for the speaker-phone)* I'll find you, Leo, I'll find you. . . . *(Finally lifts the speaker out of the basket, holds it gently, tenderly in his hands like a child, speaks soothingly to it.)* Look Leo . . . Leo, we had a little . . . some trouble with the phone, we . . . *(Realizes that he is getting no reaction from the box.)* Leo? . . . Leo? . . . *(As though the box were a friend whom he thinks might have died, shaking the box tenderly to revive it)* Leo . . . Leo, are you there? . . . Are you there? . . . It's dead. *(Turning to look at* MURRAY, *as though announcing the demise of a dear one.)* He's gone.

MURRAY   Well, don't look at me like that, Arnie; I didn't *kill* him. He doesn't *live* in that box . . . Or maybe he does.

ARNOLD   A man has a job for you so you drop him in a basket.

MURRAY   Arnie, I quit that nonsense five months ago . . .

ARNOLD   Murray, you're a *nut,* a man has a job for you, there's a hearing on Thursday . . .

MURRAY   A fool in a box telling me what's funny, a Welfare Board checking my underwear every week because I don't look good in their files . . . and *I'm* the nut, right? *I'm* the crazy one.

ARNOLD   Murray, you float like a balloon and everybody's waitin' for ya with a pin. I'm trying to put you in *touch,* Murray . . . with *real things;* with . . .

MURRAY *(angrily, taking in the office with a sweep of his hand)*   You mean like this office, *real* things, like this office? The world could come to an end and you'd find out about it on the phone. *(Pointing at two framed photographs on* ARNOLD'S *desk)* Pictures of your wife six years ago when she was still a piece, and your kids at their cutest four years ago when they looked best for the office. . . . Oh, you're in *touch* all right, Arnie.

ARNOLD *(softly, soothing)*   Murray, you're just a little excited, that's all, just relax, everything's gonna be fine . . .

MURRAY *(shouting)*   Damn it . . . get angry; I just insulted you, personally, about your wife, your kids; I just said lousy things to you. Raise your voice, at least your eyebrows . . . *(Pleading painfully)* Please, have an argument with me . . .

ARNOLD *(coaxing)*   We'll call Leo back, we'll apologize to him . . . *(MURRAY goes to the end table, picks up an apple from the bowl of fruit.)* Everything's gonna be just fine, Murray, you'll see . . . just fine.

MURRAY   Arnie?

ARNOLD   Huh?

MURRAY   Catch. *(Tosses the apple underhand across the room.* ARNOLD *catches it.* MURRAY *exits.)*

ARNOLD *(his hand out from catching the apple)*   Aw, Murray . . . *(Lowers his hand to his side; speaks quietly, alone now in the office.)* Murray, I swear to you, King Kong is *not* on top of the Time-Life Building . . .

(ARNOLD discovers the apple in his hand; bites into it. The lights fade quickly. As they dim, we hear NICK *humming and whistling. "Yes, Sir, That's My Baby." The lights go up on* MURRAY'*s apartment.* NICK'*s humming and whistling fades back so that it is coming from outside the window; the humming grows louder again after a second or two as, it would seem, he descends the fire-escape ladder from Mrs. Myers' apartment. It is early evening. No one is onstage. The apartment has been rather spectacularly rehabilitated by* SANDRA *since we saw it last. The great clutter of* MURRAY'*s nonsense collection, clocks, radios, knickknacks, has been cleared away, the books have been neatly arranged in the bookcases, a hat rack has been placed above the bureau and* MURRAY'*s hats are placed neatly on it. There are bright new bedspreads on the two beds and brightly colored throw pillows, one new curtain is already up at the windows and a piece of matching material is over the Morris chair. The beach chair and swivel chair are gone and the wicker chair has been painted gold, the table has a bright new cloth over it. Pots of flowers are on the table, the bookshelves, the file cabinets, headboard and desk; and geraniums are in a holder hanging from the window molding. The whole place has been dusted and polished and gives off a bright glow. After two lines or so of the song,* NICK *enters through the window from the fire*

escape, carrying his pajamas and school books. NICK *sees the new curtain first, and then, from his position on the window seat, sees the other changes in the apartment and smiles appreciatively.* SANDRA *enters from the kitchen, carrying a mixing bowl and a spoon. She smiles, glad to see* NICK.*)*

SANDRA   Hello, Nick . . .

NICK   Hello, lady. I came in from the fire escape. Mrs. Myers lives right upstairs. I went there after school, I . . . *(Indicating her work on the apartment)* Did . . . did you do all this?

SANDRA   Yes, Nick; do you like it?

NICK *(goes to her, smiling)*   I think it's superb. I mean, imagine my surprise when I saw it. *(Pause)* Where's Murray?

SANDRA *(happily telling him the good news)*   Nick . . . Murray went downtown to see your Uncle Arnold. He's going to get a job.

NICK   That's terrific. Hey, that's just terrific. *(*SANDRA *goes to the folded new curtains on the bed, sits down on the bed, unfolds one of the curtains, begins attaching curtain hooks and rings to it;* NICK *sits next to her, helping her as they talk together.)* See, lady, he was developing into a bum. You don't want to see somebody you like developing into a bum, and doing nutty things, right? You know what he does? He hollers. Like we were on Park Avenue last Sunday, it's early in the morning and nobody is in the street, see, there's just all those big quiet apartment houses; and he hollers "Rich people, I want to see you all out on the street for volleyball! Let's snap it up!" And sometimes, if we're in a crowded elevator some place, he turns to me and yells "Max, there'll be no *more* of this self-pity! You're forty, it's time you got *used* to being a midget!" And everybody stares. And he has a wonderful time. What do you do with somebody who hollers like that? Last week in Macy's he did that. *(He laughs.)* If you want to know the truth, it was pretty funny. *(*SANDRA *smiles.)* I think you're a very nice lady.

SANDRA   Thank you, Nick.

NICK   What do you think of me?

SANDRA   I think you're very nice also.

NICK   A very nice quality you have is that you are a good listener, which is important to me because of how much I talk. *(She laughs, enjoying him.)* Hey, you're some laugher, aren't you, lady?

SANDRA   I guess so, Nick.

NICK *(trying to make her feel at home)*   Would you like some fruit? An orange maybe?

SANDRA   No thank you, Nick.

NICK   If you want to call your mother or something, I mean, feel free to use the telephone . . . or my desk if you want to read a book or something . . . or *any* of the chairs . . .

SANDRA   I will, Nick, thank you.

NICK   O.K. *(Pause)* Are you going to be staying around here for a while?

SANDRA   I might, yes.

NICK *(he rises, picks up the pajamas and books he brought in with him; indicates apartment)*   Has . . . has Murray seen . . . all this?

SANDRA   No, not yet.

NICK *(nods)*   Not yet. Well . . . *(Goes to the window, steps up on the window seat.)* Good luck lady. *(He exits through the window, carrying his pajamas and school books, goes back up the fire escape,* SANDRA *crosses to window seat, smiling to herself.* MURRAY *enters, unnoticed by her.)*

MURRAY *(standing still at the front door, glancing around at the apartment; to himself)*   Oh God, I've been attacked by the Ladies Home Journal.

*(*SANDRA *hears him, goes to him happily.)*

SANDRA   Murray, what a nice suit you bought. How is everything, which job did . . .

MURRAY *(looking around at her work on the apartment)*   Hey look at this. You've started to get rid of the Edgar Allan Poe atmosphere.

SANDRA   Don't you like it?

MURRAY *(looking around, noticing his knickknacks are missing)-* Sure. Sure lotta work. Place has an unusual quality now. Kind of Fun Gothic.

SANDRA   Well, of course I'm really not done yet, the curtains aren't all up, and this chair won't look so bad if we reupholster . . . Come on, Murray, don't keep me in suspense, which one of the jobs did you . . .

MURRAY *(takes her arm, smiles, seats her on the chair in front of him)* I shall now leave you breathless with the strange and wondrous tale of this sturdy lad's adventures today in downtown Oz. *(She is cheered by his manner and ready to listen.)* Picture, if you will, me. I am walking on East Fifty-first Street an hour ago and I decided to construct and develop a really decorative, general-all-purpose apology. Not complicated, just the words "I am sorry," said with a little style.

SANDRA   Sorry for what?

MURRAY   Anything. For being late, early, stupid, asleep, silly, alive . . . *(He moves about now, acting out the scene on the street for her.)* Well, y'know when you're walking down the street talking to yourself how sometimes you suddenly say a coupla words out loud? So I said, "I'm sorry," and this fella, complete stranger, he looks up a second and says, "That's all right, Mac," and goes right on *(MURRAY and SANDRA laugh.)* He automatically forgave me. I communicated. Five-o'clock rush-hour in midtown you could say, "Sir, I believe your hair is on fire," and they wouldn't hear you. So I decided to test the whole thing out scientifically, I stayed right there on the corner of Fifty-first and Lex for a while, just saying "I'm sorry" to everybody that went by. *(Abjectly)* "Oh, I'm so sorry, sir . . ." *(Slowly, quaveringly)* "I'm terribly sorry, madam . . ." *(Warmly)* "Say there, miss, I'm sorry." Of course, some people just gave me a funny look, but Sandy, I swear, seventy-five percent of them *forgave* me. *(Acting out the people for her)* "Forget it, buddy" . . . "That's O.K., really." Two ladies forgave in unison, one fella forgave me from a passing car, and one guy forgave me for his dog. "Poofer forgives the nice man, don't you, Poofer?" Oh, Sandy, it was fabulous. I had tapped some vast reservoir. Something had happened to all of them for which they felt *some*body should apologize. If you went up to people on the street and offered them money, they'd refuse it. But everybody accepts apology immediately. It is the most negotiable currency. I said to them, "I am sorry." And they were all so generous, so kind. You could give 'em love and it wouldn't be accepted half as graciously, as unquestioningly . . .

SANDRA *(suspiciously, her amusement fading)*   That's certainly . . . that's very interesting, Murray.

MURRAY   Sandy, I could run up on the roof right now and holler, "I am sorry," and half a million people would holler right back, "That's O.K., just see that you don't do it again!"

SANDRA *(after a pause)*   Murray, you didn't take any of the jobs.

MURRAY *(quietly)* Sandy, I took whatever I am and put a suit on it and gave it a haircut and took it outside and that's what happened. I know what I said this morning, what I promised, and Sandra, I'm sorry, I'm very sorry. *(She just sits there before him and stares at him expressionlessly.)* Damn it, lady, that was a beautiful apology. You gotta love a guy who can apologize so nice. I rehearsed for over an hour. *(She just looks at him.)* That's the most you should expect from life, Sandy, a really good apology for all the things you won't get.

SANDRA Murray, I don't understand. What happens to Nick? What about the Welfare Board?

MURRAY *(he takes her hand)* Sandra . . .

SANDRA I mean, if you don't like the jobs your brother found for you, then take *any* job . . .

MURRAY *(he takes both of her hands . . . softly, pleading for her to understand)* Nick, he's a wonderful kid, but he's brought the God-damned world in on me. Don't you understand, Sandy, they'd be checking up on me every week; being judged by people I don't know and who don't know me, a committee of ghosts; gimme a month of that and I'd turn into an ashtray, a bowl of corn flakes, I wouldn't know me on the street. . . . *(Looks under chair.)* Have you seen Murray? He was here just a minute ago. . . . *(Looks at her, smiles.)* Hey, have you seen Murray? *(Pleading for her to understand)* I wouldn't be of any use to Nick or you or anybody . . .

(SANDRA moves away from him, goes to the window seat, leaves him kneeling at the chair. She is still holding the curtain she had been working on.)
SANDRA *(quietly)* I've had no effect on you at all. I've made no difference. You have no idea what it feels like to have no effect on people. I am not a leader. I scored very low in leadership in three different vocational aptitude tests. When I point my finger, people go the other way . . . *(Absently, she begins to fold the curtain neatly in her lap.)*

MURRAY Sandra . . .

SANDRA In grad school they put me in charge of the Structured-Childs-Play-Analysis session one day . . . *(She shrugs.)* and all the children fell asleep. I am not a leader.

MURRAY *(going to take her at the window seat; warmly, with love)* Oh, Sandy, you are a cute, jolly lady . . . please understand.

SANDRA When you left this morning, I was so sure . . .

MURRAY   This morning . . . *(He sits next to her on the window seat, his arm around her, his free hand gesturing expansively, romantically.)* Oh, Sandy, I saw the most beautiful sailing this morning . . . The *Sklardahl*, Swedish liner, bound for Europe. It's a great thing to do when you're about to start something new; you see a boat off. It's always wonderful; there's a sailing practically every day this time of year. Sandy, you go down and stand at the dock with all the well-wishers and throw confetti and make a racket with them. . . . Hey, bon voyage, Charley, have a wonderful time. . . . It gives you a genuine feeling of the beginning of things. . . . There's another one Friday, big French ship, two stacker . . .

(SANDRA has been watching him coldly during this speech; she speaks quietly; catching him in mid-air.)

SANDRA   Nick will have to go away now, Murray. *(She looks away from him.)* I bought new bedspreads at Altman's, I haven't spoken to my mother in two days, and you went to see a boat off. *(She pauses; then smiles to herself for a moment.)* My goodness; I'm a listmaker. *(She leaves him alone in the window seat.)* I have to have enough sense to leave you, Murray. I can see why Nick liked it here. I would like it here too if I was twelve years old. *(She puts the folded curtain down on a chair, picks up her jacket.)*

MURRAY *(coming toward her, warmly)*   Come on, stick with me, Dr. Markowitz, anything can happen above an abandoned Chinese restaurant.

SANDRA *(looking directly at him; quietly)*   Maybe you're wonderfully independent, Murray, or maybe, maybe you're the most extraordinarily selfish person I've ever met. *(She picks up her hand bag and starts toward the door.)*

MURRAY *(tired of begging; angrily, as she walks toward the door)*- What're you gonna do now, go back and live in a closet? It's really gonna be quite thrilling, you and Albert, guarding the Lincoln Tunnel together.

SANDRA *(turning at the door to look at him)*   I think, Murray, that you live in a much, much larger closet than I do.

MURRAY *(painfully)*   Lady, lady, please don't look at me like that . . .

SANDRA *(looking about the apartment; very quietly)*   Oh, there are so many really attractive things you can do with a one-room apartment if you're willing to use your imagination. *(Opens the door.)* Good-bye, Murray. *(She exits, MURRAY stands still for a moment; then rushes forward to the closed door, angrily.)*

MURRAY *(shouting)*   Hey, damn it, you forgot your files! *(Picks up her files from the bureau, opens the door; but she is gone.)* The management is not responsible for personal property! *(Closes the door, puts the files back on the bureau; stands at the door, looking around at the apartment.)* And what the hell did you do to my apartment? Where are my clocks? What'd you do with my stuff? Where's my radios? *(His back to the audience, shouting)* What've we got here; God damn Sunnybrook Farm! What happened to my place? *(Suddenly realizing he is still wearing a new suit, he pulls off his suit jacket, rolls it up into a tight ball, and throws it violently across the room. A moment; then he relaxes, walks casually to the window, puts his favorite hat on, sits, leans back comfortably in the window seat and smiles. He talks out of the window in a loudmock-serious voice.)* Campers . . . the entertainment committee was quite disappointed by the really poor turn-out at this morning's community sing. I mean, where's all that old Camp Chickawattamee spirit? Now, I'd like to say that I . . . *(He hesitates; he can't think of anything to say. A pause; then he haltingly tries again.)* I'd like to say right now that I . . . that . . . that I . . . *(His voice is soft, vague; he pulls his knees up, folds his arms around them, his head bent on his knees; quietly)* Campers, I can't think of anything to say . . .

   (A moment; then)

CURTAIN

ACT THREE

   In the darkness, before the curtain goes up, we hear an old recording of a marching band playing "Stars and Stripes Forever." This goes on rather loudly for a few moments. The music diminishes somewhat as the curtain goes up; and we see that the music is coming from an old phonograph on the wicker chair near the bed. It's about thirty minutes later and, though much of SANDRA'S *work on the apartment is still apparent, it is obvious that* MURRAY *has been busy putting his place back into its old shape. The curtains are gone, as is the tablecloth and the material on the Morris chair. All the flower pots have been put on top of the file cabinet. The swivel chair and the beach chair are back in view. Cluttered about the room again is much of* MURRAY'S *nonsense collection, clocks, radios, knickknacks and stacks of magazines.*
   As the curtain goes up, MURRAY *has just retrieved a stack of magazines, the megaphone and the pirate pistol from the closet where* SANDRA *had put them; and we see him now placing them back around the room carefully, as though they were part of some strict design.* ARNOLD *enters, carrying his attaché case; walks to the beach chair, sits, takes his*

hat off. The two men do not look at each other. The music continues to play.

ARNOLD *(after a moment)*   I didn't even bring a tangerine with me. That's very courageous if you think about it for a minute. *(Looks over at* MURRAY, *who is not facing him, points at record player.)* You wanna turn that music off, please? *(No reply from* MURRAY.*)* Murray, the music; I'm trying to . . .*(No reply from* MURRAY, *so* ARNOLD *puts his attaché case and hat on table, goes quickly to the record player and turns the music off;* MURRAY *turns to look at* ARNOLD.*)* O.K., I'm a little slow. It takes me an hour to get insulted. Now I'm insulted. You walked out of my office. That wasn't a nice thing to do to me, Murray . . .*(*MURRAY *does not reply.)* You came into my office like George God; everybody's supposed to come up and audition for Human Being in front of you. *(Comes over closer to him, takes his arm.)* Aw, Murray, today, one day, leave the dragons alone, will ya?And look at the dragons you pick on; Sloan, Leo, me; silly old arthritic dragons, step on a toe and we'll start to cry. Murray, I called Leo back, I apologized, told him my phone broke down; I got him to come over here tonight. He's anxious to see you, everything's O.K. . . .

MURRAY   Hey, you just never give up, do you Arnie?

ARNOLD   Listen to me, Murray, do I ever tell you what to do . . .

MURRAY   Yes, all the time.

ARNOLD   If you love this kid, then you gotta take any kinda stupid job to keep him . . .

MURRAY   Now you're an expert on love.

ARNOLD   Not an expert, but I sure as hell value my amateur standing. Murray, about him leaving, have you told him yet?

MURRAY *(softly; realizing* ARNOLD's *genuine concern)*   Arnie, don't worry, I know how to handle it. I've got a coupla days to tell him. And don't underrate Nick, he's gonna understand this a lot better than you think.

ARNOLD   Murray, I finally figured out your problem. There's only one thing that really bothers you . . .*(With a sweep of his hand)* Other people. *(With a mock-secretive tone)* If it wasn't for them other people, everything would be great, huh, Murray? I mean, you think everything's fine, and then you go out into the street . . . and there they all *are* again, right? The Other People; taking up space, bumping into you, asking for things, making lines to wait on, taking cabs away from ya . . . The Enemy . . . Well, *watch* out, Murray, they're *every*where . . .

MURRAY   Go ahead, Arnie, give me advice, at thirty thousand a year you can afford it.

ARNOLD   Oh, I get it, if I'm so smart why ain't I poor? You better get a damn good act of your own before you start giving *mine* the razzberry. What's this game you play gonna be like ten years from now, without youth? Murray, Murray, I can't *watch* this, you gotta *shape* up . . .

MURRAY   *(turning quickly to face* ARNOLD; *in a surprised tone)-* Shape up? *(Looks directly at* ARNOLD; *speaks slowly.)* Arnie, what the hell happened to you? You got so old. I don't know you any more. When you quit "Harry the Fur King" on Thirty-eighth Street, remember?

ARNOLD   That's twenty years ago, Murray.

MURRAY   You told me you were going to be in twenty businesses in twenty years if you had to, till you found out what you wanted. Things were always going to change. Harry said you were not behaving maturely enough for a salesman; your clothes didn't match or something . . . *(Laughs in affectionate memory of the event.)* So the next day, you dressed perfectly, homburg, gray suit, cuff links, carrying a briefcase and a rolled umbrella . . . and you came into Harry's office on roller skates. You weren't going to take crap from *any*body. So that's the business you finally picked . . . taking crap from *every*body.

ARNOLD   I don't do practical jokes any more, if that's what you mean . . .

MURRAY   *(grabs both of* ARNOLD's *arms tensely)*   Practical, that's right; a way to stay alive. If most things aren't funny, Arn, then they're only exactly what they are; then it's one long dental appointment interrupted occasionally by something exciting, like waiting or falling asleep. What's the point if I leave everything exactly the way I find it? Then I'm just adding to the noise, then I'm just taking up some more room on the subway.

ARNOLD   Murray, the Welfare Board has these specifications; all you have to do is meet a couple specifications . . .

*(*MURRAY *releases his grip on* ARNOLD's *arms;* MURRAY's *hands drop to his sides.)*

MURRAY   Oh, Arnie, you don't understand any more. You got that wide stare that people stick in their eyes so nobody'll know their head's asleep. You got to be a shuffler, a moaner. You want me to come sit and eat fruit with you and watch the clock run out. You start to drag and stumble with the rotten weight of all the people who should have been told off, all the things you should have said, all the specifications that aren't yours. The only thing you got left to reject is your food in a restaurant if they do it wrong and you can send it back and make a big fuss with the waiter. . . . *(MURRAY turns away from ARNOLD, goes to the window seat, sits down.)* Arnold, five months ago I forgot what *day* it was. I'm on the subway on my way to work and I didn't know what day it was and it scared the hell out of me. . . . *(Quietly)* I was sitting in the express looking out the window same as every morning watching the local stops go by in the dark with an empty head and my arms folded, not feeling great and not feeling rotten, just not feeling, and for a minute I couldn't remember, I didn't know, unless I really concentrated, whether it was a Tuesday or a Thursday . . . or a . . . for a minute it could have been *any* day, Arnie . . . sitting in the train going through any day . . . in the dark through any year. . . . Arnie, it scared the hell out of me. *(Stands up.)* You got to know what day it is. You got to know what's the name of the game and what the rules are with nobody else telling you. You have to own your days and name them, each one of them, every one of them, or else the years go right by and none of them belong to you. *(Turns to look at* ARNOLD.*)* And that ain't just for weekends, kiddo . . . *(Looks at* ARNOLD *a moment longer, then speaks in a pleasant tone.)* Here it is, the day after Irving R. Feldman's birthday, for God's sake . . . *(Takes a hat, puts it on.)* And I never even congratulated him . . . *(Starts to walk briskly toward the front door.* ARNOLD *shouts in a voice stronger than we have ever heard from him.)*

ARNOLD   Murray! *(MURRAY stops, turns, startled to hear this loud a voice from* ARNOLD. ARNOLD *looks fiercely at* MURRAY *for a moment, then* ARNOLD *looks surprised, starts to laugh.)*

MURRAY   What's so funny?

ARNOLD   Wow, I scared myself. You hear that voice? Look at that, I got you to stop, I got your complete, full attention, the floor is mine now . . . *(Chuckles awkwardly.)* And I can't think of a God-damned thing to say . . . *(Shrugs his shoulders; picks up his hat from the table.)* I have long been aware that you don't respect me much. . . . I suppose there are a lot of brothers who don't get along. . . . But in reference . . . to us, considering the factors . . . *(Smiles, embarrassed.)* Sounds like a contract, doesn't it? *(Picks up his briefcase, comes over to* MURRAY.*)* Unfortunately for you, Murray, you want to be a hero. Maybe, if a fella falls into a lake, you can jump in and save him; there's still that kind of stuff. But who gets opportunities like that in midtown Manhattan, with all that traffic. *(Puts on his hat.)* I am willing to deal with the available world and I do not choose to shake it up but to live with it. There's the people who spill things, and the people who get spilled on; I do not choose to notice the stains, Murray. I have a wife and I have children, and business, like they say, is

business. I am not an exceptional man, so it is possible for me to
stay with things the way they are. I'm lucky. I'm gifted. I have a talent for
surrender. I'm at peace. But you are cursed; and I like you so it makes me
sad, you don't have the gift; and I see the torture of it. All I can do is
worry for you. But I will not worry for myself; you cannot convince me
that I am one of the Bad Guys. I get up, I go, I lie a little, I peddle a little, I
watch the rules, I talk the talk. We fellas have those offices high up there
so we can catch the wind and go with it, however it blows. But, and I will
not apologize for it, I take pride; I am the best possible Arnold Burns.
(Pause) Well . . . give my regards to Irving R. Feldman, will ya? *(He
starts to leave.)*

MURRAY *(going toward him)* Arnold . . .

ARNOLD Please, Murray . . . *(Puts his hand up.)* Allow me once to
leave a room before you do.

*(ARNOLD snaps on record player as he walks past it to the front door;
he exits. MURRAY goes toward the closed door, the record player has
warmed up and we suddenly hear "Stars and Stripes Forever" blaring
loudly from the machine again; MURRAY turns at this sound and stands for
a long moment looking at the record player as the music comes from it.
NICK enters through the window from the fire escape, unnoticed by
MURRAY. NICK looks about, sees that the apartment is not quite what it
was an hour before.)*

NICK Hey, Murray . . .

MURRAY *(turns, sees NICK)* Nick . . . *(Turns the record player off;
puts the record on the bed.)*

NICK Hey, where's the lady?

MURRAY Well, she's not here right now . . .

NICK *(stepping forward to make an announcement)* Murray, I have
decided that since *you* are getting a job today then I made up my mind it is
time for *me* also to finish a certain matter which I have been putting off.

MURRAY Nick, listen, turned out the only job I could get in a hurry
was with Chuckles . . .

NICK *(nodding in approval)* Chuckles, huh? Well, fine. *(Then,
grimly)* Just as long as I don't have to watch that terrible program every
morning. *(Returning to his announcement)* For many months now I have
been concerned with a decision, Murray . . . Murray, you're not listening.

MURRAY *(distracted)*   Sure I'm listening, yeah . . .

NICK   The past couple months I have been thinking about different names and considering different names because in four weeks I'm gonna be thirteen and I gotta pick my permanent name, like we said.

MURRAY   Why don't you just go on calling yourself Nick? You've been using it the longest.

NICK   Nick is a name for a short person. And since I am a short person I do not believe I should put a lot of attention on it.

MURRAY   Whaddya mean, where'd you get the idea you were short?

NICK   From people who are taller than I am.

MURRAY   That's ridiculous.

NICK   Sure, standing up there it's ridiculous, but from down here where I am it's not so ridiculous. And half the girls in my class are taller than me. Especially Susan Bookwalter. *(NICK sits dejectedly in the swivel chair.)*

MURRAY *(crouching over next to him)*   Nick, you happen to be a nice medium height for your age.

NICK *(pointing at MURRAY)*   Yeah, so how is it everybody crouches over a little when I'm around?

MURRAY *(straightening up)*   Because you're a kid. *(Sits next to him.)* Listen, you come from a fairly tall family. Next couple years you're gonna grow like crazy. Really, Nick, every day you're getting bigger.

NICK   So is Susan Bookwalter. *(Stands.)* So for a couple of months I considered various tall names. Last month I considered, for a while, Zachery, but I figured there was a chance Zachery could turn into a short, fat, bald name. Then I thought about Richard, which is not really tall, just very thin with glasses. Then last week I finally, really, decided and I took out a new library card to see how it looks and today I figured I would make it definite and official. *(He takes a library card out of his pocket, hands it to MURRAY.)*

MURRAY *(looks at the card, confused)*   This is *my* library card.

NICK   No, that's the whole thing; it's mine.

MURRAY   But it says *"Murray* Burns" on it . . .

NICK   Right, that's the name I picked. So I took out a new card to see how it looks and make it official.

MURRAY *(looks at the card, is moved and upset by it, but covers with cool dignity; stands, speaks very formally)*   Well, Nick, I'm flattered . . . I want you to know that I'm . . . very flattered by this. (*NICK goes to the alcove to put his school books and pajamas away.*) Well, why the hell did you . . . I mean, damn it, Nick, that's too many Murrays, very confusing . . . (MURRAY *begins to shift the card awkwardly from one hand to the other, speaks haltingly.*) Look, why don't you call yourself George, huh? Very strong name there, George . . .

NICK *(shaking his head firmly)*   No. We made a deal it was up to me to pick which name and that's the name I decided on; "Murray."

MURRAY   Well, what about Jack? What the hell's wrong with Jack? Jack Burns . . . sounds like a promising heavyweight.

NICK   I like the name I picked better.

MURRAY *(very quietly)*   Or Martin . . . or Robert . . .

NICK   Those names are all square.

LEO'S VOICE *(from behind the door, shouting)*   Is this it? Is this the Lion's Den, here? Hey, Murr'!

MURRAY *(softly)*   Ah, I heard the voice of a chipmunk.

NICK *(going into the bathroom)*   I better go put on a tie.

MURRAY *(goes to the door; stands there a moment, looks over to the other side of the room at NICK, who is offstage in the bathroom; smiles, speaks half to himself, very softly)*   You coulda called yourself Charlie. Charlie is a very musical name.

(Then, he opens the door. LEO HERMAN *enters. He wears a camel's-hair coat and hat. The coat, like his suit, is a little too big for him. He is carrying a paper bag and a large Chuckles statue—a life-size cardboard cutout of himself in his character of Chuckles the Chipmunk; the statue wears a blindingly ingratiating smile.)*

LEO *(with great enthusiasm)*   Murray, there he is! There's the old monkey! There's the old joker, right?

MURRAY *(quietly, smiling politely)* Yeah, Leo, here he is. *(Shakes* LEO's *hand.)* It's . . . it's very nice to see you again, Leo, after all this time.

LEO *(turning to see* NICK, *who has come out of the bathroom wearing his tie)* There he is! There's the little guy! *(Goes to* NICK *carrying the statue and the paper bag.)* Looka here, little guy . . . *(Setting the statue up against the wall next to the window.)* I gotta Chuckles statue for you.

NICK *(with his best company manners)* Thank you, Mr. Herman; imagine how pleased I am to receive it. It's a very artistic statue and very good cardboard too.

LEO *(taking a Chuckles hat from the paper bag; a replica of the furry, big-eared hat worn by the statue)* And I gotta Chuckles hat for you too, just like the old Chipmunk wears. *(He puts the hat on* NICK's *head.)*

NICK Thank you.

LEO *(crouching over to* NICK's *height)* Now that you've got the Chuckles hat, you've got to say the Chuckles-hello.

NICK *(confused, but anxious to please)* The what?

LEO *(prompting him)* "Chip-chip, Chippermunkie!" *(He salutes.)*

NICK Oh, yeah . . . "Chip-chip, Chippermunkie!" *(He salutes too.)*

LEO May I know your name?

NICK It's Nick, most of the time.

LEO Most of the . . .*(Pulling two bags of potato chips from his overcoat pockets)* Say, look what I've got, two big bags of Chuckle-Chip potato chips! How'd ya like to put these crispy chips in some bowls or somethin' for us, huh? *(*NICK *takes the two bags, goes to the kitchen.)* And take your time, Nick, your uncle 'n' me have some grown-up talkin' to do. *(After* NICK *exits into the kitchen)* The kid hates me. I can tell. Didn't go over very well with him, pushed a little too hard. He's a nice kid, Murray.

MURRAY How are *your* kids, Leo?

LEO Fine, fine. But, Murray, I swear, even *they* don't like my show since you stopped writing it. My youngest one . . . my six-year-old . . . *(He can't quite remember.)*

MURRAY   Ralphie.

LEO   Ralphie; he's been watching the Funny Bunny Show now every morning instead of me. *(Begins pacing up and down.)* Oh, *boy,* have I been bombing out on the show. Murray, do you know what it feels like to bomb out in front of children? You flop out in front of children? You flop out in front of kids and, Murray, I swear to God, they're ready to *kill* you. *(Stops pacing.)* Or else, they just stare at you, that's the worst, that hurt, innocent stare like you just killed their pup or raped their turtle or something. *(Goes over to* MURRAY.) Murray, to have you back with me on the show, to see you at the studio again tomorrow, it's gonna be *beautiful.* You're the *best.*

MURRAY   I appreciate your feeling that way, Leo.

LEO   This afternoon, Murray, on the phone, you hung up on me, didn't you?

MURRAY   I'm sorry Leo, I was just kidding . . . I hope you . . .

LEO *(sadly)*   Murray, why do you do that to me? Aw, don't tell me, I know, I make people nervous. Who can listen to me for ten minutes? *(Begins pacing up and down again, strokes his tie.)* See *that?* See how I keep touching my suit and my tie? I keep touching myself to make sure I'm still there. Murray, I get this feeling, maybe I vanished when I wasn't looking.

MURRAY   Oh, I'm sure that you're here, Leo.

LEO *(pointing at* MURRAY)   See how he talks to me? A little nasty, *(Smiles suddenly.)* Well, I like it. It's straight and it's real and I like it. You know what I got around me on the show? Finks, dwarfs, phonies and frogs. No Murrays. The show: boring, boredom, bore . . . *(Cups his hands around his mouth and shouts.)* boring, boring . . .

(During these last few words, SANDRA *has entered through the partly open door.* MURRAY *turns, sees her.)*

SANDRA *(staying near the doorway; reserved, official)*   Murray, I believe that I left my files here; I came to get my files; may I have my files, please. I . . . *(She sees* LEO, *comes a few feet into the room.)* Oh, excuse me . . .

MURRAY *(cordially, introducing them)*   Chuckles the Chipmunk . . . this is Minnie Mouse.

LEO *(absently)*   Hi, Minnie . . .

SANDRA *(looking from one to the other, taking in the situation, smiles; to* LEO*)*   You must be . . . you must be Mr. Herman.

LEO *(mumbling to himself)*   Yeah, I must be. I must be him; I'd rather not be, but what the hell . . .

SANDRA *(smiling, as she turns right around and goes to the door)* Well, I'll be on my way . . . *(She exits.* MURRAY *picks up her files from the bureau, goes to the door with them.)*

LEO *(interrupting* MURRAY *on his way to the door)*   Very attractive girl, that Minnie; what does she do?

MURRAY   She's my decorator.

LEO *(looking around the apartment)*   Well, she's done a *wonderful* job! *(Indicating the apartment with a sweep of his hand)* This place is great. It's loose, it's open, it's free. Love it. Wonderful, crazy place. My God . . . you must make out like mad in this place, huh? *(*MURRAY *closes door, puts the files back on the bureau;* LEO *is walking around the apartment.)* How come I never came here before?

MURRAY   You were here last January, Leo.

LEO   Funny thing, work with me for three years and I never saw your apartment.

MURRAY   You were here last January, Leo.

LEO *(stops pacing, turns to* MURRAY*)*   Wait a minute, wait a minute, wasn't I here recently, in the winter? Last January, I think . . . *(Goes over to* MURRAY*.)* Oh, I came here to get you back on the show and you wouldn't listen, you went into the kitchen, sang "Yes, Sir, That's My Baby." I left feeling very foolish, like I had footprints on my face . . . You old monkey. *(Smiles, musses up* MURRAY'S *hair.)* You're an old monkey, aren't ya? *(Starts pacing again.)* You know what I got from that experience? A rash. I broke out something terrible . . . Minnie Mouse! *(Stops pacing.)* Minnie *Mouse! (Laughs loudly, points at the door.)* You told me her name was Minnie Mouse! I swear to God, Murray, I think my mission in life is to feed you straight-lines . . . *(Taking in the apartment with a sweep of his hand.)* It's kind of a fall-out shelter, that's what you got here, Murr', protection against the idiots in the atmosphere. Free, freer, freest . . . *(Cups his hands around his mouth, shouts.)* Free! Free! *(Takes off his coat.)* Another year and I'm gonna cut loose from the God-damn Chipmunk show. Binds me up, hugs me. Finks, dwarfs, phonies and frogs . . . *(Following* MURRAY *to the window seat)* Two of us should do

something new, something wild; new kind of kid's show, for adults
maybe . . .

MURRAY *(sitting on the window seat)* You told me the same thing
three years ago, Leo.

LEO *(sits next to* MURRAY*)* Well, whaddya want from me? I'm a
coward; everybody knows that. *(Suddenly seeing the Chuckles statue
against the wall next to him.)* Oh God! *(Points at the statue; in anguish)*
Did you ever see anything so immodest? I bring a big statue of myself as a
gift for a child! I mean, the *pure ego* of it . . . *(Covers his face with his
hands.)* I am ashamed. Murray, could you throw a sheet over it or
something . . . *(Sees* NICK, *who has just come out of the kitchen with two
bowls of potato chips.)* Mmmm, good! Here they are. *(Grabs one bowl
from* NICK'S *hand, gives it to* MURRAY. *Then* LEO *turns to* NICK, *assumes
the character and the voice of Chuckles the Chipmunk; a great mock-
frown on his face, he goes into a routine for* NICK.*)* Oh, goshes, kidderoonies, look at your poor Chippermunk friend; he got his mouff stuck.
No matter how hard I try I can't get my mouth unstuck. But maybe—if
you Chippermunks yell, "Be happy, Chuckles," maybe then it'll get
unstuck . . . *(*LEO *waits.* NICK *does not react.* LEO *prompts* NICK *in a
whisper.)* You're supposed to yell, "Be happy, Chuckles."

NICK Oh, yeah . . . sure . . . *(Glances quickly at* MURRAY; *then, a
little embarrassed, he yells.)* Be happy, Chuckles!

LEO Oh *boy! (His frown changes to a giant smile.)* You *fixed* me!
Looka my mouff! *(He jumps up in the air.)* Now I'm all fixed! *(Gets no
reaction from* NICK. NICK *stands patiently in front of* LEO.*)*

NICK *(offering the other bowl of potato chips trying to be polite)* Mr.
Herman, don't you want your . . .

LEO *(not accepting the potato chips, speaking in his own voice again,
stroking his tie nervously)* That was a bit from tomorrow morning's
show. You'll know it ahead of all the kids in the neighborhood.

NICK Thank you.

LEO That . . . that was one of the funny parts there, when I couldn't
move my mouth.

NICK Yeah?

LEO Didn't you think it was funny?

NICK   Yeah, that was pretty funny.

LEO   *(smiling nervously)*   Well, don't you laugh or something when you see something funny?

NICK   It just took me by surprise is all. So I didn't get a chance. *(Offering him the potato chips, politely)* Here's your . . .

LEO   Another funny part was when I jumped up with the smile there, at the end there. That was another one.

NICK   Uh-huh.

LEO   *(pressing on, beginning to get tense)*   And the finish on the bit, see, I've got the smile . . . *(*NICK, *looking trapped, stands there as* LEO *switches back to his Chipmunk voice and puts a giant smile on his face.)* Now I'm aaaall fixed, Chippermunks! *(Suddenly mock-pathos in his eyes.)* Oooops! Now I got stuck the *other* way! Oh, *oh*, now my face is stuck the *other* way! *(Throws up his arms, does a loose-legged slapstick fall back onto the floor. Remains prone, waiting for* NICK'S *reaction.* NICK *stands there looking at* LEO *quite solemnly.)*

NICK   *(nods his head up and down approvingly)*   That's terrific, Mr. Herman. *(With admiration)* That's all you have to do, you just get up and do that and they pay you and everything.

LEO   You didn't laugh.

NICK   I was waiting for the funny part.

LEO   *(sits up)*   That was the funny part.

NICK   Oh, when you fell down on the . . .

LEO   When I fell down on the floor here.

NICK   See, the thing is, I was . . .

LEO   *(gets up from the floor, paces up and down tensely)*   I know, waiting for the funny part. Well, you missed another funny part.

NICK   Another one. Hey, I'm really sorry, Mr. Herman, I . . .

LEO   Forget it . . . I just happen to know that that bit is very *funny.* I can prove it to you. *(Takes small booklet from pocket, opens it, shows it to* NICK.) Now, what does that say there, second line there?

NICK *(reading from the booklet)* "Frown bit; eighty-five percent of audience; outright prolonged laughter on frown bit."

LEO   That's the analysis report the agency did for me on Monday's preview audience. The routine I just did for you, got outright prolonged laughter; eighty-five percent.

MURRAY   You could try him on sad parts, Leo; he's very good on sad parts.

LEO *(goes to* MURRAY *at the window seat, shows him another page in the booklet)* Matter fact, there's this poignant-type bit I did at the Preview Theatre: "Sixty percent of audience; noticeably moved."

MURRAY   They left the theatre?

LEO *(tensely, angrily)*   There he is; there's the old joker; Murray the joker, right?

NICK   I do some routines. I can imitate the voice of Alexander Hamilton.

LEO   That's lovely, but I . . .

NICK   I do Alexander Hamilton and Murray does this terrific Thomas Jefferson; we got the voices just right.

MURRAY *(in a dignified voice; to* NICK*)*   Hello there, Alex, how are you?

NICK *(in a dignified voice; to* MURRAY*)*   Hello there, Tom; say, you should have been in Congress this morning. My goodness, there was quite a discussion on . . .

LEO   Now, that's *ridiculous.* You . . . you can't *do* an imitation of Alexander Hamilton; nobody knows what he *sounds* like . . .

NICK *(pointing triumphantly at* LEO*)*   *That's* the *funny* part.

MURRAY *(shaking his head regretfully)*   You missed the funny part, Leo.

LEO *(walking away from them)*   I'm getting a terrible rash on my neck. *(Turns to them, growing louder and more tense with each word.)* The routine I did for him was *funny.* I was workin' good in front of the kid, I know how to use my God-damn *warmth,* I don't go over with these odd kids; I mean, here I am right in *front* of him, in *person* for God's sake, and he's *staring* at me . . . *(Moves toward them, on the attack.)* It's oddness here, Murray, *odd*ness. Alexander *Ham*ilton imitations! Jaded jokes for old men. Murray, what you've done to this kid. It's a damn shame, a child can't enjoy little animals, a damn shame . . . *(Really on the attack now; waving at the apartment, shouting)* The way you brought this kid up, Murray, grotesque atmosphere, *unhealthy,* and you're not even guilty about it, women in and out, *dec*orators; had he been brought up by a *normal* person and not in this *mad*house . . .

NICK *(quietly, going toward* LEO)   Hey, don't say that . . .

LEO   A certain kind of freakish way of growing up . . .

NICK *(quietly*   Hey, are you calling me a freak? You called me a freak. Take back what you said.

LEO *(walks away from them, mumbling to himself)*   On June third I will be forty-two years old and I'm standing here arguing with a twelve-year-old kid . . . *(*LEO *quiets down, turns, comes toward* NICK, *sits on bed,* NICK *standing next to him; speaks calmly to* NICK.) See, Nicky, humor is a cloudy, wonderland thing, but simple and clear like the blue, blue sky. All I want is your simple, honest, child's opinion of my routine; for children are too honest to be wise . . .

NICK *(looking directly at* LEO, *calmly, quietly, slowly)*   My simple, child's reaction to what you did is that you are not funny. Funnier than you is even Stuart Slossman my friend who is eleven and puts walnuts in his mouth and makes noises. What is not funny is to call us names and what is mostly not funny is how sad you are that I would feel sorry for you if it wasn't for how dull you are and those are the worst-tasting potato chips I ever tasted. And that is my opinion from the blue, blue sky.

*(*NICK *and* LEO *stay in their positions, looking at each other. A moment; then* MURRAY *throws his head back and laughs uproariously.* LEO *stands; the bowl of potato chips tips over in his hand, the chips spilling onto the floor.)*

LEO *(seeing* MURRAY'S *laughter, goes to him at the Morris chair; angrily)*   Murray the joker, right? You didn't want to come back to work for me, you just got me up here to step on my face again! *(*NICK, *unnoticed by* LEO, *has gone quickly into his alcove and comes out now with his ukulele, playing and singing "Yes, Sir, That's My Baby" with great spirit.* LEO, *hearing this, turns to look at* NICK.) It's the *song.* It's the good-*bye* song. *(*LEO *grabs his hat and coat quickly, as* NICK *goes on playing, starts for front door, shouting.)* Getting *out,* bunch of *nuts* here, *crazy* people . . .

MURRAY   Leo, wait . . . *(Goes to the door to stop* LEO.*)* Leo, wait . . . I'm sorry . . . wait . . . *(*LEO *stops at the door;* MURRAY *goes down toward* NICK, *who is near the alcove, still playing the song.)* Nick, you better stop now . . .

NICK   Come on, Murray, get your uke, we'll sing to him and he'll go away . . .

MURRAY *(quietly)*   Nick, we can't . . . *(Gently taking the uke from* NICK *puts it on the window seat.)* Just put this down, huh?

NICK *(confused by this; urgently)*   Come on, Murray, let him go away, he called us names, we gotta get rid of him . . .

MURRAY   Quiet now, Nick . . . just be quiet for a minute . . . *(Starts to go back toward* LEO.*)*

NICK *(shouting)*   Murray, please let him go away . . . *(*NICK, *seeing the Chuckles statue next to him against the wall, grabs it angrily, throws it down on the floor.)* It's a crummy statue . . . that crummy statue . . . *(Begins to kick the statue fiercely, jumping up and down on it, shouting.)* It's a terrible statue, rotten cardboard . . .

*(*MURRAY *comes quickly back to* NICK, *holds both of his arms, trying to control him.)*

MURRAY   Aw, Nick, please, no more now, stop it . . .

There is a great struggle between them; NICK *is fighting wildly to free himself from* MURRAY'S *arms.)*

NICK *(near tears, shouting)*   We don't want jerks like that around here, Murray, let him go away, we gotta get rid of him, Murray, we gotta get rid of him . . .

MURRAY *(lifts the struggling* NICK *up into his arms, hugging him to stop him.)* No, Nick . . . I'm sorry, Nick . . . we can't . . . *(*NICK *gives up, hangs limply in* MURRAY'S *arms.* MURRAY *speaks quietly, with love.)* I'm sorry . . . I'm sorry, kid . . . I'm sorry . . . *(He puts* NICK *down, still holding him.)*

NICK *(after a pause; quietly, in disbelief)*   Murray . . .

MURRAY   You better go to your room.

NICK   This is a one-room apartment.

MURRAY   Oh. Then go to your alcove. *(NICK waits a moment, then turns, betrayed, walks over to his alcove, lies down on the bed.* MURRAY *looks over at* LEO, *who is standing at the front door. He walks slowly over to* LEO, *looking down at the floor; humbly)* Leo . . . hope you didn't misunderstand . . . we were just kidding you . . . we . . .

LEO *(coming toward* MURRAY, *apologetically)*   I, myself, I got carried away there myself.

MURRAY   We all got a little excited, I guess. *(Reaches out to shake* LEO's *hand.)* So, I'll see you at work in the morning, Leo.

LEO *(smiling, shaking* MURRAY's *hand)*   Great to have you back, fellah. *(Pause)* You both hate me.

MURRAY   Nobody hates you, Leo.

LEO   I hollered at the kid, I'm sorry. I didn't mean to cause any upset. I don't get along too good with kids . . .

MURRAY   Don't worry about it.

LEO   Wanna come have a drink with me, Murray? We could . . .

MURRAY   No thanks; maybe another night, Leo.

LEO   Look, after I leave, you horse around a little with the kid, he'll feel better.

MURRAY   Right, Leo.

LEO *(pauses; then comes closer to* MURRAY)   Murray . . . that bit I did was funny, wasn't it?

MURRAY *(after a moment)*   Yeah, Leo . . . I guess it was just a bad day for you.

LEO *(pointing at the Chuckles statue on the floor; quietly, but giving a command)*   You don't want to leave that statue lying around like that, huh, Murray?

MURRAY   Oh, no. *(Goes to statue obediently, lifts it up off the floor, leans it upright against the wall)*   There.

LEO   Fine.

MURRAY   See you tomorrow, Leo.

LEO *(smiles)*   Yeah, see ya tomorrow at the studio . . . *(Ruffles up* MURRAY's *hair.)* You old monkey. *(Goes to the door.)* Hey, you're an old monkey, aren't you?

(LEO exits. MURRAY stays at the door for a moment. NICK is sitting on the alcove step, his back to MURRAY.)

MURRAY *(walking over to NICK, trying to make peace with him)*   Say, I could use a roast-turkey sandwich right now, couldn't you, Nick? On rye, with cole slaw and Russian dressing . . .

(NICK does not reply. MURRAY sits down next to him on the alcove step. NICK refuses to look at MURRAY. They are both silent for a moment.)

NICK   Guy calls us names. Guy talks to us like that. Shoulda got rid of that moron. Coulda fooled the Welfare people or something . . . *(SANDRA enters through the partly open door, unnoticed by them; she stays up in the doorway, watching them.)* We coulda gone to Mexico or New Jersey or someplace.

MURRAY   I hear the delicatessen in Mexico is terrible.

NICK *(after a moment)*   I'm gonna call myself *Theodore.*

MURRAY   As long as you don't call yourself Beatrice.

NICK   O.K., fool around. Wait'll you see a Theodore running around here. *(Silent for a moment, his back still to MURRAY; then, quietly)* Another coupla seconds he woulda been out the door . . . *(Turns to look at MURRAY.)* Why'd you go chicken on me, Murray? What'd you stop me for?

MURRAY   Because your routines give me outright prolonged laughter, Theodore.

SANDRA *(after a pause)*   Four ninety-five for this table cloth and you leave it around like this . . . *(Picks up the discarded tablecloth from the chair.)* A perfectly new tablecloth and already there are stains on it . . . *(Sits on the Morris chair, starts to dab at the tablecloth with her handkerchief.)* You know, it's very interesting that I left my files here. That I forgot them. I mean, psychologically, if you want to analyze that. Of course, last month I left my handbag in the Automat, and I have no idea what that means at all. *(MURRAY leaves alcove, starts toward her.)* I think that the pattern of our relationship, if we examine it, is very intricate, the different areas of it, especially the whole "good-bye" area of it, and also the "hello" and "how-are-you" area . . . of it.

MURRAY *(standing next to her chair now, smiles warmly)*   Hello, Sandy, and how are you?

SANDRA *(looks up at him, smiles politely)*   Hello, Murray. *(Goes right back to her work, rubbing the tablecloth with her handkerchief.)* You're standing in my light.

MURRAY   Oh. *(He retreats a step.)*

NICK *(walking over to her)*   Hello, lady.

SANDRA   Hello, Nick.

NICK *(indicating her work on the tablecloth)*   Lady, can I help you with any of that?

SANDRA   Matter of fact, Nick . . . *(She stands; her arm around* NICK, *she goes to center with him.)* Nick, I don't think the effect, I mean, the overall design of this room, is really helped by all these*(Gesturing to* MURRAY'S *stuff around the bed)* these knickknacks.

NICK   You mean the junk?

SANDRA   Yes.

NICK   Yeah, not too good for the overall design.

SANDRA   If you'd just put them away in that carton there. *(She indicates a carton near the bed.)*

NICK   Sure, lady . . .

*(*NICK *goes quickly to the carton, begins to put* MURRAY'S *junk into it—some radios, a megaphone, some clocks.* SANDRA *starts putting the tablecloth on the table.)*

MURRAY *(realizes that they are taking over, moves forward, trying to halt the proceedings)*   Hey, Sandy, now wait a minute . . . *(She goes on with her work, putting a piece of material over the Morris chair. He turns at the sound of one of his radio cabinets being dropped into the carton by* NICK.*)* Listen, Nick, I didn't tell you to . . . Nick . . .

NICK *(looking up from his work)*   Wilbur . . . *(Drops a clock into the carton.)* Wilbur Malcolm Burns.

*(*SANDRA *is putting the flowers back around the room, picking up the magazines.)*

MURRAY *(protesting)* Hey, now, both of you, will ya wait a minute here, will ya just wait . . . *(They ignore him, going on with their work. He shrugs, defeated; gives up, goes over to the windows, away from them, sits down sadly in the window seat.)* Wonder what kind of weather we got out there tonight. *(Looks out of window; as usual, he can see nothing but the gray, blank wall of the building a few feet opposite; sadly, to himself)* Never can see the God-damned weather. We got a permanent fixture out there: twilight in February. Some day that damn building'll fall down into Seventh Avenue so I can see the weather. *(Leans over, begins to talk out of the window.)* Everybody onstage for the Hawaiian number, please . . . *(SANDRA, during these last few lines, has gone to the phone, dialed, listened a few moments and hung up. MURRAY hears her hang up, turns to her.)* What're you doing?

SANDRA   I just spoke to the Weather Lady. She says it's a beautiful day. *(She goes back to her work on the apartment.)*

MURRAY *(he continues to talk out the window, softly at first)*   Well, then, if you're not ready, we better work on the Military March number. Now the last time we ran this, let's admit it was pretty ragged. I mean, the whole "Spirit of '76" float was in disgraceful shape yesterday . . . O.K. now, let's go, everybody ready . . . *(As MURRAY continues to talk out the window, NICK looks up from his work, smiles, picks up a record from the bed, puts it on the record player, turns it on.)* Grenadiers ready, Cavalry ready, Cossacks ready, Rough Riders ready, Minute Men ready . . . *(The record player has warmed up now and we hear "Stars and Stripes Forever." MURRAY hears the music, turns from the window, smiling, acknowledges NICK'S assistance; turns to the window again, his voice gradually growing in volume.)* O.K. now, let's go . . . ready on the cannons, ready on the floats, ready on the banners, ready on the flags . . . *(The music builds up with MURRAY'S voice, NICK humming along with the band and SANDRA laughing as MURRAY shouts.)* Let's go . . . let's go . . . let's go . . . *(His arms are outstretched.)*

CURTAIN

FOR FURTHER CONSIDERATION

According to the discussion between Murray and Arnold at the beginning of Act Three, what motivates each of the two men? How do their views of the world differ? This play offers a catalog of satire on a variety of institutions, beliefs, and social conventions. Make a list of the things the playwright satirizes. What comments does *A Thousand Clowns* make on individuality, integrity, and loyalties to others?

Dramatis Personae: From the Watergate Transcripts

On June 17, 1972 police captured five men who had illegally entered
Democratic Party headquarters in the Watergate hotel-apartment complex in Washington, D.C. After it was determined that the Administration
attempted to coverup White House involvement in the break-in and
related events, the event led to the most celebrated series of scandals in
American political hisory. The culmination of this chain of events came
with the resignation of Richard M. Nixon from the Presidency.

The events which follow were actually recorded in the Oval Office of
the White House on March 21, 1973, between 10:12 A.M. and 11:55 A.M. in
a conversation between P (Richard Nixon, then President), D (John Dean,
White House counsel), and later H (H. R. "Bob" Haldeman, White House
Chief of Staff).

Ehrlichman—John Ehrlichman, then Assistant to the President, later
convicted for his roles in the coverup and in the break-in at the office of
Daniel Ellsberg's psychiatrist, Dr. Fielding. Ellsberg had leaked the
Pentagon Papers to the press.

Judge John J. Sirica—federal district court judge presiding over the
trial of the original Watergate conspirators and other key legal proceedings leading up to a later House Judiciary Committee vote to impeach Mr.
Nixon and Nixon's subsequent resignation.

John Mitchell—former Attorney General under Nixon and briefly
head of Nixon's Committee to Re-elect the President (CREEP) in 1972.

Hunt—E. Howard Hunt, Jr., a CIA veteran convicted in the Watergate break-in and implicated in the attempted robbery of Dr. Fielding's
office.

Chuck Colson—Charles W. Colson, a troubleshooter for Nixon later
jailed for his part in the break-in at Fielding's office.

Liddy—G. Gordon Liddy, a former White House employee convicted in the Watergate and Fielding office break-ins.

Jeb S. Magruder—The number two man in CREEP, later jailed for
obstructing justice.

Bud—Egil "Bud" Krogh, Jr., jailed for his role in the Fielding
break-in.

McCord—James J. McCord, convicted for his role in the Watergate
break-in.

Richard Kleindienst—former Attorney General convicted of misin-
forming the Senate.

Herbert W. Kalmbach—Nixon's personal attorney, guilty of selling
ambassadorships and raising campaign funds illegally.

LaRue—Frederick C. LaRue, a campaign aide and friend of Mitchell's, guilty of obstructing justice in the Watergate coverup.

Gordon Strachan—a White House aide to Haldeman, implicated in
the obstruction of justice.

Petersen—Henry E. Petersen, Assistant U.S. Attorney General at
one time in charge of the Watergate break-in investigation.

Martha—Martha Mitchell, former wife of John Mitchell.

Ervin and Baker—Senators Sam Ervin and Howard Baker of the Senate Select Committee that investigated the Watergate break-in, cover-up, and related matters.

The reader should note that this play is but an excerpt from a longer dialogue between the parties on March 21, 1972, and that this conversation was but one of several between the actors in these events.

In an Oval Office

D What I am coming in today with is: I don't have a plan on how to solve it right now, but I think it is at the juncture that we should begin to think in terms of how to cut the losses; how to minimize the further growth of this thing, rather than further compound it by, you know, ultimately paying these guys forever. I think we've got to look—

P But at the moment, don't you agree it is better to get the Hunt thing that's where that—

D That is worth buying time on.

P That is buying time, I agree.

D The Grand Jury is going to reconvene next week after Sirica sentences. But that is why I think that John and Bob have met with me. They have never met with Mitchell on this. We have never had a real down and out with everybody that has the most to lose and it is the most danger for you to have them have criminal liabilities. I think Bob has a potential criminal liability, frankly. In other words, a lot of these people could be indicted.

P Yeah.

D They might never be convicted but just the thought of spending nights—

P Suppose they are?

D I think that would be devastating.

P Suppose the worst—that Bob is indicted and Ehrlichman is indicted. And I must say, we just better then try to tough it through. You get the point.

D That's right.

P If they, for example, say let's cut our losses and you say we are going to go down the road to see if we can cut our losses and no more blackmail and all the rest. And then the thing blows cutting Bob and the rest to pieces. You would never recover from that, John.

D That's right.

P It is better to fight it out. Then you see that's the other thing. It's better to fight it out and not let people testify, and so forth. And now, on the other hand, we realize that we have these weaknesses,—that we have these weaknesses—in terms of blackmail.

D There are two routes. One is to figure out how to cut the losses and minimize the human impact and get you up and out and away from it in any way. In a way it would never come back to haunt you. That is one general alternative. The other is to go down the road, just hunker down,

fight it at every corner, every turn, don't let people testify—cover it up is
what we really are talking about. Just keep it buried, and just hope that we
can do it, hope that we make good decisions at the right time, keep our
heads cool, we make the right moves.

P   And just take the heat?

D   And just take the heat.

P   Now with the second line of attack. You can discuss this
(unintelligible) the way you want to. Still consider my scheme of having
you brief the Cabinet, just in very general terms and the leaders in very
general terms and maybe some very general statement with regard to my
investigation. Answer questions, basically on the basis of what they told
you, not what you know. Haldeman is not involved. Ehrlichman is not
involved.

D   If we go that route Sir, I can give a show we can sell them just
like we were selling Wheaties on our position. There's no—

P   The problem that you have are these mine fields down the road. I
think the most difficult problem are the guys who are going to jail. I think
you are right about that.

D   I agree.

P   Now. And also the fact that we are not going to be able to give
them clemency.

D   That's right. How long will they take? How long will they sit
there? I don't know. We don't know what they will be sentenced to.
There's always a chance—

P   Thirty years, isn't it?

D   It could be. You know, they haven't announced yet, but it—

P   Top is thirty years, isn't it?

D   It is even higher than that. It is about 50 years. It all—

P   So ridiculous!

D   And what is so incredible is, he is (unintelligible)

P   People break and enter, etc., and get two years. No weapons! No
results! What the hell are they talking about?

D   The individuals who are charged with shooting John Stennis are
on the street. They were given, you know, one was put out on his personal
recognizance rather than bond. They've got these fellows all stuck with
$100,000 bonds. It's the same Judge, Sirica, let one guy who is charged
with shooting a United States Senator out on the street.

P   Sirica?

D   Yes–it is phenomenal.

P   What is the matter with him? I thought he was a hard liner.

D   He is. He is just a peculiar animal, and he set the bond for one of
the others somewhere around 50 or 60,000. But still, that guy is in. Didn't
make bond, but still 60 thousand dollars as opposed to $100,000 for these
guys is phenomenal.

P   When could you have this meeting with these fellows as I think
time is of the essence. Could you do it this afternoon?

D   Well, Mitchell isn't here. It might be worth it to have him come down. I think that Bob and John did not want to talk to John Mitchell about this, and I don't believe they have had any conversation with him about it.

P   Well, I will get Haldeman in here now.

D   Bob and I have talked about it, just as we are talking about it this morning. I told him I thought that you should have the facts and he agrees. Of course, we have some tough problems down the road if we— (inaudible) Let me say (unintelligible) How do we handle all (unintelligible) who knew all about this in advance. Let me have some of your thoughts on that.

D   Well we can always, you know, on the other side charge them with blackmailing us. This is absurd stuff they are saying, and

P   See, the way you put it out here, letting it all hang out, it may never get there.

(Haldeman enters the room)

P   I was talking to John about this whole situation and he said if we can get away from the bits and pieces that have broken out. He is right in recommending that there be a meeting at the very first possible time. I realize Ehrlichman is still out in California but, what is today? Is tomorrow Thursday?

H   (unintelligible)

D   That's right.

P   He does get back. Could we do it Thursday? This meeting—you can't do it today, can you?

D   I don't think so. I was suggesting a meeting with Mitchell.

P   Mitchell, Ehrlichman, yourself and Bob, that is all. Now, Mitchell has to be there because he is seriously involved and we are trying to keep him with us. We have to see how we handle it from here on. We are in the process of having to determine which way to go, and John has thought it through as well as he can. I don't want Moore there on this occasion. You haven't told Moore all of this, have you?

D   Moore's got, by being with me, has more bits and pieces. I have had to give him,

P   Right.

D   Because he is making judgments—

P   The point is when you get down to the PR, once you decide it, what to do, we can let him know so forth and so on. But it is the kind of thing that I think what really has to happen is for you to sit down with those three and for you to tell them exactly what you told me.

D   Uh, huh.

P   It may take him about 35 or 40 minutes. In other words he knows, John knows, about everything and also what all the potential criminal liabilities are, whether it is—like that thing—what, about obstruction?

D   Obstruction of justice. Right.

P   So forth and so on. I think that's best. Then we have to see what the line is. Whether the line is one of continuing to run a kind of stone wall, and take the heat from that, having in mind the fact that there are vulnerable points there;—the vulnerable points being, the first vulnerable points would be obvious. That would be one of the defendants, either Hunt, because he is most vulnerable in my opinion, might blow the whistle and his price is pretty high, but at least we can buy the time on that as I pointed out to John. Apparently, who is dealing with Hunt at the moment now? Colson's—

D   Well, Mitchell's lawyer and Colson's lawyer both.

P   Who is familiar with him? At least he has to know before he is sentenced.

H   Who is Colson's lawyer? Is he in his law firm?

D   Shapiro. Right. The other day he came up and—

H   Colson has told him everything, hasn't he?

D   Yep, I gather he has. The other thing that bothered me about that is that he is a chatterer. He came up to Fred Fielding, of my office, at Colson's going away party. I didn't go over there. It was the Blair House the other night. He said to Fred, he said, "well, Chuck has had some mighty serious words with his friend Howard and has had some mighty serious messages back." Now, how does he know what Fielding knows? Because Fielding knows virtually nothing.

P   Well,—

H   That is where your dangers lie, in all these stupid human errors developing.

P   Sure. The point is Bob, let's face it; the secretaries, the assistants know all of this. The principals may be as hard as a rock, but you never know when they, or some of their people may crack. But, we'll see, we'll see. Here we have the Hunt problem that ought to be handled now. Incidentally, I do not feel that Colson should sit in this meeting. Do you agree?

D   No. I would agree.

P   Ok. How then—who does sit on Colson? Because somebody has to, don't they?

D   Chuck—

P   Talks too much.

D   I like Chuck, but I don't want Chuck to know anything that I am doing, frankly.

P   Alright.

H   I think that is right. I think you want to be careful not to give Chuck any more knowledge than he's already got.

D   I wouldn't want Chuck to even know of the meeting, frankly.

P   Ok. Fortunately, with Chuck it is very—I talk to him about many, many political things, but I have never talked with him about this sort of thing. Very probably, I think he must be damn sure that I didn't know anything. And I don't. In fact, I am surprised by what you told me today. From what you said, I gathered the impression, and of course your analysis does not for sure indicate that Chuck knew that it was a bugging operation.

D   That's correct. I don't have—Chuck denies having knowledge.

P   Yet on the other side of that is that Hunt had conversations with Chuck. It may be that Hunt told Chuck that it was bugging, and so forth and so on.

D   Uh, uh, uh, uh. They were very close. They talk too much about too many things. They were intimate on this sort of—

H   That's the problem. Chuck loves (unintelligible). Chuck loves what he does and he loves to talk about it.

P   He also is a name dropper. Chuck may have gone around and talked to Hunt and said, well I was talking to the President, and the President feels we ought to get information about this, or that or the other thing, etc.

D   Well, Liddy is the same way.

P   Well, I have talked about this and that and the other thing. I have never talked to anybody, but I have talked to Chuck and John and the rest and I am sure that Chuck might have even talked to him along these lines.

H   Other than—Well, anything could have happened. I was going—

D   I would doubt that seriously.

H   I don't think he would. Chuck is a name dropper in one sense, but not in that sense. I think he very carefully keeps away from that, except when he is very intentionally bringing the President in for the President's purposes.

P   He had the impression though apparently he, as it turns out, he was the trigger man. Or he may well have been the trigger man where he just called up and said now look here Jeb go out and get that information. And Liddy and Hunt went out and got it at that time. This was February. It must have been after—

D   This was the call to Magruder from Colson saying, "fish or cut bait." Hunt and Liddy were in his office.

H   In Colson's office?

D   In Colson's office. And he called Magruder and said, "Let's fish or cut bait on this operation. Let's get it going."

H   Oh, really?

D   Yeah. This is Magruder telling me that.

H   Of course. That—now wait, Magruder testified—

D   Chuck also told me that Hunt and Liddy were in his office when he made the call.

H   Oh, ok.

D   So it was corroborated by the principal.

H   Hunt and Liddy haven't told you that, though?

D   No.

H   You haven't talked to Hunt and Liddy?

D   I talked to Liddy once right after the incident.

P   The point is this, that it is now time, though, that Mitchell has got to sit down, and know where the hell all this thing stands, too. You see, John is concerned, as you know, about the Ehrlichman situation. It worries him a great deal because, and this is why the Hunt problem is so serious, because it had nothing to do with the campaign. It has to do with the Ellsberg case. I don't know what the hell the—(unintelligible)

H   But what I was going to say—

P   What is the answer on this? How you keep it out, I don't know. You can't keep it out if Hunt talks. You see the point is irrelevant. It has gotten to this point—

D   You might put it on a national security grounds basis.

H   It absolutely was.

D   And say that this was—

H   (unintelligible)—CIA—

D   Ah—

H   Seriously,

P   National Security. We had to get information for national security grounds.

D   Then the question is, why didn't the CIA do it or why didn't the FBI do it?

P   Because we had to do it on a confidential basis.

H   Because we were checking them.

P   Neither could be trusted.

H   It has basically never been proven. There was reason to question their position.

P   With the bombing thing coming out and everything coming out, the whole thing was national security.

D   I think we could get by on that

P   On that one I think we should simply say this was a national security investigation that was conducted. And on that basis, I think the same in the drug field with Krogh. Krogh could say feels he did not perjure himself. He could say it was a national security matter. That is why—

D   That is the way Bud rests easy, because he is convinced that he was doing. He said there was treason about the country, and it could have threatened the way the war was handled and (explitive deleted)—

P   Bud should just say it was a question of national security, and I was not in a position to divulge it. Anyway, let's don't go beyond that. But I do think now there is a time when you just don't want to talk to Mitchell. But John is right. There must be a four way talk of the particular ones you can trust here. We've got to get a decision on it. It is not something—you have two ways basically. You really only have two ways to go. You either decide that the whole (expletive deleted) thing is so full of problems with potential criminal liabilities, which most concern me. I don't give a damn about the publicity. We could rock that through that if we had to let the whole damn thing hang out, and it would be a lousy story for a month. But I can take it. The point is, that I don't want any criminal liabilities. That is the thing that I am concerned about for members of the White House staff, and I would trust for members of the Committee. And that means Magruder.

D   That's right. Let's face it. I think Magruder is the major guy over there.

D   I think he's got the most serious problem.

P   Yeah.

H   Well, the thing we talked about yesterday. You have a question where you cut off on this. There is a possibility of cutting it at Liddy, where you are now.

P   Yeah.

D   But to accomplish that requires a continued perjury by Magruder and requires—

P   And requires total commitment and control over all of the defendants which—in other words when they are let down—

H   But we can, because they don't know anything beyond Liddy.

D   No. On the fact that Liddy, they have hearsay.

H   But we don't know about Hunt. Maybe Hunt has that tied into Colson. We don't know that though, really.

P   I think Hunt knows a hell of a lot more.

D   I do too. Now what McCord does—

H   You think he does. I am afraid you are right, but we don't know that.

P   I think we better assume it. I think Colson—

D   He is playing hard ball. He wouldn't play hard ball unless he were pretty confident that he could cause an awful lot of grief.

H   Right.

P   He is playing hard ball with regard to Ehrlichman for example, and that sort of thing. He knows what he's got.

H   What's he planning on, money?

D   Money and—

H   Really?

P   It's about $120,000. That's what, Bob. That would be easy It is not easy to deliver, but it is easy to get. Now,

H   If the case is just that way, then the thing to do if the thing cranks out.

P   If, for example, you say look we are not going to continue to—let's say, frankly, on the assumption that if we continue to cut our losses, we are not going to win. But in the end, we are going to be bled to death. And in the end, it is all going to come out anyway. Then you get the worst of both worlds. We are going to lose, and people are going to—

H   And look like dopes!

P   And in effect, look like a cover-up. So that we can't do. Now the other line, however, if you take that line, that we are not going to continue to cut our losses, that means then we have to look square in the eye as to what the hell those losses are, and see which people can—so we can avoid criminal liability. Right?

D   Right.

P   And that means keeping it off you. Herb has started this Justice thing. We've got to keep it off Herb. You have to keep it, naturally, off of Bob, off Chapin, if possible, Strachan, right?

D   Uh, huh

P   And Mitchell. Right?

D   Uh, huh

H   And Magruder, if you can.

P   John Dean's point is that if Magruder goes down, he will pull everybody with him.

H   That's my view. Yep, I think Jeb, I don't think he wants to. And I think he even would try not to, but I don't think he is able not to.

D   I don't think he is strong enough.

P   Another way to do it then Bob, and John realizes this, is to continue to try to cut our losses. Now we have to take a look at that course of action. First it is going to require approximately a million dollars to take care of the jackasses who are in jail. That can be arranged. That could be arranged. But you realize that after we are gone, and assuming we can expend this money, then they are going to crack and it would be an unseemly story. Frankly, all the people aren't going to care that much.

D   That's right.

P   People won't care, but people are going to be talking about it, there is no question. And the second thing is, we are not going to be able to deliver on any of a clemency thing. You know Colson has gone around on this clemency thing with Hunt and the rest?

D   Hunt is now talking about being out by Christmas.

H   This year?

D   This year. He was told by O'Brien, who is my conveyor of doom back and forth, that hell, he would be lucky if he were out a year from now, or after Ervin's hearings were over. He said how in the Lord's name could you be commuted that quickly? He said, "Well, that is my commitment from Colson."

H   By Christmas of this year?

D   Yeah.

H   See that, really, that is verbal evil. Colson is—That is your fatal flaw in Chuck. He is an operator in expediency, and he will pay at the time and where he is to accomplish whatever he is there to do. And that, and that's,—I would believe that he has made that commitment if Hunt says he has. I would believe he is capable of saying that.

P   The only thing we could do with him would be to parole him like the (unintelligible) situation. But you couldn't buy clemency.

D   Kleindienst has now got control of the Parole Board, and he said to tell me we could pull Paroles off now where we couldn't before. So—

H   Kleindienst always tells you that, but I never believe it.

P   Paroles—let the (unintelligible) worry about that. Parole, in appearance, etc., is something I think in Hunt's case, you could do Hunt, but you couldn't do the others. You understand.

D   Well, so much depends on how Sirica sentences. He can sentence in a way that makes parole even impossible.

P   He can?

D   Sure. He can do all kind of permanent sentences.

P   (unintelligible)

D   Yeah, He can be a (characterization deleted) as far as the whole thing.

H   Can't you appeal an unjust sentence as well as an unjust?

D   You have 60 days to ask the Judge to review it. There is no Appellate review of sentences.

H   There isn't?

P   The judge can review it.

H   Only the sentencing judge can review his own sentence?

P   Coming back, though, to this. So you got that hanging over. Now! If—you see, if you let it hang there, you fight with them at all or they part—The point is, your feeling is that we just can't continue to pay the blackmail of these guys?

D   I think that is our great jeopardy.

P   Now, let me tell you. We could get the money. There is no problem in that. We can't provide the clemency. Money could be provided. Mitchell could provide the way to deliver it. That could be done. See what I mean?

H   Mitchell says he can't, doesn't he?

D   Mitchell says—there has been an interesting phenomena all the way along. There have been a lot of people having to pull oars and not everybody pulls them all the same time, the same way, because they develop self-interests.

H   What John is saying, everybody smiles at Dean and says well you better get something done about it.

D   That's right.

H   Mitchell is leaving Dean hanging out on him. None of us, well, may be we are doing the same thing to you.

D   That's right.

H   But let me say this. I don't see how there is any way that you can have the White House or anybody presently in the White House involved in trying to gin out this money.

D   We are already deeply enough in that. That is the problem, Bob.

P   I thought you said—

H   We need more money.

D   Well, in fact when—

P   Kalmbach?

H   He's not the one.

D   No, but when they ran out of that money, as you know it came out of the 350,000 that was over here.

P   And they knew that?

D   And I had to explain what it was for before I could get the money.

H   In the first place, that was put back to LaRue.

D   That's right.

H   It was put back where it belonged. It wasn't all returned in a lump sum. It was put back in pieces.

D   That's right.

P   Then LaRue used it for this other purpose?

D   That's right.

H   And the balance was all returned to LaRue, but we don't have any receipt for that. We have no way of proving it.

D   And I think that was because of self-interest over there. Mitchell—

H   Mitchell told LaRue not to take it at all.

D   That's right.

H   That is what you told me.

D   That's right. And then don't give them a receipt.

P   Then what happened? LaRue took it, and then what?

D   It was sent back to him because we just couldn't continue piecemeal giving. Everytime I asked for it I had to tell Bob I needed some, or something like that, and he had to get Gordon Strachan to go up to his safe and take it out and take it over to LaRue. And it was just a forever operation.

P   Why did they take it all?

D   I just sent it along to them.

H   We had been trying to get a way to get that money back out of here anyway. And what this was supposed to be was loans. This was immediate cash needs that was going to be replenished. Mitchell was arguing that you can't take the $350,000 back until it is all replenished. Isn't that right?

D   That is right.

H   They hadn't replenished, so we just gave it all back anyway.

P   I had a feeling we could handle this one.

D   Well, first of all, I would have a hell of a time proving it. That is one thing.

P   I just have a feeling on it. Well, it sounds like a lot of money, a million dollars. Let me say that I think we could get that. I know money is hard to raise. But the point is, what we do on that—Let's look at the hard problem—

D   That has been, thus far, the most difficult problem. That is why these fellows have been on and off the reservation all the way along.

P   So the hard place is this. Your feeling at the present time is the hell with the million dollars. I would just say to these fellows I am sorry it is all off and let them talk. Alright?

D   Well,—

P   That's the way to do it isn't it, if you want to do it clean?

H   That's the way. We can live with it, because the problem with the blackmailing, that is the thing we kept raising with you when you said there was a money problem. When you said we need $20,000, or $100,000, or something. We said yeah, that is what you need today. But what do you need tomorrow or next year or five years from now?

P   How long?

D   That was just to get us through November 7th, though.

H   That's what we had to have to get through November 7th. There is no question.

D   These fellows could have sold out to the Democrats for one-half a million.

P   These fellows though, as far as what has happened up to this time, are covered on their situation, because the Cuban Committee did this for them during the election?

D   Well, yeah. We can put that together. That isn't of course quite the way it happened, but—

P   I know, but that's the way it is going to have to happen.

D   It's going to have to happen.

P   Finally, though, so you let it happen. So then they go, and so what happens? Do they go out and start blowing the whistle on everybody else? Isn't that what it really gets down to?

D   Uh, huh.

P   So that would be the clean way—Right!

D   Ah—

P   Is that—you would go so far as to recommend that?

D   No, I wouldn't. I don't think necessarily that is the cleanest way. One of the things that I think we all need to discuss is, is there some way that we can get our story before a Grand Jury, so that they can really have investigated the White House on this. I must say that I have not really thought through that alternative. We have been so busy on the other containment situation.

P   John Ehrlichman, of course, has raised the point of another Grand Jury. I just don't know how you could do it. On what basis. I could call for it, but I—

D   That would be out of the question.

P   I hate to leave with differences in view of all this stripped land. I could understand this, but I think I want another Grand Jury proceeding and we will have the White House appear before them. Is that right John?

D   Uh, huh.

P   That is the point, see. Of course! That would make the difference. I want everybody in the White House called. And that gives you a reason not to have to go before the Ervin and Baker Committee. It puts it in an executive session, in a sense.

H   Right.

D   That's right.

H   And there would be some rules of evidence, aren't there?

D   There are rules of evidence.

P   Rules of evidence and you have lawyers.

H   You are in a hell of a lot better position than you are up there.

D   No, you can't have a lawyer before the Grand Jury.

P   Oh, no. That's right.

H   But you do have rules of evidence. You can refuse to talk.

D   You can take the 5th amendment.

P   That's right.

H   You can say you have forgotten too can't you?

D   Sure but you are chancing a very high risk for perjury situation.

P   But you can say I don't remember. You can say I can't recall. I can't give any answer to that that I can recall.

H   You have the same perjury thing on the Hill don't you?

D   That's right.

P   Oh hell, yes.

H   And the Ervin Committee is a hell of a lot worse to deal with.

D   That's right.

P   The Grand Jury thing has its in view of this thing. Suppose we have a Grand Jury thing. What would that do to the Ervin Committee? Would it go right ahead?

D   Probably. Probably.

P   If we do that on a Grand Jury, we would then have a much better cause in terms of saying, "Look, this is a Grand Jury, in which the prosecutor—How about a special prosecutor?We could use Petersen, or use another one. You see he is probably suspect. Would you call in another prosecutor?

D   I would like to have Petersen on our side, if I did this thing.

P   Well, Petersen is honest. There isn't anybody about to question him is there?

D   No, but he will get a barrage when these Watergate Hearings start.

P   But he can go up and say that he has been told to go further with the Grand Jury and go in to this and that and the other thing. Call everybody in the White House, and I want them to go to the Grand Jury.

D   This may happen without even our calling for it when these—

P   Vesco?

D   No. Well, that is one possibility. But also when these people go back before the Grand Jury here, they are going to pull all these criminal defendants back before the Grand Jury and immunize them.

P   Who will do this?

D   The U.S. Attorney's Office will.

P   To do what?

D   To let them talk about anything further they want to talk about.

P   But what do they gain out of it?

D   Nothing.

P   To hell with it!

D   They're going to stonewall it, as it now stands. Excepting Hunt. That's why his threat.

H   It's Hunt opportunity.

P   That's why for your immediate things you have no choice but to come up with the $120,000, or whatever it is. Right?

D   That's right.

P   Would you agree that that's the prime thing that you damn well better get that done?

D   Obviously he ought to be given some signal anyway.

P   (Expletive deleted), get it. In a way that—who is going to talk to him? Colson? He is the one who is supposed to know him?

D   Well, Colson doesn't have any money though. That is the thing. That's been one of the real problems. They haven't been able to raise a million dollars in cash. (unintelligible) has been just a very difficult problem as we discussed before. Mitchell has talked to Pappas, and John asked me to call him last night after our discussion and later you had met with John to see where that was. And I said, "Have you talked to Pappas?" He was at home, and Martha picked up the phone so it was all in code. I said, "Have you talked to the Greek?" And he said, "Yes, I have." I said, "Is the Greek bearing gifts?" He said, "Well, I'll call you tomorrow on that."

P   Well, look, what is it you need on that? When—I am not familiar with the money situation.

D   It sounds easy to do and everyone is out there doing it and that is where our breakdown has come every time.

P   Well, if you had it, how would you get it to somebody?

D   Well, I got it to LaRue by just leaving it in mail boxes and things like that. And someone phones Hunt to come and pick it up. As I say, we are a bunch of amateurs in that business.

H   That is the thing that we thought Mitchell ought to be able to know how to find somebody who would know how to do all that sort of thing, because none of us know how to.

D   That's right. You have to wash the money. You can get a $100,000 out of a bank, and it all comes in serialized bills.

P   I understand.

D   And that means you have to go to Vegas with it or a bookmaker in New York City. I have learned all these things after the fact. I will be in great shape for the next time around.

H   (Expletive deleted)

P   Well, of course you have a surplus from the campaign. Is there any other money hanging around?

H   Well, what about the money we moved back out of here?

D   Apparently, there is some there. That might be what they can use. I don't know how much is left.

P   Kalmbach must have some.

D   Kalmbach doesn't have a cent.

P   He doesn't?

H   That $350,000 that we moved out was all that we saved. Because they were afraid to because of this. That is the trouble. We are so (adjective deleted) square that we get caught at everything.

P   Could I suggest this though: let me go back around—

H   Be careful—

P   The Grand Jury thing has a feel. Right? It says we are cooperating well with the Grand Jury.

D   Once we start down any route that involves the criminal justice system, we've got to have full appreciation that there is really no control over that. While we did an amazing job of keeping us in on the track before while the FBI was out there, and that was the only way they found out where they were going—   .

P   But you've got to (unintelligible) Let's take it to a Grand Jury. A new Grand Jury would call Magruder again, wouldn't it?

D   Based on what information? For example, what happens if Dean goes in and gives a story. You know, that here is the way it all came about. It was supposed to be a legitimate operation and it obviously got off the track. I heard—before, but told Haldeman that we shouldn't be involved in it. Then Magruder can be called in and questioned again about all those meetings and the like. And if again he'll begin to change his story as to what he told the Grand Jury the last time. That way, he is in a perjury situation.

H   Except that is the best leverage you've got with Jeb. He has to keep his story straight or he is in real trouble, unless they get smart and give him immunity. If they immunize Jeb, then you have an interesting problem.

D   We have control over who gets immunized. I think they wouldn't do that without our—

P   But you see the Grand Jury proceeding achieves this thing. If we go down that road— (unintelligible) We would be cooperating. We would be cooperating through a Grand Jury. Everybody would be behind us. That is the proper way to do this. It should be done in the Grand Jury, not up there under the kleig lights of the Committee. Nobody questions a Grand Jury. And then we would insist on Executive Privilege before the Committee, flat out say, "No we won't do that. It is a matter before the Grand Jury, and so on, and that's that."

H   Then you go the next step. Would we then—The Grand Jury is in executive session?

D   Yes, they are secret sessions.

H   Alright, then would we agree to release our Grand Jury transcripts?

D   We don't have the authority to do that. That is up to the Court and the Court, thus far, has not released the ones from the last Grand Jury.

P   They usually are not.

D   It would be highly unusual for a Grand Jury to come out. What usually happens is—

H   But a lot of the stuff from the Grand Jury came out.

P   Leaks.

D   It came out of the U.S. Attorney's Office, more than the Grand Jury. We don't know. Some of the Grand Jurors may have blabbered, but they were—

P   Bob, it's not so bad. It's bad, but it's not the worst place.

H   I was going the other way there. I was going to say that it might be to our interest to get it out.

P   Well, we could easily do that. Leak out certain stuff. We could pretty much control that. We've got so much more control. Now, the other possibility is not to go to the Grand Jury. We have three things. (1) You just say the hell with it, we can't raise the money, sorry Hunt you can say what you want, and so on. He blows the whistle. Right?

D   Right.

P   If that happens, that raises some possibilities about some criminal liabilities, because he is likely to say a hell of a lot of things and will certainly get Magruder in on it.

D   It will get Magruder. It will start the whole FBI investigation going again.

P   Yeah. It would get Magruder, and it could possibly get Colson.

D   That's right. Could get—

P   Get Mitchell. Maybe. No.

H   Hunt can't get Mitchell.

D   I don't think Hunt can get Mitchell. Hunt's got a lot of hearsay.

P   Ehrlichman?

D   Krogh could go down in smoke.

P   On the other hand—Krogh says it is a national security matter. Is that what he says?

D   Yeah, but that won't sell ultimately in a criminal situation. It may be mitigating on sentences but it won't, in the main matter.

P   Seems we're going around the track. You have no choice on Hunt but to try to keep—

D   Right now, we have no choice.

P   But my point is, do you ever have any choice on Hunt? That is the point. No matter what we do here now, John, whatever he wants if he doesn't get it—immunity, etc., he is going to blow the whistle.

D   What I have been trying to conceive of is how we could lay out everything we know in a way that we have told the Grand Jury or somebody else, so that if a Hunt blows, so what's new? It's already been told to a Grand Jury and they found no criminal liability and they investigated it in full. We're sorry fellow—And we don't, it doesn't—

P   (Unintelligible) for another year.

D   That's right.

P   And Hunt would get off by telling them the Ellsberg thing.

D   No Hunt would go to jail for that too—he should understand that.

P   That's a point too. I don't think I would throw that out. I don't think we need to go into everything. (adjective deleted) thing Hunt has done.

D   No.

P   Some of the things in the national security area. Yes.

H   Whoever said that anyway. We laid the groundwork for that.

P   But here is the point, John. Let's go the other angle, is to decide if

you open up the Grand Jury: first, it won't be any good, it won't be
believed. And then you will have two things going: the Grand Jury and the
other things, committee, etc. The Grand Jury appeals to me from the
standpoint, the President makes the move. All these charges being
bandied about, etc., the best thing to do is that I have asked the Grand
Jury to look into any further charges. All charges have been raised. That
is the place to do it, and not before a Committee of the Congress. Right?

    D   Yeah.

    P   Then, however, we may say, (expletive deleted), we can't risk
that, or she'll break loose there. That leaves you to your third thing.

    D   Hunker down and fight it.

    P   Hunker down and fight it and what happens? Your view is that it
is not really a viable option.

    D   It is a high risk. It is a very high risk.

    P   Your view is that what will happen on it, that it's going to come
out. That something is going to break loose, and—

    D   Something is going to break and—

    P   It will look like the President

    D   is covering up—

    P   Has covered up a huge (unintelligible)

    D   That's correct.

    H   But you can't (inaudible)

FOR FURTHER CONSIDERATION

How does the kind of language that the characters use offer clues to their
intentions? What do the characters seem most interested in accomplishing
for themselves? What forces oppose them? What do the characters hope
to accomplish for the other administration members they refer to? For the
public?

    What comment does the play make on personal loyalties? Personal
integrity? Power? The interrelationships of these three? In what ways is
this play comic or farcical? Tragic? Ironic?

Part Four

Nonfiction

"And one man in his time plays many parts"

William Shakespeare

In moments of introspection many of us recognize that despite the myth of a person as a single self, we play many parts in life—student and teacher, child and parent, friend and stranger, and so on—through the limitless roles that age, circumstance, and chance seem to require of us. It is as if every human relationship required some shade of difference in who we are; and while we feel that these roles are founded on a single underlying identity, we nonetheless sense the shifting nature of self. Nineteenth-century Western people had a strong sense of self which came from the common frame of reference they found in religion and social organization. One believed in God and in the essential order of society. That was that. But the discontinuity of modern society and the fragmentation of belief have left contemporary Western people without a common belief system or point of reference. Nineteenth-century beliefs rested on an abstraction of a higher good; today, people believe only in the reality of secular goods. Where they once clung to God and the law, people now cling to their cars or their television sets. The value system which acted as the foundation for the self has shifted rapidly and radically, raising as a consequence the question of whether the self as we have long thought of it can continue.

The essays which follow offer a number of perspectives on the survival of an essential self. In "Love Was Once a little Boy," D. H. Lawrence comments on the paradoxical impact of love on personal identity and explores the role of the lover, a role we all need. His poetic analogies reveal love as a mountain, a lake, a candle, a stone, a broken jar of honey, and even as centrifugal force. He describes as well the difficult business of striking a balance between the integrity necessary to one's identity and the outward flow of self essential for love.

Thomas Harris traces, in "Parent, Adult, Child," the basic ego states of self as seen through the lens of transactional analysis. He enlarges upon his thesis with reason and abundant examples, then makes a case for how a person plays at any given moment in social intercourse one of the three roles described in his title. Avoiding the usual jargon of psychology, he illuminates the need for roles and argues for a three part concept of self. His argument proves intriguing reading.

In "Kennedy Without Tears" we encounter the personality of J. F. K. in the form of vignettes. Tom Wicker draws our attention to the inner qualities of leadership and to the loneliness, stress, and responsibility that go with it. Using adroitly chosen examples, Wicker shows us the extraordinary confidence of a natural leader, emphasizing as well the vital part that humor plays in maintaining balance in the face of immense stresses. In contrast to the lonely role of Kennedy as a patrician leader, Irene Castañeda depicts the plight of the poor immigrant multitude. Her matter-of-fact prose in "A Personal Chronicle of Crystal City" recounts how migrant Mexican families have for generations struggled from crisis to crisis, their identities shaped by sickness, hunger, and tragedy. Through the tone of her writing and the hardships she records, she demonstrates that dignity, integrity, and courage are there to call on when the individual confronts deprivation and emotional shock.

The selections next shift to one of the subthemes; the self as revealed in significant choices and expressions of values. Bertrand Russell describes in "A Free Man's Worship" a world in which science has destroyed the common belief system and replaced it with only a void, a hostile, meaningless universe. As the void also offers the opportunity for mental freedom, Russell urges people to exercise that freedom by pursuing their aspirations and by creating during the brief period of life as much beauty and meaning as they can. Only through choosing this role as a creator, he states, can a free person's hope, dignity, and identity be maintained. In contrast to Russell's abstractions and learned prose, Dick Gregory offers in everyday language an autobiographical anecdote that shows how two childhood incidents relating to shame and hate shaped his values and his sense of person. In telling of his battle to avoid the socially assigned role of the black welfare child, Gregory reveals the unfortunate extent to which society sometimes succeeds in telling us who we are.

"Farewell, My Nation! Farewell, Black Hawk!" touches upon the importance of courage and honor in the face of defeat and despair. Having fought long and hard for his people, Black Hawk faced imprisonment, humiliation, and tragedy with an equaminity born of a life of adversity. His story offers us two ways of viewing the impact of values on identity: first, in the immense differences between Indians and whites as a result of what they value and, next, in the importance of deeply held beliefs when one sees everything of personal importance lost or destroyed. Plato's famous "Allegory of the Cave" offers the classic example of experience forming the values and beliefs of the individual. The Greek philosopher raises in turn the question of what happens to the individual when the very beliefs that constitute the self suddenly prove to be only illusions. John Ciardi's "The Act of Language" concludes the subsection on values, choices, and self as he explores how through language and poetry, man reveals his innermost self.

The remaining essays deal with the second subtheme, the impact of science and technology on personal identity. Alvin Toffler tells us in the first selection that "To survive, to avert what we have termed future shock, the individual must become infinitely more adaptable and capable than ever before." In "The Accelerative Thrust" he advances his theory of how the sheer amount and speed of change around us, much of it the product of technology, place tremendous pressures on human identity. In the mass of his data, Toffler identifies the causes of much that disconcerts us, the seeming drift of society away from the known to the unknown, the discontinuity between past and present. How the self responds to this increasing load of newness appears as a critical question in contemporary society, for with the loss of familiar patterns, objects, and relationships, part of the self is lost, and more, that which remains is threatened. Toffler traces the nature of this threat and suggests in his conclusion what he feels is the only possible response to it.

In "The Obligation to Endure" Rachel Carson pursues what may prove still a larger threat, again one that humanity has created. Her essay outlines a staggering irony, that in our attempts to control nature with science and technology, we seem bent on destroying the entire ecosystem that supports us. How individuals adjust to an environment made inimical by their fellows remains one of the vexed questions of our times, one Miss Carson's essay urges us to address.

In "Politics, A Con Game" Joe McGinniss offers a first-hand look at the political implications of communications technology, what the combination of advertising tactics and television hold in store for the democratic process. He examines how in seeking the response of voters to the image rather than the person, politicians eagerly pander to the individual's longing for illusions. As McGinniss pictures it, the very character of the candidate, that same character which will make crucial decisions affecting our lives, is reduced to a pseudo-event, an amalgam of carefully contrived half truths and advertising hoopla. The identity of the human being who set out to run for office somehow gets lost in the rush to supply an image. The ramifications of what McGinniss points to go far beyond the particular candidate he pictures; they lead inevitably to an officeholder's overwhelming concern with images and to the threat this attitude poses to the entire political system. The reader may find it intriguing to compare Mr. McGinniss's analysis (published 1969) with the later actions of that same candidate as officeholder (see *In an Oval Office*).

D. H. Lawrence (1885-1930)

Few writers have ever captured passion and human motivation as well as Lawrence, nor have many approached his capacity for insights into human relationships. His novels, short stories, and poems mark him a genius, and here his ability as an essayist bears out that judgment. In this essay he examines the need of the self for love and the role love plays in human identity.

Love Was Once a Little Boy

Collapse, as often as not, is the result of persisting in an old attitude towards some important relationship, which, in the course of time, has changed its nature.

Love itself is a relationship, which changes as all things change, save abstractions. If you want something really more durable than diamonds you must be content with eternal truths like "twice two are four."

Love is a relationship between things that live, holding them together in a sort of unison. There are other vital relationships. But love is this special one.

In every living thing there is the desire, for love, or for the relationship of unison with the rest of things. That a tree should desire to develop itself between the power of the sun, and the opposite pull of the earth's centre, and to balance itself between the four winds of heaven, and to unfold itself between the rain and the shine, to have roots and feelers in blue heaven and innermost earth, both, this is a manifestation of love: a knitting together of the diverse cosmos into a oneness, a tree.

At the same time, the tree must most powerfully exert itself and defend itself, to maintain its own integrity against the rest of things.

So that love, as a desire, is balanced against the opposite desire, to maintain the integrity of the individual self.

Hate is not the opposite of love. The real opposite of love is individuality.

We live in the age of individuality, we call ourselves the servants of love. That is to say, we enact a perpetual paradox.

Take the love of a man and a woman, to-day. As sure as you start with a case of "true love" between them, you end with a terrific struggle and conflict of the two opposing egos or individualities. It is nobody's fault: it is the inevitable result of trying to snatch an intensified individuality out of the mutual flame.

Love, as a relationship of unison, means and must mean to *some extent*, the sinking of the individuality. Woman for centuries was expected to sink her individuality into that of her husband and family. Nowadays the tendency is to insist that a man shall sink his individuality into his job, or his business, primarily, and secondarily into his wife and family.

At the same time, education and the public voice urge man and woman into intenser individualism. The sacrifice takes the old symbolic form of throwing a few grains of incense on the altar. A certain amount of time, labour, money, emotion are sacrificed on the altar of love, by man and woman: especially emotion. But each calculates the sacrifice. And man and woman alike, each saves his individual ego, her individual ego, intact, as far as possible, in the scrimmage of love. Most of our talk about love is cant, and bunk. The treasure of treasures to man and woman to-day is his own, or her own ego. And this ego, each hopes it will flourish like a salamander in the flame of love and passion. Which it well may: but for the fact that there are two salamanders in the same flame, and they fight till the flame goes out. Then they become grey cold lizards of the vulgar ego.

It is much easier, of course, when there *is* no flame. Then there is no serious fight.

You can't worship love and individuality in the same breath. Love is a mutual relationship, like a flame between wax and air. If either wax or air insists on getting its own way, or getting its own back too much, the flame goes out and the unison disappears. At the same time, if one yields itself up to the other entirely, there is a guttering mess. You have to balance love and individuality, and actually sacrifice a portion of each.

You have to have some sort of balance.

The Greeks said equilibrium. But whereas you can quite nicely balance a pound of butter against a pound of cheese, it is quite another matter to balance a rose and a ruby. Still more difficult is it to put male man in one scale and female woman in the other, and equilibrate that little pair of opposites.

Unless, of course, you abstract them. It's easy enough to balance a citizen against a citizeness, a Christian against a Christian, a spirit against a spirit, or a soul against a soul. There's a formula for each case. Liberty, Equality, Fraternity, etc., etc.

But the moment you put young Tom in one scale, and young Kate in the other: why, not God Himself has succeeded as yet in striking a nice level balance. Probably doesn't intend to, ever . . .

Now we have imagined love to be something absolute and personal. It is neither. In its essence, love is no more than the stream of clear and unmuddied, subtle desire which flows from person to person, creature to creature, thing to thing. The moment this stream of delicate but potent desire dries up, the love has dried up, and the joy of life has dried up. It's no good trying to turn on the tap. Desire is either flowing, or gone, and the love with it, and the life too.

This subtle streaming of desire is beyond the control of the ego. The ego says: "This is *my* love, to do as I like with! This is *my* desire, given me for my own pleasure."

But the ego deceives itself. The individual cannot possess the love which he himself feels. Neither should he be entirely possessed by it.

Neither man nor woman should sacrifice individuality to love, nor love to individuality.

If we lose desire out of our life, we become empty vessels. But if we break our own integrity, we become a squalid mess, like a jar of honey dropped and smashed.

The individual has nothing, really, to do with love. That is, his individuality hasn't. Out of the deep silence of his individuality runs the stream of desire, into the open squash blossom of the world. And the stream of desire may meet and mingle with the stream from a woman. But it is never *himself* that meets and mingles with *herself:* any more than two lakes, whose waters meet to make one river, in the distance, meet in themselves.

The two individuals stay apart, forever and ever. But the two streams of desire, like the Blue Nile and the White Nile, from the mountains one and from the low hot lake the other, meet and at length mix their strange and alien waters, to make a Nilus Flux.

See then the childish mistake we have made, about love. We have *insisted* that the two individualities should "fit." We have insisted that the "love" between man and woman must be "perfect." What on earth that means, is a mystery. What would a perfect Nilus Flux be?—one that never overflowed its banks? or one that always overflowed its banks? or one that had exactly the same overflow every year, to a hair's-breadth?

My dear, it is absurd. Perfect love is an absurdity. As for casting out fear, you'd better be careful. For fear, like curses and chickens, will also come home to roost.

Perfect love, I suppose, means that a married man and woman never contradict one another, and that they both of them always feel the same thing at the same moment, and kiss one another on the strength of it. What blarney! It means, I suppose, that they are absolutely intimate: this precious intimacy that lovers insist on. They tell each other *everything:* and if she puts on chiffon knickers, he ties the strings for her: and if he blows his nose, she holds the hanky.

Pfui! Is anything so loathsome as intimacy, especially the married sort, or the sort that "lovers" indulge in!

It's a mistake and ends in disaster. Why? Because the individualities of men and women are incommensurable, and they will no more meet than the Mountains of Abyssinia will meet with Lake Victoria Nyanza. It is far more important to keep them distinct, than to join them. If they are to join, they will join in the third land where the two streams of desire meet.

Of course, as citizen and citizeness, as two persons, even as two spirits, man and woman can be equal and intimate. But this is their outer, more general or common selves. The individual man himself, and the individual woman herself, this is another pair of shoes.

It is a pity that we have insisted on putting all our eggs in one basket: calling love the basket, and ourselves the eggs. It is a pity we have insisted on being individuals only in the communistic, semi-abstract or generalized sense: as voters, money-owners, "free" men and women: free in so far as we are all alike, and individuals in so far as we are commensurable integers.

By turning ourselves into integers: every man to himself and every woman to herself a Number One; an infinite number of Number Ones; we have destroyed ourselves as desirous or desirable individuals, and broken the inward sources of our power, and flooded all mankind into one dreary marsh where the rivers of desire lie dead with everything else, except a stagnant unity.

It is a pity of pities women have learned to think like men. Any husband will say: *"they haven't."* But they have: they've all learned to think like some other beastly man, who is not their husband. Our education goes on and on, on and on, making the sexes alike, destroying the original individuality of the blood, to substitute for it this dreary individuality of the ego, the Number One. Out of the ego streams neither Blue Nile nor White Nile. The infinite number of little human egos makes a mosquito marsh, where nothing happens except buzzing and biting, ooze and degeneration.

And they call this marsh, with its poisonous will-o-the-wisps, and its clouds of mosquitoes, *democracy,* and the reign of love!!

You can have it.

I am a man, and the Mountains of Abyssinia, and my Blue Nile flows towards the desert. There should be a woman somewhere far south, like a great lake, sending forth her White Nile towards the desert, too: and the rivers will meet among the Slopes of the World, somewhere.

But alas, every woman I've ever met spends her time saying she's as good as any man, if not better, and she can beat him at his own game. So Lake Victoria Nyanza gets up on end, and declares it's the Mountains of Abyssinia, and the Mountains of Abyssinia fall flat and cry: *"You're all that, and more, my dear!"*—and between them, you're bogged.

I give it up.

But at any rate it's nice to know what's wrong, since wrong it is.

If we were men, if we were women, our individualities would be lone and a bit mysterious, like tarns, and fed with power, male power, female power, from underneath, invisibly. And from us the streams of desire would flow out in the eternal glimmering adventure, to meet in some unknown desert.

*Mais nous avons changé tout cela.**

I'll bet the yokel, even then, was more himself, and the stream of his desire was stronger and more gurgling, than William Wordsworth's. For a long time the yokel retains his own integrity, and his own real stream of desire flows from him. Once you break this, and turn him, who was a yokel, into still another Number One, an assertive newspaper-parcel of an ego, you've done it!

*"But we have changed all that."

But don't, dear, darling reader, when I say "desire," immediately conclude that I mean a jungleful of rampaging Don Juans. . . . When I say that a woman should be eternally desirable, *don't* say that I mean every man should want to sleep with her, the instant he sets eyes on her.

On the contrary. Don Juan was only Don Juan because he *had* no real desire. He had broken his own integrity, and was a mess to start with. No stream of desire, with a course of its own, flowed from him. He was a marsh in himself. He mashed and trampled everything up, and desired no woman, so he ran after every one of them, with an itch instead of a steady flame. And tortured by his own itch, he inflamed his itch more and more. That's Don Juan, the man who *couldn't* desire a woman. He shouldn't have tried. He should have gone into a monastery at fifteen.

As for the yokel, his little stream may have flowed out of commonplace little hills, and been ready to mingle with the streams of any easy, puddly little yokeless. But what does it matter! And men are far less promiscuous, even then, than we like to pretend. It's Don Juanery, sex-in-the-head, no real desire, which leads to profligacy or squalid promiscuity. The yokel usually met desire with desire: which is all right: and sufficiently rare to ensure the moral balance.

Desire is a living stream. If we gave free rein, or a free course, to our living flow of desire, we shouldn't go far wrong. It's quite different from giving a free rein to an itching, prurient imagination. That is our vileness.

The living stream of sexual desire itself does not often, in any man, find its object, its confluent, the stream of desire in a woman into which it can flow. The two streams flow together, spontaneously, not often, in the life of any man or woman. Mostly, men and women alike rush into a sort of prostitution, because our idiotic civilization has never learned to hold in reverence the true desire-stream. We force our desire from our ego: and this is deadly.

Desire itself is a pure thing, like sunshine, or fire, or rain. It is desire that makes the whole world living to me, keeps me in the flow connected. It is my flow of desire that makes me move as the birds and animals move through the sunshine and the night, in a kind of accomplished innocence, not shut outside of the natural paradise. For life is a kind of Paradise, even to my horse Azul, though he doesn't get his own way in it, by any means, and is sometimes in a real temper about it. Sometimes he even gets a bellyache, with wet alfalfa. But even the bellyache is part of the natural paradise. Not like human ennui.

So a man can go forth in desire, even to the primroses. But let him refrain from falling all over the poor blossom, as William did. Or trying to incorporate it in his own ego, which is a sort of lust. Nasty anthropomorphic lust.

Everything that exists, even a stone, has two sides to its nature. It fiercely maintains its own individuality, its own solidity. And it reaches forth from itself in the subtlest flow of desire.

It fiercely resists all inroads. At the same time it sinks down in the curious weight, or flow, of that desire which we call gravitation. And imperceptibly, through the course of ages, it flows into delicate combination with the air and sun and rain.

At one time, men worshipped stones: symbolically, no doubt, because of their mysterious durability, their power of hardness, resistance, their strength of remaining unchanged. Yet even then, worshipping man did not rest till he had erected the stone into a pillar, a menhir, symbol of the eternal desire, as the phallus itself is but a symbol.

And we, men and women, are the same as stones: the powerful resistance and cohesiveness of our individuality is countered by the mysterious flow of desire, from us and towards us.

It is the same with the worlds, the stars, the suns. All is alive, in its own degree. And the centripetal force of spinning earth is the force of earth's individuality: and the centrifugal force is the force of desire. Earth's immense centripetal energy, almost passion, balanced against her furious centrifugal force, holds her suspended between her moon and her sun, in a dynamic equilibrium.

So instead of the Greek: *Know thyself!* we shall have to say to every man: *"Be Thyself! Be Desirous!"* — and to every woman: *"Be Thyself! Be Desirable!"*

Be Thyself! does not mean: *Assert thy ego!* It means, be true to your own integrity, as man, as woman: let your heart stay open, to receive the mysterious inflow of power from the unknown: know that the power comes to you from beyond, it is not generated by your own will: therefore all the time, be watchful, and reverential towards the mysterious coming of power into you. . . .

FOR FURTHER CONSIDERATION

Lawrence suggests that people "sink their individuality" into things and relationships. Do you agree? If so, into what things and relationships do you sink your self? Do love and individuality always exercise opposite pulls on a person?

Thomas A. Harris (1913–)

Thomas H. Harris, M.D., practiced psychiatry in Sacramento, California, and founded the Institute for Transactional Analysis in California. Harris distinguished three active elements in each person's make-up: the Parent, the Adult, and the Child. He explores these life roles in the essay which follows, excerpted from his best-selling book I'm OK-You're OK: A Practical Guide to Transactional Analysis. *Implicit in Harris's approach is the attitude that the individual must assume responsibility for his own acts in the future, regardless of the past.*

Parent, Adult, and Child

Early in his work in the development of Transactional Analysis, Berne observed that as you watch and listen to people you can see them change before your eyes. It is a total kind of change. There are simultaneous changes in facial expression, vocabulary, gestures, posture, and body functions, which may cause the face to flush, the heart to pound, or the breathing to become rapid.

We can observe these abrupt changes in everyone: the little boy who bursts into tears when he can't make a toy work, the teen-age girl whose woeful face floods with excitement when the phone finally rings, the man who grows pale and trembles when he gets the news of a business failure, the father whose face "turns to stone" when his son disagrees with him. The individual who changes in these ways is still the same person in terms of bone structure, skin, and clothes. So what changes inside him? He changes *from* what *to* what?

This was the question which fascinated Berne in the early development of Transactional Analysis. A thirty-five-year-old lawyer, whom he was treating, said, "I'm not really a lawyer. I'm just a little boy." Away from the psychiatrist's office he was, in fact a successful lawyer, but in treatment he felt and acted like a little boy. Sometimes during the hour he would ask, "Are you talking to the lawyer or to the little boy?" Both Berne and his patient became intrigued at the existence and appearance of these two real people, or states of being, and began talking about them as "the adult" and "the child." Treatment centered around separating the two. Later another state began to become apparent as a state distinct from "adult" and "child." This was "the parent" and was identified by behavior which was a reproduction of what the patient saw and heard his parents do when he was a little boy.

Changes from one state to another are apparent in manner, appearance, words, and gestures. A thirty-four-year-old woman came to me for help with a problem of sleeplessness, constant worry over "what I am doing to my children," and increasing nervousness. In the course of the first hour she suddenly began to weep and said, "You make me feel like I'm three years old." Her voice and manner were that of a small child. I asked her, "What happened to make you feel like a child?" "I don't know," she responded, and then added, "I suddenly felt like a failure." I said, "Well, let's talk about children, about the family. Maybe we can discover something inside of you that produces these feelings of failure and despair." At another point in the hour her voice and manner again changed suddenly. She became critical and dogmatic: "After all, parents have rights, too. Children need to be shown their place." During one hour this mother changed to three different and distinct personalities: one of a small child dominated by feelings, one of a self-righteous parent, and one of a reasoning, logical, grown-up woman and mother of three children.

Continual observation has supported the assumption that these three states exist in all people. It is as if in each person there is the same little person he was when he was three years old. There are also within him his own parents. These are recordings in the brain of actual experiences of internal and external events, the most significant of which happened during the first five years of life. There is a third state, different from these two. The first two are called Parent and Child, and the third, Adult. (See Figure 1.)

These states of being are not roles but psychological realities. Berne says that "Parent, Adult, and Child are not concepts like Superego, Ego, and Id . . . but phenomenological realities."[1] The state is produced by the playback of recorded data of events in the past, involving real people, real times, real places, real decisions, and real feelings.

THE PARENT

The Parent is a huge collection of recordings in the brain of unquestioned or imposed external events perceived by a person in his early years, a period which we have designated roughly as the first five years of life. This is the period before the social birth of the individual, before he leaves home in response to the demands of society and enters school. (See Figure 2.) The name Parent is most descriptive of this data inasmuch as the most significant "tapes" are those provided by the example and pronouncements of his own real parents or parent substitutes. Everything the child saw his parents do and everything he heard them say is recorded in the Parent. Everyone has a Parent in that everyone experienced external stimuli in the first five years of life. Parent is specific for every person, being the recording of that set of early experiences unique to him.

The data in the Parent was taken in and recorded "straight" without editing. The situation of the little child, his dependency, and his inability to construct meanings with words made it impossible for him to modify,

[1]E. Berne, *Transactional Analysis in Psychotherapy* (New York: Grove Press, 1961), p. 24.

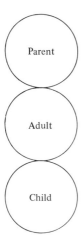

Figure 1 The Personality.

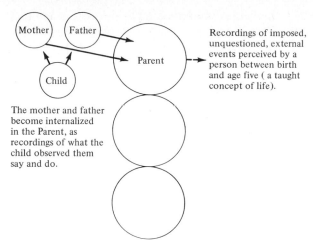

The mother and father
become internalized
in the Parent, as
recordings of what the
child observed them
say and do.

Recordings of imposed,
unquestioned, external
events perceived by a
person between birth
and age five (a taught
concept of life).

Figure 2 The Parent.

correct, or explain. Therefore, if the parents were hostile and constantly
battling each other, a fight was recorded with the terror produced by
seeing the two persons on whom the child depended for survival about to
destroy each other. There was no way of including in this recording the
fact that the father was inebriated because his business had just gone
down the drain or that the mother was at her wits' end because she had
just found she was pregnant again.

In the Parent are recorded all the admonitions and rules and laws that
the child heard from his parents and saw in their living. They range all the
way from the earliest parental communications, interpreted nonverbally
through tone of voice, facial expression, cuddling, or noncuddling, to the
more elaborate verbal rules and regulations espoused by the parents as
the little person became able to understand words. In this set of
recordings are the thousands of "no's" directed at the toddler, the
repeated "don'ts" that bombarded him, the looks of pain and horror in
mother's face when his clumsiness brought shame on the family in the
form of Aunt Ethel's broken antique vase.

Likewise are recorded the coos of pleasure of a happy mother and
the looks of delight of a proud father. When we consider that the recorder
is on all the time we begin to comprehend the immense amount of data in
the Parent. Later come the more complicated pronouncements: Remember, Son, wherever you go in the world you will always find the best
people are Methodists; never tell a lie; pay your bills; you are judged by
the company you keep; you are a good boy if you clean your plate; waste
is the original sin; you can never trust a man; you can never trust a
woman; you're damned if you do and damned if you don't; you can never
trust a cop; busy hands are happy hands; don't walk under ladders; do
unto others as you would have them do unto you; do others in that they
don't do you in.

The significant point is that whether these rules are good or bad in the light of a reasonable ethic, they are recorded as *truth* at a time when it is important to the two-foot-tall child that he please and obey them. It is a permanent recording. A person cannot erase it. It is available for replay throughout life.

This replay is a powerful influence throughout life. These examples—coercing, forcing, sometimes permissive but more often restrictive—are rigidly internalized as a voluminous set of data essential to the individual's survival in the setting of a group, beginning with the family and extending throughout life in a succession of groups necessary to life. Without a physical parent the child would die. The internal parent also is lifesaving, guarding against many dangers which, perceived experientially, could cause death. In the Parent is the recording, "Don't touch that knife!" It is a thunderous directive. The threat to the little person, as he sees it, is that his mother will spank him or otherwise show disapproval. The greater threat is that he can cut himself and bleed to death. He cannot perceive this. He does not have adequate data. The recording of parental dictates, then, is an indispensable aid to survival, in both the physical and the social sense.

Another characteristic of the Parent is the fidelity of the recordings on inconsistency. Parents say one thing and do another. Parents say, "Don't lie," but tell lies. They tell children that smoking is bad for their health but smoke themselves. They proclaim adherence to a religious ethic but do not live by it. It is not safe for the little child to question this inconsistency, and so he is confused. Because this data causes confusion and fear, he defends himself by turning off the recording.

We think of the Parent predominantly as the recordings of the transactions between the child's two parents. It may be helpful to consider the recordings of Parent data as somewhat like the recording of stereophonic sound. There are two sound tracks that, if harmonious, produce a beautiful effect when played together. If they are not harmonious, the effect is unpleasant and the recording is put aside and played very little, if at all. This is what happens when the Parent contains discordant material. The Parent is repressed or, in the extreme, blocked out altogether. Mother may have been a "good" mother and father may have been "bad," or vice versa. There is much useful data which is stored as a result of the transmission of good material from one parent; but since the Parent does contain material from the other parent that is contradictory and productive of anxiety, the Parent as a whole is weakened or fragmented. Parent data that is discordant is not allowed to come on "audibly" as a strong influence in the person's life.

Another way to describe this phenomenon is to compare it with the algebraic equation: a plus times a minus equals a minus. It does not matter how big the plus was, or how little the minus was. The result is always a minus—a weakened, disintegrated Parent. The effect in later life may be ambivalence, discord, and despair—for the person, that is, who is not free to examine the Parent.

Much Parent data appears in current living in the "how-to" category:

how to hit a nail, how to make a bed, how to eat soup, how to blow your nose, how to thank the hostess, how to shake hands, how to pretend no one's at home, how to fold the bath towels, or how to dress the Christmas tree. The *how to* comprises a vast body of data acquired by watching the parents. It is largely useful data which makes it possible for the little person to learn to get along by himself. Later (as his Adult becomes more skillful and free to examine Parent data) these early ways of doing things may be updated and replaced by better ways that are more suited to a changed reality. A person whose early instructions were accompanied by stern intensity may find it more difficult to examine the old ways and may hang onto them long after they are useful, having developed a compulsion to do it "this way and no other."

The mother of a teen-ager related the following parental edict, which had long governed her housekeeping procedures. Her mother had told her, "You *never* put a hat on a table or a coat on a bed." So she went through life never putting a hat on a table or a coat on a bed. Should she occasionally forget, or should one of her youngsters break this old rule, there was an overreaction that seemed inappropriate to the mere violation of the rules of simple neatness. Finally, after several decades of living with this unexamine law, mother asked grandmother (by then in her eighties), "Mother, *why* do you never put a hat on a table or a coat on a bed?"

Grandmother replied that when she was little there had been some neighbor children who were "infested," and her mother had warned her that it was important they never put the neighbor children's hats on the table or their coats on the bed. Reasonable enough. The urgency of the early admonition was understandable. In terms of Penfield's findings it was also understandable why the recording came on with the original urgency. Many of the rules we live by are like this.

Some influences are more subtle. One modern housewife with every up-to-date convenience in her home found she simply did not have any interest in buying a garbage-disposal unit. Her husband encouraged her to get one, pointing out all the reasons this would simplify her kitchen procedures. She recognized this but found one excuse after another to postpone going to the appliance store to select one. Her husband finally confronted her with his belief that she was *deliberately* not getting a garbage disposal. He insisted she tell him why.

A bit of reflection caused her to recognize an early impression she had about garbage. Her childhood years were the Depression years of the 1930's. In her home, garbage was carefully saved and fed to the pig, which was butchered at Christmas and provided an important source of food. The dishes were even washed without soap so that the dishwater, with its meager offering of nutrients, could be included in the slops. As a little girl she perceived that garbage was important, and as a grown woman she found it difficult to rush headlong into purchasing a new-fangled gadget to dispose of it. (She bought the disposal unit and lived happily ever after.)

When we realize that thousands of these simple rules of living are recorded in the brain of every person, we begin to appreciate what a comprehensive, vast store of data the Parent includes. Many of these edicts are fortified with such additional imperatives as "never" and "always" and "never forget that" and, we may assume, pre-empt certain primary neurone pathways that supply ready data for today's transactions. These rules are the origins of compulsions and quirks and eccentricities that appear in later behavior. Whether Parent data is a burden or a boon depends on how appropriate it is to the present, on whether or not it has been updated by the Adult, the function of which we shall discuss in this chapter.

There are sources of Parent data other than the physical parents. A three-year-old who sits before a television set many hours a day is recording what he sees. The programs he watches are a "taught" concept of life. If he watches programs of violence, I believe he records violence in his Parent. That's how it is. That is life! This conclusion is certain if his parents do not express opposition by switching the channel. If they enjoy violent programs the youngster gets a double sanction—the set and the folks—and he assumes permission to be violent provided he collects the required amount of injustices. The little person collects his own reasons to shoot up the place, just as the sheriff does; three nights of cattle rustlers, a stage holdup, and a stranger foolin' with Miss Kitty can be easily matched in the life of the little person. Much of what is experienced at the hands of older siblings or other authority figures also is recorded in the Parent. Any external situation in which the little person feels himself to be dependent to the extent that he is not free to question or to explore produces data which is stored in the Parent. (There is another type of external experience of the very small child which is not recorded in the Parent, and which we shall examine when we describe the Adult.)

THE CHILD

While external events are being recorded as that body of data we call the Parent, there is another recording being made simultaneously. This is the recording of *internal* events, the responses of the little person to what he sees and hears. (Figure 3.) In this connection it is important to recall Penfield's observation that

> the subject feels again the emotion which the situation originally produced in him, and he is aware of the same interpretations, true or false, which he himself gave to the experience in the first place. Thus, evoked recollection is not the exact photographic or phonographic reproduction of past scenes or events. It is reproduction of what the patient *saw and heard and felt and understood*.[2] [Italics added.]

---

[2]W. Penfield, "Memory Mechanisms," *A.M.A. Archives of Neurology and Psychiatry,* 67(1952): 178–198, with discussion by L. S. Kubie et al.

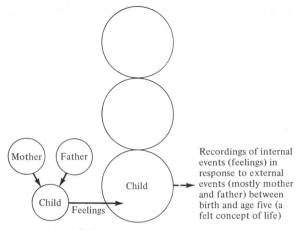

Figure 3 The Child.

It is this "seeing and hearing and feeling and understanding" body of data which we define as the Child. Since the little person has no vocabulary during the most critical of his early experiences, most of his reactions are *feelings*. We must keep in mind his situation in these early years. He is small, he is dependent, he is inept, he is clumsy, he has no words with which to construct meanings. Emerson said we "must know how to estimate a sour look." The child does not know how to do this. A sour look turned in his direction can only produce feelings that add to his reservoir of negative data about himself. *It's my fault. Again. Alway is. Ever will be. World without end.*

During this time of helplessness there are an infinite number of total and uncompromising demands on the child. On the one hand, he has the urges (genetic recording) to empty his bowels ad lib., to explore, to know, to crush and to bang, to express feelings, and to experience all of the pleasant sensations associated with movement and discovery. On the other hand, there is the constant demand from the environment, essential-ly the parents, that he give up these basic satisfactions for the reward of parental approval. This approval, which can disappear as fast as it appears, is an unfathomable mystery to the child, who has not yet made any certain connection between cause and effect.

The predominant by-product of the frustrating, civilizing process is negative feelings. On the basis of these feelings the little person early concludes, "I'm not OK." We call this comprehensive self-estimate the NOT OK, or the NOT OK Child. This conclusion and the continual experiencing of the unhappy feelings which led to it and confirm it are recorded permanently in the brain and cannot be erased. This permanent recording is the residue of having been a child. It is the *situation of childhood* and *not* the intention of the parents which produces the problem. An example of the dilemma of childhood was a statement made by my seven-year-old daughter, Heidi, who one morning at breakfast said, "Daddy, when I have an OK Daddy and an OK Mama, how come *I'm* not OK?"

When the children of "good" parents carry the NOT OK burden, one can begin to appreciate the load carried by children whose parents are guilty of gross neglect, abuse, and cruelty.

As in the case of the Parent, the Child is a state into which a person may be transferred at almost any time in his current transactions. There are many things that can happen to us today which recreate the situation of childhood and bring on the same feelings we felt then. Frequently we may find ourselves in situations where we are faced with impossible alternatives, where we find ourselves in a corner, either actually, or in the way we see it. These "hook the Child," as we say, and cause a replay of the original feelings of frustration, rejection, or abandonment, and we relive a latter-day version of the small child's primary depression. Therefore, when a person is in the grip of feelings, we say his Child has taken over. When his anger dominates his reason, we say his Child is in command.

There is a bright side, too! In the Child is also a vast store of positive data. In the Child reside creativity, curiosity, the desire to explore and know, the urges to touch and feel and experience, and the recordings of the glorious, pristine feelings of first discoveries. In the Child are recorded the countless, grand *a-ha* experiences, the firsts in the life of the small person, the first drinking from the garden hose, the first stroking of the soft kitten, the first sure hold on mother's nipple, the first time the lights go on in response to his flicking the switch, the first submarine chase of the bar of soap, the repetitious going back to do these glorious things again and again. The feelings of these delights are recorded, too. With all the NOT OK recordings, there is a counterpoint, the rhythmic OK of mother's rocking, the sentient softness of the favorite blanket, a continuing good response to favorable external events (if this is indeed a favored child), which also is available for replay in today's transactions. This is the flip side, the happy child, the carefree, butterfly-chasing little boy, the little girl with chocolate on her face. This comes on in today's transactions, too. However, our observations both of small children and of ourselves as grownups convince us that the NOT OK feelings far outweigh the good. This is why we believe it is a fair estimate to say that everyone has a NOT OK Child.

Frequently I am asked, When do the Parent and Child stop recording? Do the Parent and Child contain only experiences in the first five years of life? I believe that by the time the child leaves the home for his first independent social experience—school—he has been exposed to nearly every possible attitude and admonition of his parents, and thenceforth further parental communications are essentially a reinforcement of what has already been recorded. The fact that he now begins to "use his Parent" on others also has a reinforcing quality in line with the Aristotelian idea that that which is expressed is impressed. As to further recordings in the Child, it is hard to imagine that any emotion exists which has not already been felt in its most intense form by the time the youngster is five years old. This is consistent with most psychoanalytic theory, and, in my own observation, is true.

If, then, we emerge from childhood with a set of experiences which are recorded in an inerasable Parent and Child, what is our hope for change? How can we get off the hook of the past?

THE ADULT

At about ten months of age a remarkable thing begins to happen to the child. Until that time his life has consisted mainly of helpless or unthinking responses to the demands and stimulations by those around him. He has a Parent and a Child. What he has not had is the ability either to choose his responses or to manipulate his surroundings. He has had no self-direction, no ability to move out to meet life. He has simply taken what has come his way.

At ten months, however, he begins to experience the power of locomotion. He can manipulate objects and begins to move out, freeing himself from the prison of immobility. It is true that earlier, as at eight months, the infant may frequently cry and need help in getting out of some awkward position, but he is unable to get out of it by himself. At ten months he concentrates on inspection and exploitation of toys. According to the studies conducted by Gesell and Ilg, the ten-month-old child

> . . . enjoys playing with a cup and pretends to drink. He brings objects to his mouth and chews them. He enjoys gross motor activity: sitting and playing after he has been set up, leaning far forward, and re-erecting himself. He secures a toy, kicks, goes from sitting to creeping, pulls himself up, and may lower himself. He is beginning to cruise. Social activities which he enjoys are peek-a-boo and lip play, walking with both hands held, being put prone on the floor, or being placed in a rocking toy. Girls show their first signs of coyness by putting their heads to one side as they smile.[3]

The ten-month-old has found he is able to do something which grows from his own awareness and original thought. This self-actualization is the beginning of the Adult. (Figure 4.) Adult data accumulates as a result of the child's ability to find out for himself what is different about life from the "taught concept" of life in his Parent and the "felt concept" of life in his Child. The Adult develops a "thought concept" of life based on data gathering and data processing.

The motility which gives birth to the Adult becomes reassuring in later life when a person is in distress. He goes for a walk to "clear his mind." Pacing is seen similarly as a relief from anxiety. There is a

---

[3]Arnold Gesell and Frances L. Ilg, *Infant and Child in the Culture of Today* (New York: Harper, 1943), pp. 116–122.

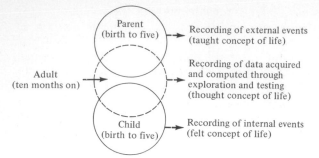

Figure 4 Gradual emergence of the Adult beginning at ten months.

recording that movement is good, that it has a separating quality, that it helps him see more clearly what his problem is.

The Adult, during these early years, is fragile and tentative. It is easily "knocked out" by commands from the Parent and fear in the Child. Mother says about the crystal goblet, "No, no! Don't touch that!" The child may pull back and cry, but at the first opportunity he will touch it anyway to see what it is all about. In most persons the Adult, despite all the obstacles thrown in its way, survives and continues to function more and more effectively as the maturation process goes on.

The Adult is "principally concerned with transforming stimuli into pieces of information, and processing and filing that information on the basis of previous experience."[4] It is different from the Parent, which is "judgmental in an imitative way and seeks to enforce sets of borrowed standards, and from the Child, which tends to react more abruptly on the basis of prelogical thinking and poorly differentiated or distorted perceptions." Through the Adult the little person can begin to tell the difference between life as it was taught and demonstrated to him (Parent), life as he felt it or wished it or fantasied it (Child), and life as he figures it out by himself (Adult).

The Adult is a data-processing computer, which grinds out decisions after computing the information from three sources: the Parent, the Child, and the data which the Adult has gathered and is gathering (Figure 5). One of the important functions of the Adult is to examine the data in the Parent, to see whether or not it is true and still applicable today, and then to accept it or reject it; and to examine the Child to see whether or not the feelings there are appropriate to the present or are archaic and in response to archaic Parent data. The goal is not to do away with the Parent and Child but to be free to examine these bodies of data. The Adult, in the words of Emerson, "must not be hindered by the name of goodness, but must examine if it be goodness"; or badness, for that matter, as in the early decision, "I'm not OK."

The Adult testing of Parent data may begin at an early age. A secure

[4]Berne, *Transactional Analysis in Psychotherapy.*

youngster is one who finds that most Parent data is reliable: "They told me the truth!"

"It really *is* true that cars in the street are dangerous," concludes the little boy who has seen his pet dog hurt by a car in the street. "It really *is* true that things go better when I share my toys with Bobby," thinks the little boy who has been given a prized possession by Bobby. "It really *does* feel better when my pants aren't wet," concludes the little girl who has learned to go to the bathroom by herself. If parental directives are grounded in reality, the child, through his own Adult, will come to realize integrity, or a sense of wholeness. What he tests holds up under testing. The data which he collects in his experimentation and examination begins to constitute some "constants" that he can trust. His findings are supported by what he was taught in the first place.

It is important to emphasize that the verification of Parent data does not erase the NOT OK recordings in the Child, which were produced by the early imposition of this data. Mother believes that the only way to keep three-year-old Johnny out of the street is to spank him. He does not understand the danger. His response is fear, anger, and frustration with no appreciation of the fact that his mother loves him and is protecting his life. The fear, anger, and frustration are recorded. These feelings are not erased by the later understanding that she was right to do what she did, but the understanding of how the original situation of childhood produced so many NOT OK recordings of this type can free us of their continual replay in the present. *We cannot erase the recording, but we can choose to turn it off!*

In the same way that the Adult updates Parent data to determine what is valid and what is not, it updates Child data to determine which feelings may be expressed safely. In our society it is considered appropriate for a woman to cry at a wedding, but it is not considered appropriate for that woman to scream at her husband afterward at the reception. Yet both crying and screaming are emotions in the Child. The Adult keeps emotional expression appropriate. The Adult's function in updating the

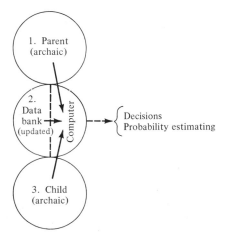

Figure 5 The Adult gets data from three sources.

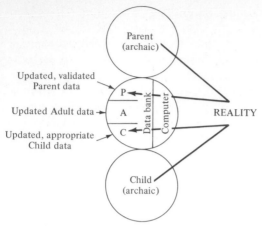

Figure 6 The updating function of the Adult through reality testing.

Parent and Child is diagrammed in Figure 6. The Adult within the Adult in this figure refers to updated reality data. (The evidence once told me space travel was only fantasy; now I know it is reality.)

Another of the Adult's functions is *probability estimating.* This function is slow in developing in the small child and, apparently, for most of us, has a hard time catching up throughout life. The little person is constantly confronted with unpleasant alternatives (either you eat your spinach or you go without ice cream), offering little incentive for examining probabilities. Unexamined probabilities can underlie many of our transactional failures, and unexpected danger signals can cause more Adult "decay," or delay, than expected ones. There are similarities here to the stock ticker in investment concerns, which may run many hours behind on very active trading days. We sometimes refer to this delay as "computer lag," a remedy for which is the old, familiar practice of "counting to ten."

The capacity for probability estimating can be increased by conscious effort. Like a muscle in the body, the Adult grows and increases in efficiency through training and use. If the Adult is alert to the possibility of trouble, through probability estimating, it can also devise solutions to meet the trouble if and when it comes.

Under sufficient stress, however, the Adult can be impaired to the point where emotions take over inappropriately. The boundaries between Parent, Adult, and Child are fragile, sometimes indistinct, and vulnerable to those incoming signals which tend to recreate situations we experienced in the helpless, dependent days of childhood. The Adult sometimes is flooded by signals of the "bad news" variety so overwhelming that the Adult is reduced to an "onlooker" in the transaction. An individual in this situation might say, "I knew what I was doing was wrong, but I couldn't help myself."

Unrealistic, irrational, non-Adult responses are seen in a condition referred to as traumatic neurosis. The danger, or "bad news" signal, hits the Parent and the Child at the same time it hits the Adult. The Child responds in the way it originally did, with a feeling of NOT OK. This may produce all kinds of regressive phenomena. The individual may again feel himself to be a tiny, helpless, dependent child. One of the most primitive of these phenomena is thought blocking. One place this can be seen is in psychiatric hospitals that have a locked-door policy. When the door is locked on a new patient, his retreat is rapid and pronounced. This is why I am opposed to treating patients in a setting where the emphasis is on parental care. Catering to the helpless Child in the individual delays the reconstructive process of restoring the Adult to the executive function.

An ideal hospital would be a comfortable motel with "play area" for the Child, surrounding a clinic building devoted to activities designed for achieving autonomy of the Adult. The nurses would not wear uniforms or serve as parents to the patients. Instead, nurses in street clothing would apply their skills and training to help each individual learn the identity of his Parent, Adult, and Child.

In our treatment groups we use certain colloquial catch phrases such as, "Why don't you stay in your Adult?" when a member finds his feelings are taking over. Another of these is, "What was the original transaction?" This is asked as a means of "turning on the Adult" to analyze the similarity between the present incoming signal producing the present distress and the original transaction, in which the small child experienced distress.

The ongoing work of the Adult consists, then, of checking out old data, validating or invalidating it, and refiling it for future use. If this business goes on smoothly and there is a relative absence of conflict between what has been taught and what is real, the computer is free for important new business, *creativity.* Creativity is born from curiosity in the Child, as is the Adult. The Child provides the "want to" and the Adult provides the "how to." The essential requirement for creativity is computer time. If the computer is cluttered with old business there is little time for new business. Once checked out, many Parent directives become automatic and thus free the computer for creativity. Many of our decisions in day-to-day transactions are automatic. For instance, when we see an arrow pointing down a one-way street, we automatically refrain from going the opposite way. We do not involve our computer in lengthy data processing about highway engineering, the traffic death toll, or how signs are painted. Were we to start from scratch in every decision or operate entirely without the data that was supplied by our parents, our computer would rarely have time for the creative process.

Some people contend that the undisciplined child, unhampered by limits, is more creative than the child whose parents set limits. I do not believe this true. A youngster has more time to be creative—to explore, invent, take apart, and put together—if he is not wasting time in futile decision making for which he has inadequate data. A little boy has more time to build a snowman if he is not allowed to engage Mother in a long hassle about whether or not to wear overshoes. If a child is allowed to be creative by painting the front room walls with shoe polish, he is unprepared for the painful consequences when he does so at the neighbor's house. Painful outcomes do not produce OK feelings. There are other consequences that take time, such as mending in the hospital after a trial-and-error encounter with a car in the street. There is just so much computer time. Conflict uses a great deal. An extremely time-consuming conflict is produced when what parents say is true does not seem to be true to the Adult. The most creative individual is the one who discovers that a large part of the content of the Parent squares with reality. He can then file away this validated information in the Adult, trust it, forget about it, and get on with other things—like how to make a kite fly, how to build a sand castle, or how to do differential calculus.

However, many youngsters are preoccupied much of the time with the conflict between Parent data and what they see as reality. Their most troubling problem is that they do not understand why the Parent has such a hold on them. When Truth comes to knock at the Parent's door, the Parent says, "Come, let us reason together." The little child whose father is in jail and whose mother steals to support him may have a loud recording in his Parent, "You never trust a cop!" So he meets a friendly one. His Adult computes all the data about this nice guy, how he gets the ball game started in the sand lot, how he treats the gang to popcorn, how he is friendly, and how he speaks in a quiet voice. For this youngster there is conflict. What he sees as reality is different from what he has been taught. The Parent tells him one thing and the Adult another. During the period of his actual dependency upon his parents for security, however tenuous this security may be, it is likely he will accept the parents' verdict that cops are bad. This is how prejudice is transmitted. *For a little child, it may be safer to believe a lie than to believe his own eyes and ears.* The Parent so threatens the Child (in a continuing internal dialogue) that the Adult gives up and stops trying to inquire into areas of conflict. Therefore, "cops are bad" comes through as truth. This is called *contamination* of the Adult.

FOR FURTHER CONSIDERATION

Compare Harris's concept of Parent, Adult, and Child with Barth's explanation of what the quack Doctor calls Mythotherapy in "The Remobilization of Jacob Horner," that is, that "everyone is necessarily the hero of his own life's story." To test your understanding of Harris's theory, try labeling which of the ego states (Parent, Adult, Child) operates in each remark in the final conversation of "Remobilization." Begin with " 'Say something' the Doctor ordered. 'Move! Take a role!' "

Tom Wicker (1926–   )

Wicker has been a highly popular political reporter for The New York Times, *a columnist, a novelist, and a free-lance magazine writer. His*

insight into political personalities derives from his wide range of acquaint-
ances in political circles.

Kennedy Without Tears.

Shortly after President Kennedy was shot, the following inscription
appeared on a plaque in one of the private bedrooms of the White House:

In this room Abraham Lincoln slept during his occupancy of the
White House as President of the United States, March 4, 1861-April 13,
1865.

In this room lived John Fitzgerald Kennedy with his wife Jacqueline
Kennedy during the two years, ten months and two days he was President
of the United States, January 20, 1961-November 22, 1963.

Before many years pass, that deliberate linkage of two Presidents,
that notice chiseled upon history by Jacqueline Kennedy, may seem as
inevitable as the Washington Monument. Already, airports and space-
ports and river bridges and a cultural center have been named for her
husband. Books about him, even phonograph records, are at flood tide
and *Profiles in Courage* has returned to the top of The New York *Times*
best-seller list. It is almost as if he had never called businessmen sons of
bitches, sent the troops to Ole Miss, the refugees to the Bay of Pigs, or
kicked the budget sky-high.

Six months after his death, John F. Kennedy is certain to take his
place in American lore as one of those sure-sell heroes out of whose face
or words or monuments a souvenir dealer can turn a steady buck. There
he soon will stand, perhaps in our lifetime—cold stone or heartless
bronze, immortal as Jefferson, revered as Lincoln, bloodless as Washington. One can imagine the graven words on his pedestal:

Ask not what your country can do for you, Ask what you can do for
your country.

What his country inevitably will do for John Kennedy seems a
curious fate for the vitality and intensity, the wry and derisive style of the
man who was the Thirty-fifth President of the United States. His wit
surely would have seared the notion of John F. Kennedy International
Airport, much less Cape Kennedy—for this was the man who once told
the great-great-grandson of John Adams, "It is a pleasure to live in your
family's old house, and we hope that you will come by and see us."

One suspects the Eternal Flame might have embarrassed him as
much as the Navy did that brilliant Pacific day last June when the strutting
admirals put him literally on a flag-draped pedestal aboard an aircraft
carrier while the band played *Hail to the Chief* and the jets screamed
overhead on taxpayers' money; one of his favorite quips, after all, was
that he had gone from Lieutenant J. G. to Commander-in-Chief without
any qualifications at all.

I can almost hear that amused Boston voice inquiring, as he once did
after reading a favorable Gallup Poll, where all those people who admired

him so much were when Congress turned down his school bill in 1961. Staring from Valhalla at himself cast in stone in the middle of some downtown Washington traffic circle, he might well whisper to earthly passersby what he once told 12,000 Democrats in Harrisburg, Pennsylvania:

"I will introduce myself. I am Teddy Kennedy's brother."

And when children rise reverently in some future Fourth of July pageant to recite the chiastic prose of the Kennedy Inaugural Address—the stirring words that raced so many pulses among that "new generation of Americans" to which he appealed—some may recall instead the same rhythm, the same rhetoric, but different words and a more subtle imagination at work:

"We observe tonight not a celebration of freedom but a victory of party, for we have sworn to pay off the same party debt our forebears ran up nearly a year and three months ago. Our deficit will not be paid off in the next hundred days, nor will it be paid off in the first one thousand days, nor in the life of this Administration. Nor, perhaps, even in our lifetime on this planet. But let us begin—remembering that generosity is not a sign of weakness and that ambassadors are always subject to Senate confirmation. For if the Democratic party cannot be helped by the many who are poor, it cannot be saved by the few who are rich. So let us begin."

Now a politician who could laugh at a parody of his noblest speech—let alone make it himself, as Kennedy did the foregoing—obviously was something more intricate in life than the mere sum of the virtues symbolized by the Eternal Flame: purity, steadfastness, warmth, light. A President delight by the political caricature of Everett McKinley Dirksen, but impatient with the solemn earnestness of Chester Bowles obviously had a wide streak of Honey Fitz down his spine; yet that same President, confronted with an adulatory mob of hundreds of thousands of cheering Europeans, could not bring himself to respond with more than a halfhearted jab of the arm from the chest—something like a halfback straight-arming a tackler, apologetically. And lest it be imagined that he was merely unemotional, remember that it was the crowd's transmitted frenzy that led Kennedy to make the inspiring but not very wise cry: *Ich bin ein Berliner!*

In the early days of Kennedy's New Frontier (there was bound to be something roguish about a man who could bring the Ivy Leaguers—and himself—to Washington with a slogan that evoked echoes of the Wild West, which appalled most of them), I thought Richard Nixon was perhaps a more interesting *man* than Kennedy. I thought Nixon was, as Conrad wrote of Lord Jim, "one of us." But Kennedy, I thought then, for all his charm and fire and eloquence, was a straightforward political man, who listened to his own rhetoric, contrived his "image" in the comforting faith that a statesman had to get elected before he could do anyone any good, and believed sincerely that his causes were not only right but actually offered solutions to human problems. I thought Kennedy had what Senator Eugene McCarthy called the perfect political mentality—

that of a football coach, combining the will to win with the belief that the game is important.

Now, I think that what Kennedy really had of that mentality was a rather peculiar form of the will to win. He wanted power, all right, but something more; "This ability," he once said, "to do things well, and to do them with precision and with modesty, attracts us all." It was a theme to which he returned—the pursuit of excellence. And as the probability of his political canonization turns toward certainty, and the sad calcification of his humanity into stone and bronze continues, there is not much football coach in the man Kennedy who recalls himself to me most strongly.

If that human Kennedy still seems to me to have been altogether too detached and too controlled to have been, as were Nixon and Lord Jim, "one of us," with all those fascinating hesitancies and inadequacies and torments out of which literature is made, nevertheless he *was* a man "of few days and full of trouble," and for all I know he may even have played "such fantastic tricks before high heaven as to make the angels weep." But the statues will tell us nothing of that.

Not many of them, for instance, will bear inscriptions drawn from his wit—that derisive, barbed, spontaneous wit, just short of mordant, that played so steadily through his speeches and recurred in such stable patterns of wording and attitude that it strikes me in retrospect as the true expression of a point of view, of a way of thinking not subject to time or circumstance or conditions.

It is astonishing, in retrospect, how constantly and boldly this Irish Catholic President, this young man so publicly committed to things like patriotism and public affairs, lampooned politicians, politics, notions, men, systems, myths, himself, even his church. When *The Wall Street Journal* criticized Nixon, Kennedy said, it was like *"L'Osservatore Romano* criticizing the Pope." And Speaker John McCormack denies that Kennedy called him "Archbishop"; "He called me 'Cardinal,'" McCormack recalls.

When the Vatican implied some criticism of Kennedy's campaign efforts to prove himself free of papal influence, Kennedy said ruefully to a pair of reporters: "Now I understand why Henry the Eighth set up his own church."

He and McKinley were the only Presidents ever to address the National Association of Manufacturers, Kennedy told that august body, so "I suppose that President McKinley and I are the only two that are regarded as fiscally sound enough to be qualified." And to the $100-a-plate guests at a glittering political occasion, he confessed: "I could say I am deeply touched, but not as deeply touched as you have been in coming to this luncheon."

Not even the Kennedy family was spared its scion's irreverence. To a dinner of the Alfred E. Smith Foundation during the 1960 campaign, he remarked:

"I had announced earlier this year that if successful I would not

consider campaign contributions as a substitute for experience in appointing ambassadors. Ever since I made that statement I have not received
one single cent from my father."

Everyone remembers his remark, upon appointing Bob Kennedy
Attorney General, that his brother might as well get a little experience
before having to practice law; not so many heard him late one night at a
Boston dinner last fall when he paid similar respects to the youthful
Edward M. Kennedy:

"My last campaign may be coming up very shortly," he said, "but
Teddy is around and, therefore, these dinners can go on indefinitely."

The Kennedy wit was so pronounced and so identifiable that it could
be reproduced with near exactitude by Ted Sorensen, his speech writer. A
deadly serious man, Sorensen's few recorded public jokes include one
perfect specimen of Kennedy-style wit.

"There will be a meeting this afternoon of representatives from
Baltimore, Atlantic City, San Francisco, Philadelphia, Chicago and other
cities interested in holding the 1964 national convention," he said in a
mock announcement to a Democratic party gathering. "The meeting will
be held in Mayor Daley's room."

In order to laugh—as the Democrats did—one had to know of course
that Richard Daley was mayor of Chicago and one of the most powerful
figures in the Democratic party—and that the competition for the
convention was cutthroat. But Sorensen, as Kennedy always did, had
tuned his derision precisely to his audience and the circumstances. The
target was the situation—Daley's power, the party's foibles, the audience's pretensions. But whatever the situation, the *point of view* remained
constant in Kennedy-style wit; it was the point of view that marked the
man.

That point of view, as these few examples show, was a blending of
amiable irreverence into a faintly resigned tolerance. It was a point of
view that did not expect too much of human beings, even of its possessor;
even less did it count heavily upon the wisdom or majesty of politicians;
and often enough the political process itself was seen with frank
disrespect. Perhaps a British M.P., but no American politician in memory
except John Kennedy, would have been capable of the devastating
"endorsement" of Senator George Smathers that the President delivered
at a fund-raising dinner in Miami Beach:

"I actually came down here tonight to pay a debt of obligation to an
old friend and faithful adviser. He and I came to the Eightieth Congress
together and have been associated for many years, and I regard him as
one of my most valuable counselors in moments of great personal and
public difficulty.

"In 1952, when I was thinking about running for the United States
Senate, I went to the then Senator Smathers and said, 'George, what do
you think?'

"He said, 'Don't do it. Can't win. Bad year.'

"In 1956, I was at the Democratic convention, and I said—I didn't know whether I would run for Vice President or not, so I said, 'George, what do you think?'

" 'This is it. They need a young man. It's your chance.' So I ran—and lost.

"And in 1960, I was wondering whether I ought to run in the West Virginia primary. 'Don't do it. That state you can't possibly carry.'

"And actually, the only time I really got nervous about the whole matter at the Democratic Convention of 1960 was just before the balloting and George came up and he said, 'I think it looks pretty good for you.' "

The audience was already in stitches, but Kennedy had saved the real barb of his wit to the last, for an astonishing punch line in which Smathers appears not only as a target but as part of an apparatus—the Presidency and its problems—that was in itself somewhat ridiculous in its pretensions:

"It will encourage you to know [Kennedy said] that every Tuesday morning . . . we have breakfast together and he advises with me—Cuba, anything else, Laos, Berlin, anything—George comes right out there and gives his views and I listen very carefully."

Nor did he stop with such small targets as Smathers. Composing a birthday telegram to his touchy Vice President, Lyndon Johnson, he once told a reporter, was like "drafting a state document."

When Prime Minister Lester B. Pearson of Canada arrived at Hyannis Port in the Spring of 1963, his reputation as a baseball expert had preceded him. The resident White House baseball nut was Dave Powers, an Irishman of jovial mien who could sing *Bill Bailey Won't You Please Come Home* with marvelous vigah at the drop of a Scotch and soda. After a chilly Cape Cod dinner, Pearson followed Kennedy into seclusion, only to find it shattered by a summons to Powers.

"Dave," the President said, "test him out."

Whereupon Powers put the Prime Minister through an exhaustive baseball catechism, while the President rocked silently in his rocking chair, puffing on a cigar inscrutably, either measuring his man or enjoying the incongruous match—or both. Back and forth flowed the batting averages, managers' names, World Series statistics, and other diamond esoterica, until finally it was Dave Powers, not Mike Pearson, who tripped on some southpaw's 1926 earned run average.

"He'll do," Kennedy said then, with some satisfaction. After which he and Pearson hit it off famously and jointly equipped Canada with nuclear warheads.

Probably the finest piece of work Kennedy did in his eight generally lackluster years in the Senate was his leadership of the fight against reform of the electoral college in 1956. He argued brilliantly for the system as it was and still is. His side prevailed for a number of sound reasons, but not least because Kennedy succeeded in convincing enough Senators that, as he put it, "Falkland's definition of conservatism is quite appropriate—'When it is not necessary to change, it is necessary not to change.' "

That might almost have been Lord Melbourne speaking: *If it was not absolutely necessary, it was the foolishest thing ever done,* Melbourne said of a Parliamentary act. Indeed, Melbourne may have been in Kennedy's mind; for in the course of that brutal exposure of all his habits and persuasions to which Americans subject their President, it was to become known that his favorite book was David Cecil's *Melbourne.*

Probably no monument of the future will record that fact; yet it ought to give biographers pause. If the Kennedy campaign of 1960 meant anything, in terms of the man who waged it, it ought to have meant that Kennedy was a man who aimed to set the country right, who saw no reason it couldn't be done, who intended to let nothing stand in the way of doing it. The President who took office that cold day in January, 1961, saying, "let us begin," seemed to promise that the nation's problems could be solved if only enough brains and vigor and determination and money were applied to them.

Why would such a man enjoy reading of Melbourne, who believed government, in fact most human effort, was futile; who counseled, *When in doubt do nothing;* who said of a proposal to reform the English municipal councils, *We have got on tolerably well with the councils for five hundred years; we may contrive to go on with them for another few years or so;* and who thought the most damaging part of reform was that it aroused extravagant hopes that government and society—even men— might actually be improved.

But perhaps Kennedy was never quite the man the 1960 campaign suggested—just as Melbourne was not quite the fogy a few random quotations might suggest. Melbourne, in fact, as his biographer pictures him, was a man of immense charm and wit, great learning, considerable understanding of human nature, and remarkable courage in going his, way—attributes that might be aspired to by any man. Certainly Kennedy possessed some of them and there is evidence to suggest that he shared to some extent Melbourne's skepticism about political and other human efforts at improving the condition of man.

The Kennedy wit certainly implies that he did. So did his remarks on a famous television interview in December of 1962, when he reviewed his first two years in office.

"There is a limitation upon the ability of the United States to solve these problems," he said. ". . . there is a limitation, in other words, upon the power of the United States to bring about solutions. . . . The responsibilities placed on the United States are greater than I imagined them to be and there are greater limitations upon our ability to bring about a favorable result than I had imagined them to be. . . . It is much easier to make the speeches than it is finally to make the judgments . . ."

And it might have been Melbourne speaking again when he said of his efforts to roll back steel prices: "There is no sense in raising hell and then not being successful. There is no sense in putting the office of the Presidency on the line on an issue and then being defeated."

A few months later, I asked Kennedy at a news conference if he would comment on what I said was a feeling in the country that his Administration seemed "to have lost its momentum and to be slowing down and to be moving on the defensive."

"*There is a rhythm to a personal and national and international life and it flows and ebbs*," Kennedy replied. He even conceded—sounding not unlike Melbourne on the Reform Laws—that "Some of our difficulties in Europe have come because the military threat in Europe is less than it has been in the past. In other words, whatever successes we may have had in reducing that military threat to Europe brought with it in its wake other problems . . ."

Later, Ted Sorensen was to publish a book that in its essence was a discussion of the limitations upon a President—the reasons why, as Kennedy wrote in a foreword, "Every President must endure a gap between *what he would like and what is possible*" (the italics are mine). Once again Sorensen had caught the spirit of his chief and reproduced it; politics was not after all simply a matter of brains and vigor and determination, or even money. Its events, life itself, flowed also from the contrary nature of men, the blind turns of chance, the inertia of custom. And in that same foreword Kennedy quoted Franklin Roosevelt as saying:

Lincoln was a sad man because he couldn't get it all at once. And nobody can.

On a more personal level, some who knew Kennedy well sensed something deeper than skepticism in him, though he was a private man who did not much reveal himself even to men who worked with him for years. He was absolutely fearless about airplanes, for instance, flying anywhere, at any time, in any weather in which he could get aloft, sleeping through anything, scarcely seeming aware that he was off the ground. Yet four persons in his family—his brother, his sister, Ethel Kennedy's parents—had died in aircraft accidents.

Kennedy sometimes discussed the possibility that he would be assassinated with members of his staff. They would be anxious to explain the details of security precautions to him, to show him that it was unlikely it could happen. "If someone is going to kill me," he would say, "they're going to kill me."

And one of those who was close to him believes that Kennedy bothered little about what he was going to do with all those years that presumably would be on his hands when he emerged from the White House at age fifty-one (assuming he won two terms).

"It didn't really concern him," the aide recalls. "He never thought he was going to live to be an old man anyway."

Yet he had his imperatives. A man owed something to the public service. He had to be a patriot. He ought to be physically fit and courageous. (Good war records received special consideration on the New Frontier, and Dave Powers remembers that Kennedy once learned by heart the citation for a medal that had been awarded to General Douglas MacArthur.) A man's job was to act, not talk—to begin, to take the first step in a journey of a thousand miles.

Kennedy has been compared to Franklin Roosevelt and he liked to pose in front of an F.D.R. portrait. In fact, some of his qualities more nearly recall Theodore Roosevelt, the apostle of the big stick, the strenuous life and the bully pulpit. Like T.R., for instance, Kennedy fancied himself in the role of national taste maker—Roosevelt picked up Edward Arlington Robinson and Kennedy adopted Robert Frost. Roosevelt let his rather rigid literary ideas get about and the Kennedys thought they ought to provide White House examples—Casals, Shakespeare and opera in the East Room—for the cultural uplift of the nation. Yet, after an American opera group had sung a scene from *The Magic Flute* in English, after a dinner for the President of India, Kennedy could confess to a group of guests: "I think they ought to sing it in the original language. It doesn't sound right any other way."

There is not much doubt that Kennedy's publicized delight in Ian Fleming's spoof-spy novels doubled Fleming's sales, although there has been no big run on Cecil's *Melbourne.* He kept green, graceful, Lafayette Square in Washington from disappearing into the capital's Great Stone Face. One of his last interests was in a plan to redeem Pennsylvania Avenue from army-surplus stores, cheap steak houses and bumbling federal architects. But it was as if art and culture were in the National Interest, like the test-ban treaty and Project Mercury; and if Kennedy was an avid reader of history, he did not seem to suffer from a great personal involvement in drama, music, art. The movies shown in the White House screening room were often the commonplace of Hollywood, and, except in the East Room, Kennedy's favorite music was more nearly Sinatra than Schönberg. As President, his first venture to Broadway took him to the slick musical, *How to Succeed in Business Without Really Trying.* Once, when he had a group of newspapermen in his house at Palm Beach, I stole a look at a stack of recordings; the one on top was a Chubby Checker twist collection.

But the imperatives of taking part, of public service, seemed, like those that moved Teddy Roosevelt, to be genuine and even profound. To the Touchdown Club of New York, he quoted with obvious approval the rather fervent view of T.R. on the matter:

"The credit belongs to the man who is actually in the arena—whose face is marred by dust and sweat and blood . . . a leader who knows the great enthusiasms, the great devotions—and spends himself in a worthy cause—who at best if he wins knows the thrills of high achievement—and if he fails at least fails while daring greatly—so that his place shall never be with those cold and timid souls who know neither victory nor defeat."

Many times, he voiced a similar sentiment in his own words. Oddly, the man of detachment, of cool wit and ironic view, preached the "long twilight struggle" in which the most certain thing was that there would be "neither victory nor defeat." Yet, the man of commitment, of action, rejected with robustious Teddy the "cold and timid souls" who had no blood and dust upon their faces. And another quotation he liked to throw at university audiences was the rhetorical question of George William Curtis of Massachusetts:

"Would you have counted him a friend of ancient Greece who quietly discussed the theory of patriotism on that hot summer day through whose hopeless and immortal hours Leonidas and the three hundred stood at Thermopylae for liberty? Was John Milton to conjugate Greek verbs in his library when the liberty of Englishmen was imperiled?"

To the students of George Washington University, Kennedy gave his own answer: "No, quite obviously, the duty of the educated man or woman, the duty of the scholar, is to give his objective sense, his sense of liberty to the maintenance of our society at the critical time."

But in the next breath he was telling the story of someone who went to Harvard years ago and "asked for President Lowell. They said, 'He's in Washington, seeing Mr. Taft.' I know that some other day, when they are asking for the President of your university, they will say that he is over at the White House seeing Mr. Kennedy. They understood at Harvard, and you understood here, the relative importance of a university president and a President of the United States."

If that was a joke, it did not come from one who often gave up "his objective sense, and his sense of liberty." Honey Fitz would sing *Sweet Adeline* until his tonsils gave out, but his grandson was never known to wear a funny hat in public. It may seem a small point, but John Kennedy maintained it literally to his dying day. On November 22, in Fort Worth, he went through the Texas ritual of being presented a cowboy hat—but steadfastly resisted the pleas of two thousand Texans that he put it on.

"Come to Washington Monday and I'll put it on for you in the White House," he joked. But even in that comparative privacy, had he reached it, he would not have worn that hat. The man of detachment had yielded himself enough; he would make his little pushing gesture at the crowds, but he would not wave his arms exuberantly above his head like Eisenhower, or thump his chest like Theodore Roosevelt.

So, despite their similarities, he was radically different from the ebullient T.R. Restraint was his style, not arm-waving. There was nothing detached, nothing ironic, about Roosevelt, who could say and believe it that in the White House "my teaching has been plain morality." Kennedy would never claim more than that he hoped he was a "responsible President"; he would not often speak on television because he believed people would tire of him and stop listening.

Sometimes it seemed, he even thought of politics, the Presidency itself, as a sporting proposition. Kennedy never tired of exhorting college students to prepare themselves for the public service, but he was seldom stuffy about it. He did not propose, he told the University of North Carolina student body, to adopt "from the Belgian constitution a provision giving three votes instead of one to college graduates—at least not until more Democrats go to college."

As the campaign of 1960 wore on, the atmosphere around the candidate sometimes seemed almost like one of those parlor games the Kennedys played so often. "Tell me a delegate and I'll tell you who he's for," Kennedy would say to members of his staff, in his best Twenty Questions manner. "Give me a state and I'll give you the delegate breakdown."

The election was so close it inhibited Kennedy; he would point out how closely divided was the country at every opportunity. Yet, he could compare his own disputed election to the plight of a Notre Dame football team that had won a game by means some thought illegal. "And we're not going to give it back," he told the National Football Foundation.

Kennedy disliked the solemn ideologues and myopic Babbitts who crowd American political life—Senator Karl Mundt of South Dakota, for instance—but he delighted in the skillful shenanigans of some who took the game of politics less seriously—even, in some cases, when the voters and taxpayers were taken too. With obvious relish, he once described the operations of the raffish but highly effective Senator Warren Magnuson of Washington as follows:

> He speaks in the Senate so quietly that few can hear him. He looks down at his desk—he comes into the Senate late in the afternoon—he is very hesitant about interrupting other members of the Senate—when he rises to speak, most members of the Senate have left—he sends his messages up to the Senate and everyone says, "What is it?" And Senator Magnuson says, "It's nothing important." And Grand Coulee Dam is built.

The night before he died, Kennedy spoke in tribute to Representative Albert Thomas in Houston, Texas. Not the least of Thomas' achievements over the years had been the enrichment of Houston with federal investments; his most recent coup had been the somewhat controversial establishment there of the Manned Spacecraft Center. Kennedy recounted a bit floridly how Thomas had helped put the United States in a position to fire into space the largest booster rocket bearing the largest "payroll" in history. As the audience laughed, Kennedy hastily corrected the word to "payload."

That slip might have embarrassed most politicians, but it obviously struck Kennedy as funny. "It will be the largest payroll, too," he added, grinning, "and who should know that better than Houston. We put a little of it right in here." Wasn't that what made the wheels go around?

Kennedy laughed out loud when he heard that Everett Dirksen had said that one of his early economic measures would have "all the impact of a snowflake on the bosom of the Potomac." He once carried a letter from de Gaulle around the White House, pointing out its elegances to his staff. It mattered not who won or lost, but how they played the game.

Even the selection of winners of the Medal of Freedom, a sort of royal honors list Mrs. Kennedy and the President invented, was not free in Kennedy's mind from the sporting balance of politics—you scratch mine and I'll scratch yours. When the painter Andrew Wyeth was selected, Kennedy—who had put up an early argument for Ben Shahn—decreed: "Next year, we'll have to go abstract."

One night on his plane, returning to Washington from a speech in Trenton, he talked about his love of boating with a group of us, and confided: "I'd really like to have that yacht Eisenhower laid up in Philadelphia [the old *Williamsburg*]. But he said he did it for economy reasons and if I took it out of mothballs now they'd never let me hear the end of it." That was how the game was played; all you could do was grin and bear it, and play the game yourself.

Thus, John Kennedy in his pursuit of excellence, his commitment to active service, spent a great deal of his short life playing and thinking politics—running and angling for office, first; pushing political solutions to social and economic problems, second. But that is not necessarily the same thing as being profoundly involved in politics; it is not the same thing as a belief in solutions or the efficacy of politics. Kennedy seemed sometimes to think of himself as taking the first steps he so often urged upon the country and the world; he would use politics, he would propose a program, not with much hope for either, but to raise a question, to start someone thinking, to bring a matter into whatever light there was.

One Saturday morning in 1963 in Los Angeles he appeared at the Hollywood Palladium to address a Democratic women's breakfast; it was the only time I ever heard *Hail to the Chief* played with a twist beat. He was supposed to make "brief remarks"; instead, he plunged in his familiar machine-gun delivery into a half hour of Democratic party evangelism so impassioned and so portentous of phrase that some of my colleagues wrote that he had "kicked off his 1964 campaign." I was so stirred by the speech that I phoned The *Times* to hold space for the full text of it. It was a "major address," I assured my editors.

When the transcript came spinning from the White House mimeograph an hour later, I thumbed through it in search of those memorable phrases, those ringing pledges, those grand calls to battle, that had rung through the Palladium. I have that transcript before me now and it confirms my disillusionment; there was nothing there, nothing but rhetoric and delivery. We had seen a performance in which J.F.K. had been playing the game unusually well.

In 1962, Kennedy proposed a Cabinet-level Department of Urban Affairs. Robert C. Weaver, the Administration's housing chief, was to be its Secretary—the first Negro to sit in any President's Cabinet. The proposal was hailed as a political masterstroke. Who could vote, in effect, against Weaver except the Southerners? And who cared about them?

In any event, a great many members of Congress voted against the proposal and it became one of Kennedy's most embarrassing defeats. Not long afterward, I asked him how it had happened.

He took a cigar out of his mouth and answered bluntly: "I played it too cute. It was so obvious it made them mad." In short, he had played the game poorly. I think he often did.

He could go before a captive audience of Democratic old people in Madison Square Garden and shed crocodile tears in behalf of his medical-care plan—and look as political and as uncomfortable as he was. Before an audience in Miami Beach from which he had little further to gain, the A.F.L.-C.I.O., he was so palpably bored, his speech was so blatantly routine and uninspired, that men of more objective political judgment might have booed him from the platform. He went into General Eisenhower's home county during the 1962 campaign and delivered a speech so demagogic and so extravagant in its claims for Democratic virtue and Republican sloth that even the General was enraged and promptly proceeded to emerge from retirement to campaign against him—a development that might have been politically important had not the Cuban crisis changed the whole picture in October. On his Western trip in the Fall of 1963—his last extended tour in the country—Kennedy looked and felt so out of place talking about conservation and nature and wildlife that the reporters following him gave him the nickname "Smokey the Bear"; it was reported by Pierre Salinger at Jackson Lake Lodge that the President actually had seen a moose from the window of his room.

Shortly after Kennedy's death, Carroll Kilpatrick and I visited J. Frank Dobie at the University of Texas and asked him what was the difference in Kennedy and Lyndon Johnson. Mr. Dobie knew Johnson well; he knew Kennedy only as most Americans knew him—as a voice on the radio, a face on the screen, a presence in the land. "Johnson is concerned with means," Mr. Dobie said at once, as if the contrast was obvious. "Kennedy was interested in ends."

A generality, perhaps, but near enough to truth to *ring* true. Kennedy played the game as a political man had to, sometimes brilliantly, often with boredom and ineptitude. But it was not then that he stirred us. Even his memorable campaign of 1960, the finest exercise of his strictly political life, was not politics-as-usual; it was outside the ordinary rules, for Kennedy was a Roman Catholic, an inexperienced younger man, something of an intellectual, who put little trust in traditional politicians, and relied instead upon his own men, his own techniques, his own personality.

Perhaps he had to move beyond the rules, get out of the game, before he really involved himself—and therefore involved other men. His trip to Europe in 1963 exhilarated him, for instance; he knew he had broken through the traditional wall of diplomatic niceties, spoken above the heads of politicians and governments, and he believed a new generation of Europeans had responded. At his death, his tax bill was mired in Congress, but its mere presentation may yet be the longest step toward lifting American economic policy out of the twin ruts of ignorance and cliche. His civil-rights bill was fumbled and botched, but he was the first American President to recognize in the out-pouring of events a "moral crisis" in race relations. The long shadow of de Gaulle darkened his European policy, but he had proclaimed on both sides of the Atlantic a commitment to the interdependence of two continents. Nobody could say there would be no nuclear war, but he had taken the "first step" of the test-ban treaty.

That is what haunts me about Kennedy—not just that he was a man of certain admirable visions, but that he had the kind of mind that could entertain vision, the kind of outlook that could put in perspective the gambits and maneuvers of the moment, see truly the futility of most means, the uncertain glory of most ends. Surely he was one of those men "educated in the liberal traditions, willing to take the long look, undisturbed by prejudices and slogans of the moment, who attempt to make an honest judgment on difficult events"; surely he tried to be one of those, to borrow his words again, who could "distinguish the real from the illusory, the long-range from the temporary, the significant from the petty. . . ."

And that is the real irony of John F. Kennedy's coming immortality. For when James Reston asked him in the Summer of 1961, during a long afternoon's talk at Hyannis Port, what kind of a world it was he had in mind, what vision he had of the future, John Kennedy—President of the United States for half a year, perpetrator of the Bay of Pigs, not long home from his "somber" meeting with Khrushehev in Vienna—could reply: "I haven't had time to think about that yet."

It is the classic story of the liberal man in politics. *I claim not to have controlled events,* Lincoln said, *but confess plainly that events have controlled me.* And perhaps it is symbolized in a compelling picture of Kennedy that comes to us from one of Washington's most imposing men.

It is a glimpse from the Cuban missile crisis of October, 1962, a period of great tension at the White House as throughout the world. The personage and the President were alone in Kennedy's oval office, discussing what in New Frontier jargon were known as "the options"; that month, the options were pretty grim.

Kennedy rose from his rocking chair, leaving his visitor seated on a sofa. The President went across his office to the French doors that opened on the terrace of the West Executive Wing. Beyond the terrace lay the famous Rose Garden, redesigned like almost everything else about the White House by the elegant stylists who had come to live there. But at its end still towered the famous magnolia planted by Andrew Jackson.

Kennedy stood for a long time, silent, gazing at the garden and the magnolia, his hands behind his back, the burden of decision almost visible on his shoulders. "Well," he said at last, "I guess this is the week I earn my salary."

The detached thinker had been brought to bay by the necessities of the moment. That questioning mind with its sensitivity to the complexity of things, to the illusory nature of answers and solutions, had come to the moment of black vs. white. That derisive and worldly wit was stilled in the sheer responsibility of choice. Action and events had overtaken contemplation and vision, and Kennedy shared the plight of Melbourne: *I am afraid the question of the Irish Church can neither be avoided or postponed. It must therefore be attempted to be solved.* And for Kennedy, that fall, humanity itself was the question.

So with his football coach's will to win, with his passion for "the ability to do things well," Kennedy had had his dreams and realized them. But I believe he stood on the sidelines, too, even while the game was going on, measuring his performance, wryly remarking upon it, not much impressed, not much deluded. Perhaps he knew all along that events would control, action overwhelm, means fail to reach ends. "There stands the decision," he wrote, "and there stands the President." Sooner or later, they would be as one.

The decisions he made, the slogans he spoke—let them be carved on the monuments. But for me his epitaph is inscribed on Dave Powers' silver beer mug, that John Kennedy gave him for his birthday last year. It reads:

> *There are three things which are real:*
> *God, human folly and laughter.*
> *The first two are beyond our comprehension*
> *So we must do what we can with the third.*

No one at the White House knew the source of those lines. I can find the words in no book of quotations. The Library of Congress has not been able to discover who wrote them. But I think I know.

FOR FURTHER CONSIDERATION

Wicker outlines a Kennedy who used humor in a variety of ways. List four or five of the uses to which JFK put his humor. In choosing to find these things funny, what values did Kennedy reveal? Given the evidence that Wicker offers, what kind of self-image do you suppose John Kennedy had of himself, that is, what did he see as his personal strong points and weaknesses?

Irene Castañeda

Responding to her daughter's request, a mother offers a chronicle of the life of a migrant family over the years. That living conditions remain in many ways as bad as ever for contemporary migrant laborers and their families comments harshly on the humanity of us all. Castañeda's unapologetic and uncomplaining description offers a fine example of simplicity as eloquence.

Personal Chronicle of Crystal City

Well daughter as I remember there was lots of Mexican families and they'd go to pick cotton—Ganado, Texas, Corpus Cristy, Agua Dulce, Kerney, and lots of other little towns. When the cotton picking was done they'd come back to their shacks—they'd start to cut spinach, tomatoe,

onion, watermelon, melon, radiches, then—in time—they started traveling to Minesota, North Dakota and Ohio, Wisconsin—to top beets—the
people who had transportation would carry people in the trucks and
charged $10.00 per person or $5.00—depending on the price they got paid
for beets. Some of the people had houses—only 2 rooms—a room to sleep
and a little kitchen. The toilets were outside or in the chaparros. The
people who couldn't get out to work the crops because they had too many
little kids, well they had adobe houses or houses made from old tin cans
that they hamered open and nailed—they'd fix a little shack. They would
sleep on the floor or make wooden benches to sleep on. Matresses weren't
very common then—there wasn't enough money to buy them.

My parents—I think they got to Crystal City in 1910—there wasn't
too much there then—they didn't sell lots. Everything was like a ranch,
cows and horses roamed loose in 1910. 1911 they brought people from
Mexico, they started to clear the land. My father was the foreman
because he was the only one who could understand English—so that's
how they started to make up lots and sell them and many people stayed.

Mother had a small house and a little tent. Once when they came to
Texas to work, father worked on the railroad, or el traque as they called,
he had an accident and lost two toes from his left foot—he was in the
hospital—when he got out the company gave him a little money and with
that they returned to Crystal City and bought a few lots—I think they
were $35.00 each.

In 1913 there was the smallpox epidemic and many people died—they
would burn the bodies. With the kind of work they did, tuberculosis was
pretty common. With spinich, you worked right in the water, people
would get wet clear up to their waist—women, men and children—
everybody all wet and the hot sun beating down on the head—they began
to get sick from tuberculosis—the doctor would say what they were sick
from and they would build little shacks for them outside of town—and
whole families died there from that sickness.

There was no cemetary for Mexicans. They would bury them in
ground that was all rocky. My father and other men collected money—
they collected and gave the first payment on a piece of ground to form a
cemetary. You paid twenty-five cents to dig a grave—that's how they
collected to keep making the payments on the place. He took the
responsibility of paying for it and he saved the papers for twenty-five
years so that no one except us Mexicans would have right to it.

Mother, from seeing the poor people die for lack of medical
attention, wanted to do something to help them and she learned, as best
she could, to deliver babies. Sometimes on the floor with just a small
blanket. Lighting was a candle or petroleum lamp—there were no electric
bulbs. Sometimes she would bring pillows or blankets from home—many
of the women had not eaten—she would bring them rice from home and
feed them by spoonfuls. The shots were a cup of hot pepper tea—to give
strength for the baby to be born—because there was no doctor. The only
one had to travel to several towns and when he arrived it was too late.

There was no school for Mexicans. That's why no one knew how to read. Mother washed other people's clothes for a dollar for a big load. She had to starch and iron it. She would earn five dollars for a week's work. When she was washing clothes she would sit us down beside her and she taught us to read Spanish.

In time people began to go out to Washington to work in asparagus, corn, warehouses, in the so-called hop. Then when that work is over, they go to the coast to pick (straw) berries, then they return to the hops—the final stage—with the whole family, and from Washington they go to Idaho in September. They stay there a month, from there they go to Texas—spending four months of the year there. So the children go to school four months in Texas and one or two in Washington. They take them out of school there then they take them out of school here and the youngsters get very confused. Many learn something—others don't—and time passes and they know hardly anything.—They grow up and keep on in the same way—journeying from here to there—from there to here—and that's the reason why the Mexican hasn't learned anything and can't have a decent job.

Your father worked for fifteen years in a plant where they made ice—then they closed it and he went to work as a carpenter in a concentration camp in Crystal City—then he contracted himself with this company to go to Vancouver, Washington in 1944 and 1945 in a construction company that made boats. We stayed in Eagle Pass—that's where the three older children started school. The war ended in 1945, many people were left unemployed.

We heard the tale of Washington—that there was lots of money, that they paid real well, and we thought about coming to Washington. We didn't have a car to travel in and this man, Eduardo Salinas used to contract people and we came with him. We didn't have much money, we paid him $25.00 for us and $15.00 for each of the children. This was the first time we had traveled. This man said that he had housing and everything for the people, but it wasn't true. We left the 13th of March of 1946 and arrived in Toppenish the 18th. On the road the truck broke down—who knows how many times. In Utah we had to stay overnight because the road was snowed in and we couldn't travel—we all slept sitting up with the little ones in our arms because we had no money to rent a motel. We were about twenty-five people in the truck, plus the suitcases and blankets and a mattress spread out inside, and some tires—we looked like sardines. Then a heavy wind came and the tarp on the truck tore in half. They tied it as best they could—and the snow falling. We finally got out of the snow and then the driver lost his way—we almost turned over. But God is powerful and he watched over us—finally we got to Toppenish. He didn't have housing—nothing—all lies that he told us. He finally found some old shacks, all full of knotholes, in Brownstown—about twenty miles outside of Toppenish—and in tents he placed all the people. It was bitterly cold—with wood stoves and wet wood.

When the hop was over, we'd lived seven months there, the boys had gotten sick, I'd gotten pneumonia and had to go to the doctor. Well—with the fright we'd had on the road, we didn't feel like returning and we decided to stay in Washington. The work ended in Brownstown and we came to Toppenish. Then we went to live at the Golding farm—this was made up of rows of shacks—without doors and all falling apart—there was only a wall between the next unit where another person lived. The houses weren't insulated—they didn't have floors, and we worked in the hop. They paid us women 75¢ per hour and 85¢ for the men. But since Jose was a carpenter he didn't work in the field. He made crates to ship hop to other places—he did other things too. That's where he had his first accident—and you know the rest—how from the time you were ten and twelve years old you worked selling pop, then in the little corner market in Granger, then in the drugstore to have money to go to school. And you know about your brothers—that they went into the service, how they went, where they went, what they did, and what they are.

I have already written to Maria, my sister, to give me more ideas about how Crystal City got started, but she says that she didn't live there very long, she married young and went to live somplace else. So now I've told you many histories—if you want the names of the Mexicans who were living in Crystal City when my mother and father arrived there, call me and I'll give you the names I remember.

FOR FURTHER CONSIDERATION

Irene Castañeda chronicles an immense amount of hardship and deprivation in her brief family biography. What impact can such experiences have in developing facets of the self, facets such as a willingness to strive, economic expectation, pride, concern for others, sense of personal integrity, self-image? What do the contents and tone of the essay suggest about these same facets in the writer?

Bertrand Russell (1872-1970)

Russell may be considered as the most influential philosopher of the twentieth century, having had a major impact on modern thought with his cogent and persuasive applications of logic. He also generated substantial influence as a political dissident, particularly with his opposition to nuclear armaments in the 1950s. In the essay which follows he offers a strong case for a positive and creative individual response to the conviction that life has no inherent meaning or purpose.

A Free Man's Worship

To Dr. Faustus in his study Mephistopheles told the history of the Creation, saying:

The endless praises of the choirs of angels had begun to grow wearisome; for, after all, did He not deserve their praise: Had He not given them endless joy? Would it not be more amusing to obtain undeserved praise, to be worshipped by beings whom He tortured? He smiled inwardly, and resolved that the great drama should be performed.

For countless ages the hot nebula whirled aimlessly through space. At length it began to take shape, the central mass threw off planets, the planets cooled, boiling seas and burning mountains heaved and tossed, from black masses of cloud hot sheets of rain deluged the barely solid crust. And now the first germ of life grew in the depths of the ocean, and developed rapidly in the fructifying warmth into vast forest trees, huge ferns springing from the damp mould, sea monsters breeding, fighting, devouring, and passing away. And from the monsters, as the play unfolded itself, Man was born, with the power of thought, the knowledge of good and evil, and the cruel thirst for worship. And Man saw that all is passing in this mad, monstrous world, that all is struggling to snatch, at any cost, a few brief moments of life before Death's inexorable decree. And Man said: "There is a hidden purpose, could we but fathom it, and the purpose is good; for we must reverence something and in the visible world there is nothing worthy of reverence." And Man stood aside from the struggle, resolving that God intended harmony to come out of chaos by human efforts. And when he followed the instincts which God had transmitted to him from his ancestry of beasts of prey, he called it Sin, and asked God to forgive him. But he doubted whether he could be justly forgiven, until he invented a divine Plan by which God's wrath was to have been appeased. And seeing the present was bad, he made it yet worse, that thereby the future might be better. And he gave God thanks for the strength that enabled him to forgo even the joys that were possible. And God smiled; and when he saw that Man had become perfect in renunciation and worship, he sent another sun through the sky, which crashed into Man's sun; and all returned again to nebula.

Yes, he murmured, it was a good play; I will have it performed again.

Such, in outline, but even more purposeless, more void of meaning, is the world which Science presents for our belief. Amid such a world, if anywhere, our ideals henceforward must find a home. That Man is the product of causes which had no prevision of the end they were achieving; that his origin, his growth, his hopes and fears, his loves and his beliefs, are but the outcome of accidental collocations of atoms; that no fire, no heroism, no intensity of thought and feeling, can preserve an individual life beyond the grave; that all the labours of the ages, all the devotion, all the inspiration, all the noonday brightness of human genius, are destined to extinction in the vast death of the solar system, and that the whole temple of Man's achievement must inevitably be buried beneath the debris of a universe in ruins—all these things, if not quite beyond dispute, are yet so nearly certain, that no philosophy which rejects them can hope to stand. Only within the scaffolding of these truths, only on the firm foundation of unyielding despair, can the soul's habitation henceforth be safely built.

How, in such an alien and inhuman world, can so powerless a creature as Man preserve his aspirations untarnished? A strange mystery it is that Nature, omnipotent but blind, in the revolutions of her secular hurryings through the abysses of space, has brought forth at last a child, subject still to her power, but gifted with sight, with knowledge of good and evil, with the capacity of judging all the works of his unthinking Mother. In spite of Death, the mark and seal of the parental control, Man is yet free, during his brief years, to examine, to criticize, to know, and in imagination to create. To him alone, in the world with which he is acquainted, this freedom belongs; and in this lies his superiority to the resistless forces that control his outward life.

The savage, like ourselves, feels the oppression of his impotence before the powers of Nature; but having in himself nothing that he respects more than Power, he is willing to prostrate himself before his gods, without inquiring whether they are worthy of his worship. Pathetic and very terrible is the long history of cruelty and torture, of degradation and human sacrifice, endured in the hope of placating the jealous gods: surely, the trembling believer thinks, when what is most precious has been freely given, their lust for blood must be appeased, and more will not be required. The religion of Moloch—as such creeds may be generically called—is in essence the cringing submission of the slave, who dare not, even in his heart, allow the thought that his master deserves no adulation. Since the independence of ideals is not yet acknowledged, Power may be freely worshipped, and receive an unlimited respect, despite its wanton infliction of pain.

But gradually, as morality grows bolder, the claim of the ideal world begins to be felt; and worship, if it is not to cease, must be given to gods of another kind than those created by the savage. Some, though they feel the demands of the ideal, will still consciously reject them, still urging that naked Power is worthy of worship. Such is the attitude inculcated in God's answer to Job out of the whirlwind: the divine power and knowledge are paraded, but of the divine goodness there is no hint. Such also is the attitude of those, who, in our own day, base their morality upon the struggle for survival, maintaining that the survivors are necessarily the fittest. But others, not content with an answer so repugnant to the moral sense, will adopt the position which we have become accustomed to regard as specially religious, maintaining that, in some hidden manner, the world of fact is really harmonious with the world of ideals. Thus Man creates God, all-powerful and all-good, the mystic unity of what is and what should be.

But the world of fact, after all, is not good; and, in submitting our judgment to it, there is an element of slavishness from which our thoughts must be purged. For in all things it is well to exalt the dignity of Man, by freeing him as far as possible from the tyranny of non-human Power. When we have realized that Power is largely bad, that man, with his knowledge of good and evil, is but a helpless atom in a world which has no such knowledge, the choice is again presented to us: Shall we worship Force, or shall we worship Goodness? Shall our God exist and be evil, or shall he be recognized as the creation of our own conscience?

The answer to this question is very momentous, and affects profoundly our whole morality. The worship of Force, to which Carlyle and Nietzsche and the creed of Militarism have accustomed us, is the result of failure to maintain our own ideals against a hostile universe: it is itself a prostrate submission to evil, a sacrifice of our best to Moloch. If strength indeed is to be respected, let us respect rather the strength of those who refuse that false 'recognition of facts' which fails to recognize that facts are often bad. Let us admit that, in the world we know, there are many things that would be better otherwise, and that the ideals to which we do and must adhere are not realized in the realm of matter. Let us preserve our respect for truth, for beauty, for the ideal of perfection which life does not permit us to attain, though none of these things meet with the approval of the unconscious universe. If Power is bad, as it seems to be, let us reject it from our hearts. In this lies Man's true freedom: in determination to worship only the God created by our own love of the good, to respect only the heaven which inspires the insight of our best moments. In action, in desire, we must submit perpetually to the tyranny of outside forces; but in thought, in aspiration, we are free, free from our fellow-men, free from the petty planet on which our bodies impotently crawl, free even, while we live, from the tyranny of death. Let us learn, then, that energy of faith which enables us to live constantly in the vision of the good; and let us descend, in action, into the world of fact, with that vision always before us.

When first the opposition of fact and ideal grows fully visible, a spirit of fiery revolt, of fierce hatred of the gods, seems necessary to the assertion of freedom. To defy with Promethean constancy a hostile universe, to keep its evil always in view, always actively hated, to refuse no pain that the malice of Power can invent, appears to be the duty of all who will not bow before the inevitable. But indignation is still a bondage, for it compels our thoughts to be occupied with an evil world; and in the fierceness of desire from which rebellion springs there is a kind of self-assertion which it is necessary for the wise to overcome. Indignation is a submission of our thoughts, but not of our desires; the Stoic freedom in which wisdom consists is found in the submission of our desires, but not of our thoughts. From the submission of our desires springs the virtue of resignation; from the freedom of our thoughts springs the whole world of art and philosophy, and the vision of beauty by which, at last, we half reconquer the reluctant world. But the vision of beauty is possible only to unfettered contemplation, to thoughts not weighted by the load of eager wishes; and thus Freedom comes only to those who no longer ask of life that it shall yield them any of those personal goods that are subject to the mutations of Time.

Although the necessity of renunciation is evidence of the existence of evil, yet Christianity, in preaching it, has shown a wisdom exceeding that of the Promethean philosophy of rebellion. It must be admitted that, of the things we desire, some, though they prove impossible, are yet real goods; others, however, as ardently longed for, do not form part of a fully purified ideal. The belief that what must be renounced is bad, though sometimes false, is far less often false than untamed passion supposes; and the creed of religion, by providing a reason for proving that it is never false, has been the means of purifying our hopes by the discovery of many austere truths.

But there is in resignation a further good element: even real goods, when they are unattainable, ought not to be fretfully desired. To every man comes, sooner or later, the great renunciation. For the young, there is nothing unattainable; a good thing desired with the whole force of a passionate will, and yet impossible, is to them not credible. Yet, by death, by illness, by poverty, or by the voice of duty, we must learn, each one of us, that the world was not made for us, and that, however beautiful may be the things we crave, Fate may nevertheless forbid them. It is the part of courage, when misfortune comes, to bear without repining the ruin of our hopes, to turn away our thoughts from vain regrets. This degree of submission to Power is not only just and right: it is the very gate of wisdom.

But passive renunciation is not the whole of wisdom; for not by renunciation alone can we build a temple for the worship of our own ideals. Haunting foreshadowings of the temple appear in the realm of imagination, in music, in architecture, in the untroubled kingdom of reason, and in the golden sunset magic of lyrics, where beauty shines and glows, remote from the touch of sorrow, remote from the fear of change, remote from the failures and disenchantments of the world of fact. In the contemplation of these things the vision of heaven will shape itself in our hearts, giving at once a touchstone to judge the world about us, and an inspiration by which to fashion to our needs whatever is not incapable of serving as a stone in the sacred temple.

Except for those rare spirits that are born without sin, there is a cavern of darkness to be traversed before that temple can be entered. The gate of the cavern is despair, and its floor is paved with the gravestones of abandoned hopes. There Self must die; there the eagerness, the greed of untamed desire must be slain, for only so can the soul be freed from the empire of Fate. But out of the cavern the Gate of Renunciation leads again to the daylight of wisdom, by whose radiance a new insight, a new joy, a new tenderness, shine forth to gladden the pilgrimless's heart.

When, without the bitterness of impotent rebellion, we have learnt both to resign ourselves to the outward rule of Fate and to recognize that the non-human world is unworthy of our worship, it becomes possible at last so to transform and refashion the unconscious universe, so to transmute it in the crucible of imagination, that a new image of shining gold replaces the old idol of clay. In all the multiform facts of the world—in the visual shapes of trees and mountains and clouds, in the events of the life of man, even in the very omnipotence of Death—the insight of creative idealism can find the reflection of a beauty which its own thoughts first made. In this way mind asserts its subtle mastery over the thoughtless forces of Nature. The more evil the material with which it deals, the more thwarting to untrained desire, the greater is its achievement in inducing the reluctant rock to yield up its hidden treasures, the prouder its victory in compelling the opposing forces to swell the pageant of its triumph. Of all the arts, Tragedy is the proudest, the most triumphant; for it builds its shining citadel in the very centre of the enemy's country, on the very summit of his highest mountain; from its impregnable watch towers, his camps and arsenals, his columns and forts, are all revealed; within its walls the free life continues, while the legions of Death and Pain and Despair, and all the servile captains of tyrant Fate, afford the burghers of that dauntless city new spectacles of beauty. Happy those sacred ramparts, thrice happy the dwellers on that all-seeing eminence. Honour to those brave warriors who, through countless ages of warfare, have preserved for us the priceless heritage of liberty, and have kept undefiled by sacrilegious invaders the home of the unsubdued.

But the beauty of Tragedy does but make visible a quality which, in more or less obvious shapes, is present always and everywhere in life. In the spectacle of Death, in the endurance of intolerable pain, and in the irrevocableness of a vanished past, there is a sacredness, an overpowering awe, a feeling of the vastness, the depth, the inexhaustible mystery of existence, in which, as by some strange marriage of pain, the sufferer is bound to the world by bonds of sorrow. In these moments of insight, we lose all eagerness of temporary desire, all struggling and striving for petty ends, all care for the little trivial things that, to a superficial view, make up the common life of day by day; we see, surrounding the narrow raft illumined by the flickering light of human comradeship, the dark ocean on whose rolling waves we toss for a brief hour; from the great night without, a chill blast breaks in upon our refuge; all the loneliness of humanity amid hostile forces is concentrated upon the individual soul, which must struggle alone, with what of courage it can command, against the whole weight of a universe that cares nothing for its hopes and fears. Victory, in this struggle with the powers of darkness, is the true baptism into the glorious company of heroes, the true initiation into the overmastering beauty of human existence. From that awful encounter of the soul with the outer world, enunciation, wisdom, and charity are born; and with their birth a new life begins. To take into the inmost shrine of the soul the irresistible forces whose puppets we seem to be—Death and change, the irrevocableness of the past, and the powerlessness of man before the blind hurry of the universe from vanity to vanity—to feel these things and know them is to conquer them.

This is the reason why the Past has such magical power. The beauty of its motionless and silent pictures is like the enchanted purity of late autumn, when the leaves, though one breath would make them fall, still glow against the sky in golden glory. The Past does not change or strive; like Duncan, after life's fitful fever it sleeps well; what was eager and grasping, what was petty and transitory, has faded away, the things that were beautiful and eternal shine out of it like stars in the night. Its beauty, to a soul not worthy of it, is unendurable; but to a soul which has conquered Fate it is the key of religion.

The life of Man, viewed outwardly, is but a small thing in comparison with the forces of Nature. The slave is doomed to worship Time and Fate and Death, because they are greater than anything he finds in himself, and because all his thoughts are of things which they devour. But, great as they are, to think of them greatly, to feel their passionless splendour, is greater still. And such thought makes us free men; we no longer bow before the inevitable in Oriental subjection, but we absorb it, and make it a part of ourselves. To abandon the struggle for private happiness, to expel all eagerness of temporary desire, to burn with passion for eternal things—this is emancipation, and this is the free man's worship. And this liberation is effected by a contemplation of Fate; for Fate itself is subdued by the mind which leaves nothing to be purged by the purifying fire of Time.

United with his fellow-men by the strongest of all ties, the tie of a common doom, the free man finds that a new vision is with him always, shedding over every daily task the light of love. The life of Man is a long march through the night, surrounded by invisible foes, tortured by weariness and pain, towards a goal that few can hope to reach, and where none may tarry long. One by one, as they march, our comrades vanish from our sight, seized by the silent orders of omnipotent Death. Very brief is the time in which we can help them, in which their happiness or misery is decided. Be it ours to shed sunshine on their path, to lighten their sorrows by the balm of sympathy, to give them the pure joy of a never-tiring affection, to strengthen failing courage, to instil faith in hours of despair. Let us not weigh in grudging scales their merits and demerits, but let us think only of their need—of the sorrows, the difficulties, perhaps the blindnesses, that make the misery of their lives; let us remember that they are fellow-sufferers in the same darkness, actors in the same tragedy with ourselves. And so, when their day is over, when their good and their evil have become eternal by the immortality of the past, be it ours to feel that, where they suffered, where they failed, no deed of ours was the cause; but wherever a spark of the divine fire kindled in their hearts, we were ready with encouragement, with sympathy, with brave words in which high courage glowed.

Brief and powerless is Man's life; on him and all his race the slow, sure doom falls pitiless and dark. Blind to good and evil, reckless of destruction, omnipotent matter rolls on its relentless way; for Man, condemned today to lose his dearest, tomorrow himself to pass through the gate of darkness, it remains only to cherish, ere yet the blow falls, the lofty thoughts that ennoble his little day; disdaining the coward terrors of the slave of Fate, to worship at the shrine that his own hands have built; undismayed by the empire of chance, to preserve a mind free from the wanton tyranny that rules his outward life; proudly defiant of the irresistible forces that tolerate, for a moment, his knowledge and his condemnation, to sustain alone, a weary but unyielding Atlas, the world that his own ideals have fashioned despite the trampling march of unconscious power.

FOR FURTHER CONSIDERATION

According to Russell, what *frees* a person to worship? How is it that *worship* as he conceives of it can free one? What differences does he observe between the worship of a *free person* and the worship of what he calls a *slave*? What does Russell mean when he says that if we are to build a temple to our own ideals, the Self must die?

Dick Gregory (1933-   )

This brief excerpt from Gregory's autobiography, Nigger, *demonstrates how experience instills values and how our choices often reflect these values. After his rise to national prominence as a comedian, Gregory turned his humor to social purpose and became a leader in the civil rights and antiwar movements. Through his actions on behalf of others, he has expressed clearly his own tolerant sense of values and his extraordinary humanity.*

I Never Learned Hate

I never learned hate at home, or shame. I had to go to school for that. I was about seven years old when I got my first big lesson. I was in love with a little girl named Helene Tucker, a light-complected little girl with pigtails and nice manners. She was always clean and she was smart in school. I think I went to school then mostly to look at her. I brushed my hair and even got me a little old handkerchief. It was a lady's handkerchief, but I didn't want Helene to see me wipe my nose on my hand. The pipes were frozen again, there was no water in the house, but I washed my socks and shirt every night. I'd get a pot, and go over to Mister Ben's grocery store, and stick my pot down into his soda machine. Scoop out some chopped ice. By evening the ice melted to water for washing. I got sick a lot that winter because the fire would go out at night before the clothes were dry. In the morning I'd put them on, wet or dry, because they were the only clothes I had.

Everybody's got a Helene Tucker, a symbol of everything you want. I loved her for her goodness, her cleanness, her popularity. She'd walk down my street and my brothers and sisters would yell, "Here comes Helene," and I'd rub my tennis sneakers on the back of my pants and wish

my hair wasn't so nappy and the white folks' shirt fit me better. I'd run out
on the street. If I knew my place and didn't come too close, she'd wink at
me and say hello. That was a good feeling. Sometimes I'd follow her all
the way home, and shovel the snow off her walk and try to make friends
with her Momma and her aunts. I'd drop money on her stoop late at night
on my way back from shining shoes in the taverns. And she had a Daddy,
and he had a good job. He was a paper hanger.

I guess I would have gotten over Helene by summertime, but
something happened in that classroom that made her face hang in front of
me for the next twenty-two years. When I played the drums in high school
it was for Helene and when I broke track records in college it was for
Helene and when I started standing behind microphones and heard
applause I wished Helene could hear it, too. It wasn't until I was
twenty-nine years old and married and making money that I finally got her
out of my system. Helene was sitting in that classroom when I learned to
be ashamed of myself.

It was on a Thursday. I was sitting in the back of the room, in a seat
with a chalk circle drawn around it. The idiot's seat, the troublemaker's
seat.

The teacher thought I was stupid. Couldn't spell, couldn't read,
couldn't do arithmetic. Just stupid. Teachers were never interested in
finding out that you couldn't concentrate because you were so hungry,
because you hadn't had any breakfast. All you could think about was
noontime, would it ever come? Maybe you could sneak into the cloak-
room and steal a bite of some kid's lunch out of a coat pocket. A bite of
something. Paste. You can't really make a meal of paste, or put it on bread
for a sandwich, but sometimes I'd scoop a few spoonfuls out of the big
paste jar in the back of the room. Pregnant people get strange tastes. I was
pregnant with poverty. Pregnant with dirt and pregnant with smells that
made people turn away, pregnant with cold and pregnant with shoes that
were never bought for me, pregnant with five other people in my bed and
no Daddy in the next room, and pregnant with hunger. Paste doesn't taste
too bad when you're hungry.

The teacher thought I was a troublemaker. All she saw from the front
of the room was a little black boy who squirmed in his idiot's seat and
made noises and poked the kids around him. I guess she couldn't see a kid
who made noises because he wanted someone to know he was there.

It was on a Thursday, the day before the Negro payday. The eagle
always flew on Friday. The teacher was asking each student how much his
father would give to the Community Chest. On Friday night, each kid
would get the money from his father, and on Monday he would bring it to
the school. I decided I was going to buy me a Daddy right then. I had
money in my pocket from shining shoes and selling papers, and whatever
Helene Tucker pledged for her Daddy I was going to top it. And I'd hand
the money right in. I wasn't going to wait until Monday to buy me a
Daddy.

I was shaking, scared to death. The teacher opened her book and started calling out names alphabetically.

"Helene Tucker?"

"My Daddy said he'd give two dollars and fifty cents."

"That's very nice, Helene. Very, very nice indeed."

That made me feel pretty good. It wouldn't take too much to top that. I had almost three dollars in dimes and quarters in my pocket. I stuck my hand in my pocket and held onto the money, waiting for her to call my name. But the teacher closed her book after she called everybody else in the class.

I stood up and raised my hand.

"What is it now?"

"You forgot me."

She turned toward the blackboard. "I don't have time to be playing with you, Richard."

"My Daddy said he'd . . ."

"Sit down, Richard, you're disturbing the class."

"My Daddy said he'd give . . . fifteen dollars."

She turned around and looked mad. "We are collecting this money for you and your kind, Richard Gregory. If your Daddy can give fifteen dollars you have no business being on relief."

"I got it right now, I got it right now, my Daddy gave it to me to turn in today, my Daddy said . . ."

"And furthermore," she said, looking right at me, her nostrils getting big and her lips getting thin and her eyes opening wide. "We know you don't have a Daddy."

Helene Tucker turned around, her eyes full of tears. She felt sorry for me. Then I couldn't see her too well because I was crying, too.

"Sit down, Richard."

And I always thought the teacher kind of liked me. She always picked me to wash the blackboard on Friday, after school. That was a big thrill, it made me feel important. If I didn't wash it, come Monday the school might not function right.

"Where are you going, Richard?"

I walked out of school that day, and for a long time I didn't go back very often. There was shame there.

Now there was shame everywhere. It seemed like the whole world had been inside that classroom, everyone had heard what the teacher had said, everyone had turned around and felt sorry for me. There was shame in going to the Worthy Boys Annual Christmas Dinner for you and your kind, because everybody knew what a worthy boy was. Why couldn't they just call it the Boys Annual Dinner, why'd they have to give it a name? There was shame in wearing the brown and orange and white plaid mackinaw the welfare gave to 3,000 boys. Why'd it have to be the same for everybody so when you walked down the street the people could see you were on relief? It was a nice warm mackinaw and it had a hood, and my Momma beat me and called me a little rat when she found out I stuffed it in the bottom of a pail full of garbage way over on Cottage Street. There was shame in running over to Mister Ben's at the end of the day and asking for his rotten peaches, there was shame in asking Mrs. Simmons for a spoonful of sugar, there was shame in running out to meet the relief truck. I hated that truck, full of food for you and your kind. I ran into the house and hid when it came. And then I started to sneak through alleys, to take the long way home so the people going into White's Eat Shop wouldn't see me. Yeah, the whole world heard the teacher that day, we all know you don't have a Daddy.

It lasted for a while, this kind of numbness. I spent a lot of time feeling sorry for myself. And then one day I met this wino in a restaurant. I'd been out hustling all day, shining shoes, selling newspapers, and I had googobs of money in my pocket. Bought me a bowl of chili for fifteen cents, and a cheeseburger for fifteen cents, and a Pepsi for five cents, and a piece of chocolate cake for ten cents. That was a good meal. I was eating when this old wino came in. I love winos because they never hurt anyone but themselves.

The old wino sat down at the counter and ordered twenty-six cents worth of food. He ate it like he really enjoyed it. When the owner, Mister Williams, asked him to pay the check, the old wino didn't lie or go through his pocket like he suddenly found a hole.

He just said: "Don't have no money."

The owner yelled: "Why in hell you come in here and eat my food if you don't have no money? That food cost me money."

Mister Williams jumped over the counter and knocked the wino off his stool and beat him over the head with a pop bottle. Then he stepped back and watched the wino bleed. Then he kicked him. And he kicked him again.

I looked at the wino with blood all over his face and I went over. "Leave him alone, Mister Williams. I'll pay the twenty-six cents."

The wino got up, slowly, pulling himself up to the stool, then up to the counter, holding on for a minute until his legs stopped shaking so bad. He looked at me with pure hate. "Keep your twenty-six cents. You don't have to pay, not now. I just finished paying for it."

He started to walk out, and as he passed me, he reached down and touched my shoulder. "Thanks, sonny, but it's too late now. Why didn't you pay it before?"

I was pretty sick about that. I waited too long to help another man.

FOR FURTHER CONSIDERATION

In the scene in the cafe where the owner, the wino, and the author appear, each person seems to operate on a different sense of values. Given the actions of each, what values does each person exhibit?

Black Hawk

This excerpt from The Autobiography of Black Hawk, *dictated to Antoine Le Clair in 1833, chronicles the spiritual pain of an Indian leader confronting the onslaught of white civilization in the early nineteenth century. In 1973 American Indians seized the Bureau of Indian Affairs in Washington, D.C., and later captured the town of Wounded Knee, South Dakota. Clearly native Americans continue to suffer from the repression, indignities, and indifference that our society inflicts on them.*

Farewell, My Nation!
Farewell, Black Hawk!

Soon after our return home, news reached us that a war was going to take place between the British and the Americans.

Runners continued to arrive from different tribes, all confirming the reports of the expected war. The British agent, Colonel Dixon, was holding talks with, and making presents to, the different tribes. I had not made up my mind whether to join the British or remain neutral. I had not discovered yet one good trait in the character of the Americans who had come to the country. They made fair promises but never fulfilled them, while the British made but few, and we could always rely implicitly on their word.

One of our people having killed a Frenchman at Prairie du Chien, the British took him prisoner and said they would shoot him next day. His family were encamped a short distance below the mouth of the Wisconsin. He begged for permission to go and see them that night as he was to die the next day. They permitted him to go after he had promised them to return by sunrise the next morning.

He visited his family, which consisted of his wife and six children. I cannot describe their meeting and parting so as to be understood by the whites, as it appears that their feelings are acted upon by certain rules laid down by their preachers, while ours are governed by the monitor within us. He bade his loved ones the last sad farewell and hurried across the prairie to the fort and arrived in time. The soldiers were ready and immediately marched out and shot him down.

[Interrupting the straight course of his account he says in melancholy:]

Why did the Great Spirit ever send the whites to this island to drive us from our homes and introduce among us poisonous liquors, disease, and death? They should have remained in the land the Great Spirit allotted to them. But I will proceed with my story. My memory, however, is not very good since my late visit to the white people. I have still a buzzing noise in my ears. . . . I may give some parts of my story out of place, but will make my best endeavor to be correct.

[Some chiefs were called upon to go to Washington to see the Great Father, who wanted them in case of war to remain neutral, promising them to let the traders sell to them in the fall goods on credit, that they might hunt and repay with furs in the spring, as the British had arranged it up to then. Everything depended for the Sac upon this institution. But—the trader refused bluntly to sell on credit.]

The war chief said the trader could not furnish us on credit, and that he had received no instructions from our Great Father at Washington. We left the fort dissatisfied and went to camp. What was now to be done we knew not. . . . Few of us slept that night. All was gloom and discontent.

[As a result of this treatment they joined the British.]

Our lodges were soon taken down, and we all started for Rock Island. Here ended all hopes of our remaining at peace, having been forced into war by being deceived. . . .

We continued our march, joining the British below Detroit, soon after which we had a battle. The Americans fought well and drove us back with considerable loss. I was greatly surprised at this, as I had been told that the Americans would not fight. . . .

On my arrival at the village I was met by the chiefs and braves and conducted to the lodge which was prepared for me. After eating, I gave a full account of all that I had seen and done. I explained to my people the manner in which the British and Americans fought. Instead of stealing upon each other and taking every advantage to kill the enemy and save their own people as we do, which with us is considered good policy in a war chief, they march out in open daylight and fight regardless of the number of warriors they may lose. After the battle is over they retire to feast and drink wine as if nothing had happened. After which they make a statement in writing of what they have done, each party claiming the victory and neither giving an account of half the number that have been killed on their own side.

[The British lose constantly. After a long time of consideration and many councils Black Hawk decides to make a treaty of peace with the "chief at St. Louis."]

The great chief at St. Louis having sent word for us to come down and confirm the treaty, we did not hesitate but started immediately that we might smoke the peace pipe with him. On our arrival we met the great chiefs in council. They explained to us the words of our Great Father in Washington, accusing us of heinous crimes and many misdemeanors, particularly in not coming down when first invited. We knew very well that our Great Father had deceived us and thereby forced us to join the British, and could not believe that he had put this speech into the mouths of those chiefs to deliver to us. I was not a civil chief and consequently made no reply, but our civil chiefs told the commissioners: "What you say is a lie. Our Great Father sent us no such speech, he knew that the situation in which we had been placed was caused by him." The white chiefs appeared very angry at this reply and said, "We will break off the treaty and make the war against you, as you have grossly insulted us."

Our chiefs had no intention of insulting them and told them so, saying, "We merely wish to explain that you have told us a lie, without any desire to make you angry, in the same manner that you whites do when you do not believe what is told you." The council then proceeded and the pipe of peace was smoked.

Here for the first time I touched the goose quill to sign the treaty, not knowing, however, that by the act I consented to give away my village. Had that been explained to me I should have opposed it and never would have signed their treaty, as my recent conduct will clearly prove. What do we know of the manners, the laws, and the customs of the white people? They might buy our bodies for dissection, and we would touch the goose quill to confirm it and not know what we were doing. This was the case with me and my people in touching the goose quill the first time.

We can only judge of what is proper and right by our standard of what is right and wrong, which differs widely from the whites', if I have been correctly informed. The whites may do wrong all their lives and then if they are sorry for it when about to die, all is well, but with us it is different. We must continue to do good throughout our lives. If we have corn and meat, and know of a family that have none, we divide with them. If we have more blankets than we absolutely need, and others have not enough, we must give to those who are in want.

[As Black Hawk could not yield to the demand of the "white chiefs" and leave his village and his graveyard, a war ensued, the so-called Black Hawk War, lasting from 1831-2. Chief Keokuk, his great antagonist, who was willing to negotiate with the whites and persuaded part of the tribe to abandon the village, caused thus a rift among the Sac.]

I looked upon Keokuk as a coward and no brave. . . . What right had these people [the whites] to our village and our fields, which the Great Spirit had given us to live upon? My reason teaches me that land cannot be sold. The Great Spirit gave it to his children to live upon and cultivate as far as necessary for their subsistence, and so long as they occupy and cultivate it they have the right to the soil, but if they voluntarily leave it, then any other people have a right to settle on it. Nothing can be sold but such things as can be carried away.

[It was at Fort Crawford that Black Hawk, in the despair of defeat, said: "Farewell, my nation! Farewell, Black Hawk!"]

The massacre which terminated the war lasted about two hours. Our loss in killed was about sixty, besides a number that was drowned. . . .

I was now given up by the agent to the commanding officer at Fort Crawford, the White Beaver [General Atkinson] having gone down the river.

On our way down I surveyed the country that had cost us so much trouble, anxiety, and blood, and that now caused me to be a prisoner of war. I reflected upon the ingratitude of the whites when I saw their fine houses, rich harvests, and everything desirable around them; and recollected that all this land had been ours, for which I and my people had never received a dollar, and that the whites were not satisfied until they took our village and our graveyards from us and removed us across the Mississippi.

On our arrival at Jefferson Barracks we met the great war chief, White Beaver, who had commanded the American army against my little band. I felt the humiliation of my situation; a little while before I had been leader of my braves, now I was a prisoner of war. He received us kindly and treated us well.

We were now confined to the barracks and forced to wear the ball and chain. This was extremely mortifying and altogether useless. Was the White Beaver afraid I would break out of his barracks and run away? Or was he ordered to inflict this punishment upon me? If I had taken him prisoner on the field of battle I would not have wounded his feelings so much by such treatment, knowing that a brave war chief would prefer death to dishonor. But I do not blame the White Beaver for the course he pursued, as it is the custom among white soldiers, and I suppose was a part of his duty.

FOR FURTHER CONSIDERATION

Black Hawk's story tells of the destruction of everything that the chieftain has fought to preserve. He faces a circumstance that would reduce a lesser personality to psychological rubble. What basic values does Black Hawk espouse? How do his choices reflect his values? Which of his values sustain him in this time of tragedy?

Jules Feiffer (1929-   )

Best known for his syndicated cartoons, Feiffer has become America's most versatile satirist. His fiction, plays, drawings and now films are unmatched in their ability to reveal the fraud and absurdity of contemporary America.

Corruption

THE EVOLUTIONARY PROCESS IN GOVERNMENT CONTINUES. WE HAVE PASSED FROM FEUDALISM TO CAPITALISM. OUR CURRENT STAGE, AS WE ALL KNOW, IS **CORRUPTION.**

CORRUPTION AS A FORM OF GOVERNMENT IS, ITSELF, WITHIN VARYING STAGES OF DEVELOPMENT. IN THE SOVIET UNION, WHERE YOU HAVE THE "**STATE**" OR "**TRICKLE DOWN**" THEORY OF CORRUPTION, IT OPERATES WITH THE **MOST** EFFICIENCY.

IN OUR **OWN** COUNTRY WE ARE IN THE TRANSITIONAL, MORE DYNAMIC PHASE—**FREE FORM** CORRUPTION. IT IS AN UNPREDICTABLE PHASE BECAUSE IT CONTINUES, SELF CONSCIOUSLY, TO DENY ITS EXISTENCE IN FEAR THAT, WERE ITS **TRUE** NATURE MADE KNOWN, IT WOULD BE OVERTHROWN.

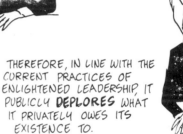

THEREFORE, IN LINE WITH THE CURRENT PRACTICES OF ENLIGHTENED LEADERSHIP, IT PUBLICLY **DEPLORES** WHAT IT PRIVATELY OWES ITS EXISTENCE TO.

AS PART OF THIS PHILOSOPHY IT OFFERS A REGULAR PROGRAM OF PLANNED EXPOSURES TO SATISFY THE PUBLIC'S APPETITE— A BUILDING INSPECTOR ONE MONTH, A CITY OFFICIAL ANOTHER MONTH—**ANYTHING** WHICH WILL MISDIRECT THE GAZE OF AN ANTI-CORRUPT CITIZENRY.

THUS THE PUBLIC IS ENCOURAGED TO THINK OF CORRUPTION AS AN UNWELCOME STRANGER IN ITS HOUSE RATHER THAN AS THE HOST.

IN THE MEANTIME, TO SOFTEN
THE PUBLIC'S ANTI CORRUPTION
NEO-IDEALISM, THERE WILL BE
A GROWING LIST OF **PEER
GROUP** EXPOSURES—
PROMINENT PRIVATE CITIZENS,
IMPORTANT BUSINESS LEADERS,
LEADING INTELLECTUALS—

WITH SO MUCH CORRUPTION
MADE SO APALLINGLY
EVIDENT, PUBLIC RESPONSE
WILL DEADEN AND WITHDRAW.
ACCEPTANCE WILL SET IN.
CORRUPTION'S TAKE OVER
WILL BE **COMPLETE**.

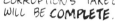

IN EVERY SCHOOL IN THE
LAND WILL BE ENGRAVED
OUR **NEW** MORAL
BANNER ————

"WHAT CAN
YOU EXPECT?
I'D DO IT
MYSELF."

John Ciardi (1916–   )

*While there are poets the equal of John Ciardi, no one has matched his
efforts as a thoughtful yet thoroughly readable commentator on poetry. He
has been a professor of English at Rutgers University and was for years
widely read as the poetry editor and critic for* Saturday Review. *His eight
books of poems and his gift for lucid commentary on poetry have won him
six major literary prizes.*

*In "The Act of Language," Ciardi explains with clarity, beauty, and
example the stuff of poetry and how it enriches us.*

The Act of Language

At the beginning of *The Divine Comedy,* Dante finds himself in a Dark Wood, lost from the light of God. It was no single, specific evil act that led Dante into that darkness but, rather, the sin of omission. Its name is Acedia, the fourth of the Seven Deadly Sins, and by us generally translated "Sloth."

In American-English, however, Sloth may seem to imply mere physical laziness and untidiness. The torpor of Acedia, it must be understood, is spiritual rather than physical. It is to know the good, but to be lax in its pursuit.

Whether one thinks of it as a sin or as a behavioral failure, Acedia is also the one fault for which no artist can be forgiven. Time, as W. H. Auden wrote in his poem titled *In Memory of W. B. Yeats:*

> *Worships language and forgives*
> *Everyone by whom it lives;*
> *Pardons cowardice, conceit,*
> *Lays its honor at their feet.*

In place of cowardice and conceit, Auden might have cited any catalogue of pride, envy, wrath, avarice, gluttony or carnality, and he could still have said that time forgives. The poet may cheat anything else and still win honor from time, but he may not cheat the poem and live.

For a man is finally defined by what he does with his attention. It was Simone Weil who said, "Absolute attention is absolute prayer." I do not, of course, know what an absolute attention is, except as an absolutely unattainable goal. But certainly to seek that increasing purity and concentration of one's attention that will lead to more and more meaningful perception, is not only possible but is the basic human exercise of any art. It must be added, however, that *in art it does not matter what one pays attention to; the quality of the attention is what counts.*

I have just made a dangerous statement; one that will probably breed protest, that will be difficult to explain, and that will turn out in the end to be only partly true. It is still necessary to make the statement first, and then to go the long way round to explaining why it is necessary, and in what way it is true.

The need to go the long way round brings matters back to another parable of poetry that one may read in Dante's opening situation. The language of parables is always likely to be apt to the discussion of poetry.

As soon as Dante realizes that he is in darkness, he looks up and sees the first light of the dawn shawling the shoulders of a little hill. (In Dante, the Sun is always a symbol of God as Divine Illumination.) The allegory should be clear enough: The very realization that one is lost is the beginning of finding oneself.

What happens next is the heart of the matter. His goal in sight, Dante tries to race straight up the hill—to reach the light, as it were, by direct assault. Note that common sense would certainly be on Dante's side. There is the light and there is the hill: Go to it. Nothing could be simpler. Nor, as Dante discovers, could anything be more false. Almost immediately his way is blocked by three beasts. These beasts—a Leopard, a Lion and a She-wolf—represent all the sins of the world. They represent, therefore, the world's total becloudment of any man's best attention, for all that has ever lured any man away from his own good is contained within them.

The three beasts drive Dante back into the darkness. There Dante comes on the soul of Virgil, who symbolizes Human Reason. In that role Virgil explains that a man may reach the light only by going the long way round. Dante must risk the dangerous descent into Hell—to the recognition of sin. And he must make the arduous ascent of Purgatory—to the renunciation of sin. Only then may he enter, bit by bit, the final presence of the light, which is to say, Heaven.

The point of the parable is that in art as in theology—as in all things that concern a man in his profoundest being—the long way round is the only way home. Short cuts are useful only in mechanics. The man who seeks mortal understanding must go the long, encompassing way of his deepest involvement.

Americans, susceptible as they are to the legend of mechanical know-how and get-it-done, may especially need to be told that there is no easy digest of understanding and no gift package of insight. May they learn, too, that "common sense," useful as it can be in its own sphere, cannot lead a man as deeply into himself as he must be led if he is to enter a meaningful experience of art or of life. Every man who looks long enough at the stars must come to feel their other-reality engulfing his mortal state, and nothing from the world's efficiencies and practicalities is specific to that awareness in him.

Poetry is written of that man under the stars in trouble and in joy, and the truth of poetry cannot be spoken meaningfully in simple common-sense assertions. In poetry, as in all our deepest emotions, many feelings and many thoughts and half-thoughts happen at once. Often these feelings and thoughts are in conflict:

We love and hate the same thing, desire it and dread it, need it and are destroyed by it. Always, too, there are more thoughts and feelings in a profound experience than we can put a finger on. What has common sense to say to such states of man? Common sense tends always to the easier assumption that only one thing is "really" happening in a man at one time, and that a simple, straightforward course of action will take care of it.

Such an assumption can only blind one to poetry. To read a poem with no thought in mind but to paraphrase it into a single, simple, and usually high-minded, prose statement is the destruction of poetry. Nor does it make much difference that one can quote poetry, and good poetry, in defense of such destruction. At the end of *Ode on a Grecian Urn,* John Keats wrote:

> *"Beauty is truth, truth beauty,"—that is all*
> *Ye know on earth, and all ye need to know.*

Heaven knows how many enthusiasts have used these lines as evidence that poetry is somehow an act of inspiration not to be measured by any criteria but an undefined devotion to "beauty," "truth" and "inspiring message."

But if beauty and truth are all that Grecian urns and men need know on earth, Keats makes evident by his own practice that a poet also needs to know a great deal about his trade, and that he must be passionately concerned for its basic elements.

Those basic elements are not beauty and truth but *rhythm, diction, image* and *form.* Certainly Keats cared about beauty and truth. Any sensitive man must care. No matter that one must forever fumble at the definition of such ideas; they are still matters of ultimate concern. But so was Dante's yearning for the light, and he discovered at once that it can be reached only by the long way round.

The poet's way round is by way of rhythm, diction, image and form. It is the right, the duty and the joy of his trade to be passionate about these things. To be passionate about them in the minutest and even the most frivolous detail. To be passionate about them, if need be, to the exclusion of what is generally understood by "sincerity" and "meaning." To be more passionate about them than he is about the cold war, the Gunpowder Plot, the next election, abolition, the H-bomb, the Inquisition, juvenile delinquency, the Spanish Armada, or his own survival.

The good poets have not generally sneered at the world of affairs. Some have, but many others have functioned well within that world. Yet the need and the right of all poets to detach themselves from the things of the world in order to pursue the things of the poetic trade have always been inseparable from their success as poets.

The poet must be passionate about the four elements of his trade for the most fundamental of reasons. He must be so because those passions are both a joy and an addiction within him. Because they are the life of the poem, without which nothing of value can happen either in the poem or to the reader. Because writing a poem is a more sentient way of living than not writing it, because no poem can be written well except as these passions inform it, and because only when the poem is so written can the beauty and truth of that more sentient way of living be brought to mortal consequence.

The act of poetry may seem to have very simple surfaces, but it is always compounded of many things at once. As Robert Frost wrote in *Two Tramps in Mud Time:*

Only where love and need are one,
And the work is play for mortal stakes,
Is the deed ever really done
For Heaven and the future's sakes.

The voice of common sense rises immediately in protest. "Mystification!" it cries. "A poem still has to *mean* something. What does it *mean?*" And the poet must answer, "Never what you think. Not when you ask the question in that way."

But how shall the question be asked? Let the questioner listen first to a kind of statement he has probably passed over without enough attention. He can find one such in Walter Pater's essay on Winckelman. "Let us understand by poetry," wrote Pater, "all literary production which attains the power of giving pleasure by its form as distinct from its matter."

He can find another in a book entitled *The Fire and the Fountain* by the English poet and critic John Press. "The essence of the poet," wrote Press, "is to be found less in his opinions than in his idiom." He may even find one in a textbook titled *Reading Poems,* in which Wright Thomas says, "The *subject* is a very poor indication of what the *poem* is"—to which I should add only that it is no indication whatever.

But if the meaning is not in the subject, what then does a poem mean? It means always and above all else the poet's deep involvement in the four basic elements of his trade. It means not the subject but the way the poetic involvement transfigures the subject. It means, that is to say, the very act of language by which it comes into existence. The poem may purport to be about anything from pussy willows to battleships, but the meaning of any good poem is its act of language.

Because it is an act of language, a good poem is deeply connected with everything men are and do. For language is certainly one of the most fundamental activities in which human beings engage. Take away a man's language, and you take most of his ability to think and to experience. Enrich his language, and you cannot fail to enrich his experience. Any man who has let great language into his head is the richer for it.

He is not made richer by what is being said. It is the language itself that brings his enrichment. Could poetry be meaningful aside from its act of language, it would have no reason for being, and the whole history of poetry could be reduced to a series of simple paraphrases.

Consider as simple a passage as the beginning of Herrick's *Upon Julia's Clothes:*

Whenas in silks my Julia goes,
Then, then, methinks, how sweetly flows
The liquefaction of her clothes.

Who can read those lines without a thrill of pleasure? But now consider the paraphrase: "I like the rustle of Julia's silks when she walks." The poetry and the paraphrase are certainly about equal in subject matter. The difference is that the poetry is a full and rich act of language, whereas the paraphrase, though faultless, lacks, among other things, measure, pause, stress, rhyme and the pleasure of lingering over the word "liquefaction."

"But what is Julia doing there?" cries that voice of common sense. "She must have something to do with the poem or she wouldn't be in it!"

The owner of that voice would do well to ponder the relation between a good portrait and its subject. The subject is there, to be sure—at least in most cases. But the instant the painter puts one brush stroke on the canvas and then another, the two brush strokes take on a relation to each other and to the space around them. The two then take on a relation to the third, and it to them. And so forth. The painting immediately begins to exert its own demands upon the painter, its own way of going. Immediately the subject begins to disappear.

All too soon, for that matter, the subject will have changed with age or will have died. After a while no living person will have any recollection of what the subject looked like. All that will remain then is a portrait head which must be either self-validating or worthless. Because the subject cannot validate the painting, he or she will have become irrelevant. All that can finally validate the portrait is the way in which the painter engaged the act of painting.

And one more thing—the good artist always thinks in long terms. He knows, even at the moment of the painting, that both he and the subject will disappear. Any good painter will be painting for the painting—for the time when the subject will have blown away into time.

So with poetry. The one final and enduring meaning of any poem lies not in what it seems to have set out to say, but in its act of language.

The only test of that act of language is the memory of the race. Bad poetry is by nature forgettable; it is, therefore, soon forgotten. But good poetry, like any good act of language, hooks onto human memory and stays there. Write well, and there will always be someone somewhere who carries in his mind what you have written. It will stay in memory because man is the language animal, and because his need of language is from the roots of his consciousness. That need in him is not a need for meaning. Rather, good language in him takes possession of meaning; it fills him with a resonance that the best of men understand only dimly, but without which no man is entirely alive. Poetry is that presence and that resonance. As Archibald MacLeish put it in his much-discussed *Ars Poetica:*

> *A poem should not mean*
> *But be.*

If the reader truly wishes to engage poetry, let him forget meaning. Let him think rather: "I shall summon great language to mind. I shall summon language so fully, so resonantly and so precisely used that it will bring all my meanings to me." Then let him turn to poetry, and let him listen to the passions of the poet's trade.

Listen to great rhythms. Here is the opening stanza of John Donne's *The Anniversarie:*

> *All Kings, and all their favorites,*
> *All glory of honours, beauties, wits,*
> *The Sun it selfe, which makes times as they passe,*
> *is elder by a yeare, now, than it was*
> *When thou and I first one another saw:*
> *All other things, to their destruction draw,*
> *Only our love hath no decay;*
> *This, no to morrow hath, nor yesterday.*
> *Running, it never runs from us away,*
> *But truly keeps his first, last, everlasting day.*

Wordly things pass away, but true love is constant, says the subject matter. All true enough and tried enough. But listen to the rhythm enforce itself upon the saying, especially in the last four lines. For present purposes, let the voice ignore the lesser accents. Let it stress only those syllables printed in capital letters below, while observing the pauses as indicated by the slash marks. And forget the meaning. Read for the voice emphasis and the voice pauses:

> *Only OUR LOVE hath no deCAY‖*
> *THIS‖no to MOrrow hath‖nor YESterday‖*
> *RUNning‖it never runs from us aWAY‖*
> *But truly keeps his FIRST‖LAST‖EVerlasting DAY.*

Not all rhythms are so percussive, so measured out by pauses, and so metrically irregular. Listen to this smoother rhythm from Poe's *Israfel:*

> *If I could dwell*
> *Where Israfel*
> > *Hath dwelt, and he where I,*
>
> *He might not sing so wildly well*
> > *A mortal melody,*
>
> *While a bolder note than his might swell*
> > *From my lyre within the sky.*

Or the rhythm may be percussive, but without substantial pauses, as in the last line of this passage from the end of Gerard Manley Hopkins' *Felix Randal,* an elegy for a blacksmith:

> *How far from then forethought of, all thy more boisterous years,*
> *When thou at the random grim forge, powerful amidst peers,*

> *Didst fettle for the great gray drayhorse his bright and battering*
> *sandal.*

Listen to the hammerfall of that last line: "Didst FEttle for the GREAT GRAY DRAYhorse his BRIGHT and BAttering SANdal."

Or listen to the spacing of the "ah" sounds as a rhythmic emphasis in the last line of this final passage from Meredith's *Lucifer in Starlight:*

> *Around the ancient track marched, rank on rank,*
> *The ARmy of unALterable LAW.*

Percussive, smooth, flowing or studded with pauses—there is no end to the variety and delight of great language rhythms. For the poet, his rhythms are forever more than a matter of making a "meaningful" statement; they are a joy in their own right. No poet hates meaning. But the poet's passion is for the triumph of language. No reader can come to real contact with a poem until he comes to it through the joy of that rhythmic act of language.

As for rhythm, so for diction. The poet goes to language—or it comes to him and he receives it—for his joy in the precision of great word choices. Give him such a line as Whitman's "I witness the corpse with the dabbled hair," and he will register the corpse, to be sure, but it will be "dabbled" he seizes upon with the joy of a botanist coming on a rare specimen. So when Keats speaks of Ruth amid "the alien corn" or when Theodore Roethke speaks of sheep "strewn" on a field, the good reader will certainly care about the dramatic situation of the poem, but he cannot fail to answer with a special joy to "alien" and to "strewn."

What, after all, is the subject as compared to his joy in such rich precision? Thousands of English poems have described the passing of winter and the coming of spring. Certainly there is little in that subject as a subject to attract him. But listen to the pure flutefall of the word choices I have italicized in the following passage from Stanley Kunitz's *Deciduous Bough,* and note how the self-delight in language makes everything immediate and new again:

> *Winter that coils in the thicket now*
> *Will glide from the field, the swinging rain*
> *Be knotted with flowers, on every bough*
> *A bird will meditate again.*

"Poetry," said Coleridge, "is the best words in the best order." How can anyone reading the Kunitz passage escape a sense that the language is being ultimately and unimprovably selected? The delight one feels in coming on such language is not only in the experience of perfection but also in the fact that perfection has been made to seem not only effortless but inevitable.

And let this much more be added to the idea of poetic meaning: Nothing in a good poem happens by accident; every word, every comma, every variant spelling must enter as an act of the poet's choice. A poem is a machine for making choices. The mark of the good poet is his refusal to make easy or cheap choices. The better the poet, the greater the demands he makes upon himself, and the higher he sets his level of choice. Thus, a good poem is not only an act of mind but an act of devotion to mind. The poet who chooses cheaply or lazily is guilty of aesthetic acedia, and he is lost thereby. The poet who spares himself nothing in his search for the most demanding choices is shaping a human attention that offers itself as a high and joyful example to all men of mind and devotion. Every act of great language, whatever its subject matter, illustrates an idea of order and a resonance of human possibility without which no man's mind can sense its own fullest dimensions.

As for rhythm and diction, so for imagery. To be sure, every word is at root an image, and poetic images must be made of words. Yet certainly there is in a well-constructed image an effect that cannot be said to rise from any one word choice, but from the total phrasing.

So for the sensory shiver of Keats' "The silver snarling trumpets 'gan to chide." So for the wonderfully woozy effect of John Frederick Nims' "The drunk clambering on his undulant floor." So for the grand hyperbole of Howard Nemerov saying that the way a young girl looks at him "sets his knees to splashing like two waves."

We learn both imagination and precision from the poet's eye. And we learn correspondences. Consider the following image from *Aereopagus* by Louis MacNeice, a poem as playful as it is serious, in which MacNeice describes Athens as a cradle of the western mind. Cradles, he makes clear, generally contain children, and all those boy-gods and girl-goddesses had their childish side:

> . . . you still may glimpse
> The child-eyed Fury tossing her shock of snakes,
> Careering over the Parthenon's ruined playpen.

It is a bit shocking to have the Parthenon spoken of as a playpen, but once the shock has passed, what a triumph there is in the figure: everything corresponds! Think how much would have been lost had the Parthenon a surviving roof, or had its general proportions or the placement of the pillars—slats—resisted the comparison. The joy of it is that, despite the first shock, nothing resists the comparison; and we find that the surprise turns out to be a true correspondence.

One of the poet's happiest—and most mortal—games is in seeking such correspondences. But what flows from them is more than a game. Every discovery of a true correspondence is an act of reason and an instruction to the mind. For intelligence does not consist of masses of factual detail. It consists of seeing essential likenesses and essential differences and of relating them, allowing for differences within the likenesses and for likenesses within the differences. Mentality is born of analogy.

Note, too, that the image-idea of "ruined playpen" does not simply happen, but is prepared for in "child-eyed." And note, further, the nice double meaning of "careering" as both "a wild rush" and "to make a career of."

A good extended image, that is to say, is made of various elements and is marked by both sequence and structure. Thus we have already touched upon the essence of the fourth element of the poet's trade: form.

There are many kinds of poetic form, but since all are based on pattern and sequence, let a tightly patterned poem illustrate. Here is Emily Dickinson's *The Soul Selects:*

> *The soul selects her own society,*
> *Then shuts the door;*
> *On her divine majority*
> *Obtrude no more.*
>
> *Unmoved, she notes the chariot's pausing*
> *At her low gate;*
> *Unmoved, an emperor is kneeling*
> *Upon her mat.*
> *I've known her from an ample nation*
> *Choose one;*
> *Then close the valves of her attention*
> *Like stone.*

Whatever the hunters of beauty and truth find for their pleasure in such a poem, the poet's joy will be in its form and management. He responds to the passion of the language for its own sparseness, to the pattern of rhyme and half-rhyme, to the flavor of the images (connotation), and to the way those flavors relate to one another. He responds to the interplay of the four-foot feminine lines (feminine lines end on an unaccented syllable) and the two-foot masculine lines (which end on an accented syllable).

And he responds, above all, to the way those two-foot lines develop in the last stanza into two boldly stroked syllables apiece (monosyllabic feet) so that the emotion held down throughout the poem by the sparseness of the language is hammered into sensation by the beat of those last two words: "Like stone"—thud! thud!

Beauty and truth are no irrelevancies, but they are abstractions that must remain meaningless to poetry until they are brought to being in the management of a specific form. It is that management the poet must love: the joy of sensing the poem fall into inescapable form, and therefore into inescapable experience. For the poet's trade is not to talk about experience, but to make it happen. His act of making is all he knows of beauty and truth. It is, in fact, his way of knowing them. His only way of knowing them.

As I. A. Richards, poet and scholar of the language, put it in a recent poem titled *The Ruins:*

> *Sometimes a word is wiser much than men:*
> *"Faithful" e.g., "responsible" and "true."*
> *And words it is, not poets, make up poems.*
> *Our words, we say, but we are theirs, too,*
> *For words made men and may unmake again.*

And now, at last, it is time to repeat the statement from which this long way round began. "In art," I said, "it does not matter what one pays attention to; the quality of the attention is what counts." It is time to amend that necessary false statement.

For it does matter where the poet fixes his attention. Attention must be to *something.* That something, however, is so casually connected with the subject of the poem that any reader will do well to dismiss the subject as no more than a point of departure. Any impassioning point of departure will do. The poet, being a man, must believe something, but what that something is does not matter so long as he believes it strongly enough to be passionate about it. What he believes, moreover, may be touched off by an image, a rhythm, or the quality of a word *in pursuit of which the subject is invented.*

The poem, in any case, is not in its point of departure, but in its journey to itself. That journey, the act of the poem, is its act of language. That act is the true final subject and meaning of any poem. It is to that act of language the poet shapes his most devoted attention—to the fullness of rhythm, diction, image and form. Only in that devotion can he seize the world and make it evident.

FOR FURTHER CONSIDERATION

What does Ciardi refer to with his phrase *"the act of language"?* To what extent is *the act of language* a revelation of self for the poet? For the reader of poetry? For the routine conversationalist? What does Ciardi suggest when he says, "The mark of the good poet is his refusal to make easy or cheap choices?"

Alvin Toffler (1928–   )

Toffler has been an editor, correspondent, free-lance writer, and academician. His explorations of the future while at Cornell and the Russell Sage Foundation have led to numerous articles in magazines and to three books: The Culture Consumers, The Schoolhouse in the City, *and* Future Shock. *The selection which follows was excerpted from the latter.*

The Accelerative Thrust

Early in March, 1967, in eastern Canada, an eleven-year-old child died of old age.

Ricky Gallant was only eleven years old chronologically, but he suffered from an odd disease called progeria—advanced aging—and he exhibited many of the characteristics of a ninety-year-old person. The symptoms of progeria are senility, hardened arteries, baldness, slack, and wrinkled skin. In effect, Ricky was an old man when he died, a long lifetime of biological change having been packed into his eleven short years.

Cases of progeria are extremely rare. Yet in a metaphorical sense the high technology societies all suffer from this peculiar ailment. They are not growing old or senile. But they *are* experiencing super-normal rates of change.

Many of us have a vague "feeling" that things are moving faster. Doctors and executives alike complain that they cannot keep up with the latest developments in their fields. Hardly a meeting or conference takes place today without some ritualistic oratory about "the challenge of change." Among many there is an uneasy mood—a suspicion that change is out of control.

Not everyone, however, shares this anxiety. Millions sleepwalk their way through their lives as if nothing had changed since the 1930's, and as if nothing ever will. Living in what is certainly one of the most exciting periods in human history, they attempt to withdraw from it, to block it out, as if it were possible to make it go away by ignoring it. They seek a "separate peace," a diplomatic immunity from change.

One sees them everywhere: Old people, resigned to living out their years, attempting to avoid, at any cost, the intrusions of the new. Already-old people of thirty-five and forty-five, nervous about student riots, sex, LSD, or miniskirts, feverishly attempting to persuade themselves that, after all, youth was always rebellious, and that what is happening today is no different from the past. Even among the young we find an incomprehension of change: students so ignorant of the past that they see nothing unusual about the present.

The disturbing fact is that the vast majority of people, including educated and otherwise sophisticated people, find the idea of change so threatening that they attempt to deny its existence. Even many people who understand intellectually that change is accelerating, have not internalized that knowledge, do not take this critical social fact into account in planning their own personal lives.

TIME AND CHANGE

How do we *know* that change is accelerating? There is, after all, no absolute way to measure change. In the awesome complexity of the universe, even within any given society, a virtually infinite number of streams of change occur simultaneously. All "things"—from the tiniest virus to the greatest galaxy—are, in reality, not things at all, but processes. There is no static point, no nirvana-like un-change, against which to measure change. Change is, therefore, necessarily relative.

It is also uneven. If all processes occurred at the same speed, or even if they accelerated or decelerated in unison, it would be impossible to observe change. The future, however, invades the present at differing speeds. Thus it becomes possible to compare the speed of different processes as they unfold. We know, for example, that compared with the biological evolution of the species, cultural and social evolution is extremely rapid. We know that some societies transform themselves technologically or economically more rapidly than others. We also know that different sectors within the same society exhibit different rates of change—the disparity that William Ogburn labeled "cultural lag." It is precisely the unevenness of change that makes it measurable.

We need, however, a yardstick that makes it possible to compare highly diverse processes, and this yardstick is time. Without time, change has no meaning. And without change, time would stop. Time can be conceived as the intervals during which events occur. Just as money permits us to place a value on both apples and oranges, time permits us to compare unlike processes. When we say that it takes three years to build a dam, we are really saying it takes three times as long as it takes the earth to circle the sun or 31,000,000 times as long as it takes to sharpen a pencil. Time is the currency of exchange that makes it possible to compare the rates at which very different processes play themselves out.

Given the unevenness of change and armed with this yardstick, we still face exhausting difficulties in measuring change. When we speak of the rate of change, we refer to the number of events crowded into an arbitrarily fixed interval of time. Thus we need to define the "events." We need to select our intervals with precision. We need to be careful about the conclusions we draw from the differences we observe. Moreover, in the measurement of change, we are today far more advanced with respect to physical processes than social processes. We know far better, for example, how to measure the rate at which blood flows through the body than the rate at which a rumor flows through society.

Even with all these qualifications, however, there is widespread agreement, reaching from historians and archaeologists all across the spectrum to scientists, sociologists, economists and psychologists, that many social processes are speeding up—strikingly, even spectacularly.

SUBTERRANEAN CITIES

Painting with the broadest of brush strokes, biologist Julian Huxley informs us that "The tempo of human evolution during recorded history is at least 100,000 times as rapid as that of pre-human evolution." Inventions or improvements of a magnitude that took perhaps 50,000 years to accomplish during the early Paleolithic era were, he says, "run through in a mere millennium toward its close; and with the advent of settled civilization, the unit of change soon became reduced to the century." The rate of change, accelerating throughout the past 5000 years, has become, in his words, "particularly noticeable during the past 300 years."

C. P. Snow, the novelist and scientist, also comments on the new visibility of change. "Until this century . . ." he writes, social change was "so slow, that it would pass unnoticed in one person's lifetime. That is no longer so. The rate of change has increased so much that our imagination can't keep up." Indeed, says social psychologist Warren Bennis, the throttle has been pushed so far forward in recent years that "No exaggeration, no hyperbole, no outrage can realistically describe the extent and pace of change. . . . In fact, only the exaggerations appear to be true."

What changes justify such super-charged language? Let us look at a few—change in the process by which man forms cities, for example. We are now undergoing the most extensive and rapid urbanization the world has ever seen. In 1850 only four cities on the face of the earth had a population of 1,000,000 or more. By 1900 the number had increased to nineteen. But by 1960, there were 141, and today world urban population is rocketing upward at a rate of 6.5 percent per year, according to Edgar de Vries and J. P. Thysse of the Institute of Social Science in The Hague. This single stark statistic means a doubling of the earth's urban population within eleven years.

One way to grasp the meaning of change on so phenomenal a scale is to imagine what would happen if all existing cities, instead of expanding, retained their present size. If this were so, in order to accommodate the new urban millions we would have to build a duplicate city for each of the hundreds that already dot the globe. A new Tokyo, a new Hamburg, a new Rome and Rangoon—and all within eleven years. (This explains why French urban planners are sketching subterranean cities—stores, museums, warehouses and factories to be built under the earth, and why a Japanese architect has blueprinted a city to be built on stilts out over the ocean.)

The same accelerative tendency is instantly apparent in man's consumption of energy. Dr. Homi Bhabha, the late Indian atomic scientist who chaired the first International Conference on the Peaceful Uses of Atomic Energy, once analyzed this trend. "To illustrate," he said, "let us use the letter 'Q' to stand for the energy derived from burning some 33,000 million tons of coal. In the eighteen and one half centuries after Christ, the total energy consumed averaged less than one half Q per century. But by 1850, the rate had risen to one Q per century. Today, the rate is about ten Q per century." This means, roughly speaking, that half of all the energy consumed by man in the past 2,000 years has been consumed in the last one hundred.

Also dramatically evident is the acceleration of economic growth in the nations now racing toward super-industrialism. Despite the fact that they start from a large industrial base, the annual percentage increases in production in these countries are formidable. And the rate of increase is itself increasing.

In France, for example, in the twenty-nine years between 1910 and the outbreak of the second world war, industrial production rose only 5 percent. Yet between 1948 and 1965, in only seventeen years, it increased by roughly 220 percent. Today growth rates of from 5 to 10 percent per year are not uncommon among the most industrialized nations. There are ups and downs, of course. But the direction of change has been unmistakable.

Thus for the twenty-one countries belonging to the Organization for Economic Cooperation and Development—by and large, the "have" nations—the average annual rate of increase in gross national product in the years 1960–1968 ran between 4.5 and 5.0 percent. The United States grew at a rate of 4.5 percent, and Japan led the rest with annual increases averaging 9.8 percent.

What such numbers imply is nothing less revolutionary than a doubling of the total output of goods and services in the advanced societies about every fifteen years—and the doubling times are shrinking. This means, generally speaking, that the child reaching teen age in any of these societies is literally surrounded by twice as much of everything newly man-made as his parents were at the time he was an infant. It means that by the time today's teen-ager reaches age thirty, perhaps earlier, a second doubling will have occurred. Within a seventy-year lifetime, perhaps five such doublings will take place—meaning, since the increases are compounded, that by the time the individual reaches old age the society around him will be producing thirty-two times as much as when he was born.

Such changes in the ratio between old and new have, as we shall show, an electric impact on the habits, beliefs, and self-image of millions. Never in previous history has this ratio been transformed so radically in so brief a flick of time.

THE TECHNOLOGICAL ENGINE

Behind such prodigious economic facts lies that great, growling engine of change—technology. This is not to say that technology is the only source of change in society. Social upheavals can be touched off by a change in the chemical composition of the atmosphere, by alterations in climate, by changes in fertility, and many other factors. Yet technology is indisputably a major force behind the accelerative thrust.

To most people, the term technology conjures up images of smoky steel mills or clanking machines. Perhaps the classic symbol of technology is still the assembly line created by Henry Ford half a century ago and made into a potent social icon by Charlie Chaplin in *Modern Times*. This symbol, however, has always been inadequate, indeed, misleading, for technology has always been more than factories and machines. The invention of the horse collar in the middle ages led to major changes in agricultural methods and was as much a technological advance as the invention of the Bessemer furnace centuries later. Moreover, technology includes techniques, as well as the machines that may or may not be necessary to apply them. It includes ways to make chemical reactions occur, ways to breed fish, plant forests, light theaters, count votes or teach history.

The old symbols of technology are even more misleading today, when the most advanced technological processes are carried out far from assembly lines or open hearths. Indeed, in electronics, in space technology, in most of the new industries, relative silence and clean surroundings are characteristic—even sometimes essential. And the assembly line—the organization of armies of men to carry out simple repetitive functions—is an anachronism. It is time for our symbols of technology to change—to catch up with the quickening changes in technology, itself.

This acceleration is frequently dramatized by a thumbnail account of the progress in transportation. It has been pointed out, for example, that in 6000 B.C. the fastest transportation available to man over long distances was the camel caravan, averaging eight miles per hour. It was not until about 1600 B.C. when the chariot was invented that the maximum speed was raised to roughly twenty miles per hour.

So impressive was this invention, so difficult was it to exceed this speed limit, that nearly 3,500 years later, when the first mail coach began operating in England in 1784, it averaged a mere ten mph. The first steam locomotive, introduced in 1825, could muster a top speed of only thirteen mph, and the great sailing ships of the time labored along at less than half that speed. It was probably not until the 1880's that man, with the help of a more advanced steam locomotive, managed to reach a speed of one hundred mph. It took the human race millions of years to attain that record.

It took only fifty-eight years, however, to quadruple the limit, so that by 1938 airborne man was cracking the 400-mph line. It took a mere twenty-year flick of time to double the limit again. And by the 1960's rocket planes approached speeds of 4000 mph, and men in space capsules were circling the earth at 18,000 mph. Plotted on a graph, the line representing progress in the past generation would leap vertically off the page.

Whether we examine distances traveled, altitudes reached, minerals mined, or explosive power harnessed, the same accelerative trend is obvious. The pattern, here and in a thousand other statistical series, is absolutely clear and unmistakable. Millennia or centuries go by, and then, in our own times, a sudden bursting of the limits, a fantastic spurt forward.

The reason for this is that technology feeds on itself. Technology makes more technology possible, as we can see if we look for a moment at the process of innovation. Technological innovation consists of three stages, linked together into a self-reinforcing cycle. First, there is the creative, feasible idea. Second, its practical application. Third, its diffusion through society.

The process is completed, the loop closed, when the diffusion of technology embodying the new idea, in turn, helps generate new creative ideas. Today there is evidence that the time between each of the steps in this cycle has been shortened.

Thus it is not merely true, as frequently noted, that 90 percent of all the scientists who ever lived are now alive, and that new scientific discoveries are being made every day. These new ideas are put to work much more quickly than ever before. The time between original concept and practical use has been radically reduced. This is a striking difference between ourselves and our ancestors. Appollonius of Perga discovered conic sections, but it was 2000 years before they were applied to engineering problems. It was literally centuries between the time Paracelsus discovered that ether could be used as an anaesthetic and the time it began to be used for that purpose.

Even in more recent times the same pattern of delay was present. In 1836 a machine was invented that mowed, threshed, tied straw into sheaves and poured grain into sacks. This machine was itself based on technology at least twenty years old at the time. Yet it was not until a century later, in the 1930's, that such a combine was actually marketed. The first English patent for a typewriter was issued in 1714. But a century and a half elapsed before typewriters became commercially available. A full century passed between the time Nicholas Appert discovered how to can food and the time canning became important in the food industry.

Today such delays between idea and application are almost unthinkable. It is not that we are more eager or less lazy than our ancestors, but we have, with the passage of time, invented all sorts of social devices to hasten the process. Thus we find that the time between the first and second stages of the innovative cycle—between idea and application—has been cut radically. Frank Lynn, for example, in studying twenty major innovations, such as frozen food, antibiotics, integrated circuits and synthetic leather, found that since the beginning of this century more than sixty percent has been slashed from the average time needed for a major scientific discovery to be translated into a useful technological form. Today a vast and growing research and development industry is consciously working to reduce the lag still further.

But if it takes less time to bring a new idea to the marketplace, it also takes less time for it to sweep through the society. Thus the interval between the second and third stages of the cycle—between application and diffusion—has likewise been sliced, and the pace of diffusion is rising with astonishing speed. This is borne out by the history of several familiar household appliances. Robert B. Young at the Stanford Research Institute has studied the span of time between the first commercial appearance of a new electrical appliance and the time the industry manufacturing it reaches peak production of the item.

Young found that for a group of appliances introduced in the United States before 1920—including the vacuum cleaner, the electric range, and the refrigerator—the average span between introduction and peak production was thirty-four years. But for a group that appeared in the 1939–1959 period—including the electric frying pan, television, and washer-dryer combination—the span was only eight years. The lag had shrunk by more than 76 percent. "The post-war group," Young declared, "demonstrated vividly the rapidly accelerating nature of the modern cycle."

The stepped-up pace of invention, exploitation, and diffusion, in turn, accelerates the whole cycle still further. For new machines or techniques are not merely a product, but a source, of fresh creative ideas.

Each new machine or technique, in a sense, changes all existing machines and techniques, by permitting us to put them together into new combinations. The number of possible combinations rises exponentially as the number of new machines or techniques rises arithmetically. Indeed, each new combination may, itself, be regarded as a new super-machine.

The computer, for example, made possible a sophisticated space effort. Linked with sensing devices, communications equipment, and power sources, the computer became part of a configuration that in aggregate forms a single new super-machine—a machine for reaching into and probing outer space. But for machines or techniques to be combined in new ways, they have to be altered, adapted, refined or otherwise changed. So that the very effort to integrate machines into super-machines compels us to make still further technological innovations.

It is vital to understand, moreover, that technological innovation does not merely combine and recombine machines and techniques. Important new machines do more than suggest or compel changes in other machines—they suggest novel solutions to social, philosophical, even personal problems. They alter man's total intellectual environment—the way he thinks and looks at the world.

We all learn from our environment, scanning it constantly—though perhaps unconsciously—for models to emulate. These models are not only other people. They are, increasingly, machines. By their presence, we are subtly conditioned to think along certain lines. It has been observed, for example, that the clock came along before the Newtonian image of the world as a great clock-like mechanism, a philosophical notion that has had the utmost impact on man's intellectual development. Implied in this image of the cosmos as a great clock were ideas about cause and effect and about the importance of external, as against internal, stimuli, that shape the everyday behavior of all of us today. The clock also affected our conception of time so that the idea that a day is divided into twenty-four equal segments of sixty minutes each has become almost literally a part of us.

Recently, the computer has touched off a storm of fresh ideas about man as an interacting part of larger systems, about his physiology, the way he learns, the way he remembers, the way he makes decisions.

Virtually every intellectual discipline from political science to family psychology has been hit by a wave of imaginative hypotheses triggered by the invention and diffusion of the computer—and its full impact has not yet struck. And so the innovative cycle, feeding on itself, speeds up.

If technology, however, is to be regarded as a great engine, a mighty accelerator, then knowledge must be regarded as its fuel. And we thus come to the crux of the accelerative process in society, for the engine is being fed a richer and richer fuel every day.

KNOWLEDGE AS FUEL

The rate at which man has been storing up useful knowledge about himself and the universe has been spiraling upward for 10,000 years. The rate took a sharp upward leap with the invention of writing, but even so it remained painfully slow over centuries of time. The next great leap forward in knowledge-acquisition did not occur until the invention of movable type in the fifteenth century by Gutenberg and others. Prior to 1500, by the most optimistic estimates, Europe was producing books at a rate of 1000 titles per year. This means, give or take a bit, that it would take a full century to produce a library of 100,000 titles. By 1950, four and a half centuries later, the rate had accelerated so sharply that Europe was producing 120,000 titles a year. What once took a century now took only ten months. By 1960, a single decade later, the rate had made another significant jump, so that a century's work could be completed in seven and a half months. And, by the mid-sixties, the output of books on a world scale, Europe included, approached the prodigious figure of 1000 titles per *day.*

One can hardly argue that every book is a net gain for the advancement of knowledge. Nevertheless, we find that the accelerative curve in book publication does, in fact, crudely parallel the rate at which man discovered new knowledge. For example, prior to Gutenberg only 11 chemical elements were known. Antimony, the 12th, was discovered at about the time he was working on his invention. It was fully 200 years since the 11th, arsenic, had been discovered. Had the same rate of discovery continued, we would by now have added only two or three additional elements to the periodic table since Gutenberg. Instead, in the 450 years after his time, some seventy additional elements were discovered. And since 1900 we have been isolating the remaining elements not at a rate of one every two centuries, but of one every three years.

Furthermore, there is reason to believe that the rate is still rising sharply. Today, for example, the number of scientific journals and articles is doubling, like industrial production in the advanced countries, about every fifteen years, and according to biochemist Philip Siekevitz, "what has been learned in the last three decades about the nature of living beings dwarfs in extent of knowledge any comparable period of scientific discovery in the history of mankind." Today the United States government alone generates 100,000 reports each year, plus 450,000 articles,

books and papers. On a worldwide basis, scientific and technical literature
mounts at a rate of some 60,000,000 pages a year.

The computer burst upon the scene around 1950. With its unprece-
dented power for analysis and dissemination of extremely varied kinds of
data in unbelievable quantities and at mind-staggering speeds, it has
become a major force behind the latest acceleration in knowledge-
acquisition. Combined with other increasingly powerful analytical tools
for observing the invisible universe around us, it has raised the rate of
knowledge-acquisition to dumbfounding speeds.

Francis Bacon told us that "Knowledge . . . is power." This can now
be translated into contemporary terms. In our social setting, "Knowledge
is change"—and accelerating knowledge-acquisition, fueling the great
engine of technology, means accelerating change.

THE FLOW OF SITUATIONS

Discovery. Application. Impact. Discovery. We see here a chain reaction
of change, a long, sharply rising curve of acceleration in human social
development. This accelerative thrust has now reached a level at which it
can no longer, by any stretch of the imagination, be regarded as "normal."
The normal institutions of industrial society can no longer contain it, and
its impact is shaking up all our social institutions. Acceleration is one of
the most important and least understood of all social forces.

This, however, is only half the story. For the speedup of change is a
psychological force as well. Although it has been almost totally ignored
by psychology, the rising rate of change in the world around us disturbs
our inner equilibrium, altering the very way in which we experience life.
Acceleration without translates into acceleration within.

This can be illustrated, though in a highly oversimplified fashion, if
we think of an individual life as a great channel through which experience
flows. This flow of experience consists—or is conceived of consisting—of
innumerable "situations." Acceleration of change in the surrounding
society drastically alters the flow of situations through this channel.

There is no neat definition of a situation, yet we would find it
impossible to cope with experience if we did not mentally cut it up into
these manageable units. Moreover, while the boundary lines between
situations may be indistinct, every situation has a certain "wholeness"
about it, a certain integration.

Every situation also has certain identifiable components. These
include "things"—a physical setting of natural or man-made objects.
Every situation occurs in a "place"—a location or arena within which the
action occurs. (It is not accidental that the Latin root *"situ"* means place.)
Every social situation also has, by definition, a cast of characters—
people. Situations also involve a location in the organizational network of
society and a context of ideas or information. Any situation can be
analyzed in terms of these five components.

But situations also involve a separate dimension which, because it cuts across all the others, is frequently overlooked. This is duration—the span of time over which the situation occurs. Two situations alike in all other respects are not the same at all if one lasts longer than another. For time enters into the mix in a crucial way, changing the meaning or content of situations. Just as the funeral march played at too high a speed becomes a merry tinkle of sounds, so a situation that is dragged out has a distinctly different flavor or meaning than one that strikes us in staccato fashion, erupting suddenly and subsiding as quickly.

Here, then, is the first delicate point at which the accelerative thrust in the larger society crashes up against the ordinary daily experience of the contemporary individual. For the acceleration of change, as we shall show, shortens the duration of many situations. This not only drastically alters their "flavor," but hastens their passage through the experiential channel. Compared with life in a less rapidly changing society, more situations now flow through the channel in any given interval of time—and this implies profound changes in human psychology.

For while we tend to focus on only one situation at a time, the increased rate at which situations flow past us vastly complicates the entire structure of life, multiplying the number of roles we must play and the number of choices we are forced to make. This, in turn, accounts for the choking sense of complexity about contemporary life.

Moreover, the speeded-up flow-through of situations demands much more work from the complex focusing mechanisms by which we shift our attention from one situation to another. There is more switching back and forth, less time for extended, peaceful attention to one problem or situation at a time. This is what lies behind the vague feeling noted earlier that "Things are moving faster." They are. Around us. And through us.

There is, however, still another, even more powerfully significant way in which the acceleration of change in society increases the difficulty of coping with life. This stems from the fantastic intrusion of novelty, newness into our existence. Each situation is unique. But situations often resemble one another. This, in fact, is what makes it possible to learn from experience. If each situation were wholly novel, without some resemblance to previously experienced situations, our ability to cope would be hopelessly crippled.

The acceleration of change, however, radically alters the balance between novel and familiar situations. Rising rates of change thus compel us not merely to cope with a faster flow, but with more and more situations to which previous personal experience does not apply. And the psychological implications of this simple fact, which we shall explore later in this book, are nothing short of explosive.

"When things start changing outside, you are going to have a parallel change taking place inside," says Christopher Wright of the Institute for the Study of Science in Human Affairs. The nature of these inner changes is so profound, however, that, as the accelerative thrust picks up speed, it will test our ability to live within the parameters that have until now defined man and society. In the words of psychoanalyst Erik Erikson, "In our society at present, the 'natural course of events' is precisely that the rate of change should continue to accelerate up to the as-yet-unreached limits of human and institutional adaptability."

To survive, to avert what we have termed future shock, the individual must become infinitely more adaptable and capable than ever before. He must search out totally new ways to anchor himself, for all the old roots—religion, nation, community, family, or profession—are now shaking under the hurricane impact of the accelerative thrust. Before he can do so, however, he must understand in greater detail how the effects of acceleration penetrate his personal life, creep into his behavior and alter the quality of existence. He must, in other words, understand transience.

FOR FURTHER CONSIDERATION

A good essayist makes his case as much with his evidence as with his organization and reasoning. Toffler's argument relies heavily on the mass and persuasiveness of his evidence. To what extent is his evidence factual, and to what extent does it appear only in the form of unsupported generalizations? Which of his examples proves most persuasive to you? Why?

Rachel Carson (1907-1964)

Carson was a marine biologist who acquired a large following with her superb book The Sea Around Us. *With* Silent Spring, *in 1962, she brought national attention to the mindless manner in which we abuse the planet we inhabit. In the years since her writing initiated major debate on environmental issues, we have witnessed the growth of environmental action groups and governmental environment agencies at all levels, and the debate rages on. What follows in essay form are the first two chapters of* Silent Spring, *as powerful and readable a polemic as ever.*

The Obligation to Endure

There was once a town in the heart of America where all life seemed to live in harmony with its surroundings. The town lay in the midst of a checkerboard of prosperous farms, with fields of grain and hillsides of orchards where, in spring, white clouds of bloom drifted above the green fields. In autumn, oak and maple and birch set up a blaze of color that flamed and flickered across a backdrop of pines. Then foxes barked in the hills and deer silently crossed the fields, half hidden in the mists of the fall mornings.

Along the roads, laurel, viburnum and alder, great ferns and wild-flowers delighted the traveler's eye through much of the year. Even in winter the roadsides were places of beauty, where countless birds came to feed on the berries and on the seed heads of the dried weeds rising above the snow. The countryside was, in fact, famous for the abundance and variety of its bird life, and when the flood of migrants was pouring through in spring and fall people traveled from great distances to observe them. Others came to fish the streams, which flowed clear and cold out of the hills and contained shady pools where trout lay. So it had been from the days many years ago when the first settlers raised their houses, sank their wells, and built their barns.

Then a strange blight crept over the area and everything began to change. Some evil spell had settled on the community: mysterious maladies swept the flocks of chickens; the cattle and sheep sickened and died. Everywhere was a shadow of death. The farmers spoke of much illness among their families. In the town the doctors had become more and more puzzled by new kinds of sickness appearing among their patients. There had been several sudden and unexplained deaths, not only among adults but even among children, who would be striken suddenly while at play and die within a few hours.

There was a strange stillness. The birds, for example—where had they gone? Many people spoke of them, puzzled and disturbed. The feeding stations in the backyards were deserted. The few birds seen anywhere were moribund; they trembled violently and could not fly. It was a spring without voices. On the mornings that had once throbbed with the dawn chorus of robins, catbirds, doves, jays, wrens, and scores of other bird voices there was now no sound; only silence lay over the fields and woods and marsh.

On the farms the hens brooded, but no chicks hatched. The farmers complained that they were unable to raise any pigs—the litters were small and the young survived only a few days. The apple trees were coming into bloom but no bees droned among the blossoms, so there was no pollination and there would be no fruit.

The roadsides, once so attractive, were now lined with browned and withered vegetation as though swept by fire. These, too, were silent, deserted by all living things. Even the streams were now lifeless. Anglers no longer visited them, for all the fish had died.

In the gutters under the eaves and between the shingles of the roofs, a white granular powder still showed a few patches; some weeks before it had fallen like snow upon the roofs and the lawns, the fields and streams.

No witchcraft, no enemy action had silenced the rebirth of new life in this stricken world. The people had done it themselves.

This town does not actually exist, but it might easily have a thousand counterparts in America or elsewhere in the world. I know of no community that has experienced all the misfortunes I describe. Yet every one of these disasters has actually happened somewhere, and many real communities have already suffered a substantial number of them. A grim specter has crept upon us almost unnoticed, and this imagined tragedy may easily become a stark reality we all shall know.

What has already silenced the voices of spring in countless towns in America? This book is an attempt to explain.

The history of life on earth has been a history of interaction between living things and their surroundings. To a large extent, the physical form and the habits of the earth's vegetation and its animal life have been molded by the environment. Considering the whole span of earthly time, the opposite effect, in which life actually modifies its surroundings, has been relatively slight. Only within the moment of time represented by the present century has one species—man—acquired significant power to alter the nature of his world.

During the past quarter century this power has not only increased to one of disturbing magnitude but it has changed in character. The most alarming of all man's assaults upon the environment is the contamination of air, earth, rivers, and sea with dangerous and even lethal materials. This pollution is for the most part irrevocable; the chain of evil it initiates not only in the world that must support life but in living tissues is for the most part irreversible. In this now universal contamination of the environment, chemicals are the sinister and little-recognized partners of radiation in changing the very nature of the world—the very nature of its life. Strontium 90, released through nuclear explosions into the air, comes to earth in rain or drifts down as fallout, lodges in soil, enters into the grass or corn or wheat grown there, and in time takes up its abode in the bones of a human being, there to remain until his death. Similarly, chemicals sprayed on croplands or forests or gardens lie long in soil, entering into living organisms, passing from one to another in a chain of poisoning and death. Or they pass mysteriously by underground streams until they emerge and, through the alchemy of air and sunlight, combine into new forms that kill vegetation, sicken cattle, and work unknown harm on those who drink from once pure wells. As Albert Schweitzer has said, "Man can hardly even recognize the devils of his own creation."

It took hundreds of millions of years to produce the life that now inhabits the earth—eons of time in which that developing and evolving and diversifying life reached a state of adjustment and balance with its surroundings. The environment, rigorously shaping and directing the life it supported, contained elements that were hostile as well as supporting. Certain rocks gave out dangerous radiation; even within the light of the sun, from which all life draws its energy, there were short-wave radiations with power to injure. Given time—time not in years but in millennia—life adjusts, and a balance has been reached. For time is the essential ingredient; but in the modern world there is no time.

The rapidity of change and the speed with which new situations are created follow the impetuous and heedless pace of man rather than the deliberate pace of nature. Radiation is no longer merely the background radiation of rocks, the bombardment of cosmic rays, the ultraviolet of the sun that have existed before there was any life on earth; radiation is now the unnatural creation of man's tampering with the atom. The chemicals to which life is asked to make its adjustment are no longer merely the calcium and silica and copper and all the rest of the minerals washed out of the rocks and carried in rivers to the sea; they are the synthetic creations of man' inventive mind, brewed in his laboratories, and having no counterparts in nature.

To adjust to these chemicals would require time on the scale that is nature's; it would require not merely the years of a man's life but the life of generations. And even this, were it by some miracle possible, would be futile, for the new chemicals come from our laboratories in an endless stream; almost five hundred annually find their way into actual use in the United States alone. The figure is staggering and its implications are not easily grasped—500 new chemicals to which the bodies of men and animals are required somehow to adapt each year, chemicals totally outside the limits of biologic experience.

Among them are many that are used in man's war against nature. Since the mid-1940's over 200 basic chemicals have been created for use in killing insects, weeds, rodents, and other organisms described in the modern vernacular as "pests"; and they are sold under several thousand different brand names.

These sprays, dusts, and aerosols are now applied almost universally to farms, gardens, forests, and homes—nonselective chemicals that have the power to kill every insect, the "good" and the "bad," to still the song of birds and the leaping of fish in the streams, to coat the leaves with a deadly film, and to linger on in soil—all this though the intended target may be only a few weeds or insects. Can anyone believe it is possible to lay down such a barrage of poisons on the surface of the earth without making it unfit for all life? They should not be called "insecticides," but "biocides."

The whole process of spraying seems caught up in an endless spiral. Since DDT was released for civilian use, a process of escalation has been going on in which ever more toxic materials must be found. This has happened because insects, in a triumphant vindication of Darwin's principle of the survival of the fittest, have evolved super races immune to the particular insecticide used, hence a deadlier one has always to be developed—and then a deadlier one than that. It has happened also because, for reasons to be described later, destructive insects often undergo a "flareback," or resurgence, after spraying, in numbers greater than before. Thus the chemical war is never won, and all life is caught in its violent crossfire.

Along with the possibility of the extinction of mankind by nuclear war, the central problem of our age has therefore become the contamination of man's total environment with such substances of incredible potential for harm—substances that accumulate in the tissues of plants and animals and even penetrate the germ cells to shatter or alter the very material of heredity upon which the shape of the future depends.

Some would-be architects of our future look toward a time when it will be possible to alter the human germ plasm by design. But we may easily be doing so now by inadvertence, for many chemicals, like radiation, bring about gene mutations. It is ironic to think that man might determine his own future by something so seemingly trivial as the choice of an insect spray.

All this has been risked—for what? Future historians may well be amazed by our distorted sense of proportion. How could intelligent beings seek to control a few unwanted species by a method that contaminated the entire environment and brought the threat of disease and death even to their own kind? Yet this is precisely what we have done. We have done it, moreover, for reasons that collapse the moment we examine them. We are told that the enormous and expanding use of pesticides is necessary to maintain farm production. Yet is our real problem not one of *overproduction?* Our farms, despite measures to remove acreages from production and to pay farmers *not* to produce, have yielded such a staggering excess of crops that the American taxpayer in 1962 is paying out more than one billion dollars a year as the total carrying cost of the surplus -food storage program. And is the situation helped when one branch of the Agriculture Department tries to reduce production while another states, as it did in 1958, "It is believed generally that reduction of crop acreages under provisions of the Soil Bank will stimulate interest in use of chemicals to obtain maximum production on the land retained in crops."

All this is not to say there is no insect problem and no need of control. I am saying, rather, that control must be geared to realities, not to mythical situations, and that the methods employed must be such that they do not destroy us along with the insects.

The problem whose attempted solution has brought such a train of disaster in its wake is an accompaniment of our modern way of life. Long before the age of man, insects inhabited the earth—a group of extraordinarily varied and adaptable beings. Over the course of time since man's advent, a small percentage of the more than half a million species of insects have come into conflict with human welfare in two principal ways: as competitors for the food supply and as carriers of human disease.

Disease-carrying insects become important where human beings are crowded together, especially under conditions where sanitation is poor, as in time of natural disaster or war or in situations of extreme poverty and deprivation. Then control of some sort becomes necessary. It is a sobering fact, however, as we shall presently see, that the method of massive chemical control has had only limited success, and also threatens to worsen the very conditions it is intended to curb.

Under primitive agricultural conditions the farmer had few insect problems. These arose with the intensification of agriculture—the devotion of immense acreages to a single crop. Such a system set the stage for explosive increases in specific insect populations. Single-crop farming does not take advantage of the principles by which nature works; it is agriculture as an engineer might conceive it to be. Nature has introduced great variety into the landscape, but man has displayed a passion for simplifying it. Thus he undoes the built-in checks and balances by which nature holds the species within bounds. One important natural check is a limit on the amount of suitable habitat for each species. Obviously then, an insect that lives on wheat can build up its population to much higher levels on a farm devoted to wheat than on one in which wheat is intermingled with other crops to which the insect is not adapted.

The same thing happens in other situations. A generation or more ago, the towns of large areas of the United States lined their streets with the noble elm tree. Now the beauty they hopefully created is threatened with complete destruction as disease sweeps through the elms, carried by a beetle that would have only limited chance to build up large populations and to spread from tree to tree if the elms were only occasional trees in a richly diversified planting.

Another factor in the modern insect problem is one that must be viewed against a background of geologic and human history: the spreading of thousands of different kinds of organisms from their native homes to invade new territories. This worldwide migration has been studied and graphically described by the British ecologist Charles Elton in his recent book *The Ecology of Invasions.* During the Cretaceous Period, some hundred million years ago, flooding seas cut many land bridges between continents and living things found themselves confined in what Elton calls "colossal separate nature reserves." There, isolated from others of their kind, they developed many new species. When some of the land masses were joined again, about 15 million years ago, these species began to move out into new territories—a movement that is not only still in progress but is now receiving considerable assistance from man.

The importation of plants is the primary agent in the modern spread of species, for animals have almost invariably gone along with the plants, quarantine being a comparatively recent and not completely effective innovation. The United States Office of Plant Introduction alone has introduced almost 200,000 species and varieties of plants from all over the world. Nearly half of the 180 or so major insect enemies of plants in the United States are accidental imports from abroad, and most of them have come as hitchhikers on plants.

In new territory, out of reach of the restraining hand of the natural enemies that kept down its numbers in its native land, an invading plant or animal is able to become enormously abundant. Thus it is no accident that our most troublesome insects are introduced species.

These invasions, both the naturally occurring and those dependent on human assistance, are likely to continue indefinitely. Quarantine and massive chemical campaigns are only extremely expensive ways of buying time. We are faced, according to Dr. Elton, "with a life-and-death need not just to find new technological means of suppressing this plant or that animal"; instead we need the basic knowledge of animal populations and their relations to their surroundings that will "promote an even balance and damp down the explosive power of outbreaks and new invasions."

Much of the necessary knowledge is now available but we do not use it. We train ecologists in our universities and even employ them in our governmental agencies but we seldom take their advice. We allow the chemical death rain to fall as though there were no alternative, whereas in fact there are many, and our ingenuity could soon discover many more if given opportunity.

Have we fallen into a mesmerized state that makes us accept as inevitable that which is inferior or detrimental, as though having lost the will or the vision to demand that which is good? Such thinking, in the words of the ecologist Paul Shepard, "idealizes life with only its head out of water, inches above the limits of toleration of the corruption of its own environment. . . . Why should we tolerate a diet of weak poisons, a home in insipid surroundings, a circle of acquaintances who are not quite our enemies, the noise of motors with just enough relief to prevent insanity? Who would want to live in a world which is just not quite fatal?"

Yet such a world is pressed upon us. The crusade to create a chemically sterile, insect-free world seems to have engendered a fanatic zeal on the part of many specialists and most of the so-called control agencies. On every hand there is evidence that those engaged in spraying operations exercise a ruthless power. "The regulatory entomologists . . . function as prosecutor, judge and jury, tax assessor and collector and sheriff to enforce their own orders," said Connecticut entomologist Neely Turner. The most flagrant abuses go unchecked in both state and federal agencies.

It is not my contention that chemical insecticides must never be used. I do contend that we have put poisonous and biologically potent chemicals indiscriminately into the hands of persons largely or wholly ignorant of their potentials for harm. We have subjected enormous numbers of people to contact with these poisons, without their consent, and often without their knowledge. If the Bill of Rights contains no guarantee that a citizen shall be secure against lethal poisons distributed either by private individuals or by public officials, it is surely only because our forefathers, despite their considerable wisdom and foresight, could conceive of no such problem.

I contend, furthermore, that we have allowed these chemicals to be used with little or no advance investigation of their effect on soil, water, wildlife, and man himself. Future generations are unlikely to condone our lack of prudent concern for the integrity of the natural world that supports all life.

There is still very limited awareness of the nature of the threat. This is an era of specialists, each of whom sees his own problem and is unaware of or intolerant of the larger frame into which it fits. It is also an era dominated by industry, in which the right to make a dollar at whatever cost is seldom challenged. When the public protests, confronted with some obvious evidence of damaging results of pesticide applications, it is fed little tranquilizing pills of half truth. We urgently need an end to these false assurances, to the sugar coating of unpalatable facts. It is the public that is being asked to assume the risks that the insect controllers calculate. The public must decide whether it wishes to continue on the present road, and it can do so only when in full possession of the facts. In the words of Jean Rostand, "The obligation to endure gives us the right to know."

FOR FURTHER CONSIDERATION

Environmentalist Ian McHarg often refers to the human brain as "the tumor at the end of the spine," indicating that our perverse pursuit of technology and science may mean the end of human beings and the death of all else on the planet. Do you agree with the idea that our intelligence and selfishness may prove our undoing, or do you feel that the human intellect is our hope for salvation against ecological disasters? What answer(s) to this question does Rachel Carson suggest?

Plato (428-328 B.C.)

Plato was perhaps the most influential philosopher in Western history and founder of the Academy, the forerunner of the modern university. A student and admirer of Socrates, he inquired into the nature of being, morality, and political principles, establishing himself as a preeminent thinker with his doctrine of forms. An application of this doctrine appears in the following selection from The Republic, *as Plato has the philosopher Socrates pursue, through a dialogue, the nature of human perceptions of reality*

The Allegory of the Cave

   Socrates: And now, I said, let me show in a figure[1] how far our nature is enlightened or unenlightened:—Behold! human beings living in an underground den, which has a mouth open towards the light and reaching all along the den; here they have been from their childhood, and have their legs and necks chained so that they cannot move, and can only see before them, being prevented by the chains from turning round their heads. Above and behind them a fire is blazing at a distance, and between the fire and the prisoners there is a raised way; and you will see, if you look, a low wall built along the way, like the screen which marionette players have in front of them, over which they show the puppets.
   Glaucon: I see.

[1]Figuratively, as in a metaphor.

And do you see, I said, men passing along the wall carrying all sorts of vessels, and statues and figures of animals made of wood and stone and various materials, which appear over the wall? Some of them are talking, others silent.

You have shown me a strange image, and they are strange prisoners.

Like ourselves, I replied; and they see only their own shadows, or the shadows of one another, which the fire throws on the opposite wall of the cave?

True, he said; how could they see anything but the shadows if they were never allowed to move their heads?

And of the objects which are being carried in like manner they would only see the shadows?

Yes, he said.

And if they were able to converse with one another, would they not suppose that they were naming what was actually before them?

Very true.

And suppose further that the prison had an echo which came from the other side, would they not be sure to fancy when one of the passers-by spoke that the voice which they heard came from the passing shadow?

No question, he replied.

To them, I said, the truth would be literally nothing but the shadows of the images.

That is certain.

And now look again, and see what will naturally follow if the prisoners are released and disabused of their error. At first, when any of them is liberated and compelled suddenly to stand up and turn his neck round and walk and look towards the light, he will suffer sharp pains; the glare will distress him, and he will be unable to see the realities of which in his former state he had seen the shadows; and then conceive some one saying to him, that what he saw before was an illusion, but that now, when he is approaching nearer to being and his eye is turned towards more real existence, he has a clearer vision,—what will be his reply? And you may further imagine that his instructor is pointing to the objects as they pass and requiring him to name them,—will he not be perplexed? Will he not fancy that the shadows which he formerly saw are truer than the objects which are now shown to him?

Far truer.

And if he is compelled to look straight at the light, will he not have a pain in his eyes which will make him turn away to take refuge in the objects of vision which he can see, and which he will conceive to be in reality clearer than the things which are now being shown to him? True, he said.

And suppose once more, that he is reluctantly dragged up a steep and rugged ascent, and held fast until he is forced into the presence of the sun himself, is he not likely to be pained and irritated? When he approaches the light his eyes will be dazzled, and he will not be able to see anything at all of what are now called realities.

Not all in a moment, he said.

He will require to grow accustomed to the sight of the upper world. And first he will see the shadows best, next the reflections of men and other objects in the water, and then the objects themselves; then he will gaze upon the light of the moon and the stars and the spangled heaven; and he will see the sky and the stars by night better than the sun or the light of the sun by day?

Certainly.

Last of all he will be able to see the sun, and not mere reflections of him in the water, but he will see him in his own proper place, and not in another; and he will contemplate him as he is.

Certainly.

He will then proceed to argue that this is he who gives the season and the years, and is the guardian of all that is in the visible world, and in a certain way the cause of all things which he and his fellows have been accustomed to behold?

Clearly, he said, he would first see the sun and then reason about him.

And when he remembered his old habitation, and the wisdom of the den and his fellow-prisoners, do you not suppose that he would felicitate himself on the change, and pity them?

Certainly, he would.

And if they were in the habit of conferring honours among themselves on those who were quickest to observe the passing shadows and to remark which of them went before, and which followed after, and which were together; and who were therefore best able to draw conclusions as to the future, do you think that he would care for such honours and glories, or envy the possessors of them? Would he not say with Homer,

'Better to be the poor servant of a poor master,'

and to endure anything, rather than think as they do and live after their manner?

Yes, he said, I think that he would rather suffer anything than entertain those false notions and live in this miserable manner.

Imagine once more, I said, such an one coming suddenly out of the sun to be replaced in his old situation; would he not be certain to have his eyes full of darkness?

To be sure, he said.

And if there were a contest, and he had to compete in measuring the shadows with the prisoners who had never moved out of the den, while his sight was still weak, and before his eyes had become steady (and the time which would be needed to acquire this new habit of sight might be very considerable), would he not be ridiculous? Men would say of him that up he went and down he came without his eyes; and that it was better not even to think of ascending; and if any one tried to loose another and lead him up to the light, let them only catch the offender, and they would put him to death.

No question, he said.

This entire allegory, I said, you may now append, dear Glaucon, to the previous argument; the prison-house is the world of sight, the light of the fire is the sun, and you will not misapprehend me if you interpret the journey upwards to be the ascent of the soul into the intellectual world according to my poor belief, which, at your desire, I have expressed—whether rightly or wrongly God knows. But, whether true or false, my opinion is that in the world of knowledge the idea of good appears last of all, and is seen only with an effort; and when seen, is also inferred to be the universal author of all things beautiful and right, parent of light and of the lord of light in this visible world, and the immediate source of reason and truth in the intellectual; and that this is the power upon which he who would act rationally either in public or private life must have his eye fixed.

I agree, he said, as far as I am able to understand you.

FOR FURTHER CONSIDERATION

What meanings does Plato assign to the terms "real" and "reality" in this essay? To what extent is the argument of Socrates an appeal to ignorance, that is, we must agree something exists unless we can prove otherwise?

Joe McGinniss (1942-0000)

The Selling of the President 1968 brought Joe McGinniss to international attention. In preparing the book he sat in on the innermost conferences of then Presidential candidate Richard M. Nixon and his campaign advisers. The alarming, funny, and often devastating story he later presented became a best seller, not simply because it criticized Richard Nixon, but because it revealed in a firsthand, behind-the-scenes account the manipulation and callousness that American politicians practice to win election from the people they promise to serve. The selection which follows is Chapter 2 from The Selling of the President 1968.

Politics, A Con Game

POLITICS, in a sense, has always been a con game.

The American voter, insisting upon his belief in a higher order, clings to his religion, which promises another, better life; and defends passionately the illusion that the men he chooses to lead him are of finer nature than he.

It has been traditional that the successful politician honor this illusion. To succeed today, he must embellish it. Particularly if he wants to be President.

"Potential presidents are measured against an ideal that's a combination of leading man, God, father, hero, pope, king, with maybe just a touch of the avenging Furies thrown in," an adviser to Richard Nixon wrote in a memorandum late in 1967. Then, perhaps aware that Nixon qualified only as father, he discussed improvements that would have to be made—not upon Nixon himself, but upon the image of him which was received by the voter.

That there is a difference between the individual and his image is human nature. Or American nature, at least.

Advertising, in many ways, is a con game, too. Human beings do not need new automobiles every third year; a color television set brings little enrichment of the human experience; a higher or lower hemline no expansion of consciousness, no increase in the capacity to love.

It is not surprising then, that politicians and advertising men should have discovered one another. And, once they recognized that the citizen did not so much vote for a candidate as make a psychological purchase of him, not surprising that they began to work together.

The voter, as reluctant to face political reality as any other kind, was hardly an unwilling victim. "The deeper problems connected with advertising," Daniel Boorstin has written in *The Image,* "come less from the unscrupulousness of our 'deceivers' than from our pleasure in being deceived, less from the desire to seduce than from the desire to be seduced. . . .

"In the last half-century we have misled ourselves . . . about men . . . and how much greatness can be found among them. . . . We have become so accustomed to our illusions that we mistake them for reality. We demand them. And we demand that there be always more of them, bigger and better and more vivid."

The Presidency seems the ultimate extension of our error.

Advertising agencies have tried openly to sell Presidents since 1952. When Dwight Eisenhower ran for re-election in 1956, the agency of Batton, Barton, Durstine and Osborn, which had been on a retainer throughout his first four years, accepted his campaign as a regular account. Leonard Hall, national Republican chairman, said: "You sell your candidates and your programs the way a business sells its products."

The only change over the past twelve years has been that, as technical sophistication has increased, so has circumspection. The ad men were removed from the parlor but were given a suite upstairs.

What Boorstin says of advertising: "It has meant a reshaping of our very concept of truth," is particularly true of advertising on T.V.

With the coming of television, and the knowledge of how it could be used to seduce voters, the old political values disappeared. Something new, murky, undefined started to rise from the mists. "In all countries,"

Marshall McLuhan writes, "the party system has folded like the organization chart. Policies and issues are useless for election purposes, since they are too specialized and hot. The shaping of a candidate's integral image has taken the place of discussing conflicting points of view."

Americans have never quite digested television. The mystique which should fade grows stronger. We make celebrities not only of the men who cause events but of the men who read reports of them aloud.

The televised image can become as real to the housewife as her husband, and much more attractive. Hugh Downs is a better breakfast companion, Merv Griffin cozier to snuggle with on the couch.

Television, in fact, has given status to the "celebrity", which few real men attain. And the "celebrity" here is the one described by Boorstin: "Neither good nor bad, great nor petty . . . the human pseudo-event . . . fabricated on purpose to satisfy our exaggerated expectations of human greatness."

This is, perhaps, where the twentieth century and its pursuit of illusion have been leading us. "In the last half-century," Boorstin writes, "the old heroic human mold has been broken. A new mold has been made, so that marketable human models—modern 'heroes'—could be mass-produced, to satisfy the market, and without any hitches. The qualities which now commonly make a man or woman into a 'nationally advertised' brand are in fact a new category of human emptiness."

The television celebrity is a vessel. An inoffensive container in which someone else's knowledge, insight, compassion, or wit can be presented. And we respond like the child on Christmas morning who ignores the gift to play with the wrapping paper.

Television seems particularly useful to the politician who can be charming but lacks ideas. Print is for ideas. Newspapermen write not about people but policies: the paragraphs can be slid around like blocks. Everyone is colored gray. Columnists—and commentators in the more polysyllabic magazines—concentrate on ideology. They do not care what a man sounds like; only how he thinks. For the candidate who does not, such exposure can be embarrassing. He needs another way to reach the people.

On television it matters less that he does not have ideas. His personality is what the viewers want to share. He need be neither statesman nor crusader; he must only show up on time. Success and failure are easily measured: how often is he invited back? Often enough and he reaches his goal—to advance from "politician" to "celebrity," a status jump bestowed by grateful viewers who feel that finally they have been given the basis for making a choice.

The TV candidate, then, is measured not against his predecessors—not against a standard of performance established by two centuries of democracy—but against Mike Douglas. How well does he handle himself? Does he mumble, does he twitch, does he make me laugh? Do I feel warm inside?

Style becomes substance. The medium is the massage and the masseur gets the votes.

In office, too, the ability to project electronically is essential. We were willing to forgive John Kennedy his Bay of Pigs; we followed without question the perilous course on which he led us when missiles were found in Cuba; we even tolerated his calling of reserves for the sake of a bluff about Berlin.

We forgave, followed, and accepted because we liked the way he looked. And he had a pretty wife. Camelot was fun, even for the peasants, as long as it was televised to their huts.

Then came Lyndon Johnson, heavy and gross, and he was forgiven nothing. He might have survived the sniping of the displaced intellectuals had he only been able to charm. But no one taught him how. Johnson was syrupy. He stuck to the lens. There was no place for him in our culture.

"The success of any TV performer depends on his achieving a low-pressure style of presentation," McLuhan has written. The harder a man tries, the better he must hide it. Television demands gentle wit, irony, understatement: the qualities of Eugene McCarthy. The TV politician cannot make a speech; he must engage in intimate conversation. He must never press. He should suggest, not state; request, not demand. Nonchalance is the key word. Carefully studied nonchalance.

Warmth and sincerity are desirable but must be handled with care. Unfiltered, they can be fatal. Television did great harm to Hubert Humphrey. His excesses—talking too long and too fervently, which were merely annoying in an auditorium—became lethal in a television studio. The performer must talk to one person at a time. He is brought into the living room. He is a guest. It is improper for him to shout. Humphrey vomited on the rug.

It would be extremely unwise for the TV politician to admit such knowledge of his medium. The necessary nonchalance should carry beyond his appearance while *on* the show; it should rule his attitude *toward* it. He should express distaste for television; suspicion that there is something "phony" about it. This guarantees him good press, because newspaper reporters, bitter over their loss of prestige to the television men, are certain to stress anti-television remarks. Thus, the sophisticated candidate, while analyzing his own on-the-air technique as carefully as a golf pro studies his swing, will state frequently that there is no place for "public relations gimmicks" or "those show business guys" in his campaign. Most of the television men working for him will be unbothered by such remarks. They are willing to accept anonymity, even scorn, as long as the pay is good.

Into this milieu came Richard Nixon: grumpy, cold, and aloof. He would claim privately that he lost elections because the American voter was an adolescent whom he tried to treat as an adult. Perhaps. But if he treated the voter as an adult, it was as an adult he did not want for a neighbor.

This might have been excused had he been a man of genuine vision. An explorer of the spirit. Martin Luther King, for instance, got by without being one of the boys. But Richard Nixon did not strike people that way. He had, in Richard Rovere's words, "an advertising man's approach to his work," acting as if he believed "policies [were] products to be sold the public—this one today, that one tomorrow, depending on the discounts and the state of the market."

So his enemies had him on two counts: his personality, and the convictions—or lack of such—which lay behind. They worked him over heavily on both.

Norman Mailer remembered him as "a church usher, of the variety who would twist a boy's ear after removing him from church."

McLuhan watched him debate Kennedy and thought he resembled "the railway lawyer who signs leases that are not in the best interests of the folks in the little town."

But Nixon survived, despite his flaws, because he was tough and smart, and—some said—dirty when he had to be. Also, because there was nothing else he knew. A man to whom politics is all there is in life will almost always beat one to whom it is only an occupation.

He nearly became President in 1960, and that year it would not have been by default. He failed because he was too few of the things a President had to be—and, because he had no press to lie for him and did not know how to use television to lie about himself.

It was just Nixon and John Kennedy and they sat down together in a television studio and a little red light began to glow and Richard Nixon was finished. Television would be blamed but for all the wrong reasons.

They would say it was makeup and lighting, but Nixon's problem went deeper than that. His problem was himself. Not what he said but the man he was. The camera portrayed him clearly. America took its Richard Nixon straight and did not like the taste.

The content of the programs made little difference. Except for startling lapses, content seldom does. What mattered was the image the viewers received, though few observers at the time caught the point.

McLuhan read Theodore White's *The Making of the President* book and was appalled at the section on the debates. "White offers statistics on the number of sets in American homes and the number of hours of daily use of these sets, but not one clue as to the nature of the TV image or its effects on candidates or viewers. White considers the 'content' of the debates and the deportment of the debaters, but it never occurs to him to ask why TV would inevitably be a disaster for a sharp intense image like Nixon's and a boon for the blurry, shaggy texture of Kennedy." In McLuhan's opinion: "Without TV, Nixon had it made."

What the camera showed was Richard Nixon's hunger. He lost, and bitter, confused, he blamed it on his beard.

He made another, lesser thrust in 1962, and that failed, too. He showed the world a little piece of his heart the morning after and then he moved East to brood. They did not want him, the hell with them. He was going to Wall Street and get rich.

He was afraid of television. He knew his soul was hard to find. Beyond that, he considered it a gimmick; its use in politics offended him. It had not been part of the game when he had learned to play, he could see no reason to bring it in now. He half suspected it was an eastern liberal trick: one more way to make him look silly. It offended his sense of dignity, one of the truest senses he had.

So his decision to use it to become President in 1968 was not easy. So much of him argued against it. But in his Wall Street years, Richard Nixon had traveled to the darkest places inside himself and come back numbed. He was, as in the Graham Greene title, a burnt-out case. All feeling was behind him; the machine inside had proved his hardiest part. He would run for President again and if he would have to learn television to run well, then he would learn it.

America still saw him as the 1960 Nixon. If he were to come at the people again, as candidate, it would have to be as something new; not this scarred, discarded figure from their past.

He spoke to men who thought him mellowed. They detected growth, a new stability, a sense of direction that had been lacking. He would return with fresh perspective, a more unselfish urgency.

His problem was how to let the nation know. He could not do it through the press. He knew what to expect from them, which was the same as he had always gotten. He would have to circumvent them. Distract them with coffee and doughnuts and smiles from his staff and tell his story another way.

Television was the only answer, despite its sins against him in the past. But not just any kind of television. An uncommitted camera could do irreparable harm. His television would have to be controlled. He would need experts. They would have to find the proper settings for him, or if they could not be found, manufacture them. These would have to be men of keen judgment and flawless taste. He was, after all, Richard Nixon, and there were certain things he could not do. Wearing love beads was one. He would need men of dignity. Who believed in him and shared his vision. But more importantly, men who knew television as a weapon: from broadest concept to most technical detail. This would be Richard Nixon, the leader, returning from exile. Perhaps not beloved, but respected. Firm but not harsh; just but compassionate. With flashes of warmth spaced evenly throughout.

Nixon gathered about himself a group of young men attuned to the political uses of television. They arrived at his side by different routes. One, William Gavin, was a thirty-one-year-old English teacher in a suburban high school outside Philadelphia in 1967, when he wrote Richard Nixon a letter urging him to run for President and base his campaign on

TV. Gavin wrote on stationery borrowed from the University of Pennsylvania because he thought Nixon would pay more attention if the letter seemed to be from a college professor.

> Dear Mr. Nixon:
> May I offer two suggestions concerning your plans for 1968?
> 1. Run. You can win. Nothing can happen to you, politically speaking, that is worse than what has happened to you. Ortega y Gassett in his *The Revolt of the Masses* says: "These ideas are the only genuine ideas; the ideas of the shipwrecked. All the rest is rhetoric, posturing, farce. He who does not really feel himself lost, is lost without remission . . ." You, in effect, are "lost"; that is why you are the only political figure with the vision to see things the way they are and not as Leftist or Rightist kooks would have them be. Run. You will win.
> 2. A tip for television: instead of those wooden performances beloved by politicians, instead of a glamorboy technique, instead of safety, be bold. Why not have live press conferences as your campaign on television? People will see you daring all, asking and answering questions from reporters, and not simply answering phony "questions" made up by your staff. This would be dynamic; it would be daring. Instead of the medium using you, you would be using the medium. Go on "live" and risk all. It is the only way to convince people of the truth: that you are beyond rhetoric, that you can face reality, unlike your opponents, who will rely on public relations. Television hurt you because you were not yourself; it didn't hurt the "real" Nixon. The real Nixon can revolutionize the use of television by dynamically going "live" and answering everything, the loaded and the unloaded question. Invite your opponents to this kind of a debate.
> Good luck, and I know you can win if you see yourself for what you are; a man who had been beaten, humiliated, hated, but who can still see the truth.

A Nixon staff member had lunch with Gavin a couple of times after the letter was received and hired him.

William Gavin was brought to the White House as a speech writer in January of 1969.

Harry Treleaven, hired as creative director of advertising in the fall of 1967, immediately went to work on the more serious of Nixon's personality problems. One was his lack of humor.

"Can be corrected to a degree," Treleaven wrote, "but let's not be too obvious about it. Romney's cornball attempts have hurt him. If we're going to be witty, let a pro write the words."

Treleaven also worried about Nixon's lack of warmth, but decided that "he can be helped greatly in this respect by how he is handled. . . . Give him words to say that will show his *emotional* involvement in the issues. . . . Buchanan wrote about RFK talking about the starving children in Recife. *That's* what we have to inject. . . .

"He should be presented in some kind of 'situation' rather than cold in a studio. The situation should look unstaged even if it's not."

Some of the most effective ideas belonged to Raymond K. Price, a former editorial writer for the *New York Herald Tribune,* who became Nixon's best and most prominent speech writer in the campaign. Price later composed much of the inaugural address.

In 1967, he began with the assumption that, "The natural human use of reason is to support prejudice, not to arrive at opinions." Which led to the conclusion that rational arguments would "only be effective if we can get the people to make the *emotional* leap, or what theologians call [the] 'leap of faith.'"

Price suggested attacking the "personal factors" rather than the "historical factors" which were the basis of the low opinion so many people had of Richard Nixon.

"These tend to be more a gut reaction," Price wrote, "unarticulated, non-analytical, a product of the particular chemistry between the voter and the *image* of the candidate. *We have to be very clear on this point: that the response is to the image, not to the man. . . .* It's not what's *there* that counts, it's what's projected—and carrying it one step further, it's not what *he* projects but rather what the voter receives. It's not the man we have to change, but rather the *received impression.* And this impression often depends more on the medium and its use than it does on the candidate himself."

So there would not have to be a "new Nixon." Simply a new approach to television.

"What, then, does this mean in terms of our uses of time and of media?" Price wrote.

"For one thing, it means investing whatever time RN needs in order to work out firmly in his own mind that vision of the nation's future that he wants to be identified with. This is crucial. . . ."

So, at the age of fifty-four, after twenty years in public life, Richard Nixon was still felt *by his own staff* to be in need of time to "work out firmly in his own mind that vision of the nation's future that he wants to be identified with."

"Secondly," Price wrote, "it suggests that we take the time and the money to experiment, in a controlled manner, with film and television techniques, with particular emphasis on pinpointing those *controlled* uses of the television medium that can *best* convey the *image* we want to get across . . .

"The TV medium itself introduces an element of distortion, in terms of its effect on the candidate and of the often subliminal ways in which the image is received. And it inevitably is going to convey a partial image— thus ours is the task of finding how to control its use so the part that gets across is the part we want to have gotten across. . . .

"Voters are basically lazy, basically uninterested in making an *effort* to understand what we're talking about . . . ," Price wrote. "Reason requires a high degree of discipline, of concentration; impression is easier. Reason pushes the viewer back, it assaults him, it demands that he agree or disagree; impression can envelop him, invite him in, without making an intellectual demand. . . . When we argue with him we demand that he make the effort of replying. We seek to engage his intellect, and for most people this is the most difficult work of all. The emotions are more easily roused, closer to the surface, more malleable. . . ."

So, for the New Hampshire primary, Price recommended "saturation with a film, in which the candidate can be shown better than he can be shown in person because it can be edited, so only the best moments are shown; then a quick parading of the candidate in the flesh so that the guy they've gotten intimately acquainted with on the screen takes on a living presence—not saying anything, just being seen. . . .

"[Nixon] has to come across as a person larger than life, the stuff of legend. People are stirred by the legend, including the living legend, not by the man himself. It's the aura that surrounds the charismatic figure more than it is the figure itself, that draws the followers. Our task is to build that aura. . . .

"So let's not be afraid of television gimmicks . . . get the voters to like the guy and the battle's two-thirds won."

So this was how they went into it. Trying, with one hand, to build the illusion that Richard Nixon, in addition to his attributes of mind and heart, considered, in the words of Patrick K. Buchanan, a speech writer, "communicating with the people . . . one of the great joys of seeking the Presidency"; while with the other they shielded him, controlled him, and controlled the atmosphere around him. It was as if they were building not a President but an Astrodome, where the wind would never blow, the temperature never rise or fall, and the ball never bounce erratically on the artificial grass.

They could do this, and succeed, because of the special nature of the man. There was, apparently, something in Richard Nixon's character which sought this shelter. Something which craved regulation, which flourished best in the darkness, behind cliches, behind phalanxes of antiseptic advisers. Some part of him that could breathe freely only inside a hotel suite that cost a hundred dollars a day.

And it worked. As he moved serenely through his primary campaign, there was new cadence to Richard Nixon's speech and motion; new confidence in his heart. And, a new image of him on the television screen.

TV both reflected and contributed to his strength. Because he was winning he looked like a winner on the screen. Because he was suddenly projecting well on the medium he had feared, he went about his other tasks with assurance. The one fed upon the other, building to an astonishing peak in August as the Republican convention began and he emerged from his regal isolation, traveling to Miami not so much to be nominated as coronated. On live, but controlled, TV.

FOR FURTHER CONSIDERATION

Is it irrevocably the nature of television that it be used to mislead voters, or can it and is it used to communicate effectively and honestly the attitudes and characters of political candidates? Must TV always sell the image, or can it let us know the person? Does television inevitably make a candidate into a pseudo-event? What impact has the cost of TV campaigning on the integrity of elected officials?

Glossary of Terms

Alliteration The repetition of like consonant sounds at the beginning of successive words. For example, "Perfect pearl, a pleasure for princes," or "The lone and level sands stretch far away."

Antagonist The force or forces opposing the protagonist; often a combination of exterior and internal forces; sometimes one or more other characters.

Apostrophe A special form of poetic personification where the speaker addresses something nonhuman as if it were human. As in Keats's "Ode on a Grecian Urn," "Thou foster-child of silence," or Paul Simon's line, "Hello darkness my old friend."

Assonance The recurrence of similar internal vowel sounds. For example, "So we'll go no more a-roving."

Chorus From the Greek word meaning "dance." In Greek drama, a group of singers. Choragus is the chorus leader who acts as spokesman. Aristotle says "The chorus, too, should be viewed as one of actors," and so it should, for the chorus describes setting and circumstances and comments on the characters and the action.

Connotation Whatever a word or phrase suggests (as opposed to what it states outright). For example, the word "wall" may connote many things, among them a barrier, a need for security, an unwillingness to communicate, a lack of trust, and a person's interest in ownership.

Convention A commonly recognized or agreed upon understanding between the author and his or her audience as to the circumstances the audience must accept to receive the story.

Denotation   The direct, accepted, precise meaning of a word. For example, the word "darkness" denotes the absence of light.

Denouement   At the end of a story, the unraveling of the complication or plot: the disposition of pending conflicts and the explanation of the fate of characters.

Diction   The choice of words in a work of literature.

Exposition   That part of a play or story (usually at the beginning) which introduces characters, setting, and conflict; exposition also informs the reader or spectator of whatever must be known about what has gone on before the time of the story (antecedent action).

Foot   Two or more syllables linked to show stress or emphasis. (′)

Feet	*Example*
Iambic	abóve
Anapestic	entertaín
Trochaic	límit
Dactylic	límitless
Spondaic	eýebrów
Pyrrhic	xx (requires more than one word)

E.G., Shall Í compáre thée tó a súmmer's daý?

Shakespeare's line has five iambic feet; hence, iambic pentameter, the rhythm of the line.

Foreshadowing   An event, remark, or occurrence which hints at what will actually occur later in a story. Often ironic.

Free verse   Poetry that lacks rhyme or set meter.

Imagery   A word or group of words stimulating the reader's senses and creating a mental image. For example, "broad bellying sails."

Irony   A statement or situation which states one thing but suggests something very different or even opposite. Often used as a form of humor or sarcasm.

Metaphor   A description of one thing in terms of another, adding a new view of something. A comparison that gives the attributes or characteristics of one thing to something we do not ordinarily consider as having them. For example, "all experience is an arch where through gleams that untraveled world."

Meter   The number of feet in the line establishes the meter.

1 foot—monometer
2 feet—dimeter
3 feet—trimeter
4 feet—tetrameter
5 feet—pentameter
6 feet—hexameter
7 feet—heptameter
8 feet—octameter

Onomatopoeia   A word which sounds like what it is. For example, "burp," "honk," "hiss," "crash," "slither," "drip."

Oxymoron   A metaphor which contradicts itself. For example, "darkest noon," "the little giant."

Personification   A metaphor attributing human characteristics to something non-human. As when Donne writes, "The pregnant bank swelled up to rest/The violet's reclining head."

Plot   The sequence or chain of events in which a conflict unfolds.

Point of view   The viewpoint through which a reader learns the events of a story. In *first person* point of view the narrator is himself a character in the story and therefore limited in what he can know or recount. In *third person omniscient* point of view an all-knowing narrator who exists outside the story tells of the events and the characters. *Third person limited* point of view varies in that the all-knowing narrator is limited to the thoughts and actions of one character at a given place in the story. *Stream of consciousness* is a particular point of view in which the reader encounters the unbroken flow of thought from the mind of a character.

Protagonist   The leading character in a story; the hero or heroine.

Recognition   In fiction or drama, a change from ignorance to knowledge. From Aristotle's *Poetics.*

Reversal   In fiction or drama, the change of a situation to its opposite. From Aristotle's *Poetics.*

Rhyme   An effect achieved when the same concluding sound of a word is repeated For example, "blow," "snow." End rhyme occurs when the repeated sounds appear at the ends of lines. For example, in Shakespeare's Sonnet 18:

> So long as men can breathe, or eyes can see,
> So long lives this, and this gives life to thee.

Imperfect rhymes approximate similar concluding sounds of words: for example, "thought," "not"; or "opposed," "sowed." Internal rhyme occurs when a word in the middle of the line rhymes with the word at the end, for example, "At an *age* to now unloose his *rage.*"

Simile   A metaphor employing "like" or "as." For example, "O, my Luve's like a red red rose."

Sonnet   A poem of fourteen lines centering on one basic sensibility. Two standard types of sonnets appear: (1). The Italian or Petrarchan sonnet, grouping eight lines (a quatrain) by means of the rhyme scheme *abba, abba,* and six subsequent lines with various rhyme patterns (*cde, cde,* or *cdc, cdc*). (2.) The Shakespearian, English, or Elizabethan sonnet, grouping three quatrains (*abab, cdcd, efef*) with a final couplet (*gg*).

Stanza   A group of lines in a poem; equivalent to a paragraph in prose.

Symbol   An object, attribute, person, or thing which suggests something else because of a relationship or common understanding. For example, a river might symbolize the beginning, maturation, movement, change, and end of life.

Theme   The concept, idea, or comment on life suggested by a work of literature. For example, the theme of *Oedipus the King* might be said to deal with power and pride blinding man. Because a reader or playgoer brings much of a personal nature to the experience of a work of literature, disagreements often occur regarding the theme of a piece of literature.

Tone   The feeling or attitude an author exhibits toward his or her subject. Tone is suggested rather than stated.